Mexico
a travel survival kit

Mexico – a travel survival kit
2nd edition

Published by
Lonely Planet Publications
PO Box 88, South Yarra, Vic 3141 Australia
PO Box 2001A, Berkeley CA 94702 USA

Printed by
Colorcraft, Hong Kong

Photographs
Doug Richmond

First Published
1982

This edition
October 1985

National Library of Australia
Cataloguing in Publication Data

Richmond, Doug
Mexico, a travel survival kit

2nd ed.
Includes index
ISBN 0 908086 76 8

1. Mexico – Description and travel – 1981– - Guide-books. I. Title.

917.2'04834

Doug Richmond is an inveterate traveller who has lived and worked in Mexico intermittently since the mid-1940s. Early on, he discovered that the amount of money he spent determined how much travelling he could enjoy, so he made a study of travelling on the cheap. This experience and a life-long interest in Mexican history – particularly the Mexican-American War – led him to write this guidebook. His other writing has included travel guides to Central America and Baja California, as well as illustrated feature articles. When not travelling, Doug lives near Guadalajara, Mexico.

Contents

Contents

Introduction

I've long thought that the official motto of the United Mexican States should be *'No hay regulas fijas'* ('There are no fixed rules'). This saying prevails throughout the fabric of Mexican life from the Customs guard at the border to the menu at a favourite restaurant. More than any single factor this is enough to make Mexico more unlike the rest of North America – and Europe as well – than Costa Rica, Spain or Chile.

The majority of the people are Spanish-speaking *mestizos,* a mixture of indigenous tribes and Europeans, with a generous sprinkling of all the other races and nationalities under the sun. But there are still more native-language-only speakers – people living entirely outside the money economy – in Mexico today than there are inhabitants in Guatemala.

Mexico has about 80 million people, half of whom are 15 years of age or younger. The 1981 World Almanac lists the unemployment and under-employment rate as approximately 50%. For some reason the current World Almanac has absolutely nothing to say on the subject, but things aren't improving. The disparity in wealth between the very rich and the very poor is extreme, and the gap appears to be widening. But there is probably no group of people on earth that treats the stranger in its midst as warmly as the Mexicans do, and everywhere the person who makes mistakes – inevitable – in his or her attempts at speaking Mexican Spanish will be gently corrected, not ridiculed as is the individual who essays poor French in Paris.

Mexico is an industrialized country in which mechanical devices, from water closets to locomotives, seem to take a malicious delight in breaking down at the most inopportune times, a situation that seems to bother no one unduly. When something becomes *discompuesto* it is regarded by the locals as a petty annoyance not worth becoming upset about. This remark applies whether we are talking about a two-room hotel in a little no-plaza tank town out in the wilderness or a posh establishment on the Reforma in the heart of Mexico City.

And there is no country on earth that can offer so much to the foreign traveller for so little money as Mexico.

Facts about the Country

HISTORY

It is difficult to pinpoint exactly the date that can truly be said to be the beginning of modern Mexico, but I would place it as Good Friday, 1519, the day on which Hernan Cortés arrived on the foreshore of what became Villa Rica de Veracruz, and a more sanguine and hard-bitten little group of freebooters has probably never existed before or since.

Something like 500 men and 16 horses arrived from Cuba in several ships, ships which Cortés promptly burned to discourage dissension, backsliding and desertion among the other ranks. In effect, this single act ensured the success of the undertaking as it forced the Spaniards to conquer or die, and conquer they did. Most of them, and especially the officers, were scions of impoverished lesser nobility and they tended to hail from Extramadura and, to a somewhat lesser degree, from Andalucia. Both regions were, and are, noted more for their lack of opportunity and general poverty than for anything else. This pattern of emigration from Spain to the New World persisted for centuries and is largely responsible for the fact that Mexican Spanish differs sharply from the Castilian dialect which is the language of the so-called 'better classes' in Spain.

At the time he made his propitious landing Cortés had absolutely no idea of the immense number of Indians he was facing, in point of fact he and his men were pitted against hundreds of thousands of Aztecs alone, plus uncounted hordes of other tribesmen. The Aztecs were the dominant nation, but their rule was maintained through constant warfare with their neighbours, a situation on which Cortés and his men capitalized neatly, fostering alliances as they went, often after pitched battles.

Cortés was greatly aided in his conquest of Mexico – by which I mean the Aztecs – by the fact that the Indians regarded both the Europeans and their horses with superstitious awe which lasted until the Spaniards had a fairly secure toehold on the Aztec capital of Tenochtitlán and had made the Aztec emperor, Moctezuma, prisoner. To give some idea of the magnitude of the task let me point out that Tenochtitlán was larger than either the London or Paris of the time, with an estimated 300,000 or so inhabitants, and the Spanish had fewer than 500 men under arms, including priests, with half that number disabled by diarrhoea. Which is not to say that the Aztecs simply gave up their cause without a struggle. There were continuing battles and skirmishes between the Spaniards and Indians, and also between Cortés' forces and other Spaniards sent out from Cuba to punish him.

On St John's Day, 24 June 1520, there occurred a battle between the Europeans and the Aztecs, during the course of which Moctezuma was struck in the head by a flung stone and killed. The cause of this fight is forgotten, but there is every reason to suspect that the Aztecs were irritated beyond endurance by the Spaniard's edict prohibiting human sacrifice. By 30 June things were looking very bad for Cortés, so he began a retreat under cover of darkness over a causeway to Tacuba with a force consisting of three to four thousand Tlaxcala Indian allies and about 1000 Europeans – by this time he had received some reinforcements. The retreat was intended to be secret, but a wakeful Indian woman saw their flight and sounded the alarm. Thousands of Indians were killed in the ensuing battle, along with several hundred Spaniards. The Europeans put up an excellent rear guard action and the upshot of it was that Cortés wound up with about 400 European survivors, approximately the number with which he had mounted his expedition. The retreat is remembered in Mexican history books as the *Noche Triste* (Sad Night), and the bloody causeway is commemorated on the maps of modern Mexico City as the street 'Puente de Alvarado'(Alvarado's Bridge), in honour of Cortés' second-in-command.

About a year later, after numerous battles with members of the various Indian tribes and the addition of around 200 more European reinforcements, Cortés was back at Tenochtitlán. He defeated the Aztecs once and for all and effectively made himself ruler of Mexico. He tore down the temples which the Aztecs had used for human sacrifices and used the stones to construct churches and homes – the foundation of what is now the world's largest city.

Although the Conquistadores' stated purpose in conquering Mexico was to spread the word of God and convert the Indians, and only incidentally to make money, I suspect that the latter endeavour was probably regarded privately as the most compelling; and those early Spaniards who survived wound up fabulously wealthy. Many of them returned to their native Extramadura and built immense

mansions, some of which are still in use by their descendants in Cáceres and Mérida.

Then followed 300 years of Spanish colonization and rule in Mexico, years which the energetic Spaniards put to very good use. Nearly every city of any consequence in the country was surveyed and planned during the 16th century, and the plans approved in Spain.

New-world Spanish cities were built around a central plaza on which were located the church and government offices, with the remaining frontage being taken up by the establishments of the leading merchants and professional people, a system which is followed to this day. In time, these bare-ground plazas, originally used much of the time for parade grounds, acquired stately trees, ornate fountains and, almost always, bandstands. Now they are both the central park and the focal point for social activities and provide much of modern Mexico's charm. Called the *plaza, zócalo, plaza de armas, jardín* or *parque centro*, it is the single feature that sets a Spanish-designed town apart from its equivalent in the United States and Canada. And about the nastiest thing one can call a Mexican town these days is a 'no-plaza village', for without a zócalo a town in Mexico doesn't really amount to a whole lot.

It didn't take very long for the general population to take on its present ethnic characteristics, for the virile Spaniards soon mixed with the indigenous population and created the mestizo, today the predominant ethnic group in the country by a wide margin. The degree of inter-mixture is amazing when you consider that there were never more than 20,000 Spaniards in New Spain at any one time.

Spain was an efficient ruler. It had to be, for it controlled Mexico for some 300 years; but the way it looked on Mexico as a cow to be milked irritated the upper-class Mexicans no end. For example, only *Peninsulares* or *Gachupines* (the Mexican term for Spaniards born in Spain) could hold high office. All wine had to be shipped in from the mother country, although it was well known that the colony was able to make wines of equal quality. The Spanish rule of thumb was 'What is good for Spain is good for Mexico.'

Eventually these, plus hundreds of other perceived indignities, became too much for the Mexicans to bear. A parish priest, one Miguel Hidalgo y Costilla, raised the cry for Mexican independence – the famous *Grito* repeated each 14 September by the leading political lights of the country, both national and local: 'Long live the Virgin of Guadalupe! Death to the Gachupines!'

Unfortunately Father Hidalgo was a much better schemer and plotter than he was a soldier, and it didn't take too long for the hated Gachupines to capture and execute him along with three of his cohorts and put their heads up on hooks at the four corners of the Alhóndiga, a large public granary in Guanajuato.

The rebels persevered, and in 1821 Mexico became a free and independent nation. The years that followed, characterized by political fecklessness, were typical of the freed Spanish colonies in North, South and Central America. For example, when Mexico became a nation it inherited the Spanish government holdings and a very efficient tax-collection system, but by means of diligent mismanagement it was able to dissipate its wealth and default on its foreign obligations within a very few years. In 1836 the fledgling Republic lost a great deal of its holdings when Texas revolted. Mexico was unable to overcome the Texans who were outnumbered by about the same ratio as the Aztecs had outnumbered the Spaniards some three centuries previously.

By 1846 relations between the United States and Mexico had reached an impasse over unpaid debts – a perennial problem besetting countries dealing with Mexico then and now – and Mexican mistreatment of US citizens residing in Mexico, among other things. The Mexicans in turn were incensed by the United States' annexation of the Republic of Texas which had been a free nation for a decade. There were dozens of other differences. Most people today believe the ensuing war was a one-sided mismatch with the odds greatly favouring the United States, but such was by no means the case. In fact, European military experts and politicians were sure that Mexico would win the war hands-down and in very short order. Mexico had a modern, supposedly well-trained army, a dashing officer corps, flamboyant uniforms and a very short supply line, whereas the United States was blessed with none of these supposed advantages.

When the war got under way, Santa Ana, the disgraced one-legged politician-cum-soldier who had been instrumental in losing Texas for the Mexicans, was in exile in Cuba. He promptly contacted the US government and suggested that he be smuggled into Mexico where he was sure he could persuade the government to call off hostilities on terms favourable to the US. The United States ostensibly fell in with his line of reasoning and returned him to Mexico via Veracruz – probably the dirtiest and most subtle trick a country at war ever played on an enemy.

Immediately upon Santa Ana's arrival in Mexico, he convinced the government to appoint him commander-in-chief of all Mexican forces, and also to make him president several times. By means of gross ineptitude in the way military operations were conducted, the Mexicans managed to lose the crucial battles of Buena Vista, Cerro Gordo and the ultimate struggle for Mexico City itself. This not only cost them the war, but also the parts of their northern territory that eventually became the US states of California, Arizona, Utah and Nevada, plus parts of New Mexico, Colorado and Wyoming.

Incidentally, this war is pretty much neglected in history lessons in the schools of both the United States and Mexico, although it was the most important struggle ever undertaken by either of the antagonists.

In 1857 a full-blooded Zapotec Indian from Oaxaca named Benito Juárez, whose statue today graces nearly every plaza in Mexico, took over as president and a three-year civil war began. It ended with the Juaristas passing laws disestablishing the Catholic Church as the official religion. Civil registration of marriages, births and deaths became compulsory, and the huge wealth of the Church was expropriated.

Juárez was still running the country when the French, with the assistance of Spain and England, invaded Mexico for the same old reason – non-payment of justly contracted debts. That is, England and Spain were strictly on a bill-collecting mission, but the French were after bigger game – the whole country. To this end they installed as emperor one Maximilian of Austria who should have been suspicious of the whole enterprise when he discovered that he would have to give up his claim to the Austrian crown if he accepted the crown of Mexico.

The result was that Mexico got another emperor – its second – and for a while Maximilian ruled Mexico, and fairly ably, too. Among the monuments to his brief reign is Mexico City's famous Reforma, the boulevard he conceived and executed as the focal point of the city, patterned after the Champs Elysees in Paris. Another enduring legacy of Emperor Maximilian is the *Code Napoleon*, still the basis of Mexican law. However, Maximilian and his scatty wife, Carlotta, had badly misjudged Mexico and the determination of the Mexicans and, worse, he had lodged his trust in a French emperor, Napoleon III. When push came to shove, Napoleon abandoned his protegé to his fate: to be stood up on a hill between two of his faithful generals and shot. The hill is called The Hill of Bells (Cerro de las Campanas) and is located on the outskirts of Queretaro. There is a little chapel on the spot now, built by the Austrians, and called, appropriately, 'the Chapel of Expiation'.

Díaz, who had served as a general under Juárez, followed his leader as president. Like Juárez, he was an Indian, and he ruled Mexico with an iron fist for some 30 years. These were the three decades during which the Republic made the greatest material advances since the days of Spanish rule. Under Díaz' aegis, railroads were built, highways constructed and many of the capital improvements serving Mexico today were created. But the poor suffered at the expense of the rich, and in 1911 they put on their armbands, took up their 7 mm Mausers and threw the rascals out.

The revolution had as its avowed aim the alleviation of the miserable conditions of the poor (especially the rural poor); the redistribution of land; and the destruction of the huge *haciendas* (estates). The rallying cry of one of its leaders, Emiliano Zapata, 'Tierra y Libertad!' ('Land and Liberty!') is still a force in the land. The revolution lasted until 1917, with flare-ups until the 1930s, and during that period Mexico essentially lapsed into anarchy. This is the period many people still think of when you mention Mexico. It was the land of *bandidos* and crossed bandoliers and big hats and wiry horses. During the final days of the revolution the country was plagued by roving gangs of bandits; the sacking of towns and the robbery and murder of wayfarers was commonplace. And it was during this final period that some of the most bloody fighting occurred between the religious fanatics known as the Cristeros and the proponents of secular government.

During the late 1930s Mexico expropriated the oil industry which was to prove a bonanza 40 years later when an immense pool of oil was discovered in the area around Villahermosa and Coatzalcoalcos. The country now ranks among the leading oil-producing nations, but this has done the average Mexican very little good. One reason for this is that under Mexican law the oil belongs to the state and not to the owner of the land over the oil. This means that an oil strike is just about the worst thing that can befall a small landowner, and as a direct result hundreds of farmers and ranchers lost their land.

It also encouraged the government to go on a spending spree that resulted in a total debt of some US$80 billion, a staggering amount for what is essentially a dirt-poor, overpopulated country. Naturally the result of this spending did José Fulano, the Mexican John Doe, little or no good, although it did enrich lots of politicians. Now the pendulum has swung the other way and essentially the International Monetary Fund is managing the finances of the country. José Fulano is feeling the pinch. But I will be the first to admit that if it weren't for the oil strike Mexico would probably have gone bankrupt a long time ago.

Mexico has always had a tendency to squander huge amounts of scarce money on projects that are unnecessary, never completed, and poorly conceived in the first place. For example, Mexico is dickering to buy a dozen F-15 war planes from the United States, despite the fact that it has no enemy worth mentioning and only one or two airports in the country from which these ultra-modern aircraft can operate. Another case is the huge steel mill at Las Truchas, a Pacific coast town that doesn't even appear on most maps. The mill was apparently designed with Ouija boards and everything about it was totally wrong – it is located far from existing or potential markets, and its machines didn't work well together (sometimes not at all). All in all the government admits to spending about US$4 billion on this white elephant which is still woefully inefficient and totally incapable of producing steel competitively.

A legacy of colonial rule is buried in the psyche of Mexican politicians to this day, and most politicos look on public office as a licence to steal for themselves, their families, and their supporters. The tourist will likely first encounter this at the border when the immigration officer casually requests a dollar or two for providing a document that is plainly printed *gratis!* in large letters. Done in precisely this way the payment is called *mordita*, which translates as 'little bite', and it's done all over the country at all levels of government.

The mordita is often confused with the *propina* by the visitor, but the two are entirely different. The mordita is a demanded bribe, while the propina is a gratuity, a tip. To put it another way, the traffic cop demands a mordita; a waiter or a cab driver earns a propina. The traffic policeman who is lucky can make maybe 1500 pesos a day, but the brother of a recent president is rumoured by his fellow countrymen to have wound up with millions of US dollars acquired via morditas.

Today Mexico has a stable government dominated by a single party, the Partido Revolucionario Institutional, commonly abbreviated PRI and pronounced 'Pree'. To give the semblance of multi-party rule, PRI actually supports the other political parties with sub rosa donations – not too large, of course. It is thoroughly understood by all concerned that PRI runs – and milks – Mexico.

The president, currently Miguel de la Madrid, is elected to a six-year term, and one of the most important planks in the Constitution of 1917 is 'no re-election'. This is so highly regarded in Mexico that it is not uncommon to encounter streets named 'No Re-election'. The president of Mexico has a great deal more power than his counterpart in the United States, which is bad for the country in a way because each president tends to junk the programs of his predecessors. For instance, during the 1950s the president embarked on a program of replacing the machinery in the inefficient sugar industry, but before the machinery could be installed his term ended, and the incoming president simply forgot the whole thing.

When the expensive machinery arrived from here and there around the world it was not unpacked, or even properly stored. In the early 1970s President Díaz-Ordaz remembered it, but by this time it was nothing but a mass of rusted junk, so of course the whole thing was forgotten. Forgotten, that is, until 1980 when the world price of sugar soared and Mexico was not only unable to take advantage of the higher price but couldn't make enough sugar for its own needs and had to use some more oil money to buy sugar.

There are hundreds of these stories and as you travel in Mexico you will encounter dozens of examples of inefficient planning and execution such as the new, modern cement plant that has never crushed a piece of limestone, or the dozens of idle locomotives in Guadalajara that were cannibalized because nobody ordered replacement parts while the government-owned railroads are chronically short of motive power.

CLIMATE & GEOGRAPHY

A great deal has been written about the various climates of Mexico, complete with tables giving the average temperatures for each month of the year at various locations, but the traveller has to remember only two things: The lower the altitude and/or the closer the ocean the hotter and muggier the climate; and the higher the elevation and/or the greater the distance from the ocean the more salubrious the climate.

The Spaniards were well aware of the effect of altitude on climate. To this day Mexico has no large city on the coast and the few ports all serve an inland metropolis in the high country behind them. Veracruz on the Gulf of Mexico and Acapulco on the Pacific serve Mexico City. Guaymas serves the prosperous state of Sonora, and the factories, mills and smelters of Monterrey and Saltillo now get their ocean freight through Tampico.

Mexico, the fourth largest country in the Americas, is shaped sort of like a cornucopia with a bump near the small end jutting out into the Caribbean. It begins by running south from the US border, then curves more and more toward the east and finally to the north so that Merida, Yucatan, is slightly farther north than Mexico City and due south of New Orleans. The Sierra Madre Oriental and the Sierra Madre Occidental mountain ranges run parallel to the two coasts. Between them is a high mesa containing Mexico's most important cities and the most interesting places. Beyond Mexico City the two ranges merge and continue down into Central America as one.

This quirk of geography makes Mexico the ideal place for the independent traveller. As every experienced wanderer knows, extremes of weather can do more than any single factor to ruin a trip, but in Mexico a drastic change in the weather can be had for the trifling price of a short bus ride.

This climatic variability makes it difficult to recommend clothing – radically different outfits are needed for the different altitudes, but the Central California-style clothes I wear pretty well cover the whole spectrum.

The strip of land along the United States frontier is mostly uninteresting, with the possible exception of the area next to the California border. Except for those arriving in Mexico via the Tijuana crossing – far and away Mexico's busiest port of entry – very few travellers stay even overnight in a Mexican border town.

LANGUAGE

Latin-American Spanish varies considerably from that spoken in Spain, and within Latin America there are again variations.

Mexicans, while having the natural distaste of any people to hearing their language treated with disrespect or worse, ignored, are remarkably willing to help those who make an effort.

Below is a bare bones guide for those who know no Spanish at all.

Pronunciation

a	a in *cart*
e	a in *late*, or e in *get*
i	ee in *feet*
o	o in *rope*
u	oo in *loot*
y	a vowel when alone or at end of a word; like ee in *feet*
b	between vowels sounds like *bw*
c	before e and i like s in *sit*; otherwise like k
d	like in *dog*, but less decisive
g	before e and i like h in *hat*; otherwise like g in *go*.
h	always silent
j	like h in *hat*
ll	usually like y in *yet*
ñ	like ni in *onion*
qu	like k in *kit*
r	strongly trilled, like Scottish r
rr	very strongly trilled
s	generally like s in *sit*
v	tends to be like b in *bad*
x	usually like in *taxi*; before a consonant, like s in *sit*. In Indian words often like ch in *loch*

The Basics

yes	*si*
no	*no*
please	*por favor*
thank you	*gracias*
thank you very much	*muchas gracias*
don't mention it	*no hay de qué*
excuse me	*perdone*
danger of death	*peligro de muerte*

Greetings & Civilities

Good morning	*Buenos dias*
Good afternoon	*Buenos tardes*
Good evening	*Buenos tardes*
Good night	*Buenas noches*
Good-bye	*Adiós*
Have a nice trip	*Hasta luego*

Questions

where	*dónde*
where is	*dónde está*
where are	*dónde están*
when	*cuándo*
what	*qué*
how	*cómo*
who	*quién*
why	*por qué*

Simple Phrases & Queries

I don't undertand
  No comprendo
Can you help me, please?
  Puede usted ayudarme, por favor?
I'd like a ticket to . . .
  Quiero un billete para . . .
Where are the toilets?
  Dónde está el baño?
How much is it?
  Cuánto es?
What time is it?
  Qué hora es?
Can you tell me where .... is?
  Puede decirme don'da está ....?
Where can I cash a travellers' cheque?
  Dónde puedo cambiar un cheque de viajero?

Days of the Week

Sunday	*domingo*
Monday	*lunes*
Tuesday	*martes*
Wednesday	*miércoles*
Thursday	*jueves*
Friday	*viernes*
Saturday	*sábado*

Time

hour	*hora*
minute	*minuto*
half an hour	*media hora*
day	*el dia*

week	*la semana*	24	*veinticuatro*
yesterday	*ayer*	25	*veinticinco*
10 o'clock	*las diez*	26	*veintiséis*
		27	*veintiisiete*
		28	*veintiocho*
Numbers		29	*veintinueve*
		30	*treinta*
0	*cero*	31	*treinta y uno*
1	*uno*	32	*treinta y dos*
2	*dos*	33	*treinta y tres*
3	*tres*	40	*cuarenta*
4	*cuatro*	50	*cincuenta*
5	*cinco*	60	*sesenta*
6	*seis*	70	*setenta*
7	*siete*	80	*ochenta*
8	*ocho*	90	*noventa*
9	*neuve*	100	*cien*
10	*diez*	101	*ciento uno*
11	*once*	110	*ciento diez*
12	*doce*	120	*ciento veinte*
13	*trece*	200	*doscientos*
14	*catorce*	300	*trescientos*
15	*quince*	1,000	*mil*
16	*dieceséis*	1,100	*mil cien*
17	*diecisiete*	2,000	*dos mil*
18	*dieciocho*	3,000	*tres mil*
19	*diecinueve*	10,000	*deiz mil*
20	*veinte*	50,000	*cincuenta mil*
21	*veintiuno*	100,000	*cien mil*
22	*veintidós*	1,000,000	*un millión*
23	*veintitrés*	1,000,000,000	*mil millones*

Facts for the Visitor

MONEY

The peso is the Mexican monetary unit. In this book it is written as M$. In Mexico it is indicated by $, identical to the sign used for the US and other dollars. Under some circumstances this can cause confusion, so occasionally the peso amount may be followed by MN, which means *Moneda Nacional* (national money). $1000MN translates as a thousand Mexican pesos – other countries use pesos too. But US$100 can also be written $100US, or $100dls, or even $100MA, this last meaning *Moneda Americano*.

The peso is divided into 100 centavos, abbreviated ctvos now and then. Because of the debasement of the peso, 20-centavo coins are the smallest you are likely to encounter, and they're quickly disappearing. Other coins are the 50-centavo (occasionally referred to as a *toston*), and one, five, 10, 20, 50 and 100-peso coins, these last two recently introduced and still in short supply.

Approximate exchange rates are:

US$1	=	M$218
A$1	=	M$148
£1	=	M$260

Before the devaluation early in 1982, the rate had been around 25 to the US dollar. As the peso will probably continue to drop sharply, it is advisable to change US dollars for pesos only as needed.

Because of Mexico's extremely close economic ties with the US, the United States' dollar is well known and readily negotiable almost anywhere in Mexico, but other currencies such as Swiss or French francs, or British pounds, are unfamiliar to the locals, especially in the smaller, out-of-the-way places, and could very well cause problems come conversion time. It is technically illegal to use foreign currency in Mexico, but you wouldn't

know it around the US border where dollars are as common as pesos.

Cash is easier to convert than travellers' cheques, but try to avoid offering torn banknotes. Even in the fair-sized city of Lagos de Moreno several banks refused to exchange a torn US$100 bill simply because it was ripped halfway across its face. (In fact a ragged US banknote is worth just exactly the same as one in pristine condition.) I usually carry cash on my travels in US$50 and $100 bills concealed in a leather money belt that looks just like any other belt a man uses to hold up his pants. These belts are available in luggage stores, men's shops, Easy Going and L L Bean, among others. (See Sources section.) If you get one be sure that the zipper-closed hidden pocket inside the belt is long enough for its intended purpose.

It is important to always have a few small-denomination Mexican bills and about 100 pesos in coins. The smaller businesses, and a few large ones, are chronically short of cash and unable to come up with change for bills as small as M$100. Out in the hinterlands it is always wise to have a few 500 and 1000-peso notes in reserve. Getting caught with nothing smaller than a M$5000 bill, worth about US$20, might just lead to a frantic scurrying if it happens outside of banking hours. If you get caught in this situation good bets for change are bus companies, gas stations and large hotels, although the latter will as not charge a bit for their trouble.

Travellers' cheques are not nearly as acceptable and readily negotiable as their vendors would lead you to believe, and the farther one gets from large cities the less acceptable they are. Even in a major city like Guadalajara banks might not want to cash them for non-depositors. They are accepted by the larger tourist-oriented hotels such as the Sheraton, Fenix and Holiday Inn, but these places tend to charge a hefty fee for the service and at some you even have to be a guest which can make it an awfully expensive way to get a travellers' cheque cashed.

When a bank condescends to accept travellers' cheques at all it may only do so as a service for depositors. It isn't all that hard to open an account in a Mexican bank, but it will probably take a couple of hours, at least, and require the counter-signatures of half the bank's staff, including the managing director. If you are going to spend some time in a given area it would be worth opening an account for the sake of convenience, if nothing else. But I would make it a practice to keep my peso account low because of the extreme likelihood of additional devaluation.

Credit cards are not too popular in Mexico, although they are gradually catching on. Part of the reason for the lack of acceptance is that a local must have an extremely high income to qualify for a card, which puts cards out of reach for the vast majority of the people. The most popular credit cards are the bank credit cards – Visa and Mastercharge – but their use is pretty well limited to the more expensive establishments. American Express comes in a distant third, followed by Diner's Club and Carte Blanche. Credit cards are not generally accepted for bus, ferry and train tickets, but airlines accept them as a matter of course. Many travellers carry an American Express card so they can receive mail at Amex offices, but in Mexico this is not too important because the country is so huge and there are so few American Express offices. Experienced travellers simply receive their mail at their hotel or via the *Lista de Correos* at the local post office.

In your travels around Mexico you will see sign after sign touting the extremely high interest rates paid on deposits in banks and other financial institutions. At the time of this writing almost any bank will pay 50-60% on deposits. But before putting your money into this sort of deposit be aware that you will be at the not-so-tender mercies of the government and any sort of devaluation could wipe out your high interest overnight. Actually the real advantage in doing this sort of investing is that Mexico has tough secrecy laws, which means that they don't make a practice of informing foreign governments – and especially the US government – of financial transactions, so that a non-Mexican citizen is left to decide for himself whether or not he will declare his gains to the tax collectors back home. The Mexican government withholds its own tax out of the interest, but this is a mere bagatelle compared to the vicious bite of the English-speaking countries.

Finally, the black market. I haven't forgotten it, but as the peso is freely exchangeable at the moment, banks are the place to exchange money. The exception is the travellers coming through the US-Mexican border. On both sides of the border *casas de cambio* (money exchange houses) are offering from four to eight more pesos per dollar than the 'official' exchange rate.

STREET ADDRESSES

Addresses in Mexico can be extremely confusing. There is almost no such thing as a numbering system, and it is far from uncommon for a building to have two or three street numbers, all computed using different systems. Or no system at all. As streets are fairly easy to find, and are also easy to show on a map, I have elected to dispense with street numbers where possible, preferring to locate a place as being between two cross streets, opposite the main bus station, near the cathedral on the same side of the street, or any way I think will simplify things for the wayfaring stranger.

If you have occasion to correspond with the publisher or myself about a place, please stick to the same system of locating by the block rather than the street number.

HOTELS

In Mexico the minimum wage is around M$1000 a day in most states, and a lot of workers don't even make that much. This means that a M$800– or M$900-a-night hotel room is beyond the wildest dreams of the majority of the locals. And a travelling mechanic, small-time salesman, truck driver or minor civil servant simply does not rate an expense account that will accommodate a M$1000 hotel room or a M$600 lunch.

Therefore Mexico must of necessity have a lot of low-priced, respectable hotels, inexpensive fixed-price lunches and bargain-rate transport. These facilities are intended primarily for the local inhabitants, but the foreigner is more than free to take advantage of them. Not only free, but royally welcomed in most cases. Best of all, as a rule the traveller is treated much better in a M$800-a-night (room with bath) hotel than in one of the many M$7500-a-night 'international' houses that won't even give you a smile or a kind word when you register. It is the smaller hotels intended for locals that will probably help the motorcyclist get his or her steed up over the threshold and into the lobby for the night, or will describe how to catch the bus for Tlaquepaque for M$20 rather than take a taxicab for 50 times as much.

In Mexico many of the smaller hotels are actually converted mansions left over from colonial times, with flower-bedecked patios and high, high ceilings. In the range of M$500 and up you can count on an attached bath most of the time, although the water may never get very warm. But the expensive hotels don't necessarily have hot water either, and they seldom spend much design time on ambience. Small hotels catering to the local population very rarely have anyone who speaks anything other than Spanish, but this no great problem. Hotels are anxious to do business, and will understand perfectly when you ask for a room in English, German, Japanese or Tagalog. 'If you don't want a room, why are you standing there with your bag in front of the reception desk?' is their line of reasoning.

By and large the smaller the town the less expensive the hotel, and there are instances where it will actually pay to stay at a smaller outlying town rather than a major city. In Mexico I seldom pay more than M$1100 a night for a room with attached bath, and most of the time I pay around M$800 or even less. Say around US$4.

In this book I have tried to list hotels in the region of M$600 to $1200 single most of the time. There are many cheaper hotels, down around M$400 or even less, but these leave too much to be desired in the eyes of most travellers. 'Single', by the way, means one person in a room. 'Double' is two people to a room. As a Mexican family is liable to be fairly large there are hotels that make it a policy to rent to large groups, say three to six people, but they are beyond the scope of this book in most instances. And the price charged for two people will be partially determined by whether one wants a double bed or a pair of twins, which cost more.

Hotel rates are price controlled in Mexico, and you will probably see a price list posted in your room – usually on the back of the door to the hall or patio. If you are charged more than the stated price, however, don't jump to the conclusion that you're being ripped off. Because of ferocious inflation the government has relaxed or revised its rulings in many cases. If there's no list in your room you can see a copy in the office, but it will probably be a waste of time. You'd be better off looking at the house and the room and deciding for yourself if the place suits your pocket and your inclinations without recourse to price lists. After about a week in small hotels in Mexico you will be able to tell almost by walking past what the rates are likely to be.

Even when the rates are as posted you can often get a lower price by polite haggling. Or the establishment may have automatically shown you the most expensive room in the place because they assume this is what a rich tourist wants. It is no disgrace to ask for something cheaper – it's a way of life for the locals. So don't hesitate to ask for a cheaper room if you think one might be available. Just ask, 'Tiene otro cuarto mas barato?'

My favourite type of hotel is a Spanish-built converted mansion, the older the better. These have thick stone walls and are usually built around a shady central courtyard that often boasts flowers and a fountain. These heavy walls have a sort of thermal flywheel effect in that they take all day to heat and in turn give the warmth back during the chill of the night. This is important because fuel is terribly expensive by local standards and most buildings, young or old, do not have heating facilities. And this applies to the super deluxe hotels, too.

Air-conditioning usually costs extra, sometimes as much as M$500 a night, but many rooms come with a big, slow-turning ceiling fan, often provided with a five or 10-speed switch. I prefer the fan hands-down because the air-conditioner often makes noise more than it cools, and I have yet to encounter a Humphrey Bogart fan (remember *Casablanca*?) that didn't work on most of its speeds. The trick is to turn the fan on when you retire, and crawl under a single sheet. The sheet shields the body from the direct blast of the fan which would otherwise leave you chilled in some areas and sweating-hot in others.

Electricity is expensive in Mexico, and even in fairly expensive hotels the room lighting – usually only a 25-watt bulb – is rarely adequate for reading. The solution is to carry your own 60 or 75-watt bulb. However, don't expect to use devices drawing eight or 10 amperes or more – the wiring and fuses simply aren't up to the job. I've known several travellers who caused fulmination and consternation by attempting to use their hand-held hair dryers in small-town hotels.

Hotels are so inexpensive in Mexico that I'm completely at a loss to account for the popularity of motor homes and huge house trailers in Mexico. These outfits cost an arm and a leg to own and operate and are an awful lot of trouble, too, because the campgrounds they require aren't at all common in Mexico. When finally located they are invariably on the outskirts of town where land is cheap, away from the centre of town which is where the action is and which is the most charming part of the area.

I have tried to list hotels in locations where there are lots of hotels in a similar price range. This will give the first-time traveller more opportunity to find a vacant room if the ones I recommend are full. And I have made an effort to list hotels in locations that are easy to find. In Guadalajara, for instance, I give you a selection in sight of the main bus station as well as some more conveniently located houses uptown.

Hotel Prices

In some cases I simply walked up and asked the clerk the price of a single room with bath; in others the classification was based on what I actually paid. In no case did I endeavour to dicker about the price, and I applied a minimum of Spanish. In other words, I made every effort to appear as an ordinary wayfarer with not too much experience in the country. I wouldn't be surprised to hear that the next prospective guest was quoted an entirely different price, either higher or lower. As I said, there are no fixed rules.

Up to M$600 a night	inexpensive
to M$1500 a night	moderate
to M$2500 a night	expensive
to M$3500 a night	very expensive
Over M$3500 a night	wildly expensive

Restaurants are classified similarly, based on the cost of the *comida corrida* or an order of the standard *enchiladas Suizas* served by about 90% of the restaurants in Mexico:

Up to M$300	inexpensive
to M$500	moderate
to M$750	expensive
to M$1000	very expensive
Over M$1000	wildly expensive

Prices generally are compared to prices in Mexico, not the rest of the world. For instance, a dinner costing US$10 in San Francisco probably wouldn't amount to a whole lot, but that would be about M$2500 and would be up in the higher brackets in Mexico. And if I say something is expensive, I mean by Mexican standards, not those of the United States, the UK or West Slobbovia.

Currency conversion concerns some travellers a great deal. I spend only the local currency no matter what country I'm in, but for those to whom it is a concern, here's a simple technique using a pocket calculator: Pesos are quoted as so many to the US dollar. Enter this in the calculator and punch the 'divide' key, then the = key. The answer will immediately appear as a decimal. That is the value of the peso in dollars. What you are doing is solving for the reciprocal. Not all pocket calculators are capable of this function, so before buying a shirt-pocket calculator for travel use, enter a 2, then the divide sign, then the = sign. The answer will be 0.5 if the calculator can solve for reciprocal. This check only takes a few seconds and is immeasurably easier than pawing through the instructions. There are also special calculators programmed for currency conversion, but for my money a small, all-purpose calculator works just as well. I suggest the kind that is powered by a small photo cell, rather than a battery-driven model. Sunlight is very much available in Mexico, whereas calculator batteries can be awfully hard to locate.

IVA, pronounced 'ee-vah', means *Impuesto al Valor Agregado*. This sales tax of sorts can run as high as 15%, and is added to the charges on almost every bill. Smaller establishments aren't required to charge it – the government's acknowledgement of the difficulties in collecting from the myriads of push-cart peddlers and hole-in-the-wall merchants. They are supposed to pay a flat rate and recover this from their customers in the form of higher charges. In practice, most of the street peddlers simply slip through the cracks of the system.

ENTRY FORMALITIES
Because Mexico actively solicits tourist business crossing the border is relatively easy, especially for US citizens. A 'tourist permit', often miscalled a 'pasaporte' by immigration officials, good for a maximum of 180 days – not six months – may be issued on proof of US citizenship, and the *Migración* people will accept almost anything on paper as documentary proof, even a California driver's licence.

Canadians also do not need passports and are admitted for 90 days on proof of citizenship. Nationals of most other countries must present a passport and will get a permit for 90 days, or for a shorter period extendable to 90 days.

Tourist permits are also issued by consulates and the various non-border tourist offices, though nothing much will be gained for US citizens except wasted time. And for those arriving in Mexico via commercial airlines or steamship, things are easiest of all – the carrier takes care of the paperwork.

A warning: tourist permits must be stamped and/or issued when you enter Mexico. Mexico regards this as a responsibility of the traveller, and at many border crossings the *Migración* officers ignore people crossing the border, leading many tourists to believe they are home clean and dry. The catch comes some 50-100 km south of the border at an inspection point. It might result in backtracking to get this vital piece of paper.

Even though US and Canadian citizens

do not need a passport in Mexico I feel that all travellers should carry passports outside their own country. For one thing, a passport is usually required for financial transactions such as cashing travellers' cheques. For another, it is a great help when picking up mail at the post office. Also, people often change their travel plans. If you happen to be in Yucatán you might just decide to go through Belize to Guatemala, visit Tikal on the way, and return to the US via Comitán and San Cristóbal de las Casas where the weather is cooler and the scenery more interesting than that of Mexico's east coast. Without a passport there is very little chance that you would be admitted to either Belize or Guatemala.

The regulations for US citizens entering Mexico from Belize or Guatemala vary from time to time, and it may be necessary to obtain a tourist permit from a consulate rather than at the border. This has happened to me a couple of times, and I have also been issued a 180-day permit at Ciudad Cuauhtémoc as a matter of course. Non-US citizens would be well advised to take no chances and apply at the Mexican consulate first.

Working in Mexico

The 180-day (or less) tourist permit is the most practical of all Mexican travel documents and most Americans residing in Mexico are actually using the temporary tourist permit rather than suffering the additional paperwork necessary to obtain the more complicated *residencia* permit. Similarly, students planning to enter one of Mexico's dozens of schools would, in most cases, be well advised to opt for the easily-obtained tourist permit rather than the student permit.

Mexico is one of the most xenophobic of nations, and getting a work permit is next door to impossible for foreigners, except for language teachers sponsored by an accredited school, and artists, writers, photographers and the like. Even if you fall into one of the latter categories you will probably find getting a permit more trouble than it is worth. Also it is extremely important to realize than an artist working in Mexico under a work permit is usually forbidden to sell his or her output on the local economy. I know a fellow who was deported because he made the mistake of photographing and writing – in English yet! – a brochure for one of the local luxury hotels.

Customs

Mexico is fairly lenient about the amount and type of goods a tourist is allowed to bring in, and as a rule of thumb anything that strikes the Customs official as reasonable will be passed without a second glance. But be warned that smuggling into Mexico by Mexican nationals is one of the most severe problems facing the government and there is a great deal of pressure on the customs people to eliminate the practice. It is forbidden to bring in such commonplace items as toasters, calculators, stereos, portable radios and so on. If you travel with one of those big cassette-radio ghetto blasters the odds are it will be confiscated on the spot.

When travelling from Tijuana or Mexicali toward Guadalajara you will encounter an inspection station out in the middle of nowhere in the desert east of Sonoita where all vehicles are stopped and the travellers and their belongings are inspected. You must have your tourist permit or other documents; otherwise there is an excellent chance you will wind up retracing your route at least as far as Sonoita. And while you are going through the customs part of this inspection take a careful look at the rooms full of stereos, computers and so on that travellers before you have donated to the greater good of the government.

ELECTRICITY

Electric service in Mexico is nominally the same as in the US – 117 volts, 60 hz. Outlets take the common parallel-bladed plugs found on US appliance cords, except that a U-ground outlet is extremely rare. Light bulbs are the same US 'regular' with Edison Medium Screw bases. Bayonet-type bases similar to European ones are rarely encountered. Voltage goes up and down like a yo-yo and can get so low at times that a NiCad battery charger won't work. In fact, constant-voltage transformers are almost standard equipment for owners of television sets to prevent low voltage from shrinking the picture to postage-stamp size, or even eliminating it altogether.

FOOD

Most Mexican breakfasts are the approximate equivalent of the Continental breakfast favoured by Europeans and weight-watchers, and a popular selection is *café con leche* (coffee with hot milk) with *pan dulces* (small semi-sweet cakes). The latter are generally placed in a wicker basket on the breakfast table, and you pay for what you eat.

Mexico prefers to take its main meal of the day at lunch, usually served during the first half of the afternoon. If dinner is eaten it is the same fare as lunch – separate menus are almost unheard of – and it is served until quite late, say 10-11 pm in the larger cities. The eating bargain for lunch, sometimes available at dinner as well, is the multi-course *comida corrida* (set meal). Some places list it as *menu turistico*. Usually the comida corrida offers four or five courses, with a limited selection of entrees, and it costs about half as much as the same items when ordered a la carte, or even less.

Maíz (in English, corn or maize) is the basic ingredient of the native diet. Anyone returning to Mexico after an absence of some years will immediately discover that tortillas and tamales taste much stronger than before. This is because Mexico has, for economic reasons, ceased importing white corn from the US and switched to the much cheaper yellow corn grown primarily for livestock food. The yellow corn has much more 'corn' flavor than the

white. It is sold through the network of government-operated stores called *Conasupos* which you will see in almost every town with a population over 1000. Originally the stores were intended as a cut-rate alternative to the price-gouging village stores, and to this day they primarily sell the necessities of life at subsidized prices.

The majority of Mexican dishes are not very 'hot' – contrary to returning tourists' wild tales. But be very, very cautious in applying the contents of the small bowls of *salsa* (sauce) that grace most dining tables in homes and restaurants. These can vary in intensity from bland to blistering, with absolutely no difference in appearance. Proceed with extreme caution until the degree of heat is ascertained.

There is no standardization in Mexican cooking, and a given dish may differ drastically from what has gone under the same name in another area, or even in another restaurant just up the street. Take the well-known tortilla as a prime example. In most of Mexico it is a corn-based unleavened pancake, almost identical to the chapatti of India in size and shape. But in parts of the state of Sonora tortillas are made of wheat flour, about one to two mm thick, and as much as 45-50 cm in diametre. Because of their extreme thinness and their large diameters these tortillas must be hand made and are gradually losing popularity as a result, but they are really good and should be sought out and enjoyed at every opportunity.

Don't expect the sort of 'Mexican' food in a restaurant in Mexico that you get in a US 'Mexican restaurant'. The latter serve what is basically Tex-Mex food, with about as much relation to the real thing as chop suey bears to Mandarin cooking.

The food in the expensive restaurants and deluxe hotels is very seldom Mexican at all. The Mexicans themselves call this cuisine 'international' and it is about the same as you might reasonably expect to find in establishments of like quality anywhere in the world, except that in

Mexico the standard of cooking is somewhat lower than in London, Paris, Milan or Barcelona.

The most economical – and often the best – food can be found either in the town market itself or somewhere close by. Another place for inexpensive, reasonably well-cooked meals is in the little restaurants that tend to spring up around the central bus terminals. The terminals always have their own restaurants, usually cafeteria-style, but most local travellers tend to regard these as too expensive and/or their food as inferior, so these little restaurants have come into being. Some are so small that only the actual kitchen is under the roof, and the customers either stand around outside eating out of their hands, or the *patrona* has brought a couple of tin tables and a few chairs from her home for her customers' convenience.

Dishes from other parts of the world are working their way into the native menus. *Hamburguesas* (hamburgers) and pizza are two examples that come to mind, but there are others. The former is now a staple in almost every hole-in-the-wall beanery in Mexico, although here, too, the Mexican penchant for non-standardization comes into play, and what a tourist who orders a hamburguesa receives is sometimes a complete surprise.

Vegetarians are in paradise when they visit Mexico. The markets are chock-a-block with organically-grown fruits and vegies fresh from the fields. There are many fruits and vegetables unknown outside Mexico that are deserving of wider distribution. And street-corner vendors peddle sliced and chopped produce ready to eat so you are even saved the necessity of strolling down to the market with your Swiss army knife.

Beer

Mexicans are justifiably proud of their beer, which perfectly complements their cuisine. It is customarily served very cold, as befits a warm country. There are around 30 different brands, many of which have a limited, local distribution. Leon Negro, for example, is a local beer brewed in Merida and seldom seen outside of Yucatán, Campeche and Chiapas. In my opinion Superior is the best nationally distributed beer in the country. It is brewed at various locations and is available in almost every town in the country. My second choice is always Bohemia, which used to be called an ale, but to me it is an out-and-out lager, albeit an excellent one.

Among the other beers, Corona de Baril is my third choice. It is not a draft beer at all and takes its name from the shape of its bottle. Dos Equis is a dark beer and is extremely popular with Americans, but it has a slight apple flavor which in my opinion is completely out of place in beer. Indio is another dark beer apparently intended to compete with Dos Equis – not very good, but at least there is no apple taste. Carta Blanca is made in the image of the weak, tasteless beers of the United States.

Tres Equis comes in two varieties, *clara* (light) and *oscura* (dark). It is not universally distributed. Theoretically the clara should resemble Superior – they're made by the same company – but to me it doesn't, nor does the oscura taste much like Dos Equis to me, but this may well be due to the packaging – I detest canned beer. Modelo and Tecate are two beers generally put up in cans, although the makers of Tecate have recently seen the light and are beginning distribution in two different designs of glass bottles. I've tried a few bottled Tecates and find the beer vastly improved.

Mexican beers can run a bit higher in alcoholic content than US beers, which with the enhancing effect of Mexico's high altitudes can cause acute embarrassment if you overestimate your capacity.

Wine & Spirits

Wine is not too popular in Mexico as it really doesn't go too well with local food, but there are some excellent wines made in Mexico, although this statement will stir up a lot of argument from people who have spent time in the Republic. The problem is that Mexicans are pretty well adjusted to beer and treat wine the same way. Wine should be stored on its side or with the cork down, kept at temperatures lower than convenient for most stores and restaurants in Mexico, and be drunk before it has an opportunity to over-age. In Mexico it tends to be mishandled all along the line, so it is wise not to order wine in a restaurant unless you are reasonably certain of the vendor's ability to provide unspoilt wine. Don't assume that because you are dining in a fancy restaurant on 'international' food that the wine will be up to standard. I've been served so much bad wine in Mexico that I very rarely order it any more.

If you are served a bad bottle of wine in a restaurant, treat it just as you would in London, Stockholm or San Francisco – send it back. And don't accept a bottle of wine unless it is opened at table. Mexicans, not knowing much about wine, are prone to shove the cork back in a returned bottle and try it on the next customer.

Be that as it may, the wine is sometimes excellent when it leaves the winery, and nearly always good, no matter how it winds up on the table. The most reliable way to buy wine in Mexico is from the large supermarkets that are springing up in the larger cities and doing a huge volume of business. Because they have a rapid turnover their table wines are rarely on the shelf long enough to spoil. Mexican cities generally have lots of parks which are ideal for picnics, and what is a picnic without wine? I buy a bottle of Urbino, Vergél, Los Reyes, or Cotillón at the nearest *supermercado*, along with the other ingredients – Mexican supermarkets have a much wider range of merchandise than do their counterparts in the US with their 101 brands of cereals – and take myself to the nearest shady park bench for a meal that beats almost any restaurant's.

Mexico is the home of tequila and its

close relative, mescal, either of which is likely to come with a worm in the bottom of the bottle. The advantage of these two beverages from the standpoint of the local resident is that they can be had dirt cheap, and the average Mexican is totally unable to understand their popularity with foreigners. In an ordinary bar that doesn't have much tourist business you will completely confuse the bartender if you order a Margarita. If you feel you can't live without one of these concoctions you should locate a saloon catering to the tourist trade, usually to be found in or near an expensive hotel, and with prices to match.

Brandy is now very popular in Mexico, with a fair number of brands from which to choose. My personal favourite is Viejo Vergél, with Presidente, Gran Vergél and San Marcos close runners-up.

Imported liquors are terribly expensive. Wines, for instance, run five and six times as much as the Mexican brands, and the same is true of hard liquor, although many well-known brands are actually made in Mexico.

Soft Drinks

Coca-Cola (called Coca by the locals) and Pepsi-Cola are universally available, usually at very low prices. Fruit-flavoured carbonated drinks are also extremely popular, and they come in a plethora of flavors. Would you believe apricot and apple, for instance? Mexicans love sweets, and their soft drinks, including Coca and Pepsi, are loaded with sugar. If, like me, you dislike excessive sweetness, you can order *agua mineral* (mineral water) – *con gas* (carbonated) or *sin gas* (non-carbonated). Agua mineral is the correct term, but some people will perhaps understand better if you ask for Agua Tehuacán.

RESTROOMS (Toilets)

Public restrooms in Mexico are located in railroad stations, bus terminals, markets, airports and ferry terminals, although the railroad stations are generally accessible only around actual train time. Unfortunately these facilities are rarely right downtown, which is the focal point of the towns and cities, so feel free to use those of the large tourist hotels which operate restrooms for the public as an adjunct of the bar. Another safe bet is the franchised quick-food emporiums such as Denny's and VIPs. They, like the tourist hotels, make it a point to keep their restrooms spic and span. The central bus terminals vary widely in cleanliness. Some are surgically clean, others would gag a maggot, but they have one great, compelling advantage over some other facilities – they never close.

For a man, the friendly corner bar is a good bet, but in many towns women are absolutely not permitted on the premises. Not that most women would want to use the facilities even if they were admitted because as often as not the urinal is just a trough at one end of the room, or the wall itself. As with most things in Mexico there is an exception, and that is the 'Ladies Bar' – watch for the sign.

Uniformly of low sanitary standards are the restroom facilities at the public markets. These are accessible during ordinary market hours, which may be from 4 am to as late as 10 pm. These are really intended for the market people, but outsiders are never turned away. And most always the way is barred by an elderly person requesting money. For those urgently seeking relief a peso or five is a small price to pay for a piece of toilet paper and an opportunity.

Papel higienico (toilet paper) – if available at all – is manufactured strictly as a fill-in during slack times at the sandpaper works, so it is a good idea to always carry a small packet of Kleenex tissues. The locals make do in markets and some other public places with ordinary newspaper. Among other serious technical disadvantages newspaper has a tendency to plug drains, which is why so many toilets have a wastepaper basket standing alongside them for used toilet paper. Be prepared for abuse if you are responsible for stopping up the toilet by failing to make use of the basket.

TOBACCO

The cigarette industry is alive and thriving in Mexico, using home-produced tobacco. *Cigarros* (cigarettes) are available in domestic brands as well as in locally-manufactured foreign brands. Cigarettes are fast-moving items and they are generally in fairly good condition when purchased. The same cannot be said of *puros* (cigars) or pipe tobacco which are usually allowed to dry out in the shop to the point of being unusable.

Sanborn's stores are about the best places in Mexico to buy smokers' supplies.

HEALTH

Diarrhoea has been a severe problem with foreigners in Mexico since at least 1519. It is variously called the 'Toltec Two-step', 'Montezuma's Revenge', or just plain *turista*, and is the same complaint known as 'Delhi Belly', 'Malta Dog' and other appellations. Diarrhoea affects travellers all over the world. It has been the subject of a great deal of study over the years, some of it voluntary, both within and without Mexico. At various times I've heard it attributed to 'the water', the change in diet by people unaccustomed to the lard used in Mexican cooking, local spices, blown dust, high altitude, and a goodly number of other things. My guess is that at various times and with different people the cause may be all of these, or none. Some escape unscathed, and others fold up like a Swiss army knife.

I've read books and magazine articles that recommend – in all seriousness – dipping green vegetables in a disinfectant solution before eating, boiling all water and taking all sorts of inconvenient precautions to ward off the evil complaint. And I have on several occasions traveled with people who followed these recommendations to the letter, and in almost every case they wound up deathly sick. My preferred remedy for the complaint is a liquid called Kaomycín, available from every drug store in Mexico. It is a mixture of antibiotic and Kaopectate tasting pretty much the same as the latter. The trick is to take a big swig, say about 15-25 ml, at the first sign of the trots, followed by another in two or three hours. If it doesn't cure the complaint it will at least mitigate the problem. If the internal difficulties get out of hand to the point where cramping begins, Kaomycín will still alleviate the misery. This is a specific that treats both the disease and the symptoms.

Lomotil is also popular. Again available at every chemist's shop, it is an opium derivative that treats the symptoms rather than the disease, and many travellers swear by it. I don't, for I've been told by several Mexican physicians that simply stopping the diarrhoea without getting to the basic problem might very well make things worse.

Entero-vioformo is still found in a few drug stores, and many travel books, usually the older ones, recommend it. This compound is actually a vermifuge and not a diarrhoea medicine. Some years back the Japanese found that Entero-vioform affected the optical nerves and was actually causing blindness. Since then it has been barred from most markets in the civilized world, but it is still to be found in a few drugstores in Mexico, especially in rural areas. There the farmers buy it by the bucketful to use on livestock.

Turista should not last longer than about three days. If it persists you may have something more serious which requires treatment by a physician.

Two mosquito-borne diseases are endemic in Mexico, although more of a problem for the locals than the casual sojourners. The most serious is malaria, called *paludismo* in Spanish. Anti-malaria medicine works but has to be taken for a considerable period before and after exposure. It is widely available in the United States, but requires a prescription. If your personal physician knows much about tropical medicine he or she is the one to see, but is a very rare bird. The best places in the United States to find a person knowledgeable about such medicines are clinics operated for seamen in most seaports, tropical medicine clinics found in a few scattered locations, and travellers' clinics such as the one at San Francisco International Airport. This last is open 24 hours a day and is probably the best of its kind in the country. Besides offering the usual emergency treatment, they are equipped to give inoculations on the spot for every disease for which shots are available. Otherwise it is best to seek the recommendation of a physician or a first-class pharmacy in Mexico.

The other mosquito-carried disease is seldom fatal, but one of the most miserable ailments around. Its rightful name is 'dengue fever' but it is better known as 'breakbone fever', and a more fitting description would be hard to devise.

The best way to avoid these two complaints is to avoid being bitten by mosquitoes, and this is best accomplished by keeping well slathered with a bug repellent containing a high percentage of DEET. The more inert ingredients in bug dope and the less DEET, the more often it will have to be applied. I use 75% and 100% DEET supplied by REI. An evening application is good for all night. If you have trouble locating a high-concentration product at your local pharmacy, REI is listed in the Sources section.

Though it does harbour the Revenge – which by no means bothers all visitors – and the abovementioned mosquito-carried diseases, Mexico is a relatively healthy place. For the rare medical complaint more serious than turista Mexico offers excellent facilities. The government makes a concerted effort to see that every village has a physician and at least a small hospital. To this end medical students are assigned to remote towns for a year before they are licenced to practice. In effect this means that a little no-plaza village way out in the boonies might take better care of a patient than a physician in one of the more affluent cities who hasn't cracked a textbook in 33 years. (Medical schools in Mexico are good enough to attract a large number of students from the US, and there are so many English-speaking medical students that there is even a 'Students' Wives' Club' in Guadalajara.)

Nearly all medicines available in Europe, Canada and the US are available in Mexico, usually under the same names, although the Spanish pronunciation will sometimes cause confusion. The safest bet is to take your medicine bottle to the *farmacia* for a refill if the label has a typewritten list of the contents. A prescription is unnecessary for almost anything you can possibly need. Pharmaceutical items are price-controlled by the government and are generally much cheaper than in the US.

For eyeglass wearers it is a good idea to carry a copy of your optical prescription – optometrists are thick on the ground in Mexico. Lacking a prescription, if you have the misfortune to break a lens, gather up the pieces very carefully. The skilled optician will often be able to deduce the prescription by working from the shards. Getting an eye examination and a new prescription won't cost very much, probably about 25% of the US price, although here it will help immeasurably to know the Spanish pronunciation of the letters on the eye chart. Optical shops, by the way, usually have their own in-house lens grinder, and thus are able to offer very rapid service. All types of lenses are available, including Photo-grey.

BOOKS

There have been dozens of excellent books published on Mexico over the years. The following are a few I have used and enjoyed.

The War With Mexico, Justin H Smith (published by Peter Smith). This is the definitive book on the Mexican-American war, the most important war ever fought by either of the countries involved.

Terry's Guide To Mexico, updated by James Norman (Doubleday 1972). This is the best general guidebook ever written on Mexico, although by now it is some 15 years or so out of date. There have been six other editions since 1909 and any of them is well worth reading.

Peoples' Guide to Mexico, Carl Franz (John Muir Publishing Company). Latest edition. An excellent book by a writer who really knows the country. More a set of suggestions for getting along and staying out of jail than a guidebook. It is very popular with the younger travellers who tend to use VW vans in their travels. Recommended for entertainment as well as for its practical advice.

Mexico, a General Sketch, Pan American Union (1911). Much information about the country at the end of the Diaz regime.

Six Faces of Mexico, edited by Russell C Ewing (University of Arizona Press, 1966). The best book I know for getting an overview of the country. Intended as a textbook, but available in many libraries.

The Easy Guides to Mexico City, Acapulco, Guadalajara, etc, Richard Bloomgarden (Editur SA, Lago Silverio No 224, Mexico 17, DF). At last count there were 20-odd of the Easy Guides, all specializing in a small region, city, or even a church. Priced in US currency (presently US$1.95 to 3.95). Available in Sanborn's in most cities and just about any place English-speakers can be expected to accumulate. Some have gone through a dozen revisions, and all are quite up-to-date. Definitely recommended.

El Chingoles, Primer Diccionario de Lenguaje Popular Mexicano, Pedro Maria de Usandizaga y Mendoza (Costa-Ami

Editores, S A, Soto 62, Mexico 3, DF Mexico). If you have even dimly remembered high-school Spanish this book will enchant, entertain and amuse you, and perhaps give rise to a few belly laughs. One of the funniest books I ever read.

The Tropical Traveller, John Hatt, Pan (UK) and Hippocrene (US). Not a book on Mexico per se, but rather a general guide to travel in the lands between the Tropic of Cancer and the Tropic of Capricorn. Full of good advice and handy tips. I don't agree with his penchant for large, heavy, hard-sided wheeled suitcases, but that's all right – John probably doesn't wholly agree with me, either.

AIM newsletter. For the last couple years or so I've been subscribing to a very informative newsletter. A bimonthly, it is published and mailed in Mexico. Each issue concentrates on a specific area, and being a recently researched newsletter with short lead time, it is replete with up-to-date information. The cost is a mere US$10 per year (six issues) and is a very good bet for anyone seriously interested in Mexico, although it is slanted more toward the prospective resident than the independent traveller. Address: Apartado Postal 31-70, Guadalajara 45050, Jalisco, Mexico.

The Mexico City *News*. This is an English-language newspaper distributed nationwide. It offers both national and international coverage. Although I read Spanish-language papers while in Mexico, I also make it a point to read the News as its point of view is somewhat different from that of the more closely-controlled Spanish-language papers intended for the locals. They tend to be heavy on political handouts.

Atención. If you are going to stay in San Miguel de Allende for any length of time make it your first order of business to stop at the Colibri bookstore on the plaza and pick up a copy of *Atención,* a weekly bilingual paper that specializes in local information.

The Bantam New College Spanish & English Dictionary. Finding a dictionary of Mexican Spanish is awfully difficult. There are lots of Spanish-English dictionaries, but Mexicans don't speak Spanish Spanish, which is what most of the books feature. This book is larger than it should be because it is printed on pulp paper instead of high-quality paper, hence it is not really pocketable. But it is the only dictionary I can recommend. The very best book of this type is the Velásquez dictionary, but it weighs about a kg and is not portable unless you put wheels on it like those on some suitcases.

COMMUNICATIONS

Mexico has door-to-door mail service in all but the tiniest towns and there is no reason at all why you can't have your mail sent to your hotel, assuming you expect to be there a few weeks. 'Poste Restante' or 'General Delivery' is *Lista de Correos* in Mexico, literally 'Mail List'. In many places people receiving letters have their names inscribed on a public list. This saves having to wait in line some minutes to find out if there is mail today. Mexico uses the Spanish system of personal nomenclature, in which the mother's name is listed last, preceded by the father's name. This means that a Mexican clerk will automatically file a letter for 'John Wesley Noble' under 'W' and not 'N'. If you use only two names it can eliminate a mite of confusion now and then.

Both air mail and surface mail are slow, either in or out, but by and large air mail is the least slow of the two, although it wouldn't be wise to bet on it. In fact, Mexican mail service is so inferior to that of the US (which in turn is far worse than that of Great Britain) that Mexican businesses in border towns habitually receive their mail at the nearest post office on the American side of the line. The slight nuisance involved in crossing the border to pick up their daily mail is far outweighed by the better service.

Packages either in or out of Mexico are usually more trouble than they're worth. Coming in the risk of loss is high, and you will probably have to go to the Customs office to pick it up. Going out is almost as bad, and a package sent to a foreign destination must be inspected by the Customs people before it can be accepted by the Post Office. If for some odd reason somebody sends valuables to Mexico they should be sent by registered mail to prevent pilferage – and the best of luck to you.

There is a story about a mail collector responsible for gathering letters from pillar boxes. He always started out his morning rounds with a pocketful of small rocks. As he came to each box he would drop a pebble through the slot and by careful listening could tell whether there was enough mail inside to make it worthwhile to open the box. I have never seen this with my own eyes, but I've been told about it so many times that I'm convinced it happened somewhere. And to anybody knowing Mexico at all it sounds perfectly logical.

Telegraph & Telephone

In Mexico a telegram is delivered the way a telegram is meant to be delivered, by a young man on a bicycle or small motorcycle. There are telegraph offices – using mostly the old clickety-clack system – in almost every town in the country, regardless of how remote or isolated.

Things have changed, however. In early 1984 some Mexican telegraph offices were refusing to accept telegrams for the US, and a telegraph operator told me it was because Western Union hadn't been paid for delivering them for some time.

There is a different sort of problem with receiving money by wire. The government-operated telegraph service doesn't deliver the money to the addressee for at least a week, and sometimes over two weeks. During the time it is holding the money it has full use of it, a considerable item in a land where interest rates are up around 50-60% a year. The quickest way to get money in Mexico appears to be having it transferred by a bank.

Telephone service is another kettle of fish entirely. Long-distance calls originating in Mexico are usually made in a telephone 'store' which is either a business devoted entirely to telephone calls, or an area in a store or restaurant set aside for this specific use. Establishments offering this service have a blue-and-white telephone sign outside with the words *Larga Distancia* (Long Distance) prominently displayed. Special international operators are supposed to speak English, but the easiest way to place an international call seems to be to write the country, state, city, area code and telephone number on a piece of paper and hand it to the attendant. Once the call is placed the quality of the transmission is surprisingly good, travelling as it does over a modern Japanese-built microwave relay system. International calls placed in Mexico cost an arm and a leg, and it makes no difference at which end they are paid. If possible, it is usually more economical to arrange for international calls to be made from the other end.

But don't get yourself in a position that requires telephone communication. In December 1984, I spent two frustrating hours trying to call the United States from Oaxaca. The GTE pay phone simply kept swallowing 20-ctvo pieces as fast as I could find them, and finally the attendant and I decided it wasn't going to work.

SHOPPING

Whole books have been written advising the affluent traveller on 'How to Shop in Mexico', as if anyone needs a guidebook on how to spend money. But shopping seems to be a major preoccupation for some travellers so here are a few of my expensively-won thoughts on the subject:

Some areas in the country are famous for certain products that are almost exclusively sold to tourists. Taxco is a prime example. At one time it was a wealthy silver-mining camp, but with the exhaustion of the mines it fell on evil times and almost became a ghost town. This condition persisted until a young American, Bill Spratling, came along and developed a silver handicraft industry. As the market for sterling silverware is severely limited in Mexico, Spratling aimed the local output square at the tourist market, and in order to provide a source of supply encouraged the rehabilitation and conversion to hotels of many of the beautiful old mansions. What with one thing and another, Taxco has become a mecca for the wealthy traveller, and generally the prices are a reflection of this. Not that Taxco is necessarily a rip-off, but be aware that the silverware is sold by the troy ounce and the price works out very dear indeed. Aside from the silver racket Taxco is an interesting and charming place well worth visiting for itself.

A thriving commerce in 'pre-Columbian' artifacts is centered around the various ruins such as Palenque and Chichén-Itzá. You may be approached by a swarthy man who looks fearfully over his shoulder before pulling an earth-stained figurine out of his side pocket and offering it for sale, together with the information – in English – that he dug it up yesterday while plowing his maize field. This is probably true, but he will probably omit to mention that he buried it the previous spring in order to impart the authentic aged appearance. And even if the Chac-mol or whatever it is happens to be authentic – unlikely to say the least – both the US and Mexico take an extremely dim view of people other than accredited scholars and museums owning pre-Columbian art.

Querétaro is famous worldwide for its opals, and invariably anyone who looks like a foreigner will be offered a selection of stones done up in a grubby handkerchief. They will appear to be quite cheap to the uninitiated, but not when you remember that making opals out of old Coca bottles has developed into a folk art around Querétaro.

A major cottage industry in Mexico is making forged 'designer labels', and there are fancy stores in Mexico City selling goods with the trademarks of Cartier and Gucci that bear absolutely no relation at all to their famous namesakes. (These stores have been sued time and again for trademark infringements but to no avail.)

There are lots of things for sale in Mexico that are both economical and practical, but they are seldom sold in the places likely to be frequented by the average package-tour customer. An exception to this are the blankets, ponchos and serapes peddled off people's backs around the zócalos of Oaxaca, although this is actually a rather poor place to buy because the vendors know only too well that most foreigners aren't aware of the local price structure or don't know how to bargain.

One last observation on shopping: remember that certain items are both fragile and bulky, such as the very practical clay *cazuelas* (cooking pots), and the beautiful lacquerware for which the region around Pátzcuaro is justly renowned. Transportation should be considered prior to purchasing. If you do buy something too big to pack in your bag do as the local people do: pack your purchases in a corrugated box with lots of newspaper padding and tie the box securely so that the rope becomes a handle. Take the box to the bus station and check it on your ticket. At layover points simply check the box at the left-luggage counter while you do your sightseeing.

Mexico is famous for its genuine vanilla extract, and it is a popular item with tourists who visit Veracruz and other east coast cities. But beware, there have been a number of recent instances of the 'pure' vanilla being adulterated with a tastealike toxic plant, and several deaths have occurred. Skip the vanilla.

Other shopping suggestions are scattered throughout this book under the headings of the various towns.

WHAT TO TAKE

First, avoid taking huge, heavy, ungainly suitcases, especially those equipped with wheels. I have travelled for months at a time with a shoulder tote bag as my only luggage, which easily qualifies as cabin luggage on planes.

Considerable pains should be taken with the selection of the tote bag, for nothing can take the fun out of a trip quicker than a bag unsuited for the specific type of travel. A common mistake is picking a bag that is too large. In a temperate climate nobody needs much stuff.

A few travellers still persist in using unnecessarily huge framed packs which from the rear make them look like walking pagodas and are too big to be carried aboard aircraft. Another serious disadvantage in Latin America is that the locals associate pack wearers with *jipis* (hippies) and the mass influx of them during the late '60s and early '70s. Discrimination can be rather subtle, such as being informed that a hotel is full when in fact rooms are immediately available for other travellers. If you really need to be able to carry your gear on your back, some packs have concealed straps so they can double as conventional luggage .

Camping gear is a waste of time in Mexico. Campgrounds as in Europe are virtually unknown, and camping out in the boonies for one or two people is actually foolhardy. Hotel rooms are so cheap that they make camping unprofitable. Cooked food ditto.

Among your personal articles I recommend taking 'Chapstick' lip balm (sometimes hard to find in Mexico), an emergency flashlight with spare bulb, a box of wax matches or a disposable lighter, a dozen purse-size packets of Kleenex, half a dozen Band-aids and a small traveller's clothesline.

I carry my passport and maps in my tote bag, my tourist permit and Mexican currency in my wallet, a small Spanish/English dictionary in my pocket, and my foreign currency in the concealed pocket of my belt.

WHAT TO WEAR

Clothing worn in Mexico is predominantly casual and much the same as is worn in comparable climates all over the world. For both men and women this usually means blue jeans or slacks with a sweater or shirt. A coat or jacket may be useful as the climate demands. Beachwear is never worn on the street away from the beach. A head covering is advised for women visiting churches.

The *guayabara* shirt rates a special paragraph. It is a man's shirt, although now and then you may see a woman wearing one. It is square-bottomed, and always worn outside the pants. The thing that makes a guayabara a guayabara, however, is its fancy embroidered or appliqued design. The guayabara can be worn anywhere, any time, but it really comes into its own at night when it doubles as a jacket on all but the most formal occasions.

It is considered a breach of good manners for anyone, male or female, to go barefoot on the street unless desperately and obviously impoverished. The very practical *guarache* (also spelled huarache), a sandal with a sole made out of a piece of retired tyre and with a top made of woven leather strips, is regarded as the footwear of the lower classes and is not too often encountered these days in the cities, but they are cheap, cool and comfortable, and a well-made pair of guaraches will wear like a bottle of Tabasco sauce. In the US they cost around US$30, but in Mexico they cost about a fifth of that.

But note, guaraches are not worn with socks.

Regarding native dress, Mexicans deeply resent tourists dressing up like Indians, and this includes the pajama-like peasant garb. As one *campesino* put it, the first thing to do to become an Indian is to skip eating for three days.

SOURCES

The best travel equipment shop I know is Easy Going, 1400 Shattuck Avenue, Berkeley, California 94700, USA; tel (415) 843-3533. Concentrating on accoutrements for the independent traveller, they stock such hard-to-find goodies as elastic clotheslines, 'Patria' maps of the various Mexican states, shirt-pocket calculators for converting currency values, little plastic bottles for liquids, money belts and numerous other stashes.

Other stores are:

L L Bean, Freeport, Maine 04033, USA. Everything I've bought from Bean's gave good value for the money. The Bean catalogue is worth perusing for its entertainment value and was the model for Stewart Brand's *Whole Earth Access Catalog*.

Recreational Equipment Incorporated (REI). PO Box C-88125, Seattle, Washington 98188, USA, with stores scattered from Anchorage, Alaska to Denver, Colorado. One of the best sources for high-quality outdoor equipment.

A SHORT ITINERARY

This is my suggestion for anyone with only a week or so to spend in Mexico.

First, fly direct to Guadalajara and check into a hotel. Try to get the early-arrival Mexicana plane from the US west coast which arrives in Guadalajara about 6 am. Spend most of the first day wandering around the Mercado Libertad, the finest market in Mexico, or strolling the new downtown *paseos* (walkways).

The next day simply stroll around town and take in the sights – Guadalajara is as good a walking town as Barcelona – not omitting Avenidas Chapultepec and Niños Heroes.

On day three catch a trackless trolley on Federalismo and ride out to Tlaquepaque, admittedly a tourist trap but an enjoyable one. That afternoon catch a bus to Lagos de Moreno and stay overnight, with dinner at the *Pastor*.

Start out early the next morning and catch a bus to Guanajuato, arriving before noon. If the town isn't brim-full you could overnight there, but if it seems crowded have a look round and then catch a bus over the hill to Dolores Hidalgo, which is rich in Mexican history and has a pleasant economy hotel on the Plaza Central.

In the morning catch a bus for San Luis de la Paz if you are interested in ghost towns, and then another bus or a cab to Pozos. But if ghost towns don't appeal then head for San Miguel de Allende early in the morning to arrive well before noon.

A day is usually enough for San Miguel, so the next morning catch a bus for Querétaro or Mexico City. Try to overnight in Querétaro because it is a nice little city with a convenient museum almost on the Plaza Central. If possible stay in the Gran Hotel right on the plaza and smack dab in the centre of things.

For Mexico City it is important to arrive early, particularly during the Christmas/New Year and Easter/Holy Week seasons when travel can get awfully difficult.

If I could I'd stay in Cuernavaca rather than Mexico City because there is almost no smog there. Those interested in sociology may want to make a side trip to Tepoztlán, a town utterly charming in itself and also the location of a number of sociological studies. There are many buses to cover the short distance.

Try Cuernavaca for at least half a day and then meander on down to Taxco, probably the most photogenic city in the country. And if you've never seen Acapulco, then by all means continue on down the hill. You can usually find an economical place to stay downtown near the zócalo.

Getting There

BY AIR

Mexico City is the hub for a number of international airlines, and direct flights are available to Europe, the United States, Canada and Central and South America. There are also flights to Yucatán and the Pacific Coast resorts. From Europe, flying direct to Mexico is the fastest way, but also the most expensive. It is usually cheaper to fly to Miami or Los Angeles on a cut-rate plan and then continue on to Mexico via another carrier.

From Los Angeles and San Francisco, Mexicana Airlines operates a popular one-class night flight, nicknamed *El Tecolote* (The Owl), to Guadalajara and Mexico City. This is usually the cheapest way from the United States west coast and is extremely popular with Mexicans themselves, but check around because occasionally other airlines offer cut-price promotional fares on this and other routes into Mexico. Because air fares are usually in a state of flux, try a good travel agent who is familiar with Mexican flights, or better yet, try several because it is far from uncommon to get a different fare with each inquiry.

BY LAND

Bus service in the US and Canada is nowhere near as good as Mexico's, but it does offer a low-priced alternative to flying. All the US border cities of any size are served by one or both of the two major US companies, and their stations are generally close to the border. Greyhound, for example, will actually haul you to the new central bus station in Tijuana from either San Diego or Los Angeles, but once inside Mexico you have to travel via Mexican carrier. (See 'Getting Around' for details.)

From the San Diego airport there is city bus service to San Ysidro, a part of San Diego right on the border. Although it entails a transfer, the service is an economical way to get to Tijuana.

The 'Tijuana Trolley' that runs from the Amtrak station in San Diego to the border is extremely popular. On the Tijuana Trolley you wind up at about the same place as the local bus, a short walk from Mexico but a long way from the new bus terminal on the east side of town. The Tijuana Trolley operates from 5.30 am, with the last departure from the border at 9 pm. Trains run every 20 minutes.

From San Ysidro you simply follow the signs to cross the international border into Mexico. If you plan on going much past the immediate border area pick up your tourist permit at the *Migrácion* office on your right. To reach the main tourist section keep on going around the igloo and when you see the pedestrian causeway ahead of you cross the street and get on it and cross the Tijuana River. At the far end is the old Tres Estrellas bus station, now largely unused. Continue straight ahead for a couple of blocks or so to the Hotel Nelson and turn left on Revolucion. You will know you are on the right street by the proliferation of hawkers, touts and schlock shops.

The new central bus station is way out toward the airport, and there is now little or no bus service between it and the old Tres Estrellas station downtown and the new place, so if your destination is deeper into Mexico than the border zone, the best bet is to take Greyhound or, perhaps handier, the shuttle bus that leaves from the Amtrak station. Remember, it is about a M$1000 cab ride from Avenida Revolucion out to the bus station.

For practical purposes there is no US rail service to Mexico so I will omit any remarks about that mode of transportation except to say that Amtrak, the US passenger train operator, is expensive, run by the government and apparently not especially interested in hauling people to the border so they can spend their money in a foreign country.

Overland from the USA

There are four main routes from the US into the interior of Mexico: through Baja California from Tijuana and then by ferry or air across the Sea of Cortés; from Tijuana around the northern end of the Sea of Cortés, meeting the route south from Nogales at Santa Ana; south from Juárez down the high-altitude backbone of the country; and south from Nuevo Laredo down through Monterrey and San Luis Potosí. There is actually a fifth route, running down the east coast to Poza Rica and then up to Mexico City, but it is hot, sultry and uninteresting in summer, and subject to bone-chilling northers during the winter.

Getting Around

Of all the countries I've had the pleasure of visiting, Third World included, Mexico has far and away the best public transport system. Some of it, such as the railroads and the ferry system, is government owned and operated, while the intercity buses, some airlines and the taxicabs are in private hands. Oddly enough, it all works fairly well, and parts of the transport system give excellent service, far exceeding what you ordinarily encounter in the USA and Europe. It's cheap, too.

One important thing to remember while traveling in Mexico is that all transportation times are officially quoted in four-digit, 24-hour time.

TRANSPORT PRICES

Bus fares have been rising steadily in peso terms, but compared to those in the US and Europe they are still downright bargains. Currently bus fares in Mexico are in the vicinity of M$2.25 to $2.50 a km, with not too much difference between first and second class. Even deluxe travel, in huge four-axle buses, costs but a trifle more.

Long-distance rail fares are lower than bus fares, except for Pullman with berth which works out to about M$4.80 per km. Ordinary first class comes out at around M$1.80 and second class (not recommended except for the desperate) is less than a peso, calculated on the basis of equivalent highway km, which can vary considerably from rail distances.

BY AIR

Because the distances are so great and surface travel fairly slow due to the terrain, Mexico has developed an extremely efficient network of air routes, with service to almost every city of over 50,000 inhabitants in the country. Equipment is modern and well maintained, and – wonder of wonders – the airlines stick pretty close to schedule. However, air travel has the disadvantage of being vastly more expensive than surface travel, and it is no way to see the sights.

Air fares are from six to eight times bus fares over the same routes.

BY ROAD

Taking an automobile to Mexico can be disconcertingly expensive, and a nuisance as well.

To begin with, only 'Mexican Auto Insurance', issued by local underwriters, is recognized in Mexico. This specialized variety of extortion is sold at all US-Mexico border crossings and by Sandborn's, of McAllen, Texas. All types of coverage are available, including collision (no collision for cars 15 years old or older), but the important one is public liability and property damage in amounts in excess of that required by Mexican law. The cost is modest; fortunately increasing the amount of PL and PD doesn't cost much more than the minimum. And it's a good investment if only for the additional peace of mind it provides. This specialized insurance is not a requirement in Mexican law, but the driver must bear in mind that in Mexico automobile accidents are handled under the criminal code and in case of an accident an uninsured driver may languish in jail for six or seven months or even longer – and a Mexican jail is no summer cruise. Mexican drivers, many of whom simply can't afford insurance, cope with the problem in a unique way that isn't readily available for the tourist: they depart the scene of an accident with maximum velocity. This ploy is generally impractical for the foreigner.

The average Mexican is quite honest, but he or she also holds to the belief that people interested in retaining their property will make an effort to protect it. Many hotels, therefore, offer 'secure

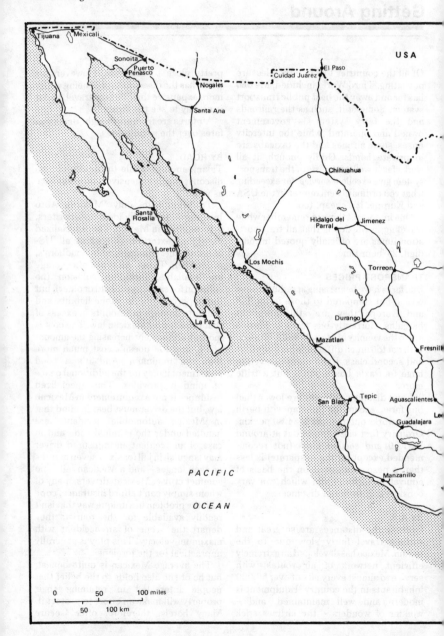

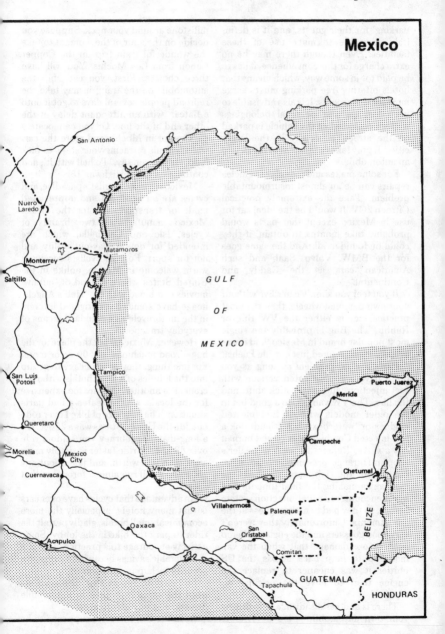

Mexico

San Antonio

Nuero Laredo

Matamoros

Monterrey

Saltillo

GULF

OF

MEXICO

San Luis Potosi

Tampico

Queretaro

Morelia

Mexico City

Cuernavaca

Veracruz

Puerto Juarez

Merida

Campeche

Chetumal

BELIZE

Acapulco

Oaxaca

Villahermosa

Palenque

San Cristabal

Comitan

Tapachula

GUATEMALA

HONDURAS

parking' for their guests, and it is definitely advisable to make use of these facilities. Even though there may be no extra charge for this convenience, it has to be paid for in some way, which means that hotels offering free parking must charge more for their rooms. It is also advisable to keep luggage and personal belongings well concealed when the vehicle is parked on the street, especially in the larger cities. It only takes a moment to break into an automobile.

For some makes and models of vehicles repairs can be an almost insurmountable problem. Take the extremely practical Citroen 2CV. It would be the ideal car for use in Mexico except that parts would probably take months to obtain, if they could be found at all. And the same goes for the BMW, Volvo, Saab and such American cars as the Caddy and Continental.

If you feel you simply can't live without your own personal wheels, then the most practical car is either the VW Bug or Rabbit. The Bug is probably the single most popular brand in Mexico, and it was actually manufactured just outside Puebla.

Parts are no problem so long as you don't have a sophisticated version with fuel injection, automatic stick shift, and the like. The VW van is also a good bet in the older models without fuel-injected engines or 'waterboxes'. A friend took a fuel-injected Combi to Mexico and burned out a valve. Repairs in the VW dealer's shop in Durango presented no problem, but when the job was finished the mechanics making the final tune-up had never encountered a fuel-injection system before, so they had to make a guess at the adjustments. Unfortunately they weren't very good guessers and the engine suffered such severe damage that when the van managed to limp back across the US border it was cheaper to replace the engine than to have the original re-repaired.

There is another disadvantage to driving your own automobile – it's a veritable millstone around your neck. Suppose you decide on the spur of the moment to take the wonderful train trip up the Copper Canon from Los Mochis. You will have three choices. First, you can ship the automobile on the train; it may take the railroad people several days to get it onto a flatcar, with an attendant delay at the other end of the line. Or you can locate a parking lot in Mochis and store the car, which entails retracing your steps to pick it up. Or you can say, 'To hell with it', and continue on down Highway 15.

Mexico is a motorcyclist's paradise, and cycles are an accepted and appreciated mode of transportation for the locals. Mexico manufactures two brands of cycles, Islo and Carabella, which are intended for day-in, day-out utility and not for sport. Foreign cyclists receive a warm welcome in Mexico, unlike in the United States where a flood of 'outlaw' movies combined with the 'Hell's Angels' image have somewhat mitigated interest in the motorcycle as a standard means of everyday transport.

However, Mexico is not the place for the huge 'road machines' of 500 cc or more. For one thing, they're too heavy to get up into the lobbies of a lot of hotels without a crane. For another, they are too expensive for the locals, which creates a bad parts situation. The best size of bike I ever rode outside the United States was a 250cc. On a long-distance journey you seldom ride over 80 kph; to ride faster is simply more work than it is worth, and just about any 250cc bike will run almost forever at that speed.

An advantage that cycles have over cars is that many hotels, especially the more economical small hotels, gladly permit the rider to park the bike in the lobby. Some actively encourage this practice. This is a considerable savings because an expensive security lockup is unnecessary.

I'm sorry to report that motorcyclists need the same insurance as automobile drivers, and pay identical rates.

As in the US, there are supposed to be

three grades of gasoline. High-octane and unleaded are theoretically available, but as these expensive fuels are mostly unused by the locals there is little incentive for stations to keep them in stock and often either or both will be impossible to locate. But the peoples' gas, Nova (no fooling, 'No va' means 'No go!'), is universally obtainable and very cheap by US and European standards at around M$34-38 a litre.

Automobiles adjusted for high-octane fuel may require a change in the ignition timing to be able to cope with Nova, but it is well worth the slight effort involved as the other fuels cost about twice as much. If you can find them.

A word about gas stations. As I pointed out, Mexico averages out as a pretty honest country, but the gas station attendants nationwide could give lessons to Arab rug peddlers when it comes to fraud and trickery. Failing to roll the pump's meter back after serving the previous customer and chronic short-changing of customers unfamiliar with Mexican money are commonplace and most foreign motorists – including myself – have been stung at one time or another by a Mexican gas-pump jockey. For some reason these tricks are seldom used against motorcycle riders, another slight plus for the bikes.

When you bring a vehicle into Mexico the government demands that you take it out again. Period. There are many sad tales of motorists who were involved in serious wrecks and had to put their junk on a truck and haul it to the border.

BICYCLES

A very few extremely hardy souls – the same types who climb Everest – ride their bicycles to Mexico – but it is by no means a popular means of travel for foreigners, although locals use bicycles extensively for going to and from work. When riding the highway the cyclist who desires long life and happiness keeps a wary eye over one shoulder for traffic, and gets off the pavement well in advance. To do otherwise is to invite death and destruction, for the trucks, buses and automobiles pay a licence fee for the use of the roads and are bloody well going to use them.

TAXIS

Taxis are available in even the smallest and most remote villages, including those that don't appear on the very best of highway maps. In most instances taxis in Mexico are a rare bargain compared to those in Europe or the rest of North America. But riding a cab in Mexico is not quite the same as riding one in London, Paris, Barcelona or even San Francisco. Some taxis are metered, some are metered but add a more-or-less fixed surcharge, some add a percentage of the meter reading to the total fare, and some are totally unmetered. This last includes taxis that have cloth hoods over the meters. These are mostly found in Mexico City and are intended strictly for the tourist trade. Needless to say they are expensive by any standard, triply so by local custom.

Taking the unmetered first, you should agree on the fare before entering the cab, otherwise there is no practical limit to what the driver will feel free to charge. Tourists wax highly indignant about this, but it is a custom of the country, and only an inquiry is required if you want to avoid it. With an agreed price the driver ordinarily keeps his end of the bargain, even if it actually costs him money out of his pocket. But I know one traveller who pretends ignorance of Spanish and has the driver write the price on a card.

I once caught a cab from Plaza San Fernando in downtown Mexico City out to the airport, normally a 15 to 20-minute ride. We got trapped in a gigantic traffic jam and wound up taking an hour and a half. Nevertheless, the driver only asked for the fare which we had fixed beforehand, though obviously he was losing his shirt on the deal, so I thought it only right to triple the fare.

Where there is a surcharge to the metered fare there will usually be a sign – occasionally it will even be in both English and Spanish – to that effect. A taxi with an inoperative meter – not all that uncommon – should be treated as an unmetered taxi and the usual haggling should take place prior to boarding, if possible.

In some places, notably Mexico City, taxis come in several sizes, and you would logically assume that a VW Bug would command a lower fare than a huge Ford Fairlane. In fact they charge about the same, but for reasons of speed and agility the Beetle is the odds-on favourite for one or two people with little baggage. These little cabs have no front passenger seats and are technically licenced for two people, and of course they aren't with the Fords, Dodges and Chevvies when it comes to baggage space.

Some of the larger bus stations, mostly in Mexico City, have a kiosk that sells coupons good for one taxi ride. These are handy and eliminate a lot of misunderstandings. The kiosks are located in the concourse and are highly visible. You just tell the person in the booth your destination, and he or she immediately fills out the ticket and assesses the fare. Then go out to the taxi rank and pick a cab. It is best to tell the driver if there is no hurry, because ride-sharing is the rule rather than the exception, and the last passenger out often gets a guided tour of parts of the city he or she would ordinarily never see.

INTERCITY BUSES

Foreign travellers in Mexico all too seldom ride intercity buses, and in so doing are depriving themselves of a great deal of enjoyment and also passing up the opportunity to save a considerable amount of money over driving, renting a car, flying or whatever. Travelling by bus is an unrivalled way to get the feeling of the real, non-tourist Mexico and is probably the greatest bargain around. The first-class fare is around M$2.50 per km and second class slightly less.

Travellers from north of the border and Europe may ignore the advantages of bus travel because they've been told Mexican buses are clapped-out converted school buses with small livestock mixed in with the paying customers. Or else because they can't figure out how to cope with the multiplicity of operating companies and routes, together with the universal absence of printed timetables.

To begin with, Mexico has a very progressive bus-building industry that exports to the rest of Latin America, and the *Hecho en Mexico* intercity bus is at the very least the equal of the best equipment used in this service anywhere in the world. Most of the coaches have two axles, some have three and a few even have four. Air-bag 'springs' are universal. This means that the 'ride' of a Mexican bus is vastly superior to that of an automobile over the country's often-bumpy highways.

I'm talking specifically about the equipment used on long-distance runs, say from Juárez to Mexico City, or from Tijuana to Guadalajara, and not of the short-haul runs that trickle out over the countryside from every city of any size in Mexico. These long-distance buses, either first or second class, definitely do not haul pigs and chickens in the passenger compartment, although most operate on a no-holds-barred concept when it comes to the things stowed in the possum-belly beneath the floor between the axles.

All first-class buses, and some second-class ones as well, operate on a reserved-seat basis, so it is advisable to purchase your ticket ahead of time. There are a couple of definite advantages in so doing. First, the earlier you buy and make your reservation the greater your selection of seats and the less chance of getting sandwiched in one of the first two seats (Nos 3 and 4) opposite the driver, which are deficient in leg room. Secondly, you have the greatest chance of getting on a bus when you want to, for buses are sometimes filled many hours prior to departure time, especially true around

Christmas and New Year. I was quoted a one-week waiting period for ADO buses from Oaxaca to Veracruz one Christmas. Delays can be even more annoying during Easter Holy Week, which the Mexican takes much more seriously than Christmas or New Year.

Advance reservations are not so important at towns on the US-Mexican border because they are the points of origin for so many runs into the interior. For example, I once had no difficulty in obtaining the seat of my choice on a coach out of Nogales, Sonora for Mazatlán a couple of days before Good Friday, but the bus was completely filled at Magdalena, 80 km to the south, and took on no more passengers until my companion and I disembarked and made room for two replacements.

As recently as 18 years ago central bus stations were extremely rare; instead, down-at-the-heel restaurants, ratty cantinas and grocery stores doubled as 'bus stations' where the coaches simply pulled up and loaded and unloaded passengers in the mud in the middle of the street. This situation still exists in a few places, but during the last decade there has been an intensive construction program aimed at providing modern central bus terminals for every large city, plus many small ones. These new *Centros de Autobuses* look more like international airports than conventional US-style bus stations. They have long lines of ticket counters along one side of the concourse, and shops selling everything a traveller could logically be expected to buy on the opposite side. These shops routinely deal in everything from office machine repairs to saddles, with an emphasis on local products. For example, in Celaya there are several shops that dispense nothing but *cajeta*, a syrupy, caramel-flavoured confection for which the area is justly famous. Stops on the long-distance buses are nearly always at these terminals with their (mostly) clean restrooms and ample and economical eating facilities.

One feature of most central bus stations

that may disconcert the stranger is the person stationed at the entrance to the restrooms soliciting contributions and/or selling toilet paper. He or she is not a beggar in any remote sense of the word and anyone taking advantage of the facilities should not begrudge a peso or five donation. These people have the job of keeping the place clean and most of the time they do an excellent – or at least a fair – job. *Sanitarios* operated in this fashion are generally somewhat cleaner than 'free' installations.

With the exception of those in Mexico City, most of the bus terminals are within fairly easy walking distance of the *zócalo* (plaza), making them ideal for the traveller who doesn't object to a 15 or 20-minute walk through colourful streets.

With so many competing lines at the big *Centros* it is generally easy to pick a departure time that exactly suits you. Or if one line is full it is usually a simple matter to make a connection with one of the others. Unlike the old-time makeshift stations, the modern terminals almost always boast baggage-checking facilities so you can check your luggage and then stroll around unburdened by dunnage.

Bus tickets are for a specific company, often for a specific bus, and usually cannot be used on a competing line. However, the people at the ticket counters often have an informal agreement of cooperation. If one company is fully booked the clerk is likely to ask the competitor at the next counter if they have any seats. In this way you will often get a seat on short notice with very little trouble.

There is an exception to the above, of course. You may buy an Estrella Blanca ticket good for about 20 bus lines. These are subsidiaries – look at the back of an Estrella Blanca ticket and you'll see what I mean. There are a few others that operate like this, but not many.

Most of the new central terminals handle all classes of buses in the same part of the terminal, which can be a terrific advantage. If the first-class seats are all taken you will usually be able to get a seat on one of the vastly more numerous second-class coaches. For example, at Querétaro I have often arrived on a first-class bus and seldom spent more than half an hour waiting for a bus out to San Miguel de Allende, although admittedly it was probably a second-class Flecha Amarilla.

This brings me to what, for foreigners, can be the most confusing part of travelling on Mexican buses: buying tickets. A very important item in a traveller's kit is a good road map. (Hallwag is recommended.) Unfortunately, many road maps are woefully short of detailed information, omitting smaller towns along the main highways and fairly large ones off to the side. My qualifying test for a Mexican road map is to see if it shows Choix – north-east of Los Mochis, Tequila, about 30 km north-west of Guadalajara on CN-15 – and Patzcuaro, about 60 km south-west of Morelia. If some or all of these are missing I assume lots of others are too, and start looking for another map.

A road map really comes into its own at the larger bus stations where there may be lots of bus lines, each using a slightly different route to reach a given destination. With a map you can pretty much pick out the most interesting route. Another use for the road map is in the actual ticket buying. Instead of struggling with unpronounceable place names you simply point to your destination and indicate with your fingers the total number of *boletos* (tickets) you want. Stopovers are not ordinarily permitted, so if you want to take a break in your journey simply buy a ticket to the intermediate destination and plan on purchasing another ticket on a later bus for the next leg of your journey.

In addition to knowing the location of towns the bus will touch it helps to be able to read the stations' signs. Below are a few of the more common words you'll see.

asiento	seat
boleto (not billete)	ticket
caballeros	gentlemen
cada	each
corto	short, about the same as directo
cuota	Literally 'quota' but in this instance it means toll road/freeway.
damas	ladies
directo	direct
equipaje, guarda, guarda equipaje or guardaria	baggage check room
hombres	men
llegada	arrive, arrivals
mujeres	women
puntos intermedios	intermediate points
regreso	return
sala de espera	waiting room – also translates as hoping room
salida	departure or exit
sanitario	toilet
senoras	women
1a	1st, as in first class
2a	2nd, as in second class

CAR RENTALS

So far I've made no mention of renting a car. This is because I've had poor luck going this route in Mexico and I've talked to many people who have had similar problems. There are a number of rental firms doing business in Mexico, both international and local, but their efficiency seems to fall by the wayside under the Mexican sun, and it is common to encounter 'lost' reservations, no cars available as promised, and a host of other petty annoyances. And to put the frosting on the cake, if you do succeed in finally renting a car, and it actually doesn't break down, it will prove to be an extremely expensive proposition when compared to other means of land transport available to the traveller.

BY RAIL

Contrary to the usual practice in most countries, railroad fares are even lower than bus fares, and trains connect all major cities in Mexico, although they miss a number of tourist spots such as Puerto Vallarta, Cancun and Acapulco. Mexico City is the hub for railroads as it is with the highway system. Due to the extremely low fares, and also because so many travellers are rail fans, trains are fairly popular with foreigners. Most of Mexico's railroads were constructed in the latter part of the 19th century under the Diaz regime. British-built by and large, they have served Mexico well, but as almost all of them are strictly single-track operations, lacking modern train-control equipment, under today's conditions they are tremendously overloaded.

As the cost of rail travel is subsidized for the benefit of the poor, the second-class coaches are usually crowded, hot, smelly and uncomfortable, with small children whooping and hollering and dashing up and down the aisles at all hours of the day and night. But first-class coach costs only a little more than second, and in most instances you can even obtain reserved seating. As there are no standees – theoretically – you are usually spared the horrible overcrowding that is common on second-class cars. Most first-class coaches are supposed to be air conditioned, but don't take air conditioning too seriously in Mexico. Even lacking air conditioning, first class is a great improvement in every way over second which never has air conditioning. There are also sleeping cars, mostly ex-US Pullmans, with the conventional US-style upper and lower berths, roomettes and so on, but when you go Pullman the price advantage is lost though the comfort is improved by a factor of eight or nine.

Trains are much slower than buses, even if they manage to stick to their schedules, which doesn't happen all that often. Mexican trains are much given to mysterious pauses out in the midst of nowhere, and running on time is more the exception than the rule. It is by no means uncommon for a train from Mexicali to pull into Guadalajara 10 hours or more behind schedule.

Very few Mexican trains can be depended on to carry dining cars, although several may have lunch counters, so the experienced rail traveller packs a bountiful picnic hamper at the market before embarking. An alternative to the hamper is to buy food from the hawkers who swarm aboard trains at almost every station, peddling tamales, tacos, tortas and other Mexican-style quick foods, including cold beer and soft drinks.

There would be more tourist travel on Mexican railroads from the US border if the American passenger service, Amtrak, made better connections with its southern counterpart. During the heyday of US rail travel it was possible and enjoyable to climb aboard a Pullman in Chicago and get off in Mexico City, but with the deterioration of rail passenger service in the US this is now an impossibility.

FERRIES

A government-owned and operated ferry system connects Baja California with the mainland. Ferries cross between Mazatlán and La Paz, and between Guaymas and Santa Rosalia. As befits the considerable distances involved they are full-fledged, ocean-going vessels, equipped to carry vehicles up to and including large 26-wheel truck-and-trailer combinations. Because they are intended more for internal commerce than the tourist trade it is not uncommon for several private automobiles to be left languishing on the dock to make room for a truckload of agricultural products. Normally they operate three days a week in each direction, with one day off for restocking, repairs and R&R for the crew. They are quite reliable when it comes to leaving at the advertised time and stick pretty close to their schedules, although they are often a little late at their destinations on account of weather conditions, fouled bottoms or engine-room problems.

Most passengers, domestic and foreign,

elect to travel as deck passengers in the spacious lounges although stateroom service, purported to be air conditioned, is available for a considerable surcharge. When I tried a stateroom several years back my cabin was on the port, or sunny, side, so I thanked my lucky stars for the air-conditioning. However, the air-conditioning packed it at about the same time the spring lines were cast off, and my comfortable stateroom soon got hot enough to bake scones. I spent the remainder of the trip in the lounge where I am sure I was the highest-paying passenger.

Baja California

TIJUANA

(elevation six metres, population 1,200,000)

Tijuana, Baja California, is one of the most popular international border crossings in the world, with millions of people going through each year. It is a free port for both individuals and merchandise, and formalities are at an absolute minimum for people and motor vehicles going no farther south than Ensenada or farther east than Mexicali. Travellers going beyond these points will avoid hassles if they pick up their documents at the government offices just beyond the gate on the right after crossing the fence. Motorists will save trouble if they enter Mexico in one of the far right lanes and are prepared to stop after about 50 metres to pick up their documentation.

Tijuana is no longer the 'booze-and-broad' centre it once was, and it will be difficult if not impossible to find one of the famous donkey acts that attracted the sailors from Dago and Pedro of yore. Today it is a thriving commercial centre, deriving much of its income from trading, importing and exporting, and small-part assembly work contracted by American manufacturers desiring to take advantage of Mexico's low wage scales. As are almost all Mexican border towns, it is rather more expensive than the average Mexican city, and about as charming as Erie, Pennsylvania.

Avenida Revolución, the main tourist shopping street of Tijuana, is living proof of the old adage that nobody ever went broke catering to the poor taste of the American public. Chartered buses bring loads of blue-haired ladies across the border for a day's shopping and adventure as a regular occurrence. The shopkeepers on Revolución are masters of the hard sell and could put a Phoenician shares peddler to shame.

Places to Stay

There is little necessity for overnighting in Tijuana, but for those who must there are three small labourers' hotels to the left as you leave the old Tres Estrellas bus station. All are in the same block, and are inexpensive.

A better shot in every way but price is the venerable *Hotel Nelson*, which not too long ago was the tallest building in town. To reach it, continue straight along for a couple of blocks or so after you leave the causeway. Primarily a commercial travellers' hotel, it is about the best bet for a reasonably priced place to stay in Tijuana. Its only real disadvantage is that it is fairly noisy for someone fresh from the US, although not particularly so by Mexican standards. Also, it is nowhere as new as it looks, and is expensive.

Places to Eat

Tijuana is not too bad for eating. As you swing around the igloo by the border there are usually taco wagons, fruit stalls, etc. These are inexpensive.

For a typical sit-down Mexican meal it is hard to beat the restaurant in the *Hotel Nelson*. As in all Mexican home-style restaurants, a foreigner ordering *bifstek* under the impression he will get North American-style beefsteak will be bitterly disappointed. Stick to the standard fare, such as *enchiladas* and *carne asada* and you will do OK. Prices are moderate.

Up Revolución a few blocks is the *Hotel Cesar* and the restaurant of the same name, where the Caesar salad is popularly supposed to have originated. Whether or not there is any truth to the legend, the Cesar is a good place for a snack or a beer or even a meal. It is very popular with the local business types, and expensive.

The *Rosarito Beach Hotel* is an old, well-maintained resort 35 km south of Tijuana on the bay side of Highway 1. Built lavishly at the height of the Art Deco fad, it resembles a cross between an old grand hotel and a moving picture palace on Detroit's Harper Avenue. Just looking around the place is worth the trip. (A magnificent grand ball is held each New Year's Eve – make reservations good and early.) The place seems popular with off-duty police from San Diego and Los Angeles. Lunch and breakfast are usually served around the pool, either in a glassed-in auxiliary dining room or between the pool and the beach under an *arco* (arch). The food is not bad, although admittedly ambience at the Rosarito counts for more than quality of food. Dinners in the original inside dining room with the heavy dark tables are quite good. Don't be afraid of having to shuck a *langosta* (salt-water crayfish, often miscalled lobster) – the waiter does it very deftly at tableside. Very expensive.

As with most resort hotels, the grounds are infested with overpriced shops selling all sorts of tourist gimcrackery. I priced a litre bottle of Viejo Vergil brandy and it came out at about US$10. No way, José. On the return trip I went through the town of Rosarito Beach and bought an identical bottle for around US$4.25 and received a novelty leather key ring and a kind smile to boot.

This is a good place to reach by private automobile. It is about 20 minutes from the border unless you have the misfortune to get mixed up in Tijuana's poorly marked freeway entrance system, in which case it will probably take around 45 minutes. Take the Cuota and get off just as you reach the second set of toll booths.

Which is not to say it isn't accessible by bus. You might be able to buy a ticket on an Ensenada-bound Tres Estrellas bus, but I prefer to catch a local ABC bus. In either case, get a ticket to 'Rosarito Beach Sur'. Otherwise you might wind up at the north end of the little town of Rosarito Beach and be faced with a walk of about four km.

Getting There & Away

Most travellers enter Tijuana on their way to or from the far western US. How to get there from the States is described in the Getting There chapter.

The easiest way to get to the new Central de Autobuses is to take a bus from the San Ysidro or San Diego Greyhound bus stations, but it is possible, of course, to reach the bus station from Tijuana itself. In that case the most practical way is to take a taxi, but it is expensive – around M$1200 or more, because the terminal is way out by the international airport, well worth a US$6 hack ride.

Although a few buses still leave from the old Tres Estrellas station in downtown Tijuana, it is being phased out gradually, and the safest bet is simply to go out to the new station right off.

There is no rail service.

ENSENADA

(elevation two metres, population 200,000) Ensenada is slightly over 100 km south of Tijuana. It is very popular as a resort for residents of San Diego, Los Angeles, and California generally, and as a result has a thriving tourist-oriented business. The tourists who visit Ensenada are, generally, more knowledgeable than those who take the package tours and Love Boats to the resorts along the 'Mexican Riviera'. As a result many of the shops price-mark their merchandise, having found that Americans won't take the time to dicker, and as the competition is on a dog-eat-dog basis, Ensenada's prices for Saltillo serapes, Taxco silver and Oaxaca pottery are about the best in Mexico.

Ensenada, more than any other non-border town in Mexico, is geared to the US dollar, and is the only non-border town where nearly all transactions can be carried out in that currency. In fact this practice is encouraged, because keeping transactions in US currency protects the business people from the vast devaluation that has recently taken place, and more devaluation is expected at any moment.

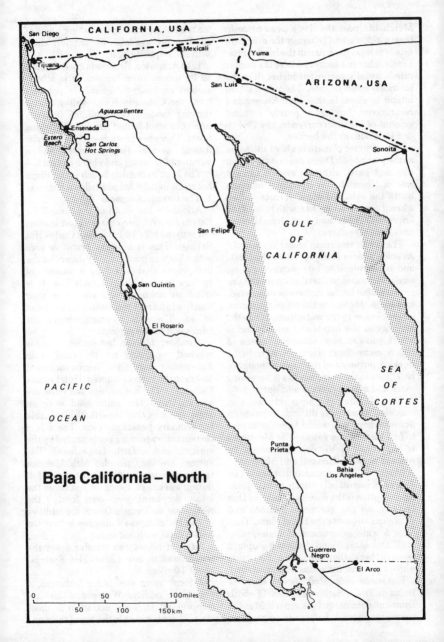

Baja California – North

CALIFORNIA, USA

San Diego
Tijuana
Mexicali
Yuma
San Luis
ARIZONA, USA
Aguascalientes
Ensenada
Estero Beach
San Carlos Hot Springs
Sonoita
San Felipe
GULF OF CALIFORNIA
San Quintin
PACIFIC OCEAN
El Rosario
SEA OF CORTES
Punta Prieta
Bahia Los Angeles
Guerrero Negro
El Arco

0   50   100 miles
0   50   100   150km

Merchants post the day's peso price in their windows, and generally the exchange rate is at least the equal of the border rate, a real oddity in a country where the border rate is usually somewhat higher than the interior exchange rate. Therefore if you intend to go no farther than Ensenada I recommend buying a purely nominal amount of Mexican currency, say US$10 or $15 worth, at the border.

The summer climate is about the same as the part of San Diego nearest the ocean (the nice part), although winters can get raw at times. In my opinion Ensenada beats the other Mexican resorts hollow when it comes to weather, with little of the oppressive heat and high humidity so prevalent elsewhere.

There are two main shopping streets. Avenida Juárez is the scene for the locals and is the place to buy picnic supplies, work clothes, auto parts, good mountain-grown coffee beans, either raw or roasted, and so on. Mateos is the tourist-oriented street closest to the waterfront. It has the majority of the hotels and motels and is where you can buy 'souvenirs' (some of which come from Hong Kong), belts, buckles, pottery and gewgaws, although of recent years the merchandise is becoming more and more practical and durable.

The 'Monterrey' shop stocks clay cazuelas, items quite difficult to locate on Juárez where you would logically expect to find them in every store. The Monterrey is just south of Victor's Restaurant on Mateos between Riveroll and Miramar.

Much of the merchandise sold on Juárez is admittedly cheap tourist junk. An exception is the wares at the Artes Don Quijote, on the corner of Mateos and Gastelum, opposite the Hotel Plaza. They offer a wide assortment of high-quality stuff. One of my friends bought a couple of blouses here that she wore for years without resewing the seams. Recommended.

Ensenada is located on the shore of Bahía de Todos Santos, and fishing – both sport and commercial – is superb. Many of the weekenders in Ensenada come down

for the fishing, and sport-fishing boats of all sizes are available for charter, along with the requisite gear.

Like Acapulco, Ensenada doesn't make all its money from tourism. It is a busy seaport, especially for agricultural products from the Colorado River Valley, and a thriving modern boat-building industry turns out steel-hulled commercial fishing boats. There is a great deal of commercial fishing, several fish canneries and a number of freezing and chilling plants.

The best swimming beach is the Playa Estero, about 9½ km south down Highway 1. The turnoff is signed.

About 3½ km south of the turnoff for Estero Beach is an unpaved road leading left into the hills 19 km to San Carlos Hot Springs. This is a rather primitive area with a bathing pool made by damming the little creek that is fed by a number of springs located along a fault line. It is relatively unknown and you bring your own food and fuel and camp for a weekend or so. There is a small charge for admission to the springs.

Another, fancier hot-spring area is reached by going up the road from Ensenada toward Ojos Negros for about 26 km to the turnoff marked 'Hotel Aguas Calientes'. The hot springs and hotel are 8½ km from the main road over an unpaved track that is perfectly navigable for ordinary passenger cars. There is a restaurant, swimming pools heated by the springs, and a fairly large hotel. The springs are very popular with Mexican families on weekends, almost never full during weekdays. I suggest you do as the locals do: bring your own food – the restaurant isn't much. One of the oddities of the Hotel Aguas Calientes is that the toilets flush with hot water.

Intrepid hikers can wander down the arroyo trail to San Carlos Hot Springs, about 10 rough km.

A local 'must see' is La Bufadora, a geological oddity. Water and air are compressed by wave action in a small cave. There is a vent in the top of the cave, and a pillar of water periodically jets into the air, like Old Faithful. This can really be spectacular, although the degree of action varies considerably, depending on the wind and the state of the tide. La Bufadora is at the end of a 22-km signed and paved road that branches west at Maneadero, south of Ensenada.

Out on Cárdenas – the street that parallels Mateos on the west side – and just past the river a few blocks from downtown, are the now-restored remains of what was one of the most glamorous, renowned and infamous gambling joints in North America. It was owned by General Abelardo Rodríguez, a local lad who went on to become the multi-millionaire ex-president of Mexico. After the general passed away, gambling was banned and the place fell into disuse. It suffered the ultimate indignity of being colonized by squatters, with the extensive grounds serving at one time as goat pasture. Now it is being used for receptions, high-school graduations and the like, with talk of ultimately converting it into a museum. Definitely worth a visit.

Right in back of the old gambling hall, on Mateos, is the location of the tech inspection and the starting point for the Baja 1000 Race, a shadow of its former grandeur but still the most noteworthy public entertainment in this part of the world.

A sort of general store of indigenous artifacts is located at the northern edge of town. It's called *El Nuevo Nopal*, and carries everything from Taxco silver to murals made of tiles assembled something like a jigsaw puzzle to create a long-lasting indoor/outdoor wall decoration. These tile pictures are seen all over Mexico, often on very old buildings, but very seldom are available in stores nowadays. And best of all, the prices at the Nopal are right. Even if you don't intend to buy, the store is worth a look because the New Nopal will give you a good line on current prices and quality. It is about four km north of the main part of town on the

beach side of the road to Tijuana and is recommended.

Places to Stay

Ensenada entertains hundreds of thousands of tourists every year and is gradually tilting toward the expensive deluxe side in the way of hotels, but there remain a number of lower-priced establishments.

As you go toward the centre of town from the bus station keep an eye out for Calle 3a and the *Piso del Norte* hotel. It is a small green-fronted hotel that hasn't been open too long and so doesn't fill as quickly as most. The street number is 724 and it is located just north of Riveroll. Moderate.

Back in the days before the Transpeninsular Highway, Numero Uno, was built, many of the back-country travellers made their headquarters at the *Pancho Motel* – we called it the Rancho in those days – on Alvarado and Calle Segunda. It was cheap and there was adequate enclosed parking. Now a couple of new additions have been added, so parking verges on the impossible as a result. The Pancho is a long block off the tourist street, Mateos, so it is quiet for Mexico. To get there, go south on Mateos to the Pemex gas station, then left down the hill. The Pancho is at the next corner. The rooms in the old section along the right as you enter are more like small Mexican residences than the usual motel, but the new section is typical Mexican Miracle Modern with little sparklers set in the rough-finished ceilings. Prices are moderate.

The *Hotel Royal* on Castelum above Mateos has a bath house as part of the operation, so the clients are reasonably assured of getting a hot bath. Moderate prices and enclosed parking.

The biggest and oldest out-and-out hotel in Ensenada is the *Hotel Plaza* on Mateos at Castelum. Closed for too long by an exasperating strike, it is open once more. The Plaza dates back to the days of Clara Bow and Tom Mix and staying there is like stepping back into the pages of time. Yet the prices are moderate.

A new hotel, the *Colonial*, has recently opened its doors on Miramar in the first block above Mateos. Look for the white-on-black imitation antique sign sticking out of the side of the building. So far the prices are moderate and look to stay that way.

Drivers of recreational vehicles have a more difficult time in Ensenada and I suggest they go either to San Carlos Hot Springs or up the hill to the *Aguas Calientes*, the latter an especially good choice during the summer months. With the latter there will be a slight extra charge for the use of the hot tubs, but that should be of slight consequence.

Places to Eat

Ensenada is one of the best eating towns in Mexico, with bitter competition between the various restaurants. It is the only city in Mexico I know where well-financed restaurants are constantly going broke.

Because of systematic mismanagement of the domestic dairying industry, most coffee is served with Carnation evaporated milk (produced in the US) as a milk substitute.

Victor's Cafe on Mateos between Riveroll and Miramar is an old standby, extremely popular for breakfast with early-rising fishermen, both amateur and professional. It is usually the first restaurant in town to be open and ready for business. Moderate.

There are three seafood restaurants shoulder-to-shoulder below Mateos on Macheros. They are all pretty similar. In the evening, tables are put on the shady sidewalk in front. All in all, I prefer to eat inside where I don't have to constantly duck the elbows of passersby. Their waiters make a habit of systematically waylaying prospective customers, too. Macheros is only about 50 metres long below Mateos, so don't hesitate to stroll down on an inspection trip. Moderate to expensive.

In the same neighbourhood, on Cardenas – the street that runs between Mateos and along the bay – and just north of Macheros,

is the *Restaurant Bar Santo Tomas* which features seafood, steak and quail. Quail (*codorníz*) is a rare and delicate item on the menus of Mexican restaurants, so if you're hankering after a really deluxe dinner some night then the Santo Tomás is your spot, although I will admit the food is not quite up to the ambience. The restaurant is a regular stop on the nightly rounds of the mariachi bands and is popular with local families out for a night on the tiles. Very expensive, but worth it if you're in the mood.

Anyone writing about Ensenada is remiss if he or she doesn't mention *Hussong's Cantina*, easily the best-publicized saloon in Mexico. Their T-shirts, which they sell very profitably, are seen all over the world. This is an ordinary Mexican bar distinguished from all the others by these facts: they don't have unisex restrooms, they permit women on the premises, and they can claim real antiquity – the bar dates back to 1892. It is located on Ruiz above Mateos.

But for real economy restaurants you can't beat the little places across from the bus station in Ensenada. If the previous night was a bibulous occasion and you're feeling a mite under the weather, then the place for you is the *Loncheria La Terminal*, almost directly across the street from the front of the bus station. It has a big red 'Menudo' painted across its green front. La Terminal serves other dishes besides menudo, and it is inexpensive.

If you're just plain hungry, or feel the need of a quick snack before resuming your journey, then along the same row of storefronts is the *Barbacoa El Rancho*. I don't know of anything that makes a better taco than well-prepared barbacoa and the El Rancho does it almost as well as the Parilla in Chihuahua. Inexpensive and recommended.

The cheapest breakfast in town may be found by going out the front door of the Ensenada bus station and turning left. Go down to the next street by the traffic light and there you'll find the *Panadería Ele*, a little bakery where you can buy your supply of pan dulces a lot cheaper than at any restaurant. A bottle of Coca from the grocery diagonally across the street from the station will complete your meal – Coca goes almost as well as coffee with pan dulce.

At long last Ensenada has a new and clean supermarket made to order for fix-it-yourselfers. It is on Gastelum up the street from Mateos and the Plaza hotel. This Mexican market is typical in that it sells everything from hootch to spatter-ware pots, and at the same time is an oddity in that it is a very business-like operation, as if the owner had been trained at Kroger's or Safeway. Recommended.

I've saved the best for the last. Danny MacMurray (my son) swears that Ensenada has the best seafood in the world on its street corners. There must be a dozen barrows selling 'sea food coktails' based on just-dug clams. Prices and flavors vary, of course, but a large glass of clam cocktail usually runs from US$.75 to $1.50. One of these and a bottle of sweating-cold Bohemia beer makes a superlative and inexpensive snack – double the above and you have a fine, cheap meal.

Getting There & Getting Around

The Central Bus Station is on Riveroll between Calle Decima and Calle 11. To get downtown go out the front door and turn right. Mateos is about the tenth cross street and at one time was called Calle Primera.

SAN QUINTÍN

(elevation six metres, population 25,000)
San Quintín is a new, sans-plaza town strung along Highway 1 about 187 km south of Ensenada. It's the last place for automobile drivers to stock up on picnic supplies for a long way.

About a hundred years ago Bahía San Quintín was the site of a couple of ill-starred attempts at colonization by British and American companies. A flour mill was built and a narrow-gauge railroad was constructed some 32 km northward toward San Diego, its intended destination. After a number of lives and fortunes were lost the promoters gave up the game and today all that remains to show for the work, money and human misery is an old Turner steeple-type compound steam engine from London and the remnants of the graveyard. The village and pier established by the colonists is slightly over four km south of the steam-powered mill, and another 3½ km south will bring you to the old graveyard. A dam was constructed across an arm of the bay in front of the mill, but when and what for I have been unable to ascertain.

Places to Stay & Eat

There are two motels side by side at Bahía San Quintín at the site of the old mill, *Ernesto's* and *El Molino Viejo*. Both have restaurants and boat rentals; both are expensive. The signed turnoff for the bay is about two km south of San Quintín, but the rest of the 7½-km route isn't very well marked, so it is inadvisable to attempt the trip after dark – there is a maze of roads in the area and even during the day they look pretty much alike. In wet weather the road disintegrates and it's foolhardy to try the trip in an ordinary vehicle.

EL ROSARIO

This small town has been a traditional stopping place since the 'road' through Baja was merely a pair of sandy ruts. Now the businesses are mostly operated by the heirs of Señora Anita Espinoza, the doyenne of Espinoza's Place. El Rosario is a fairly reliable fuel-and-food stop about 60 km below San Quintín.

Immediately below the town you will see your first *cirio*, a unique desert plant that looks like a green carrot growing upside down with its big end stuck in the ground. My late friend, Joseph Wood Krutch, called the plant a 'boojum', and the name has persisted among the English-speaking desert rats. Except for a very small and inaccessible patch across the Sea of Cortés in Sonora there are no cirio plants anywhere else in the world.

ARROYO CATAVINA

This is a not-very-wide spot on the road located about 320 km south of Ensenada. It has a Presidente Hotel and a usually non-functioning gas station. I mention the town here because once in a rare while you might need a place to stay between Guerrero Negro and Ensenada.

RANCHO SANTA YNEZ

Rancho Santa Ynez is a couple of km south of Arroyo Cataviña. A working ranch, it was capably operated for many years by a remarkable woman, Josefina, and her two tall cowboy nephews. The ranch served meals and put up travellers using the old, unimproved trail – mostly as a convenience after the fashion of the American Old West. Check with the ranch before putting up at the Presidente. If the owners still welcome visitors, accommodation will be cheaper and the people will be more interesting than those at the posh place up the road.

Santa Ynez has an airstrip and can be counted on to have a supply of aviation gasoline, which works perfectly well in any gasoline engine.

BAHÍA LOS ANGELES

(elevation two metres, population 1000)
A thriving little community on the Sea of Cortés, Bahía Los Angeles is almost entirely the result of the efforts of Antero Díaz to wrest a living from what was originally a barren wilderness. The nearby mine of San Juan and the associated mill at Las Flores are about 10 km from the settlement. Early on, Señor Díaz established an airstrip on the sound theory that not enough fishermen and back-country loafers would essay the old road to make his operation successful. Today there is a paved road to his door, but Bahía Los Angeles is still popular with fliers and offers fishing, hiking and swimming.

Places to Stay & Eat

There is a motel/hotel and restaurant operated by the Díaz family. There is also a store for general supplies. Because of the isolation, things are somewhat more expensive than in Ensenada, but not exorbitantly so. Camping on the beach is perfectly acceptable, and is free.

GUERRERO NEGRO

(elevation three metres, population 10,000)
The town has sprung up to service one of the largest salt evaporation works in the world. Guerrero Negro was for many years almost the only source of steady employment in Central Baja California and a magnet for the young people of the economically depressed towns of the area. Today it is a fairly large community offering all services, including hotels, restaurants, automobile repair shops and so on. It is about three km west of the Transpeninsular Highway, measuring from the 28th Parallel Monument.

EL ARCO

(elevation 500 metres)
When the new highway was built in the early '70s, it missed El Arco by about 40 km, so a new road was built and paved. The new branch is a long way form the original, which came out by the Rancho Los Angeles (no relation to Bahía Los Angeles). Unfortunately, the new paving job is by far the worst part of the government's efforts in Baja California, and a side trip to El Arco is definitely not recommended.

There isn't much to see anyway; El Arco is in the process of becoming a ghost town. Originally there was a mine here, developed by North American interests about 50 years ago. The mine soon closed due to a combination of labour unrest and scarcity of gold. Since then, El Arco has survived by acting as a small supply centre for the outlying ranches and even smaller towns. Construction of the new road put the final nail in El Arco's economic coffin by eliminating through traffic and by making it relatively easier for local residents to do their shopping in Guerrero Negro.

SAN IGNACIO
(elevation 275 metres, population 1200)
San Ignacio is a true oasis, and I doubt there is a sight in the world as welcome as its date palms as you come south over the burning hot desert during the summer months. The town was named after San Ignacio de Loyola, the founder of the Society of Jesus; contrary to what you may read, it was founded by the diligent Jesuits.

People have lived on the site since long before recorded history; an estimated 5000 Indians were living in the vicinity when the Spaniards arrived. Originally the town was called Cadacaaman, and the official name of the place is still San Ignacio de Cadacaaman, but everyone calls it simply San Ignacio. The Jesuits established their mission in 1728 (although it is known that Father Piccolo visited the site as early as 1716), and during the following 25 years San Ignacio served as a base for the exploration of the wild and desolate area. Disease reduced the number of Indians to around 100, but San Ignacio, unlike most of the old missions, was never abandoned. The present residents are largely descendents of immigrants from Sonora and Jalisco who began to arrive in the 1830s.

The date palms that contribute so much to the beauty of the town are another legacy from the Jesuits, and were probably introduced around the early 1760s.

The town itself was built according to the standard Spanish design for New World settlements, with a functional, tree-shaded plaza fronting the church and its outbuildings. The church itself is an exquisite example of frontier construction, built of hewn lava blocks with walls 1½ metres thick. The buildings surrounding the plaza are mostly over 200 years old, although many have been repeatedly rebuilt and only the original stone facades preserved.

The population has been essentially static for many years. There is virtually no opportunity for employment, and for many years San Ignacio's principal export has been its young people. Guerrero Negro probably has more people from San Ignacio than San Ignacio itself does.

If you have the opportunity to visit only one town in Baja California, by all means make San Ignacio your choice. But note that it gets hotter than the hinges of Hades during the summer, so it is best to visit in late fall, winter, or early spring.

Places to Eat
The best restaurant in town is *Oscar's Place*. It serves plain Mexican country fare and is expensive.

The restaurant in the *Presidente* does a capable job, unlike the hotel itself. It runs heavily to steak, which is cut in the North American style. The cook truly understands fish, which when available is the best choice. Very expensive.

The most convenient and economical restaurant in San Ignacio is the new restaurant on the Plaza, hard by the Conasupo. Called the *Loncheria Chalita*, the restaurant is actually the former living room of the family who lives there. There is no menu, and what you eat is generally what the family eats (in the manner of a boarding house, except there are no set meal times). The arrangement works better than it sounds, because the cooking is good and the family is cheerful. Inexpensive.

Getting There
San Ignacio is a stop on the north-and-south bus routes, although once in a while a driver, pressed for time or just feeling disagreeable, will disembark his passengers in San Lino on the main highway. Automobilists often miss San Ignacio altogether, mistaking San Lino for it and overlooking the sign at the intersection. San Ignacio is two km from the main highway over a paved branch road. Bus tickets are sold in the Conasupo.

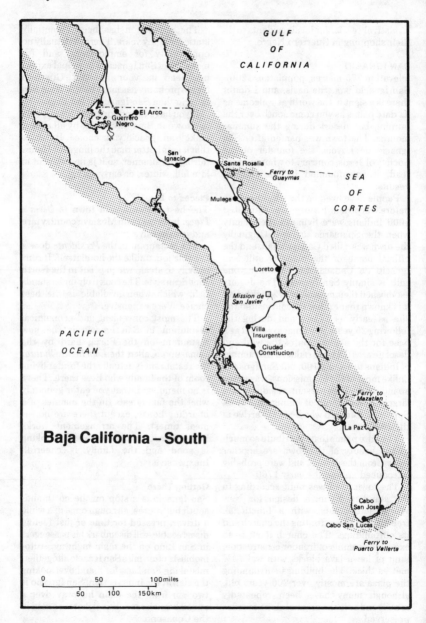

GULF
OF
CALIFORNIA

El Arco
Guerrero
Negro

San
Ignacio

Santa Rosalia

Ferry to Guaymas

SEA
OF
CORTES

Mulege

PACIFIC
OCEAN

Loreto

Mission de
San Javier

Villa
Insurgentes

Ciudad
Constiucion

Ferry to
Mazatlan

La Paz

Baja California – South

Cabo
San Jose

Cabo San Lucas

Ferry to
Puerto Vellerta

0   50   100 miles

50   100   150 km

SANTA ROSALÍA

(elevation two metres, population 12,000)
It all began when a rancher from Santa
Agueda, one Rosas Villavicencio, made a
rich copper discovery and initiated mining
in the region. In the 1880s a number of
local mines and prospects were consol-
idated under the Rothschilds' banner and
operated as the Boleo mines for almost
exactly 70 years. The Rothschilds pulled
out in the '50s and their operation was
taken over by Mexican interests who
operate to this day. The original copper
mine has been expanded to include
manganese and other minerals.

During WW I the German sailing fleet in
the Pacific was interned in the little
harbour for the duration.

The church is of interest because it was
prefabricated in Europe, used in a World's
Fair, and then shipped here. Its exterior is
of galvanized steel.

The older frame houses in the central
part of town were built by the French as
company-owned housing, and are of a
pattern familiar to anyone who has visited
the South Pacific.

Rail fans will be interested in the relics
of the meter-gauge steam-powered railroad
that was constructed before the turn of the
century to serve the mines and smelter.
One locomotive is on display at the wye in
the centre of town, and more equipment,
including a couple of antique Industrial
Brownhoist hooks, is on display in a sort of
open-air museum about 500 metres north
along the highway.

Stand in the street facing the Hotel
Central and look to your left and you'll see
what I believe to be the best example of
French Colonial architecture in Mexico. A
large, verandahed frame building with a
sheet-iron roof, it is one of the most
interesting buildings in town. Today it is
used as the city hall.

Places to Stay & Eat

The best hotel in Santa Rosalía is the
ancient *Hotel Central*, reached from the
wye by going along the one-way street

leading away from the beach for two or
three blocks, a six-minute walk. It is a relic
of the days of the French, a frame
structure, and as Santa Rosalía can get
very hot in summer check to make sure
there is a functioning fan in your room
during hot weather. Moderate.

The *Olvera Hotel* is hard by the wye on
the one-way street that goes toward the
beach, right at the pedestrian overpass. It
is in an extensively remodeled French
building, so summer visitors are advised
to check for a working fan before overnighting during the hot months. Inexpensive.

Santa Rosalía is famous for its mining
activities and not its cuisine, but there are
a couple of acceptable restaurants in
town. One is the restaurant in the Hotel
Central which actually advertises 'French
cuisine'. Be that as it may, it is still a pretty
good place to eat. Expensive.

Another is the old *Tokio Cafe* on the left
side of the street leading away from the
bay. I've been putting my feet under a
table at the Tokio since 1965 when it was
located a few blocks down the street.
Originally operated by an affable Japanese,
it served Mexican food with Asian overtones. Times have changed, though, and
the little Asian touches have mostly
disappeared, but it is still a good place for
straight Mexican cooking. Moderate.

Getting There & Away

There is regular ferry service from Santa
Rosalía to Guaymas, with three round
trips a week. This is the shortest crossing
to the mainland and also the cheapest.
The ferry leaves at night and arrives in
Guaymas early in the morning.

The route from Tijuana to Guaymas via
Santa Rosalía is about 150 km shorter in
land distance than going around the
northern end of the Sea of Cortés. The
cost is about the same, but the trip down
through Baja is much more interesting,
and offers the chance to visit Ensenada
and San Ignacio.

If you miss the boat to Guaymas the

hotel rooms are cheaper in Santa Rosalía than anywhere up and down the Peninsula, so waiting for the next ferry isn't too costly. Also, in the case of a lengthy stopover, you can easily catch a bus to Mulegé or Loreto.

The ferry terminal is on the bay side of the highway a hop, skip and jump south of the wye.

In addition to the ferry, Santa Rosalía is a stop on all the bus routes on the Transpeninsular Highway, and to this end there is a new bus terminal a few hundred metres south of the ferry terminal. It is just beyond the Pemex gas station. Walking time from the wye: 12 minutes.

MULEGÉ

(elevation two metres, population 4500)
Mulegé is about 60 km down the road from Santa Rosalía, and is drier and cooler. Located near the mouth of the Arroyo Santa Rosalía (really a small stream and not an arroyo at all), which provides water for crops, the town occupies the site of a former Indian community called Caamanc-ca-galeja. Its modern history begins with the construction of a mission, Santa Rosalía de Mulegé, in 1705 by the Jesuits. The present mission church was built in 1766 by another Jesuit, Father Escalante. This was one of the last Jesuit constructions prior to their expulsion by the Spanish crown.

Today Mulegé is a pleasant town, and because of the availability of a small amount of fresh water there are date palms dating from the days of the Jesuits, along with truck farming. There is also excellent fishing, and the Club Aereo was built so that foreigners could fly in to wet their lines. The small, attractive palm-shaded plaza only dates back to about 1965. You will also find a supermarket, Pemex gas station, hotels and several general stores. A laundromat is located under the Hotel Terrazas.

If all you're looking for is a beer or a meal you won't even have to walk down into town; the two restaurants on the wye

average out as almost as well as those down the hill.

Places to Stay

The *Hotel Vieja Hacienda* is still doing business on the plaza, but Al Cuesta has lost interest to some extent. It used to have a sign that said 'Broken English Spoken', but now it should have a sign like the one in the English pub that said 'Under Indifferent Management'. The Old Hacienda is looking a little tacky at the moment because it experienced earthquakes a couple of times in 1983. It is, however, in a convenient location. The swimming pool, though much appreciated during the summer, replaced the beer licence. Prices vary considerably, so the hotel is both moderate and expensive.

About 75 metres down from the Hacienda is the *Hotel Las Casitas*, also called 'Jorge's' by the English-speaking locals. Very expensive.

Turn left by the supermarket on the corner as you come into town, and in a couple of short blocks you will come to the fairly new *Hotel Terrazas* on the hill overlooking the town. Lots of room to take a chair out on the roof and and loaf. About the nicest place in town to my mind, but it's ridiculously expensive.

There are also a couple of *casas de huespedes* on the one-way street going out of town. To reach them from the plaza, go along the street that goes past the supermercado a couple of blocks and turn left a block past the supermarket. They are side by side about a block up the hill. They're called the *Manuelita* and the *Nachita*. Both advertise economical prices and hot water; the latter claim is to be taken with several grains of salt. Inexpensive.

Places to Eat

Mulegé used to have only one or two restaurants, and they were usually closed. Things have improved no end, and today the locals' favourite place is the *Restaurante Candil*. This small restaurant has a menu with a surprisingly large selection. It is located in the short block between the plaza and the supermercado. Moderate.

Right on the plaza is the *Restaurante Maranatha Especialidad en Pollos Rostizados.* They have a number of items besides roast chicken, although the menu is nowhere as extensive as the Candil's. Moderate.

The restaurant in the hotel/bar *Las Casitas* is somewhat fancier than those above, and often the food is as good as that of the Candil. But it is the place for those who feel a great need for a white tablecloth and/or a few mixed drinks. And the Casitas makes it a point to have a competent bartender behind the plank. Very expensive.

For dining on the cheap, stock up at the local supermarket and picnic on the plaza

Getting There & Getting Around

The highway misses Mulegé. The bus stop is up at the wye where the big trucks park. The town is off to the east of the highway out of sight, but just follow the signs. The plaza is about 75 metres to the right of the supermercado on the corner below the Pemex gas station, but if you're driving you will have to go to the next corner and double back – the small town is modernizing itself with one-way streets. From the wye to the plaza is about a km. Walking time one way is 10 minutes, the other way 15 minutes.

LORETO

(elevation two metres, population 4000)
This is probably the oldest European settlement in the three Californias, but it was pretty much abandoned for a number of years. It was established by the Jesuit Superior Juan María Salvatierra during the days when California was a theocracy so absolute that even the Spanish soldiers sent out to garrison the country were individually vetted by the Order. Over the door of the church is carved (in Spanish): 'The Head and Mother of Missions in Upper and Lower California'. The inscription dates from the days when Loreto was 'Capital of all the Californias' – you can try out this bit of trivia on your friends.

When the Jesuits were expelled in 1768 their operation was taken over by the Franciscans, and it was from here that Padre Junipero Serra left to begin his life's work of establishing missions in Alta California. Today Alta California is known simply as California.

Places to Stay & Eat

The best place to eat, especially for breakfast, is the *Hotel Presidente.* Breakfasts there are moderate, but otherwise it is overly expensive.

Getting There

Loreto is 135 km south of Mulegé and just off the main highway. Apart from road transport there is also scheduled air service, and lots of fishermen fly their own planes in from the US and stay at the Flying Sportsman Lodge.

MISIÓN DE SAN JAVIER

From just south of the turnoff to Loreto there is a signed branch road leading west 34 km to the old Misión de San Javier. This is the best example of Jesuit stone construction in Baja California. It was built for the ages in an arid location, and stands today just as the good fathers finished it, with almost no deterioration even though there has been no maintenance or restoration work in the intervening years.

The mission itself sits at the end of a double row of houses facing each other across a broad street – complete with non-operating fountains – a sort of elongated zócalo. San Javier is the scene of a pilgrimage each year on 6 December that draws (mostly) back-country people for about a week of socializing and drinking. If you are in the area around this time it is definitely worth a visit.

LA PAZ

(elevation three metres, population 140,000)

Up until WW II, La Paz was a pearl-fishing centre, but for some unknown reason the pearls played out about the time of Pearl Harbor. I can remember the day when a stroll around town took you past patio after patio decorated with complete hardhat diving outfits deteriorating in the blazing sun.

With the sudden expiration of the pearl fishing, La Paz lost population and was saved from extinction only by being the territorial capital and by some desultory shipping. The road down the peninsula was all but impossible for the average tourist, and the few motorcycle riders and other intrepid types who did manage to cope with the 1500 km of desert trail were not big spenders by any stretch of the imagination.

The current boom really started with the advent of regular ferry service to and from Mazatlán, on the mainland, in the '60s. The airport was improved and scheduled services to the US began at about the same time, bringing in a flood of tourists, and for the first time in memory 'full' signs began to appear in hotel lobbies. Then in 1973 the paving of the Transpeninsular Highway was completed at last, making it practical for families in softly-sprung US-made automobiles to drive through Baja from end to end. New hotels were constructed up and down the highway by the Presidente chain, and La Paz began a hotel-building spree that continues unabated to this very day.

With all its building, La Paz has concentrated its low-price housing around the plaza, especially the economy hotels which are all within 10 minutes' walk of the zócalo.

If you happen to arrive in La Paz by night the plaza will surprise you. Unlike most plazas that are dimly illuminated by the penny-pinching town fathers, the

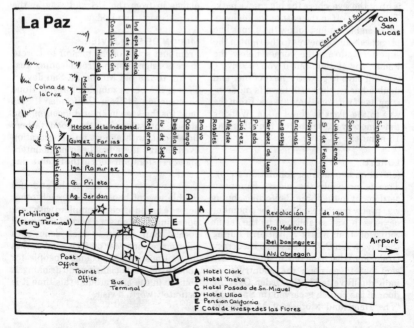

A Hotel Clark
B Hotel Yneka
C Hotel Posada de Sn. Miguel
D Hotel Ulloa
E Pensión California
F Casa de Huéspedes las Flores

zócalo at La Paz is brilliantly illuminated by dozens of sodium-vapour bulbs concealed in the old pebbled-glass globes. It is a rare sight.

On the plaza is the Libreria Coromuel, which stocks a few English-language paperbacks and also the Mexico City daily newspaper, *The News*, in English. This is the first bookstore with English-language books south of San Diego that I know of.

Places to Stay

Even with all the new rooms that have been added over the past decade, La Paz still fills up and sometimes travellers have to accept rooms they would not normally have chosen. Low-priced places are concentrated around the plaza, and the economical hotels are all within a short walk of the zócalo. There are quite a number of *viajero* (traveller) hotels, mostly clustered within a few blocks of each other south of the plaza.

The *Hotel la Purisima*, on 16 de Septiembre between Revolución and Serdan, is an older house dating back to at least the early '60s, though it doesn't look its age. It has four stories and an elevator. Located close to downtown, it is expensive.

The *Hotel Yneka*, on Madero between the plaza and 16 de Septiembre, is an economy hotel that sheltered a whole generation of travellers over the old truck trail. It has recently had a facelift and is now two stories built around a patio that doubles as a lobby and parlor. All sorts of gimcracks now line the walls of the *zaguán* (entrance) where the desk is located, including a breast drill, lots of deer antlers not necessarily in pairs, a wood-spoked iron-tyred wheel from a child's goat cart or an antique pram, a small collection of padlocks together with a large assortment of non-matching keys. And much much more. Otherwise it is the same old Yneka I know and love, except the price has gone up. Moderate.

The *Hotel Posada de San Miguel* is on Belesario Dominguez near 16 de Septiembre, across from the army barracks and hard by the old market which is now a shopping arcade. View this one from across the street to get the full Arabic effect of the handsome tiled facade. Moderate.

The *Hotel Cristine*, formerly the Hotel Mouron, is on 16 de Septiembre between Madero and Revolución de 1910. Built in 1971, it looks much older. It is a two-storey family-style hotel and considerably larger than it appears from the sidewalk. To get a fix on its true size head back through the zaguán past the desk to the patio. Moderate.

The *Hotel Ulloa* is identified at night by a bright electric sign reading 'Brandy Presidente Hotel'. It's on Serdan between Bravo and Ocampo. The front rooms of the two-storey structure include balconies overlooking the street and the schoolyard across the way. Moderate.

The single-storey *Pensión California Casa de Huéspedes* on Degollado between Madero and Revolución has a sign that states (in Spanish), 'This is not a hotel. It is a home for our guests'. The neighbourhood is fairly quiet, especially at night, and is not too far from the plaza. The hotel is built around the plant-filled patio of a former private home. Moderate.

Hotel San Carlos is on the corner of 16 de Septiembre and Revolución de 1910, but you actually enter on 16 de Septiembre and climb a flight of stairs to the lobby. Although the San Carlos is on one of the busiest intersections in town it is likely to have rooms because it is so hard to locate. Expensive.

The *Casa de Huéspedes las Flores*, on Revolución de 1910 between the plaza and 16 de Septiembre, is a typical, no-frills *casa de huéspedes* (guest house). It also doubles as a bath house, so hot water should be no problem. Inexpensive.

The *Hotel Santana* is one of the newer hotels, and a little farther out than most on Revolución de 1910 between Juárez and Pineda. The Santana is housed in a three-storey building with a clean appearance due to the bright white paint, orange *rejas* (grating) and beige trim. As usual, it is built around the patio. The neighbourhood is fairly quiet by day, dead quiet at night. The Santana is far enough from the zócalo so it takes a bit longer than most to fill, and against all reason it is cheaper than the Prado (deleted this issue), and in my opinion a far better deal, but it is still expensive.

Directly in back of the new city hall on the plaza is the little *Hotel Central*, aptly named indeed. This hotel, with its brick and cream facade, is a find – there aren't too many inexpensive hotels in La Paz.

Places to Eat

Like all boom towns, La Paz is an expensive place in which to eat – even the market is more expensive than elsewhere. The following places used to be dirt cheap; recently their prices have gone up a lot, but they are still lower than the better-publicized places down on the Malecón.

Restaurant Cielo Azul, on Bravo between Ramirez and Altamarino, has had a facelift but at the rear it is still the same old Cielo Azul of yore. One of the waiters used to be a wrestler called 'El Jipi Sucio' (The Dirty Hippy) who was full of stories about his nomadic life. The *Blue Heaven* does very well these days with *higado Mexicana* (liver with tomatoes and spices), and generally gives excellent value for the peso. Moderate.

The *Restaurante de la Rosa* is another Mexican-style restaurant that I can recommend. It's a little place next door to the Cielo Azul, serving *machaca* (dried beef), *pozole* (hominy stew) and so on. Moderate.

One of the new markets, at Degollado and Revolución de 1910, has rather more elabourate restaurant facilities than most of its kind, but is still inexpensive. There is another new market on Bravo between Prieto and Ramirez. It is mostly a meat market, but also has restaurant facilities, again inexpensive. These new markets, by the way, are the result of the destruction of the original market, the one with all the

character, to make way for a miniscule shopping arcade, complete with a gushing fountain in its middle.

The *Café Olimpia* is across the street from the Hotel La Purisima on 16 de Septiembre between Revolución and Serdan, and it's the best place to eat near the plaza. The bakery next door is actually part of the café. The locals are well aware of the Olimpia's merits and at times it is damned hard to get a seat, even if the facilities have been enlarged by the addition of a few card tables on the sidewalk. Both good and moderate in price.

Antojito El Mexicano, on 16 de Septiembre near Serdan, specializes in menudo, burritos and other home-cooked specialties, and makes a big thing of its comida corrida. Moderate.

Getting There

La Paz is the transport hub of Baja California Sur. It has scheduled air services to mainland Mexico and to the United States.

Paved roads lead north to Tijuana and the US, and south to the Cabos.

There is a new bus station on the outskirts of town where, except for the arterials, the streets aren't even paved, far beyond practical walking distance. Take a cab – it only costs M\$350.

There is ferry service from La Paz to Mazatlán. The terminal is actually at Pichilingui, about 14 km along the western shore of Bahía de La Paz, but there is a ticket office for the government ferries in downtown La Paz at Victoria and La Paz. Look for the sign that says 'Caminos y Puentes Federales de Ingresos y Servicios Conexos'.

From time to time there is a ferry to Topolobampo, the seaport for Los Mochis, Sinaloa, but the route suffers from lack of patronage which causes service to be discontinued until some other optimist takes over. I mention it only because it is shown on so many maps.

CABO SAN LUCAS & CABO SAN JOSÉ

Cabo San Lucas is the southernmost tip of Baja California. It has received a good deal of tourist-oriented publicity because it is the site of several super-high-price hotels. Originally it was visited by big game fishermen such as the late Bing Crosby and his sidekick, Phil Harris, but there aren't enough big game fishermen in the world to make a large hotel complex worthwhile. Now the publicity is aimed at everyone with the price of an airplane ticket and the yen to sit around the pool, drink margaritas, and touch up their tans.

Cabo San José, on the other hand, is not a popular tourist destination, and its hotels cost about a fourth as much as those in its sister city along the beach. San José is a town of about 3500 and has all the services of an isolated Mexican community, including liquor stores, bank, gas station, hotels, restaurants, and so on.

Getting There

There is frequent bus service from La Paz by paved road. Cabo San José is 185 km, Cabo San Lucas 215 km from La Paz.

The twice-a-week ferry service between the Cabos and Puerto Vallarta has been 'temporarily discontinued' due to lack of patronage, but it was always a lot more convenient, even for those actually bound for Puerto Vallarta, to take the ferry from La Paz to Mazatlán. There are more ferries, for one thing; and for another the ferry terminal at the Cabos is out in the middle of nowhere between the communities. If you miss a ferry the hotels at the Cabos are more expensive and inconvenient than is staying in La Paz.

The West Coast

The West Coast route, via Baja California, Mexicali or Nogales, is the preferred land route for the majority of travellers visiting central Mexico and beyond. Most tourists begin at Tijuana. Directions for reaching the new bus station were given previously.

It is vitally important to get your Mexican tourist permit at the border. Mexico has *Migración* check points along the roads leading down from the border, and if the mood of the inspectors happens to be bad they are perfectly capable of sending foreigners back to the border to pick up a permit, or even of throwing them in the slammer.

MEXICALI, Baja California

(elevation three metres, population 320,000)

Mexicali, the capital of the state of Baja California, is one of the hottest places in North America during summer. It is also the northern terminal of the railroad running along the West Coast to Mexico City.

At one time there was a connecting railroad, the San Diego and Arizona Eastern, running to Tijuana, but a number of washouts caused by a severe storm gave its owner, Southern Pacific, an excuse to discontinue the service. The tracks are still in place, however, and I suspect the line may be reinstated because Tijuana is getting so large and generates so much business.

Trains generally depart around noon for Guadalajara and Mexico City. First class is somewhat cheaper than bus, and the second-class fare is about half the price of a bus ticket, but I definitely don't recommend Mexican second-class trains to any but the most poverty-stricken foreigners. Second-class travel is like making a trip in the cargo compartment of a garbage truck with the denizens of a home for disadvantaged children. First class is better, and reserved-seat first class not bad at all, but be warned that Mexican air-conditioning in general is unreliable, and that on trains it is especially prone to breakdowns. Train travel in Mexico is only recommended for dyed-in-the-wool rail fans.

For the most up-to-date information on train service write to: Ferrocarril Sonora Baja California, Post Office Box 231, Calexico, California 92231, USA. The railroad maintains this box in the US because getting mail this way is much more efficient than receiving it via the Mexican postal system. But regardless, don't expect a sudden reply.

SONOITA, Sonora

(elevation three metres, population 15,000)

Sonoita is 266 km east of Mexicali and almost due south of Gila Bend, Arizona. It is where the road branches off for Puerto Peñasco. All buses stop here, but more important to the traveller heading south, at the eastern edge of town there are customs and immigration inspection stations. Their official name is 'Aduana Fronteriza'.

Although the immigration people are empowered to issue tourist permits at the Sonoita station, they have been known to refuse to do so for one reason or another, which means that the wayfarer caught short had to retrace the trip – and forfeit the bus ticket – to a station closer to the border.

The customs station is there primarily to check the belongings of Mexican citizens for such contraband as transistor radios, tape recorders, TV sets and other prohibited items, and the check on the foreigner is perfunctory, to say the least. But be prepared – both customs and immigration agents have it within their power to make it extremely uncomfortable

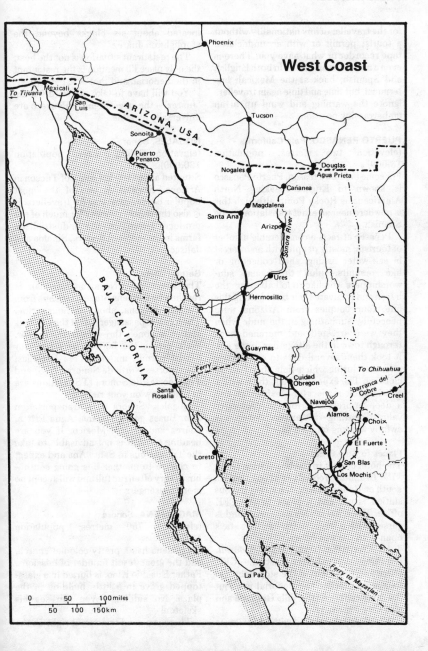

for the traveller of any nationality without a tourist permit or with an undeclared tape recorder or what have you. There is even a notice to this effect, in both English and Spanish, back at the Mexicali bus terminal, but time and time again travellers ignore the warning and wind up in an embarrassing position.

PUERTO PENASCO, Baja California

(elevation two metres, population 13,000)

For some unknown reason, Puerto Peñasco is known to English-speaking North Americans as Rocky Point, although this is nowhere near an exact translation of the Spanish.

Peñasco attracts a considerable number of tourists, mostly people with an interest in salt-water fishing, shell collecting or like pursuits, plus the usual sun-worshippers who like to loll about on the beach and cultivate their tans. (Along this line, four couples from Arizona were peacefully sunbathing in the nude when they were arrested and marched back through town in the altogether to the jail. It took them several days to effect their releases, during which time they had no clothing. The experience left them with a considerable respect for Mexican law and a deep appreciation for the protective value of clothing – a Mexican hoosegow is awfully wearing on bare skin.)

Places to Stay & Eat

The hotel closest to the bus station is the *Villa Granada Hotel*. It is about two km south on Benito Juárez, the street the bus station is on, and a block to the CFE office. The hotel is very expensive and is cursed with a large, noisy bar that stays open until the wee hours.

An alternative is the *Motel Señorial*. Continue along Juárez past the CFE office and turn right at the stop light. Go four more blocks. The Señorial is about the same calibre as the Villa Granada and also very expensive.

A trailer park, marked with a big sign, is located about six blocks beyond the stoplight on Juárez.

The restaurant situation is not the best; the only place I'll mention is the restaurant in the Señorial, and that is expensive.

You will have to take my word for the 'Juárez' – the street signs in Penasco are universally illegible.

NOGALES, Sonora

(elevation 2039 metres, population 120,000)

Situated about 100 km south of Tucson in Arizona, Nogales is one of the most popular border crossings for travellers. It is also the export gateway for much of the produce grown on the industrialized farms in the states of Sonora, Sinaloa and Jalisco.

Getting There

The sister city, Nogales (Arizona), is reached by Citizens Stage Lines bus from Tucson, Arizona, about an hour's ride. The bus lets passengers off at the Citizens station a stone's throw from the border. Walk across the border, pick up your tourist permit, and the Tres Estrellas, Transportes Norte de Sonora (TNS) and Transportes de Sonora (TS) stations are in plain view on your right.

Nogales, Sonora is a transportation hub. Buses go to Tijuana, Agua Prieta, Juárez and central Mexico. If you are heading south it is not advisable to take the Tijuana bus to Santa Ana and expect to change to another bus going south – buses very often run full and will accept no more passengers.

MAGDALENA, Sonora

(elevation 750 metres, population 16,500)

Magdalena has a pretty colonial church, and the great Jesuit founder of missions, Father Eusebio Kino, is buried in a glass-topped grave in a little building in the plaza. No kidding – you can see his skeleton!

There is a good restaurant right on the

Top: Mexico's traffic laws are frequently disregarded; note the cart on the road beyond this sign.
Left: Dancers at a local fiesta near Actopan, Hidalgo.
Right: Baja California has been called the world's biggest cactus garden.

Top: Mules and donkeys are still Mexico's basic form of transport in the country.
Bottom: In Merida horse-drawn carriages are still popular, and not just for tourists.

plaza, *El Tecolote.* It used to have huge cages filled with every kind of bird imaginable, with one notable exception – there were no owls (*tecolotes*).

Very few travellers visit Magdalena. The town proper lies off to the west of the highway and therefore goes unnoticed by both drivers and bus travellers, but it is a charming little town and deserves more attention.

AGUA PRIETA, Sonora
JANOS, Chihuahua

The height of the pass over the road between Agua Prieta, Sonora and Janos, Chihuahua is given by a roadside sign as only 1790 metres, but it is enough to cause the pass to be closed by snow several weeks each winter.

This is a relatively new way of crossing the mountains. Primarily a truck road, it reduces over 1000 km from the Monterrey-Tijuana trip. Detouring into the United States would accomplish the same thing, but many Mexican trucks are too large to operate in the United States – I saw one rig coming over this pass with 46 tyres on the road!

For some reason the Mexicans have installed *vibradores* at each end of the several bridges to slow traffic. They aren't really all that severe, but the truck drivers take them very seriously. In case you're driving, be prepared for a sudden drastic slowing of big trucks for no apparent reason out in the middle of nowhere.

SANTA ANA, Sonora

(elevation 750 metres, population 5000) Santa Ana is located at the junction of the Mexico City-Nogales and Mexico City-Tijuana roads. Changing buses here will often save a mite of time for those travelling on the south side of the international border between Tijuana and Juárez for reasons of economy.

There are essentially two bus stations in town – Pacifico's and another one that serves all the other companies. They are only a block apart, but not actually within sight of each other. Ask the bus station personnel or any passerby for directions.

SONORA RIVER VALLEY

An alternative route south to Hermosillo is via the new paved road running south from Cananea along the Sonora River to Ures, and then west to Hermosillo. This road is so new that it doesn't appear on too many maps, and as yet there is very little traffic and very few big trucks to dodge, a situation that will change with time. This route is more interesting than the CN-15 highway, and for people coming from Douglas, Arizona it is somewhat faster.

The towns here, more than almost anywhere in Mexico, have Indian names, and the accent falls on the third-from-the-last syllable rather than the next-to-the-last as per the usual Spanish practice. Watch the accent marks. Examples: Bácoachi, Bácanora.

Of all the little towns along the Sonora River Valley, Arizpe is far and away the most interesting. Originally a mission, it developed into a full-fledged church centre when mines were established in the area.

In 1776 a Spanish officer named de Anza led several hundred Mexican families to establish what is now known as San Francisco, California. Contrary to many published reports the expedition did not start from Arizpe; but Arizpe received de Anza's bones and they rest today in a glass-topped grave in the church near the plaza.

Arizpe is the most progressive of any of the old towns along the river, due mostly to the good offices of a recent mayor. The streets are paved, the various businesses are required to put up signs – most of the towns in the region look more like ranches than towns – and there is even an animal control officer who arrests livestock daring to crop the plants on the plaza.

There are three hotels, a number of restaurants, a gas station, grocery stores and a stated population of around 3700, probably counted on a Saturday night.

One restaurant on the plaza, the *Kan-Kún*, is worthy of recommendation. I've eaten there a number of times and have never had a bad meal. Straight Sonora fare – this one caters to the locals.

HERMOSILLO, Sonora
(elevation 237 metres, population 320,000)
Hermosillo, the capital of the state of Sonora, is blistering hot in summer, and the only people who overnight here are the adventurers who come down via the scenic route through Arizpe and Ures.

Hermosillo is due to become Mexico's next industrial boom town; the United States' Ford Motor Company is constructing a new automobile factory here, which will give the local economy a welcome shot in the arm. The planned plant has been widely publicized in the US, but what hasn't been publicized is that it won't build Fords – it will build Mazda parts.

The new Central de Autobuses is on the outskirts of town with nothing in view but a few hills covered with mud shacks. The station has post office and telegraph facilities, a restaurant and the usual amenities.

Places to Stay
The *Hotel Monte Carlo*, Sonora at Juárez on a corner of the Jardín Juárez, is adding a third floor. For the benefit of those arriving in the midst of a red-hot summer, it advertises 'York' air conditioning. This well-run establishment is expensive, but worth it.

The sky-blue *Hotel Royal*, around the corner from the Monte Carlo, is considerably down in price but lacks the quality of the Monte Carlo. Moderate.

Between the Royal and the Monte Carlo is the *Casa de Huéspedes Colonial*. It's painted a bilious orange so it's hard to overlook, and is the most economical place I've been able to locate. Be warned, it's not the Paris Ritz, or even the Cairo Hilton in ambience, but the rates are low.

Hotel Lourdes, Oaxaca near Juárez, toward the avenue from the plaza, is unprepossessing but economical. The style is Mexican Miracle Modern. Inexpensive.

The *Hotel San Andres*, Oaxaca near Juárez, is another low-price hotel, older than the Lourdes and not quite as well maintained. Moderate.

Places to Eat
There are any number of country-style restaurants in this neighbourhood, but the unchallenged best, and my favourite in Hermosillo, is the *Restaurante Monte Carlo* in the hotel of the same name. The restaurant is run well by knowledgeable people who know their business thoroughly. For instance, if you order a bottle of Agua Tehuacán, it will be ice-cold, served with a glass of small ice cubes and a twist of lime! Expensive.

While you are in the area, take note of the shining white teeth of the locals in the neighbourhood, not all that common in Mexico.

The fairly new *Restaurant La Central*, across the street from the bus station, is a much better place in both food and service than the greasy spoon in the station proper. Moderate.

Getting Around
To reach the plaza near the low-priced hotels, technically the Jardín Juárez, cross the street in front of the bus station and catch a bus marked 'Ranchito'. It turns right onto a broad avenue and is eventually joined by railroad tracks which run down the centre divider. After the railroad tracks end, the bus turns left onto a narrow, one-way street called Juárez. Get off at the plaza a couple of blocks along Juárez and pay the driver M$20 on leaving. Just toss the coins onto the rug on the dashboard.

To return to the bus station, go back out onto the avenue, the Bulevar Transversal, and catch another Ranchito bus going from left to right. To walk is 20 minutes.

GUAYMAS, Sonora

(elevation two metres, population 150,000)

Guaymas, 135 km south of Hermosillo, is the first town you hit coming south down the west coast that can be called a destination in any sense of the word. It is primarily a fishing port, with a fine harbour, and has the usual boat-building and repair businesses. It has been trying to build up its tourist business for years, but without any beaches to offer sun lovers it hasn't had much luck.

Guaymas is a relatively new town, founded as Guaymas de Zaragoza in 1769. Because of its fine harbour, it prospered early on, and was the shipping point for the ranches and rich mines in the interior of Sonora. The town has had many masters. In the beginning, of course, it was Spanish and so rich that it attracted the attentions of one Count Gaston Raouset de Boulbon who twice tried to sack the town. On the second attempt the Count was captured and suffered the usual end – he was executed by the local commander, General Yanez. The French were back again during Maximilian's short reign, and during the American Civil War Guaymas served as a trans-shipment point for supplies for the Union forces in Arizona Territory. With the Revolution of 1910 and the accompanying anarchy, Guaymas fell into financial doldrums from which it took decades to recover.

Places to Stay

As Guaymas itself is not popular with tourists it should follow that there are lots of economical hotels around for the local trade, but it doesn't quite work that way.

The old *Hotel Rubi*, at Serdan and Calle 29, is a good example. It is definitely overpriced, but when the Hotel Malema closed there wasn't a lot of choice left. The Rubi has been accumulated rather than built, and you may need a guide to find your room. Very expensive.

Be warned: the bar in the Rubi serves small, 200-ml bottles of beer, an insult to a thirst on a hot day.

The *Hotel Ana*, near the plaza, may be a good, reasonably priced hotel. It looks like it, but I have still never found anyone in attendance, so maybe it is always full.

The *Hotel Impala* (née Malema) is on Rodriguez and Calle 29, four blocks from the bus stations. It is the best place in town and the air conditioning works, as well it should, for the hotel is very expensive.

The *Hotel America* is up the hill on Alemán (if the street numbering were consistent Alemán would be Calle 20) three blocks on the corner of Avenida 18. As you approach from Serdan there is no sign visible, but the sign can be seen from the other side, and the odd-looking building is painted a pastel blue so it is hard to miss. Expensive.

The *Casa de Huéspedes*, on Serdan between Calles 25 and 26, is the best bet of all in the way of economy. In Europe it would be called a pension, but don't expect European standards of quality. Inexpensive.

Places to Eat

Guaymas has long been noted as a seafood town, but in recent years the quality has dropped as prices have risen.

The old standby has long been the *Chichén Itzá*, now on the Malecon near the Rubi, but even this old reliable has suffered some deterioration in recent years. Expensive like the other fish restaurants.

When the Impala Hotel was the Malema it had the premier restaurant in Guaymas and served the best *pescado Veracruzana* in Mexico. Apparently the original crew scattered while the hotel was closed during the battle between the heirs. Now that it has been recycled into the Impala it isn't quite as good as it used to be, but it ranks well in the forefront of Guaymas' restaurants, and improves with each passing year.

La Flor de Michoacán, on Calle 19

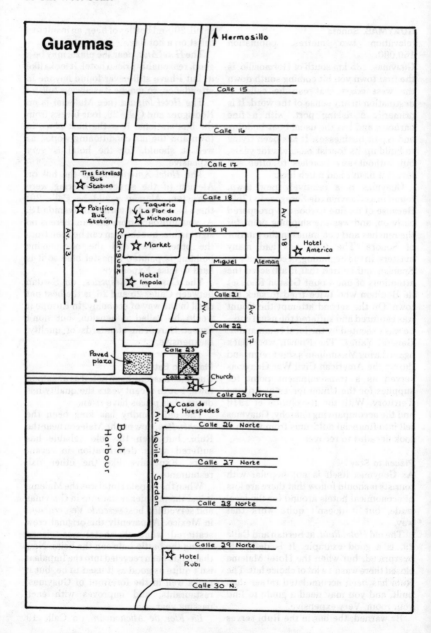

across the street from the market, is a little taqueria that does a better than average job of taco building. Inexpensive.

Unfortunately Guaymas doesn't run heavy to markets, but there are several ample ladies who serve meals in the market at rock-bottom prices. The little market is at Calle 19 at Rodriguez. Inexpensive.

Another place for a hearty and economical snack is *Las 1000 Tortas*, on Serdan between Calle 19 and Aleman. Inexpensive.

For do-it-yourselfers in the eating department there is a good supermarket at the corner of Calle 18 and Serdan. Enter through the liquor store.

Getting Around

There are two bus stations, right across the street from each other on Calle 18. To get downtown turn left as you leave the Tres Estrellas, TNS and TS station, or turn right as you leave the Pacifico station. In two blocks you will come to Serdan, the main street. Turn right and you are in the business section.

Getting There

Guaymas is a stop on the bus lines running north and south along CN-15, the west coast route.

Although there is an airport large enough to handle big jets, the flights to and from Guaymas are mostly local flights by Mexican carriers, and flying in and out of Guaymas from the United States can be frustrating in the extreme.

There is thrice-weekly ferry service to Santa Rosalia in Baja California. This is the shortest of the three ferry routes connecting Baja California with the mainland. The ferry terminal is some distance south of Guaymas and, although I have walked it, I prefer to take a cab – the fare is only around M$200 or so.

The Mexicali-Guadalajara-Mexico City trains stop here.

CIUDAD OBREGÓN, Sonora

(elevation 70 metres, population 160,000)
This town is located about 114 km south-east of Guaymas in the midst of thousands of hectares of irrigated fields. It was built during the agricultural boom caused by damming the Rio Yaqui; the water was used for power and for irrigating the fertile plain between the Sierras and the Sea of Cortés. Ciudad Obregón was named after the one-armed general and president of Mexico who got along well with the Yaqui Indians and who successfully grew chick-peas in the vicinity. In fact, Obregón was called 'The Garbanzo King' at the time. Nowadays Ciudad Obregón sells farm machinery, mills and stores grain, cans and packs vegetables and becomes larger and more prosperous year by year.

Places to Stay

In looking for quarters in town, I suggest you take a cab from the bus station to the *Hotel Kuraci* on Calle 5 de Febrero Sur. This is about the handiest and cheapest hotel in Obregón, which favours expensive hotels. Moderate.

Within walking distance of the bus station is the *Hotel Martinez*. To get to the Central Camionera the bus leaves Route 15 and goes west on a divided street for 15 or 20 blocks. The Martinez is off the divided street, Calle 200, and some six or eight blocks before you reach the bus station. Watch for a small, old-fashioned electric sign shaped like an arrow on the north side of the street and pointing north. Moderate.

NAVAJOA, Sonora

(elevation 35 metres, population 80,000)
Navajoa is a vast improvement over Obregón as a stopping point on the long trek south. It is about 67 km down the road south-east of Obregón. The reason most people stop here is that it is the jumping-off place for Alamos, 53 km by paved road to the east in the foothills of the Sierra Madre Occidental.

Places to Stay

Navajoa has a number of hotels, some of them up in the M$3000-a-night range, but it also has the *Hotel America*. This hotel is about six blocks back toward Obregón from the bus stations on Calzada de Revolución, the street the Pacifico bus station is on. Except for the noise of the buses, which continues 24 hours a day, the America is a safe bet as an inexpensive hotel.

To reach the *Hotel Aduana* go out the front door of the Tres Estrellas station and turn right on Ignacio Allende. The Aduana is in the next block. Those who stayed in the Aduana years ago wouldn't recognize the place. The old hotel has been completely recycled into a new and modern viajero hotel, a vast improvement over the original structure, but I miss the mural of the old town and smelter of Aduana, Sonora, that used to grace the lobby. Moderate.

Places to Eat

The best place to eat in Navajoa is at one of the stands across the Calzada from the TNS station. This area is actually another bus station for some of the many long-nosed buses that serve the outlying small towns over dirt roads. My favourite among these stands is the one that says simply 'Birria de Cabrón', but they are all good, and very inexpensive.

For a cooling beer on a summer afternoon, try the economical place across the street in front of the Tres Estrellas station on Allende. It's the one with the sign reading 'Carta Blanca'. The name of the establishment is *Mariscos a la Jojarrita*, but I've never seen anything but cerveza sold there.

Avoid the joint to your left as you leave the TNS station. The not-too-cold beer is overpriced by a factor of 2.5!

Getting There

Navajoa is a minor transportation hub. In addition to the long-distance carriers, local buses depart across the street from the TNS station, but the bus that goes up the hill to Alamo is probably the one that will interest the average traveller.

The Alamo bus leaves from a second-class bus terminal about a 20 to 25-minute walk from the Tres Estrellas station. To reach it, go out the front door of the Tres Estrellas station and turn right. Go two or three blocks and turn right again, then left at the next corner. The little second-class station is straight ahead.

ALAMOS, Sonora

(elevation 389 metres, population 10,000)

A falling-down ruin only a few years ago, Alamos has been repaired and restored by wealthy Americans who buy old buildings for the proverbial song and then spend thousands of dollars restoring them to their former glory. As one of Mexico's National Monuments, the town does not suffer the tawdry plastic construction that has defaced so many once-beautiful Mexican cities.

A few km back toward Navajoa, and just south of the road, is La Aduana (from whence the hotel in Navajoa takes its name), the site of the smelter that separated the silver from the ore that came from the mines around Alamos for hundreds of years. If you are interested in industrial archaeology a visit to La Aduana and an observant eye will give you considerable insight into the art of ore-dressing and its changes over the centuries. As improvements in smelting techniques required different physical structures the old ones were simply abandoned. The last operation took place around half a century ago, and there is still a complete power-house dating from that time, with the original Fairbanks-Morse C-O engine in place, looking as if it could be started again any day.

La Aduana has a church with a large cactus growing out of the wall, and there is a story about an apparition of the Virgin manifesting on the site and pointing out a large silver vein. The little town is also the scene of an important fiesta of the region's Mayo (not Maya) Indians. This is held each year on 20 November, and during the fiesta the old ghost town returns to life with a vengeance!

Places to Stay

There are very few hotels in Alamos; the only one that can be depended on to be open is the *Hotel Tesoro*, and it is ridiculously expensive.

For years Alamos had a moderately priced hotel, the *Portales*, right on the little plaza. Unfortunately the Portales has been defunct for several years, although it is still being listed in guidebooks.

But all is not lost. Stand in the street facing the Portales and on your right you will see the *Henrique Hotel*. It caters primarily to the locals – the sort of foreigner who settles in Alamos wouldn't set foot in the Henrique! I've never had occasion to stay there but the clerk assured me the Henrique was moderate.

Places to Eat

Alamos is not an eating-out town and restaurants are few because people eat in their own and each other's homes. The best I've done is a tin table in the little market, which was inexpensive.

Getting There

See Navajoa section for information on location of the Alamos bus station.

LOS MOCHIS, Sinaloa
BARRANCA DEL COBRE

(elevation 75 metres, population 100,000)

Most foreigners stop in Los Mochis to transfer to the train or railcar that goes up through the Barranca del Cobre to Chihuahua. The Barranca is considerably larger than the Grand Canyon of Arizona, although by no means as spectacular. The railroad, Chihuahua al Pacifico (now nationalized), was originally conceived as the shortest freight route between the American heartland and the Pacific. Today it mostly hauls Mexican products to and from the little seaport of Topolobampo, 22 km west of Los Mochis. At the other end the CHP terminates at the border town of Ojinaga, across the Rio Grande (Rio Bravo to Mexicans) from Presidio, Texas.

The trip is exceedingly popular with both the ordinary tourist and the out-and-out rail fans who make the 650-km trip between Mochis and Chihuahua in large numbers, for this is truly one of the great train rides of the world. The railbed is blasted from the side of the mountain for hundreds of km, and there are over 30 tunnels. The passenger equipment is standard USA (retired) or Fiat diesel-propelled railcars called Autovías. Some of the standard cars are equipped with observation domes, and the trains using them are called 'Vista Trens'.

Rail fans have loud and impassioned arguments as to which is superior, a Vista Tren, Autovía or regular passenger train. I've ridden all three at one time or another and enjoyed them equally.

At the upper end of the canyon is the little town of Creel, unusual for a Mexican community in that it is mostly built of Abe Lincoln-style log cabins. Many experienced Barranca fans take the train only to Creel and return to Mochis the following day, claiming there is little to be gained by taking the train on into Chihuahua through flat farming country. The trains stop at Divisadero for the benefit of photographers and view-enjoyers. From the lookout at Divisadero you can see across the canyon into the mouths of three major canyons, equally deep. The one on the northern side is La Barranca del Cobre, the middle one is La Santa Sinforosa and the most southerly is El Cañon de Balojaque, known to many English-speakers as Urique – God knows why?

The CHP is not operated solely for the benefit of the tourist business. Its primary purpose is to provide access to an

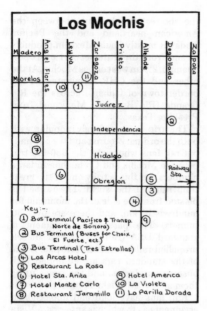

Los Mochis

Key:-
1. Bus Terminal (Pacífico & Transp. Norte de Sonora)
2. Bus Terminal (Buses for Choix, El Fuerte, ect)
3. Bus Terminal (Tres Estrellas)
4. Los Arcos Hotel
5. Restaurant La Rosa
6. Hotel Sta. Anita
7. Hotel Monte Carlo
8. Restaurant Jaramillo
9. Hotel America
10. La Violeta
11. La Parilla Dorada

Streets shown: Madero, Angel Flores, Leyva, Zaragoza, Prieto, Allende, Degollado, Zapata, Morelos, Juárez, Independencia, Hidalgo, Obregón, Railway Sta.

extremely large, otherwise inaccessible area, rich in minerals and forest products, and to allow ocean freight to move into the interior of the northern part of the country from the Pacific. Passengers are hauled as a convenience to the travelling public, and the railroad doesn't put itself too far out of its way for their benefit, Mexican or foreign. The CHP also transports automobiles, but it usually takes an extra day or two at each end for loading and unloading, and the service is expensive.

The best way to get tickets for the Copper Canyon trip is to go out to the railroad station in Los Mochis. Theoretically they are available from local travel agents, but I've been told of monumental foul-ups by people who attempted this. It is important to remember that railroad time is an hour ahead of local time. Many disappointed would-be passengers have stood at the station with tickets in their hands looking at the empty tracks an hour after the train has been and gone.

As with all schedules, the CHP feels perfectly free to change train times at will, but generally speaking a morning train from either Chihuahua or Mochis is the way to sight-see, and an evening train is for those who for one reason or another are interested in transportation more than in scenery.

The CHP station in Los Mochis is way out from the centre of town. A cab costs about M$350, or there is a bus available for a lot less. Catch it near the Tres Estrellas station on Obregon. It's green and the fare is around M$20.

Places to Stay
From the Tres Estrellas bus station, the *Los Arcos Hotel* is around the corner to the left on Allende. The blue-fronted Los Arcos represents excellent value for money and tends to fill up early on, so check as soon as possible. Moderate.

Down on Allende past the Los Arcos is the *Hotel America,* long a favourite with automobilists because of the lock-up parking lot around in back. Expensive.

Hotel Monte Carlo, on Angel Flores between Independencia and Hidalgo, is a big, older hotel that looks as if it should be inexpensive, but isn't. However, it makes quite a point of having air-conditioning that works. Expensive.

Hotel Santa Anita, on Leyva between Hidalgo and Obregón, gets the bulk of its business from the tour packagers who always offer 'first-class accommodations', which translates as 'overpriced' and means that at least one employee speaks a language that sounds something like English. I include it here because it makes an excellent landmark. Ridiculously expensive.

Up in Creel a number of hotels have been established to cope with the train passengers who don't want to continue on to Chihuahua. Most of them, including the new *Parador*, are in the M$3000 to $5000-a-day class.

An exception to this sweeping statement is the tiny *Hotel Korachi*, near the station. Because it is small and low priced it is often full of penny-wise travellers, and if you intend to overnight there I suggest you wire a reservation from Mochis stating the day and train on on which you expect to arrive. Moderate.

There is also a fancy hotel at Divisadero, apparently for the benefit of people who take package tours. Ridiculously expensive.

Places to Eat

There are lots of economy restaurants around the Tres Estrellas de Oro bus station in Los Mochis. My favourite is the *Rio Rosa*, across Obregón from the station. It serves hearty meals for country people, featuring such Central Mexican items as *chilaquiles* (casserole of corn tortillas in tomato sauce), *cocida de rez* (beef stew), *picadillo* (spiced hamburger), *flan* (custard) and a fantastic *rico pozole* (hominy stew). Moderate.

Those using Pacifico or TNS buses aren't quite so fortunate. The best way they can go is the *La Parilla Dorada*, which contrary to the name is painted lavender. It's diagonally across the street and is almost as good as the Parilla up the hill in Chihuahua. Expensive.

The *Madrid*, on Obregon at Leyva, has been good for many years. Despite the name, it's really mostly Mexican, rather than Spanish. Moderate.

At a tiny public market on Los Mochis, on Independencia between Degollado and Zapata, there are several good little restaurants intended primarily for the market people, but all comers with money are welcome, making this the cheapest place to eat in town. Inexpensive but with ambience.

Getting There

To get there, you should use the frequent bus service. And the Chihuahua al Pacifico railroad. However, the north-south railroad station for Los Mochis is up the hill at San Blas, Sinaloa (not the San Blas in Nayarit which is much better known). Local air service is also available.

SAN BLAS, EL FUERTE & CHOIX, Sinaloa

The north-south railroad station serving Los Mochis is at San Blas, some 40 km away. If you find yourself there waiting for a train the wait can be trying. The station lunch room doesn't amount to very much, and eating is definitely better in central San Blas, about one km away.

El Fuerte, on the other hand, is worthy of a visit in its own right. It is 78 km inland from Los Mochis at an altitude of 400 metres. This charming, unpublicized sister city of Alamos never did become a ghost town, nor did it become an Americanized National Monument, although most of the buildings date from colonial days. There is a large grassy plaza with the usual ornate bandstand and an unusual matched pair of fountains that work. El Fuerte gets no play at all from the usual run of tourists but is well known among the bass-fishing brotherhood perpetually seeking world-record fish at the nearby man-made lake.

About 50 km beyond El Fuerte, on the same black-topped road, is the only town in Mexico with a French name (to my knowledge). Choix is nestled up against the foot of the Sierra Madre Occidentales, and serves as a supply and outfitting point for the ranchers, loggers, miners and prospectors of the region. A busy place, it has several small hotels and a multitude of shops selling everything it takes to run a ranch or a mine. The population is about 3500, altitude about 600 metres, and climate much better than that of either Alamos or El Fuerte.

Places to Stay & Eat

The *Hotel San José* in El Fuerte is in the block on Juárez after the intercity bus stop, between 16 de Septiembre Norte and Constitución. The San José is your basic country stopping place and is inexpensive.

Continuing along Juárez to Constitución and turning right will put you on Obregón – Constitución changes its name – and in a block and a half you will reach the *Hotel*

San Francisco, a good, viajero-type hotel. A couple of blocks from the bus stop, now it isn't so noisy. Built around the patio of a great house, it is equipped with air conditioners that work. Moderate.

The restaurant in the San Francisco serves Mexican dishes and is as good as any in town. Also moderate.

Another hotel and restaurant combination is the vastly more costly *Posada Hidalgo*, a recycled mansion with a ramp allowing horse-drawn coaches to deliver their passengers to the door, which is unique in my experience in that it is not on the ground floor. The Hidalgo is very popular with international sport-fishermen and dove shooters, and is well worth a look. It's just off the plaza on the street that runs past the church and continues past the side of the newly-overhauled city hall. Need I add that the Hidalgo is ridiculously expensive?

Getting There

All three towns are customarily reached by bus from Los Mochis. The buses leave from a little station in back of the market on Degollado between Juárez and Independencia. Not all buses make all three towns, so always check to see if the Choix bus, for instance, will halt at El Fuerte.

MAZATLÁN, Sinaloa

(elevation three metres, population 250,000)
Mazatlán is the northernmost destination along what the publicity people are pleased to miscall the Mexican Riviera, but as with most Mexican resorts it has a lot more going for it than the vagaries of the tourist business. In addition to the highly visible tourist hotels along the Malecón, enterprises there include coffee roasting, fishing, beer brewing, boat building and repairing, shipping, canning and a host of others contributing to the economic base.

As in all coastal resorts, the tourist business is concentrated on the beaches. Mazatlán has a couple of beaches close to the downtown area, and it is common to see people in bathing suits, robes and zoris carrying their suntan oil, books, bumbershoots, beach chairs and so on past the plaza. As is the case all over Mexico, women are expected not to walk around in bikinis, and people naturally wear robes, or skirts and tops, when away from the beach. As I said, it is by no means an equivalent of the Riviera.

Many of the older residences between the beach and the downtown area are actually empty and falling down, but that is because they are owned by older women whose husbands have died. The widows will neither rent nor sell the houses, and, as there is no tax on unoccupied residences, they just sit empty. They give Mazatlán an elderly air, but actually the town is relatively new. About the time of Maximilian some Germans made Mazatlán their base for selling agricultural machinery, and the town as it is now dates from then.

For some years a hermit has lived in the towers of the Mazatlán cathedral. Separated from his wife, Pablo Vargas wandered into the church one day and asked Monsignor Trinidad if he could sweep the floor in return for something to eat. The regular bell-ringer had recently died, so the Monsignor asked him if he would accept the job of bell-ringer. Señor Vargas climbed the towers and has not come down since. He is a salaried employee of the cathedral and is fed by the church; his pay is sent to his children and grandchildren because living in the towers he has no need for money. High in the towers, Vargas escapes much of the town's oppressive summer heat, and when it rains he simply retreats into a tiny stone shelter. He has rigged ropes so he can ring the four bells from inside without venturing out into the rain.

At 21 de Marzo 904, near Serdan, across the street from the Hotel Vista del Mar, is a beautiful, well-maintained Buddhist temple, striking in its brilliance. It is a reminder of the days when the Chinese were a well-heeled minority here.

Mexico once had a sizeable Chinese population, but the Chinese had the unfortunate habit of working hard and investing with foresight, a combination of traits which allowed them to become very successful, and Mexico in its wisdom expelled most of them about 50 years ago.

Places to Stay

As do most of the older resort/commercial towns, Mazatlán has a number of inexpensive hotels located downtown and fairly distant from the beach.

The *Hotel Vialta*, on Azueta between Hidalgo and Estrada, is built around a patio in Mexican Modern style. Moderate.

The *Hotel Victoria*, Azueta at Estrada, on the other hand, is built around its parking lot. It is far, far from palatial, but inexpensive.

Casa Familiar Aurora is on Azueta between Estrada and Ocampo. This family-style Mexican-type hotel is better for groups of two or more, in which case it is inexpensive.

The *Hotel San Lorenzo* is on 21 de Marzo between Serdan and Azueta. Because it is on a seldom-used side street, it is one of the last economical hotels in Mazatlán to put up the 'completo' sign. Moderate.

The *Hotel Villa del Mar* is nowhere near the sea, being a block or so from the plaza. It's an old favourite of mine; I've stayed there off and on since 1967. I'd stay oftener, but it puts the 'full' sign up early, most days. You'll find it at Serdan and 21 de Marzo. Expensive, but just barely.

The *Hotel Freeman*, on the Malecón near Olas Atlas, was one of the first beach hotels and I stayed there when the sites of most of the fancy hotels along the beach were goat pastures. I prefer the front rooms with the balconies overlooking the ocean and catching the trades. Because it's at the unfasionable end of the beaches, the Freeman is merely expensive.

There are a number of hotels in view from the bus station, plus a number of

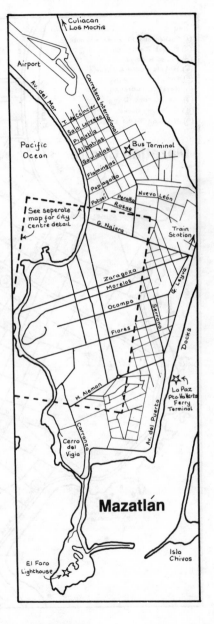

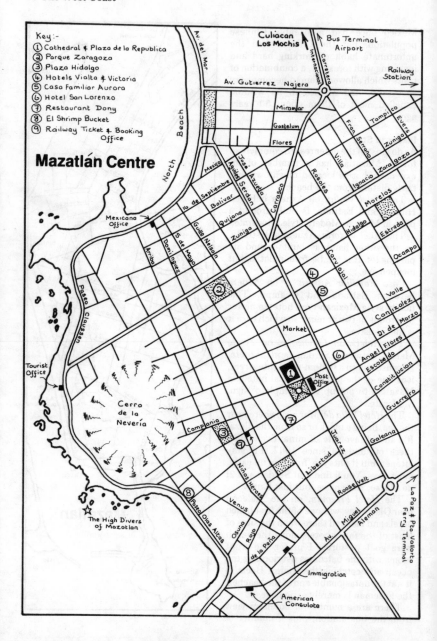

Key:-
1. Cathedral & Plaza de la Republica
2. Parque Zaragoza
3. Plaza Hidalgo
4. Hotels Vialta & Victoria
5. Casa Familiar Aurora
6. Hotel San Lorenzo
7. Restaurant Dony
8. El Shrimp Bucket
9. Railway Ticket & Booking Office

Mazatlán Centre

concrete-built food stalls. Across the street is the *Hotel Economica*, slightly misnamed because it is expensive. It is a new house built to take advantage of the flow of customers from the almost equally new bus station.

The *Hotel Fiesta*, along the same street at 306 Rio Tamazula, is also new. It's slightly cheaper than the Economica, but still expensive.

There are two new hotels across the street from the first-class section of the Central de Autobuses. The one on the left, the *Hotel San Geronimo*, is yellow with a blue sign, with the entrance on the left beside the restaurant. The hotel is small – only two floors – which recommends it. Moderate.

Next door to the Geronimo is the *Hotel Imperidor*. The three-storey building is white with blue ornamental surrounds accenting the windows. I talked with several clients and they all felt it gave good value for the money. Moderate.

The best bet in the neighbourhood is the *Hotel Esperanza*, on the hill above the station on Carretera Internacional. Go out the front door of the bus station and you'll be on Río Tamazula. Turn left and go up to the stop light and you will be on the Carretera. The Hotel Esperanza is now to your left and across the street. During daylight hours the Esperanza stands out because its brick-trimmed facade is painted bile green. Moderate.

It is worth noting that these economy-model hotels near the bus station are actually quite close to the beach. Go out the front of the bus station and turn right on Rio Tamazula and the beach is only two or three blocks away.

Places to Eat
Being a minor fishing port Mazatlán offers good seafood, but for some reason this substance is expensive in Mexico, and in Mazatlán M$500 for a shrimp cocktail, and M$450 for an octopus ceviche, are by no means unusual along the beaches, and only slightly less downtown.

The restaurant *Doney*, which I have recommended without reservation for years, has moved as predicted to one of the most charming commercial restorations I've seen anywhere. Without a doubt the transplanted and enlarged Doney is the very best oil-cloth joint in Mexico. I fully expect to see it described in print as a 'gem of colonial design' (which of course it isn't). It is a pity they didn't transfer their previously tight operation; in the new place the inventory control, service and procedures are lousy. The Doney is now at the corner of Cinco de Mayo and Mariano Escobedo.

All is not lost, however. The *Restaurant Los Faroles* at Flores and Carnival, a block or so from the new Doney, is a worthy successor to the old place. I ordered a 'Mexican plate', something nobody in his or her right mind would do – and it was excellent! Contrary to usual Mexican practice in which the customers are expected to fill in the hollows with cheap tortillas, there was simply too much to eat. Moderate.

The *Café Oriental*, 'specializing in chop suey', is on Serdan between Estrada and Ocampo. The chop suey notwithstanding, the Oriental has provided a welcome change of pace from standard Mexican fare for many years. Moderate.

El Shrimp Bucket, on the Malecón (Olas Atlas) at Flores, in the La Fiesta hotel, is part of a chain. Some people like its laboured cuteness with such menu listings as 'moo' for beef and 'oink' for pork. But they have music for dancing and there will be lots and lots of people there for you to practice your English on. Ridiculously expensive.

As usual, the cheapest eats in town – and almost the cheapest in Mexico – are served by the market vendors. Go into the market on the Ocampo side at the entrance across the street from the Banco Provincial and turn left up the stairs immediately before you get into the market proper. There are several restaurants on a balcony overlooking the

land because Baja California is much more interesting than the haul through Sinaloa and Sonora. During the summer there can be more passengers than capacity, and sometimes people wind up camping out for a day or so in order to get tickets. The crossing takes 15 or 20 hours and is usually calm. Ferries leave during the late afternoon and arrive in La Paz in time for breakfast. Or lunch. The information number is 1-24-54, but if no one answers go down to the foot of Serdan and ask there – it is about a 10-minute walk from the plaza.

Bus service, both long distance and local, is excellent. The buses cover all the heavily travelled west coast routes, as well as a route inland to Durango.

Because of the booming package tour business, plus a continuing barrage of special low promotional fares, more people come by air, mostly from California, than by train, bus and private automobile combined. The international airport for Mazatlán is about 30 km from town. A taxi costs M$1200, but somewhat lower-priced limousine service is supposed to be available. Those arriving by plane generally go directly to one of the super-expensive 'beach hotels' that line the Malecón.

street. They are very difficult to find and thus attract few foreign customers.

Skip the restaurant in the bus station if the stands outside along Río Tamazula are open. These are permanent concrete structures, and the women who run them are fiercely proud of their undoubted ability to put out a better meal for less money than the big cafeteria in the station. Prices vary but at the most are moderate, and often less.

Getting There

Mazatlán is on the main north-south route between Tijuana/Nogales and Guadalajara/Mexico City. The railway station is located on the east side of town, quite some distance from the plaza, but very few foreigners arrive by rail, barring the occasional rail fan who doesn't object to travelling the hard way.

Mazatlán is the mainland terminus for the ferry crossing the Sea of Cortés to La Paz. This is a good way to get to or from California in the US if you are travelling by

Getting Around

Mazatlán has regular taxi service, plus a unique vehicle called a *pulmonía*, which translates as 'pneumonia'. This is a three-wheeled vehicle driven by a tiny gas engine, based on the Cushman metermaid special. As the Cushmans wear out they are replaced by recycled VWs. A pulmonia can carry three passengers and is obviously much cheaper to operate than a standard full-size taxi, but the fares do not necessarily reflect this bit of economics. Haggle and bargain before you get in, otherwise the driver is perfectly within his rights in charging to the limit of his imagination. These toy taxis work only within the central area and do not go out to the airport. And I have seen them refuse a fare to the railroad station!

The city bus service is first rate. To get downtown from the Central Camionera (about an hour's walk), go out the side of the station, pass the lunch stands onto Calle Río Tamazula and turn left. Go up the street to the traffic light at the Carretera Internacional, walk right for a block and catch the bus in front of the bank. Buses should pick up passengers at Rio Tamazula, but many drivers are reluctant to stop for a lone fare and miss the light as a result, so it's better to walk the short distance to the next stop where there are almost always people waiting. The bus downtown is marked 'Centro Morelos' and goes down by the market on Serdan, the main drag of Mazatlán. For the return, catch it one block over on Azueta. Just about any bus on Azueta winds up going out the Carretera.

Around the bus station you will probably notice small pickup trucks equipped with a couple of seats running fore and aft. These are *peseros* that shuttle between the bus station and downtown, and unlike the buses, adhere to no fixed schedule. If you are going downtown and one happens to be available, grab it – a pesero will be quite a bit quicker than fiddling around with the bus.

Side Trip to Durango
It is 318 km from Mazatlán to Durango, and the road is one of the most spectacular in Mexico. Branching off the coast road at Villa Unión, about 25 km south of Mazatlán, it climbs 1625 metres through rugged mountains. At times the pavement winds along a ridge with not even room for shoulders and with hundreds and hundreds of metres of sheer nothing on each side. If you happen to be afflicted with acrophobia, then by all means make the seven-hour trip at night. There are lots of buses originating in both Mazatlán and Durango, so it is not ordinarily a problem to get a seat.

Cutting up to Durango is a good bet any time you are fed up with the coastal route, and it is a short cut to the interesting colonial cities of the high mesa, such as Sombrerete and Zacatecas.

Side Trips to Copala & Concordia
Copala and Concordia are two small communities on the mountainside south and east of Mazatlán. Much older than Mazatlán, they have the kind of picturesque calmness one associates with Old Mexico. There are regular tourist trips run from Mazatlán – you'll see signs advertising them in the hotels and travel agencies around town. But for maximum economy combined with the utmost in freedom I suggest you do as I do, take a bus from the central bus station. As both cities are on the route up the hill to Durango – CN40 – it is possible to cover them both in a single day. If you're bound for Durango it is practical to visit Copala and/or Concordia and then continue on up the hill. Women are advised to wear shoes with low, broad heels. Both cities have lots of cobblestoned streets left over from colonial days.

In Concordia – closest to Mazatlán – ceramics manufacturing has replaced mining as the main source of income. It is a pleasant little place and well worth a visit. With its altitude of about 600 metres it has a more salubrious summer climate than Mazatlán.

If you are short on time, or the weather is just too, too hot, then I suggest you go to Copala. This town, with an altitude of 700 metres, bears about the same relation to Mazatlán as Cordoba bears to Veracruz. Copala is somewhat over 400 years old and was one of the first gold mining operations in Mexico. The local residents take quite a bit of pride in their little city and have renovated the old church on the plaza as well as a number of other buildings. My favourite restaurant is *Daniel's*, on the eastern side of town. Note the old mine entrances nearby. There is another perfectly acceptable restaurant called *The Butter Company of Copala* (!) that does a brisk trade with the day-trippers up from Mazatlán.

Above The Butter Company is the town's sole hotel, the *Posada San José*, with antiques in most of the rooms, no locks on the doors and the communal bath a few metres down the hall. The locals assure me that there will 'soon' be a new hotel, but they've been telling me that for about 10 years, so I'm not really counting on it.

TEPIC, Nayarit

(elevation 915 metres, population 150,000)
Tepic is the place to abandon the main north-south coastal route for branch-line trips to Puerto Vallarta or San Blas, Nayarit. It is best to arrive in Tepic in the morning, but if you have to overnight, the *Hotel Tepic* – which can be seen from the back of the bus station – is not a bad house, and the rates are moderate. The restaurant in the hotel is on the inferior side.

The *Hotel Nayarit* is next door to the Tepic and not very different in quality, but costs considerably more and is therefore more likely to have a vacancy. Expensive.

If you turn left as you leave the bus station and then turn right at the second stoplight, and then left at the next stoplight, you will be on Juárez. Follow Juárez for two or three blocks and you will come to the *Hotel Juárez* with a blue-and-red-on-white sign. Highly visible and inexpensive.

Continue on Juárez for 10 or 15 minutes and you will come to the state capital. Turn right and another 10 minutes will bring you to the plaza. A taxi back will cost M$150-200.

If you want to take a bus downtown, go out the front door of the bus station and catch a a bus travelling from right to left marked Tepic-Fresno-Jalisco.

As you come into the bus station from the buses, you will see two restaurants and

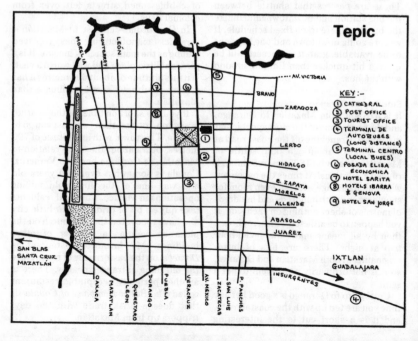

KEY:-
① CATHEDRAL
② POST OFFICE
③ TOURIST OFFICE
④ TERMINAL DE AUTOBUSES (LONG DISTANCE)
⑤ TERMINAL CENTRO (LOCAL BUSES)
⑥ POSADA ELISA ECONOMICA
⑦ HOTEL SARITA
⑧ HOTELS IBARRA & GENOVA
⑨ HOTEL SAN JORGE

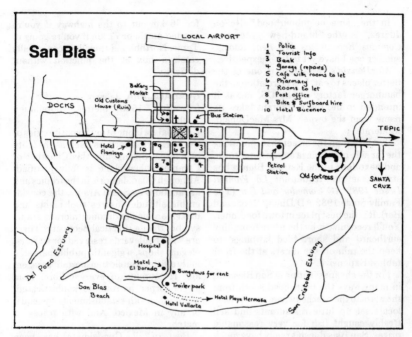

San Blas

1 Police
2 Tourist Info
3 Bank
4 Garage (repairs)
5 Cafe with rooms to let
6 Pharmacy
7 Rooms to let
8 Post office
9 Bike & Surfboard hire
10 Hotel Bucenero

a *guardaria* (checkroom). I prefer the restaurant on the right-hand side as you enter.

SAN BLAS, Nayarit
(elevation 1.5 metres, population 40,000)
People usually refer to San Blas as a 'village' – but to me there is no such thing as a village that has more than 40,000 people! San Blas was founded by the Spaniards as a ship-building centre, and many of the bottoms used in the Oriental trade were built here. As that was back in the days of wooden ships, time and termites have long since erased all traces of this activity. Old San Blas, on the little hill overlooking the town, has the remnants of the usual fort, but lack of maintenance and the roots of the tropical vegetation have pretty much demolished it.

At the foot of Juárez, the main street, is the remains of the old Spanish customs house, a good subject for photography.

As in most other small Mexican coastal towns, you can swim, loaf, cultivate a tan and spend part of a day taking photographs of the fort and customs house.

Places to Stay & Eat
The *Hotel San Blas* is a couple of blocks off Juárez, the street that brings you into town. It is well marked with signs facing the incoming traffic. Built around a patio, with 35 rooms, it is fairly new. An interesting feature is the belvedere at the end of the second floor interior balcony overlooking the patio where travellers regale each other with tales of adventure and derring-do. Moderate.

The *Hotel Flamingo* is along Juárez beyond MacDonald's restaurant. One of the oldest in town, and a step up in quality from the San Blas, it is hard to overlook with its white facade, black-painted rejas and blue trim. Expensive.

In the same neighbourhood, also on Juárez, is the brand-new enterprise *Comidas Economicas We Rent Rooms*, another one I have yet to try. Inexpensive.

MacDonald's restaurant is one of the better places to eat. It is no relation to the hamburger factory in the US, nor is it intended to be; the restaurant takes its name from the owner, Mrs MacDonald. Moderate.

To the left on the street that runs along the far side of the plaza as you enter town, and next door to the Estrella Blanca bus station, is the restaurant *La Familia Desde 1982 AC Comedor and Bar* (The Family Since 1982 AD Dining Room and Bar). It is the best place in town for dinner. You'll recognize it by the white front, tiny surfboard and short tiled 'awnings' to keep the rain off the diners at the front tables. Expensive.

For the cheapest eating in San Blas,and in many ways the best, head south from the plaza to the beaches where enterprising locals set up little restaurants and sell freshly caught fish for very reasonable prices. San Blas doesn't really have much of a market area, and these stands take the place of market eating.

Getting There & Away

Although it is possible to take a bus from the north and get off at the junction of the side road to San Blas, the procedure is risky because so many of the buses are too loaded to stop for more passengers. The safest procedure is to continue on into Tepic and then double back on a bus originating there. There are so many buses that getting a seat out of Tepic is ordinarily no problem.

Getting out of San Blas often poses more problems. Although it is a second-class bus the dragon at the main bus station stops selling tickets when the seats are all filled, and will curtly inform prospective passengers that the next autobus will be in X number of hours. Not to worry. Simply go out, get aboard the bus and be prepared to stand in the aisle

for 36 km out to the highway if you're headed north, or 71 km if you're going to Tepic. Northbound travellers can usually catch a bus at the junction without difficulty.

GUADALAJARA, Jalisco

(elevation 1540 metres, population 3,500,000)

Guadalajara is one of my favourite cities of the world. It advertises itself as the 'City of Eternal Spring' and this Chamber of Commerce hyperbole is fully justified. Although Guadalajara is in the tropics and as far south as Saudi Arabia, the considerable altitude ensures cool nights and makes an air conditioner more a status symbol than a practical necessity. There are wide boulevards reserved for walkers, elegant shops, a gigantic public market, a fairly efficient public transportation system and restaurants of every calibre, from street-corner barrows to sophisticated, white-tablecloth establishments the equal of any in Mexico. And with prices to match.

Best of all, Guadalajara has been working for some years now on a plan that will eliminate the smoking buses from the downtown area and make more pedestrian walkways, and at last the plan is bearing fruit. The three big plazas were disassembled piece by piece so that parking lots and a vehicle tunnel could be built beneath them, after which they were reassembled in their original form. Block after block was turned into vehicle-free malls, and smart shops the equal of anything in Mexico City replaced the tacky originals. Nothing like this has been done in North America.

University of Guadalajara

The University of Guadalajara is on Juárez at Tolsa. Housed in a former Jesuit monastery, it is of interest mainly for the mural by José Clemente Orozco in the lantern of the main building's lecture hall. In addition there are some excellent though little-known murals by Siquerios and Cuevas in the chapel. Guadalajara is very much a university town, with numbers of Americans enrolled in the medical school, so many that there is even an American Students' Wives' Club providing social outlet for the mostly non-Spanish-speaking women.

Templo Expiatorio

The Templo Expiatorio, Madero at Tolsa, is across the street from the university. It is often miscalled a cathedral by Americans labouring under the impression that any large, imposing ecclesiastical structure is a cathedral. One of the finest buildings erected in Mexico since colonial times, it is built of hand-hewn reddish stone using old-world techniques. It is well worth visiting for the stained-glass windows alone.

Instituto Cultural Mexico Norte America

The Instituto Cultural Mexico Norte America, Tolsa at Miguel Blanco, close to the templo, is a language and art school that teaches English and Spanish, among other cultural services. At the back of the extensive patio is an inexpensive snack bar open to all. A fine place to practice English or Spanish (or Spanglish!) with the students.

American Consulate

The American Consulate is on Progreso between Libertad and Lopez Cotillo. The Ben Franklin Library is on Libertad in the same building, and it carries a catholic selection of periodicals plus the usual run of fiction and nonfiction. It's a home away from home for the more literate expatriate Americans.

Alliance Francaise

French-speaking sojourners hungry for the sound of their own language will appreciate the Alliance Francaise, out on Lopez Cotillo between Robles Gil and Athena. The Alliance is housed in a handsome, tasteful and unusual building.

Teatro Degollado

The Teatro Degollado, on Degollado between Hidalgo and Morelos, is a European-style opera house and one of the architectural gems of Guadalajara. The School of Theatrical Arts of the University usually presents a *folklorico* each Sunday at the unlikely hour of 10 am – a must-see for any visitor. The programs change from time to time and I've had the pleasure of attending five performances with no two alike. Most tourists automatically buy the most expensive main-floor seats, but the next-cheaper ticket gives me a choice of boxes above the heads of the main-floor audience. Recommended enthusiastically.

Museo Regional de Guadalajara

The Museo Regional de Guadalajara occupies an old seminary on Liceo between Calles Independencia (not Calzada Independencia) and Hidalgo. As with most Mexican museums it leans heavily toward dark oil paintings of former bishops, government officials and just plain ordinary wealthy men and determined-looking women. Aside from this, the museum is one of a kind. Especially interesting is the building itself, a magnificent example of Spanish ecclesiastical construction of the late 1600s.

Mercado Libertad

The Mercado Libertad, on the Calzada Independencia at the foot of Juárez, is another Guadalajara must-see. It is huge as only the public market of a very large city can be, bigger than the market in Mexico City which is broken up into a number of smaller, more manageable units. On first seeing Libertad anyone would justifiably assume it is a very old place, but in truth it dates back only to 1959, although there has been a market at the site since before the Spaniards arrived.

Plaza Tapatio

Beside the Mercado Libertad is the small,

triangular Plaza Tapatio, also known as La Plaza de las Mariachis because the various *mariachi* bands meet here of an afternoon while getting ready for their nightly round of music-making. Mariachi music originated in Guadalajara in the middle of the 19th century. Originally the bands played for weddings, and the word 'mariachi' is a pochismo derived from the French word for marriage. Now they play for anyone with a few pesos to spend, and most of them do it very well indeed. The wee plaza is a good place to have a snack and a cold beer while listening to the bands practising.

Hospicio de Niños

The Hospicio de Niños, also called Hospicio Cabanas after its founder, is reached from the left side of the market, opposite the Plaza de las Mariachis and across the new pedestrian overpass. The Hospicio was supposedly designed by Tolsa and is a huge place with about 25 patios. It is a working orphanage and interesting in itself, but most visitors see it to view the famous Orozco murals, among the master's best efforts. The boisterous orphanage children wore off the bottom of many of the murals, and Orozco repainted them shortly before he died.

The Hospicio is being overhauled, but visitors are permitted while the work is in progress. The new Plaza Tapatios fronts the Hospicio and is one of the finest plazas in Mexico. The plaza is effectively a continuation of the Calle Morelos which from a distance of several blocks looks as if it runs right into the front door of the Hospicio.

Tlaquepaque

Tlaquepaque is a must on most tourist itineraries, including the all-in guided tours. At one time it was a small suburb of Guadalajara, but as the city grew it reached out and surrounded the place. It has a fine plaza and is well worth the time and effort it takes to go out there.

Tlaquepaque is noted for its glass and

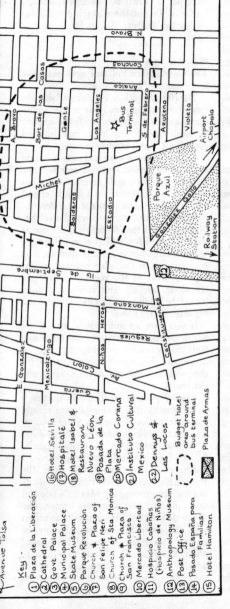

Key:-
1. Plaza de la Liberación
2. Cathedral
3. Govt. Palace
4. Municipal Palace
5. State Museum
6. Parque Revolución
7. Church & Plaza of San Felipe Neri
8. Church of Sta Monica
9. Church & Plaza of San Francisco
10. Mercado Libertad
11. Hospicio Cabañas (Hospicio de Niños)
12. Anthropology Museum
13. Post Office
14. Posada España para Familias
15. Hotel Hamilton
16. Hotel Sevilla
17. Hospitalé
18. Hotel Isabel & Restaurant Nuevo Léon
19. Posada de la Plata
20. Mercado Corona
21. Instituto Cultural Mexico
22. Dennys & Los Locos

Budget hotel area around bus terminal

Plaza de Armas

ceramics 'factories' and potential customers are urged to visit them. Note, however, that some 25 years ago writer James Norman said, 'Not too many years ago this one-industry town produced charmingly decorated, fragile pottery. Today the craft has been largely industrialized and debased and Tlaquepaque is now the chamber-of-ceramic-horrors of Mexico'. It is the same today, and just about anything you see in one of the shops in Tlaquepaque can be purchased cheaper – with a bit of dickering – from one of the vendors at the Mercado Libertad.

My favourite way of getting there is to stroll out Juárez to Federalismo and catch a trackless trolley, known locally as the 'metro', running in a tunnel beneath the street.

Shopping

Shopping in Guadalajara is probably the best in Mexico, and that includes Mexico City. There are large department stores on and off Juárez, right downtown, plus specialized leather-goods shops, charro outfitters and even a few guayabarras-only stores in Juárez itself. An ever-growing number of downtown streets have been closed to motor vehicles and the Juárez sidewalks have recently been widened about a meter at the expense of the street.

One of the finest shopping centres in North America, the Plaza del Sol, is readily accessible via the trackless trolley that runs beneath Federalismo.

There are a large number of bookstores in Guadalajara. *Librerias Gonvill* is a chain with outlets all over the city. My favourite bookstore is *El Libro Barato* on Guerra between Juárez and Lopez Cotillo. That's where I pick up a few copies of *El Chingoles* for friends every time I'm in town.

You can find flown-in US newspapers, *Time, Newsweek*, and a small selection of overpriced paperbacks at the newsstand off the lobby of the *Hotel Fenix* at 16 de Septiembre and Lopez Cotillo, but the best bet in town is *Sanborn's*, out on Vallarta. To get there catch a trackless trolley on Juárez. Watch for it on the right.

Places to Stay

The Guadalajara Yellow Pages has close to 20 pages of hotel listings.

The *Hotel Hamilton*, on Madero between Ocampo and Galeana, was my favourite for years. It's downtown where the activity is, and though the rent has jumped recently it is still moderate.

Recently I have switched my affiliation to the *Hotel Sevilla*, on Prisiliano Sanchez between Ocampo and Guerra. Somewhat larger than the Hamilton, it is quieter and a trifle more expensive, but still moderate.

Somewhat more economical than either of the above is the *Hospidaje* (pension) at the corner of Blanco Miguel and Ocampo. Quite a large house for a hospidaje, it is recognizable by the ochre paint on its flat facade. Most of the regular clients are travelling workers and country people, including families, in for a day or two in the big city. Inexpensive.

If you have an automobile, the *Motel Isabel* on Montenegro between Tolsa and Belgicia is within walking distance of downtown. I wouldn't recommend it for the non-motorist because it is overly expensive.

Travellers with families anticipating a fairly lengthy stay in Guadalajara should look over the *Posada España para Familias*, on Lopez Cotillo at the corner of 8 de Julio – hard to miss with its brilliant green facade. It is often full but inexpensive.

Almost across the street from the Posada España is the charming *Posada de la Plata*, not named for Mexico's popular local product but after the owner, one Senor de la Plata. This is one of the nicest small hotels in Mexico, and the several people I've met who stayed here raved about its virtues. But I'm sorry to have to admit I've never been fortunate enough to stay here – when I arrive in town it always seems to be *completo*. I suggest you at least tantalize yourself by peeking in through the front door/grille at the patio. Moderate and recommended – if you're lucky enough to get in.

On the side of the Mercado Libertad above the Plaza de las Mariachis is the *Hotel Imperio*. It is still reasonably priced, but probably not for long. Moderate.

All along the Calzada Independencia from the market toward the Central de Camiones there are small hotels. A few years back they were inexpensive but with inflation they became expensive, and now with devaluation they are mostly inexpensive and moderate. They are side by side, so checking them out isn't too much effort.

The *Hotel Sonora-Sinaloa*, on Dr R Michel at Gante, is near the bus station, but not visible from it. A dive, admittedly, but inexpensive.

There are nine hotels visible from the front of the Central de Camiones, mostly moderate, with a few in the expensive range. If there are plenty of vacancies, shop around until you find one that suits, but if not, check into the first one with a vacancy and use it as a base until more suitable quarters are located.

Places to Eat

Guadalajara is a first-rate eating town, and sometimes seems to have restaurants on every corner. These are some of my favourites:

Right downtown is the *Mercado Corona*, the small market on Hidalgo between Santa Monica and Zaragoza. Occupying a stand within the market is a large restaurant as market restaurants go, the *Carnes Asadas en su Jugo*. Instead of the carne asada, with or without juice, I have their *tacos al pastor*, which they do quite well. These translate as 'shepherd's tacos' and are made with beef cooked on a revolving vertical spit. The browned meat is continually sliced off the roast as it cooks and is used in the tacos. Inexpensive.

A plaque on the old balustrade in front of the Corona says: 'Don Antonio Flores was hung, drawn and quartered here by the despotic Spanish in 1812'.

Out toward Tolsa and the university there is the *Nuevo León*, on Libertad beyond Tolsa by the branch post office. This is a really good Mexican-style restaurant serving such hard-to-find northern specialties as *cabrito al horno* (baked kid), the best south of Chihuahua and Sonora. Expensive.

At the *Instituto Cultural Mexico*, Tolsa at Miguel Blanco, the snack bar in the patio is open to everyone. Inexpensive.

The local YWCA, called *Asociación Cristiana Femenina*, is on Montenegro between Belgicia and Argentina, near the Motel Isabel. It doesn't run a hotel, but it offers an economical restaurant and welcomes male, female and atheist customers. It has a soda fountain, too. Inexpensive.

Back toward the city centre a good place for lunch is the *El Greco* restaurant on Lopez Cotillo at the corner of Penitenciaria. This is a family operation popular with the business types from the surrounding offices. Despite the name, El Greco serves Mexican, not Greek fare. Moderate.

For vegetarians, the *Gran Comedor Vegetarano*, down the street on Lopez Cotillo between 8 de Julio and Martinez, is good news. Despite its cream front with red rejas, it's not very conspicuous because it is not well marked. The restaurant serves good, inexpensive food.

Mexico is noted for its fine baked goods, and *Postres de Mexico* on Guerra between Cotillo and Madero is one of the best around. Moderate.

The *Café Latino*, next door to the Hamilton Hotel on Madero between Ocampo and Galeana, is that rarity that makes *café con leche* the way it should be, with espresso coffee and hot steamed milk served separately in individual containers so you can mix your own. Beer comes icy-cold with a frosted mug rather than the usual warm glass. Moderate.

Next to the telegraph office, in a recycled church at Colón and Moreno, is an open-air cafe that is definitely the place for afternoon people-watching over a refreshment or two. I suggest you do your eating elsewhere, though. Moderate.

There is a *Denny's* on Juárez at 16 de Septiembre if you're feeling homesick. The standard fare includes hotcakes, hamburgers, pie and some Mexican dishes such as chilaquiles. The waitresses here are inclined to huddle around the coffee machine while their hapless customers are perishing from coffee deprivation. Clean restrooms. Expensive.

For a more economical alternative to Denny's, go around to the back of Denny's on 16 de Septiembre and into the shopping gallery by Gonvill Books, then upstairs to the *Fuente de Sodas los Locos*, which serves about the same sort of food as Denny's in an open-fronted restaurant overlooking one of the busiest intersections in town. This is a good place to read the Sunday papers over breakfast. Moderate.

Another place in essentially the same neighbourhood that rarely, if ever, sees a foreigner is the *El Palomar Restaurant* on Sanchez between Ocampo and Guerra, across the street from the Sevilla hotel. This is a plain restaurant for people who match. It is small and usually very busy. Good and inexpensive.

The *Madoka Café*, Martinez just off Juárez, has been around a long time and is a Middle Eastern coffee house. The front is usually devoted to chess and the back to dominoes. It is a place for the drinking of coffee (and beer), the meeting of friends, the reading of newspapers, the arguing of politics and the eating of meals. They serve first-rate espresso from a six-pump machine and pretty good food from an extensive menu. All in all, the Madoka is a rather odd establishment for Mexico, and a pleasant one. Moderate.

The cheapest restaurant in any town is almost always at the market, and in Guadalajara the *Mercado Libertad*, Juárez at Calzada Independencia, has dozens of them. They are mostly along the first floor balcony. See if you can locate one featuring *gorditas* – thick corn tortillas fried, slit open and stuffed with goodies of the customer's choice. Two gorditas and a bottle of Coca (beer is no longer sold in the market) make a very inexpensive and extremely filling meal.

Almost directly across from Sanborn's, on Vallarta at San Martín, is *La Baguette*, the best bakery in town. The intake end of the commercial pass-through oven is right in the sales room. As the name implies, the bakery sells first-rate French bread, plus some very good pastries and fruit cakes during the Christmas season.

To really pinch pesos, it is hard to beat shopping at the Gigante supermarket on Juárez at Martinez for picnic ingredients. Everything – meat, bread, mayonnaise and even a selection of domestic and imported wines – is available at quite reasonable prices. After shopping, a good place for a picnic is at the park just beyond Federalismo, about three blocks out along Juárez.

Getting There

Guadalajara's transport system is excellent with railroad passenger service and hundreds of buses a day with direct service to most larger cities in northern Mexico – buses and trains in Mexico go to, but not through, Mexico City. There is also direct air service in all directions from the international airport.

The most popular way of getting to Guadalajara from outside Mexico is by air. There are many scheduled flights each day, and usually a number of cut-rate promotional fares. The most popular regular flight is Mexicana's night flight, called 'El Tecolote', (the owl) from San Francisco and Los Angeles. It arrives in Guadalajara at about 6.30 am, just in time to begin a day's activities.

Airport baggage-handling techniques in Mexico are generally inefficient, and in Guadalajara they are a total disaster. Luggage is hauled to the terminal on little carts and tossed through a long hole in the side of the building onto iron-covered shelves for the passengers to paw through. I'm told this is due to be improved by the addition of standard carousels.

Guadalajara International Airport is about 20 km from the city centre and the taxi fare will take your breath away – around M$1200. A more economical alternative is offered by the VW van service, called *colectivos*, that take passengers downtown for around M$350.

Better still – for passengers who are not overburdened with luggage – is to go out the front of the terminal, turn right and walk about 500 metres to the Guadalajara-Chapala highway. Cross the highway and flag down a northbound bus. The road is travelled by both local and through buses, and there is frequent service.

Getting Around

At the front door of the railroad station, the street that runs slightly to the left is 16 de Septiembre, called Revolución by the locals. It will take you to Juárez and the Zona Central. The street that goes beside the park on the right is Calzada Independencia; it leads to the Mercado Libertad.

To get downtown from the bus station, go out the front and through the parking lot to the street. Turn right. Continue north in a direct line, passing the circle and monument at Calzada Independencia, after which you will be on Corona which in turn will take you to Juárez and downtown.

Walking time from either the bus or railroad station to downtown is about 15 minutes.

Many of the rickety old buses have been replaced with new trackless trolleys, and for the traveller one of the most useful routes takes you out Juárez/Vallarta practically to the arch. This is the most interesting and nicest part of the city.

CHAPALA, Jalisco

(elevation 1572 metres, population 30,000)
About 20-30,000 Americans live in the vicinity of Guadalajara – there are no hard figures – and a large percentage of them live in and around Chapala, some 50 km south of Guadalajara.

Originally Chapala was a sleepy little community of agricultural workers and fishermen, but more and more it is becoming the home-away-from-home for retirees from the US and Canada, mostly military types and salespeople. The attractions are a good year-round climate and cheap living, though inflation is rapidly eroding the latter advantage.

Chapala has the usual US-style amenities, including an American Legion post, and constitutes an English-speaking colony in Mexico. The majority of the expatriates do not trouble themselves to learn the national language, and one of the best-selling books locally is one that purports to explain to housewives how to communicate with 'your Spanish-speaking maid'. The book explains such vital operations as how to toast bread and prepare typical midwestern meals.

But Chapala is basically a pleasant little town, although most people who settle here when they retire move back to Canada or the States when the monotony becomes unbearable.

The church at the foot of the main street is interesting – it has two towers quite different in size, although somewhat similar in appearance. It seems that a few years ago a mild earthquake toppled one of the originals, and the church authorities seized the opportunity to build a grander model. They are enough alike to fool people into thinking both towers are the originals.

Almost close enough to Chapala to be considered a part of it is Ajijic and its neighbour, Jocotepec, about 17 km farther along the lake shore. Although Chapala is known as a retirement centre, these two towns actually have a few working writers and painters in residence, but it is the same old story – artists discover a place, hangers-on move in and soon the prices are too high for the original residents.

For the casual traveller I recommend making a day trip of Chapala and its environs from Guadalajara. You can easily come down on one of the early buses and return the same evening.

The bus service between Guadalajara and Chapala is excellent, with never more than half an hour's wait. A recent innovation has been the inclusion of VW Combis in the bus fleet. These command a slight extra fare, but they leave when full and are somewhat faster than most.

There is also mini-bus service along the lake, which makes getting to and from Ajijic and/or Jocotepec from Chapala a cinch. However, anyone intending to visit all three communities should also plan on overnighting somewhere along the line, in which case I suggest the *Motel Las Casitas*, quite near the centre of Ajijic. Moderate at the moment.

Places to Stay & Eat

If you have to stay overnight in Chapala, it's the *Gran Hotel Nido Restaurante y Cantina*. Located at the foot of the divided main street the bus station is on, it's a 15-minute or so walk from the bus station. The Nido (nest) is a small brick hotel with quite large rooms about a block from the shore. The dining room is nicely situated in the patio and is even popular with Mexican families down from the big city for Sunday. The hotel and restaurant are both moderate.

To get to another quality restaurant in Chapala, go down the main street past the Nido to the Malecón and turn left. You should be able to see the *Cazadores Restaurant*. It's part of a chain of deluxe restaurants and is situated in an artistically converted residence, worth a look-see even if you have no intention of eating. Very expensive.

Eating in Chapala restaurants is somewhat cheaper than in Guadalajara, but store-bought food is 15-20% higher. No, I can't figure it out either, although several local retiree-residents offered many theories on the subject.

SAN JUAN DE LOS LAGOS, Jalisco

(elevation 1863 metres, population 35,000)

San Juan de los Lagos is about 150 km east of Guadalajara and is another place that should be visited on a day-trip basis, not because it is uninteresting or overly expensive, but because while it is just another easy-going town most of the time, it has occasional spurts of frenetic activity which make it intensely interesting and fill the hotels to the rafters.

San Juan makes its living primarily from the Image of the Virgin of San Juan de los Lagos, housed in the big Parroquia on the plaza. The image is said to have miraculous powers and is the motivation for several pilgrimages each year, the most important of which brings people in large groups on foot for hundreds of km. They camp along the way in an atmosphere reminiscent of the great pilgrimages to Santiago Campostela during the Middle Ages, or the pilgrimage to Mecca. The fiesta culminates on 5 January and is the major event of San Juan's year, but there is a lesser fiesta 1-16 August, and a sort of quasi-commercial festival that lasts about a month around 20 November. This one has cockfights, bullfights and all sorts of hucksters working out of tents and peddling everything from cheap baubles for charm bracelets to quite high-quality serapes. The last formal fiesta starts on 28 November and lasts until 8 December. Oh, yes – there is the usual minor celebration around Christmas time.

During the various fiestas there isn't a prayer of obtaining a hotel room; they're all taken by families who come back year after year and occupy the same rooms.

It isn't too practical to commute from Guadalajara but it is practical from every standpoint to stay down the road in Lagos de Moreno and commute the 50 km or so. There are lots of buses and efficient central terminals.

To get to the plaza from the bus station, go left out of the waiting room and then turn left again at the highway. Go downhill to the Posada de la Plata sign on the right and turn right, heading for the spires of the Parroquia. Walking time is under 20 minutes. Taxi fare is about M$350, so walking is definitely worthwhile.

Restaurants are no problem. I simply pick one of those on the far end of the plaza from the Parroquia.

LAGOS DE MORENO, Jalisco

(elevation 1949 metres, population 40,000)

Lagos de Moreno is located 200 km east of Guadalajara at the intersection of two highways that have always been among Mexico's busiest, the east-west road between Guadalajara and San Luis Potosi and the north-south road between Juárez and Mexico City. In the days of the stagecoach it was an important stop, and even today it derives much of its income from the services it provides for the highway traffic. To augment the traditional income from transportation, Lagos also has a number of plants processing agricultural products, mostly milk, and is a supply centre for the surrounding farmers and cattle ranchers.

Note that the highways completely miss the town, except for the outskirts, and because of this few but the locals know about Lagos de Moreno – a great pity.

Although Zacatecas advertises itself as 'the most colonial city in Mexico', I'd give the title to Lagos. Most of the buildings in Lagos date from colonial times, and there have been almost no buildings constructed since in the central part of town, except for the market which is off to one side and out of general view. With the exception of the market building itself, any construction that has taken place since the exodus of the Spanish has been designed to blend with the overall motif.

There is a handsome pink stone church on the attractive plaza, and the plaza itself has lots of bright green laurels trimmed to cylindrical shapes, a topiary design that

complements perfectly the angularity of the church and other buildings surrounding the plaza.

Recently the well-planned Calzada Pedro Moreno and the Paseo Ribera – essentially the same thing – along the river have been refurbished and restored to their 1880s elegance. And at the end of the overhaul job the high-squirting fountain worked.

The best time to get a feel for Lagos is on a balmy Sunday evening, for the conservative city still clings to the old custom of the *paseo*, a sort of mating ritual in which the young men circle the plaza in one direction and the young ladies in the other. The scene is quite decorous and there is, of course, an abundance of eagle-eyed chaperons.

Places to Stay

In addition to being a charming place for a honeymoon or for writing a book, Lagos has a number of inexpensive hotels.

As you come in from the bus station along Calzada Pedro Moreno, just after you reach the fountain, make a right turn and you will see the *Hotel Victoria*, a building with window frames made of concrete and steel, now sporting a coat of dark maroon paint on the facade. Popular with truck drivers. Moderate.

The *Hotel Paris*, on the zócalo opposite the church, is actually a huge ex-private home, and what a home it must have been. The lobby measures a full 50 metres from the front door to the back, and as you come through the entrance you are struck by a fancy split staircase leading up to the first floor that looks like a set left over from an old Busby Berkeley musical. Most of the rooms remained large even after the modern bathrooms were installed. The Paris doesn't survive on its hotel business – most of its money is derived from the little bar in front. The Paris is inexpensive.

On the left side of the plaza as you face the church is the much plainer *Hotel Plaza*, also a converted private home but one that was nowhere near as grand as the

Paris. The Plaza is much better managed than the Paris. Inexpensive.

Going up in ambience and price we have the *Hotel Colonial*, also in an old mansion, on Hidalgo, the street running in front of the church and a block over. The Colonial is owned by the local veterinarian who has spent a good deal of money and thought on its restoration. Expensive and the best in town.

Places to Eat

The best place in town to eat, and the most popular, is the *Restaurante Pastor*, on Hidalgo to the left of the church as you face it. It is the gathering place for lanky men with rope-burned hands and big cowboy hats who do not look anything at all like the general conception of Mexicans. Photo-murals on the walls are worth a trip to the Pastor in their own right. They were made by a local photographer, and are of local scenes. The Pastor has a diversified menu, including fish, which is almost always available. The owner speaks English. Moderate.

La Troje on the plaza serves good food, and I've eaten there several times, but it is somewhat more expensive than the Pastor and not all that much better. Expensive.

The restaurant in the *Hotel Colonial* has the largest seating capacity in town. It does a pretty good job of cooking, but is inconsistent. Expensive.

The Hotel Paris has opened a new restaurant called – what else? – *The Versailles*, considerably better than their previous effort. Inexpensive.

As usual, the cheapest place in town for a good meal is at one of the stands in the market, up a few blocks on Juárez, the street the Hotel Plaza is on.

One reader remarked:

La Rinconada Restaurant is a wonderful little restaurant. It's family-owned and operated and I wouldn't hesitate to say it had the best food and the best atmosphere of any place I found in the country. To the left three blocks as you leave the Hotel Paris.

– Craig R Gillispie

Getting Around

To get to the plaza from the bus terminal, turn left as you leave the front door and cross the bridge over the Rio Lagos. At the far end of the bridge on the left is a narrow ramp leading down to a paved walkway along the river bank – the Paseo de Ribera. In time this becomes the Calzada Pedro Moreno and a sort of long park. At the far end keep on the right side of the Calzada and it becomes Hidalgo and goes past the Hotel Colonial to the Plaza. Walking time is an enchanting 15 minutes.

QUERÉTARO, Querétaro

elevation 1877 metres, population 300,000

This is one of Mexico's most beguiling larger colonial cities, head and shoulders better than San Luis Potosí and about the same size.

The main street of Querétaro is Corregidor, which runs beside the Alameda and near the bus terminal. The museum (Museo Regional de Querétaro) is on Corregidor across from the little Plaza de la Constitución with its statues of Mexican heroes. The Constitución, by the way, used to be the city market until the market was moved a number of blocks west of downtown.

The museum is housed in the former Convento de San Francisco de Assisi – the authorities had the good taste to leave the old building pretty much as it was in 1700 when it was only a hundred or so years old. The building itself is a fine example of Spanish design and construction, and is of more interest to me than the many paintings of important colonial personages. Of general interest is the material relating to the ill-fated Maximilian, including his coffin, a *diligencia* and an assortment of artifacts dating from colonial days. The original name of the museum was the 'Museo Pio Mariano', and it still appears that way on a few maps.

The lovely little Plaza Independencia, a couple of blocks east of the museum, contains a statue of one Don Juan de Urrutia, the man responsible for bringing potable water to Querétaro back in the 1730s. In recognition of his achievements Don Juan was made the Marques de Villa del Villar del Águila. The plinth bears a plaque stating that the statue was knocked down by a cannonball in 1867. It was rebuilt in 1892.

Also on the plaza is the Palacio Municipal, once the home of La Corregidora, the heroine of the 1810 revolt. Doña Josefa was the wife of the Spanish Corregidor (a post similar to mayor) and learned the conspiracy had been discovered. She immediately sent word to Allende and Hidalgo. This occurred on 15 September, 1810, and effectively touched off the revolution. She is the one referred to on obsolete Mexican money and around Querétaro as 'La Corregidora' without additional identification. This is why Querétaro refers to itself as 'La Cuña de Independencia' – the Cradle of Independence.

Querétaro is the closest large city to the opal workings at Tequisquiapan, about 20 km from San Juan del Río to the south. There are always people wandering around the streets with handfuls of 'opals' done up in old bandannas, looking for a monied stranger.

If you are interested in buying – and occasionally bargains are to be found – I suggest you first go up to the Casa de las Artesanias of the State of Querétaro. Located on Libertad about 50 metres off Corregidor, it is a good place to get a line on opal values, both uncut and polished. You can also find out about jewellery and all sorts of small objets d'art. A close study of the merchandise offered will give you a pretty good line on local values and might even stop you from investing in a chunk of heat-treated glass.

Maximilian & the Hill of Bells

Those with a macabre and/or historical turn of mind may wish to visit the Templo de la Cruz and the attached convent which served as Maximilian's prison while he

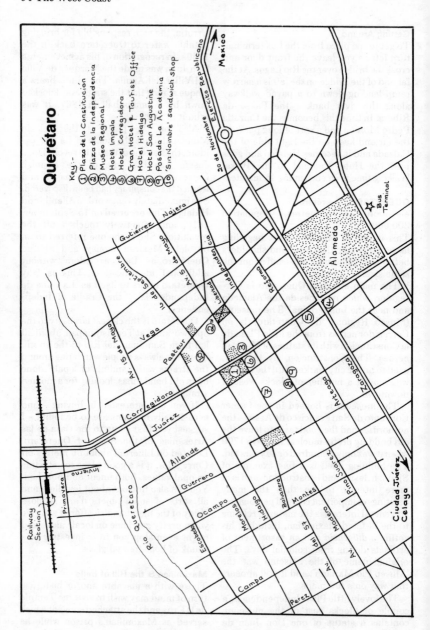

Querétaro

Key :-

① Plaza de la Constitución
② Plaza de la Independencia
③ Museo Regional
④ Hotel Impala
⑤ Hotel Corregidora
⑥ Gran Hotel + Tourist Office
⑦ Hotel Hidalgo
⑧ Hotel San Augustine
⑨ Posada La Academia
⑩ 'Sin Nombre' sandwich shop

was awaiting Juárez's signature on the execution orders. Conducted tours are run each half-hour with lectures – in Spanish – on the history of the old convent. If you don't understand Spanish it is still interesting for the opportunity to view the old buildings. To reach the Templo go east on Independencia about seven blocks from Corregidor.

You may even wish to go out to the west edge of town to the Cerro de la Campana where the luckless Maximilian, a romantic to the very last, met an inglorious end with his two faithful generals, Mejia and and Miramon. Today the spot is marked by a small brownstone chapel, the Templo de Expiación, built by Austria many years after the sanguinary event. The interior is lined with pictures of Maximilian and his dotty wife, Carlotta. Many locals know it as 'La Capilla de Maximiliano' – Maximilian's Chapel.

To reach the Cerro de la Campana, go out Corregidor to Morelos, the third street north of the Plaza Principal, and turn left. Follow Morelos about 12 (long) blocks, crossing a traffic circle near the end. At the end of Morelos, turn right, then left at the next street and follow it uphill to the Templo. Walking time is about 35 minutes.

Places to Stay

The hotel situation in Querétaro is fairly good, and not weighed too heavily in favour of the high end of the scale.

As you walk up Corregidor from the bus station you will see the big new *Hotel Impala* on the left side opposite the Alameda. The conventional rooms are expensive, but not as much as you might expect from appearances as the hotel was built long enough ago to have pretty well paid for itself by now.

The *Hotel Corregidor* on Corregidor in the middle of the next block past the Impala is smaller, older and cheaper. A conventional two-storey house, it is easy to see and often full. Moderate.

The plain, unpretentious *Gran Hotel*, on the main plaza, has been a mainstay for travellers for at least 40 years. It is far from deluxe, but I've stayed there off and on for over 20 years and can't recall ever running out of hot water, which is more than I can say about the Presidente chain. The small marble-topped tables in the lobby are for use by the local domino players, and bitterly contested games take place there each afternoon. Moderate.

The *Hotel Hidalgo*, on Madero between Juárez and Allende, proves that with determination one can make a sow's ear out of a silk purse. The hotel is an old mansion and uses the patio for a public parking lot. I've stayed there out of simple necessity but far prefer the Plaza or the Gran. Moderate.

The *Hotel Plaza* is on the main plaza diagonally across from the Gran. It is built in another old house, but the conversion came off far, far better than the Hidalgo a block away. Moderate.

The *Hotel San Agustín* is on Suarez on the opposite side of the block from the Hidalgo. Being a block farther away from the plaza than several other downtown hotels puts the San Agustín pretty well out of the high rent district. Moderate.

Almost directly across Suarez from the San Agustín is the *Posada la Academia*. It is easy to overlook because the entrance is an ordinary iron-gated storefront, one among many. More a casa de huéspedes than a hotel, and a find – I'd about given up on finding a really economical place to stay in Querétaro anywhere near the plaza. It is usually full. Inexpensive.

The *Posada Colonial* on Juárez between the former market, now Plaza de la Constitución, and General Artiaga, is also known as the *Calzontzi*. The hotel is small and economical. Inexpensive.

In the next block from the above-mentioned Colonial is the *Posada Juárez*. It's in the same general category and price range. Inexpensive.

For those arriving by rail, almost directly across the street from the station is the *Posada la Nacional*, an inexpensive stopping place.

Places to Eat

As with any large city, Querétaro has a myriad of restaurants. Below are a few in which I've eaten at one time or another.

Handiest for bus travellers is the cafeteria in the Terminal de Autobuses, one of the best bus station restaurants in Mexico. It is the only one I can name offhand where someone is constantly cooking tortillas so the customers can enjoy them fresh, as opposed to the usual machine-made and reheated ones dispensed in almost all bus station restaurants. At any time the cafeteria has about a dozen people in the serving line and by no means are all of them bus passengers. An organist provides live music for the diners' pleasure. The restaurant does a huge business. Moderate.

The bus station is a 15-minute walk each way from the centre of town – too far to go for standard Mexican fare, so I usually eat at such places as the tiny *Fonda Santa Elena*, on Paseo Libertad. The ceiling height is the largest dimension of the dining room, and seating for 18 includes five stools to be used at the short counter when the four tables are occupied. There is no menu; just peek over the counter into the bubbling pots on the stove. Inexpensive.

Restaurant Izar, on Calzada Zaragoza, across the Alameda and opposite the bus station, is a family operation with most of the trade coming from the small shops in the vicinity. Standard workers' fare and inexpensive.

The restaurant in the Gran Hotel snags most of the travelling salesperson trade, a recommendation in itself. Moderate.

The *Flor de Querétaro*, on the main plaza beneath the Plaza Hotel, is a favourite place for breakfast. It is very popular with local business people. Moderate.

Getting There & Getting Around

Querétaro is located on the heaviest-travelled bus route in Mexico, and there are hundreds of buses a day to and from Mexico City, Guadalajara, Juárez, San Luis Potosí, Monterrey, Reynosa, Morelia and Pátzcuaro. It is also the ideal jumping-off place for San Miguel de Allende.

To get uptown from the bus station, go out the front and across the pedestrian overpass and turn left, then right at the next street, Corregidor. The main plaza is straight ahead. Walking time is about 15 minutes.

The railroad station is about the same distance from the Zona Centro as the bus station, but in the opposite direction. To get to the main plaza from the station, go out the front door and turn left. Go past the beautifully preserved 4-6-2 steam locomotive to the end of the block and turn right on the street that makes an easy left curve. At the bridge it becomes Juárez and will lead you to the main plaza.

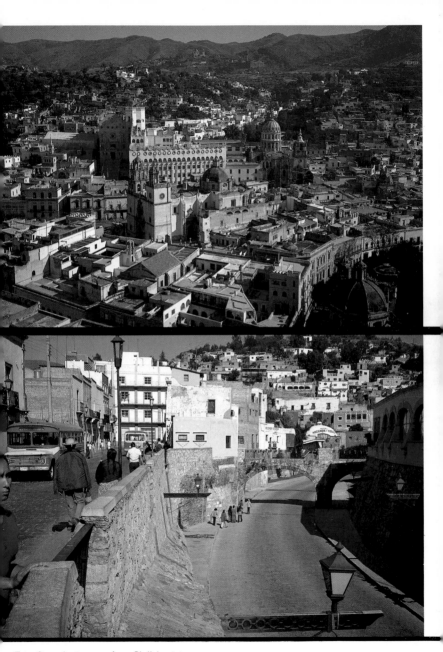

Top: Guanajuato, seen from Pipila's statue.
Bottom: View from the bridge over the subterranean roadway in front of the bus station in Guanajuato.

Top: The San Francisco church at Real de Catorce.
Left: The entrance to La Valenciana, at one time one of the world's richest mines.
Right: The church at Dolores Hidalgo.

The High Road from Juárez to Mexico City

The road from Juárez spends much of its time following the eastern edge of the Sierra Madre Occidentales. Never dropping below 1130 metres, it is the coolest summer route across northern Mexico, though in the winter it can get colder than a bartender's heart. It traverses some interesting cities and is the second most popular route into the interior, after the west coast route from Tijuana.

CIUDAD JUÁREZ, Chihuahua
(elevation 1120 metres, population 1,000,000)

Ciudad Juárez on the border opposite El Paso, Texas, has a good Central de Autobuses and excellent connections to almost anywhere in northern Mexico, including Tijuana via the new road between Janos and Agua Prieta.

After a number of years of hoofing it from the border crossing I am forced to conclude that the very best way to get to the bus station is to catch a taxi in El Paso. Be sure to stop and pick up your tourist permit when you enter Mexico. Lacking it, you will probably be turned back from a check point located out in the middle of nowhere.

Many travellers will find it a bit more convenient to catch a Mexican bus to the terminal from either the Greyhound or Trailways bus stations in El Paso. Somewhat more time-consuming than the taxi, the bus is cheaper. It stops at the immigration office so you can get yourself documented for the trip on down into Mexico.

The first town that catches any tourist traffic is Chihuahua, not so much for itself as because it is some 380 km south of the border, a good day's travel by any means. Instead of taking the main road, an alternate way to get to Chihuahua from Juárez is by bus via Nuevo las Casas Grandes, a town named after the nearby ruins of Las Casas Grandes. This route lies through flat countryside to Janos, originally a Spanish *presidio* (fort) established to protect the area's ranchers from Apache and Comanche depredation. In later years Janos was a settlement for a number of Mormon families from Utah, who emigrated in search of greater religious freedom so they could continue their practice of plural marriage. Today their descendants still live in the same vicinity in peace and prosperity, operating their own schools and sending their children north to Brigham Young University.

NUEVO LAS CASAS GRANDES, Chihuahua
(elevation 1481 metres, population 35,000)

This thriving little city serves as a supply point for the miners, ranchers and loggers of the area and is also an important shipping point on the railroad. The ruins of Las Casas Grandes are extremely interesting. Last occupied around 1500 AD, they are the most northerly trace of Mesoamerican culture, and the northernmost example of pyramid building. The ruins are about 7½ km south of the town proper, and quite extensive, covering almost 100 hectares. While not very spectacular, they are at least as interesting to me as the 'developed' pyramids to the south that are better publicized and more tourist-oriented.

Nuevo las Casas has no real plaza, and is laid out much like any midwestern US small town. There is railroad passenger service. The bus service is excellent, and includes a line that runs across the continental divide to Tijuana, Baja California. This is the last highway crossing to the west for 1300 km – the next crossing point is the Durango-Mazatlán road.

Places to Stay

The TNS buses stop on Obregón, one block south of the inexpensive *Hotel Juárez*. If you're not particularly taken with the looks of the Juárez, do as I now do and continue on to the next street north, Cinco de Mayo, and turn left. Cross the railroad tracks and the *Hotel California* is a few doors to the right.

Everything about the California is new except the name. The original frame structure caught fire and burned to the ground as I was checking in a few years back. The all-new hotel is of 'fireproof' construction. It has also been retrofitted with a modern heating system which works just fine – Las Casas gets almighty cold and windy in winter. The California is the only hotel I know of in Mexico with a US midwestern-type storm door setup. Moderate and recommended. Oh, yes – if you select the California as your home-away-from-home, be sure to remember your room number, even if you have to write it down on a wallet card. The California has the strange habit of having at least two and usually three numbers on each key.

Places to Eat

Café Juárez, across Obregón from the Hotel Juárez, is mostly a quick-food place. It is open 24 hours and is inexpensive.

If, however, you leave the TNS station and turn right, then left at the next street, Calle 16 de Septiembre, you will find the *Restaurant El Napolito*. It serves an extensive menu of typically Mexican dishes such as fried tongue and barbacoa a la Mexicana, though beer is not served. Inexpensive and recommended.

Not exactly a restaurant is the *Bar California*, across the common from the Hotel California. They serve a delicious fish salad lunch, an ideal summer arrangement when the temperature routinely reaches 40°C.

CHIHUAHUA, Chihuahua

(elevation 1430 metres, population 800,000)

Chihuahua is the capital of the largest and wealthiest state in Mexico, but more importantly to the foreigner, it is the first and most logical place to overnight on the road south from Juárez, and it is a transportation junction. From here you can take the Chihuahua al Pacifico railroad down to Los Mochis through the famous Copper Canyon. Trout fishers come here to fish the cold-water streams that gush down the eastern flank of the Sierras.

The Cathedral is worth seeing and unusual for Mexico in that the interior is more interesting than the exterior. It is a big building and was far and away the tallest structure in the city until the recent spurt of high-rise hotel building. Its twin spires loom 45 metres above the Plaza de la Constitución. The main altar is supported by 16 elaborate columns. The decorations are impressive but one can only imagine what they were like before the Reform Laws of the 1850s took their toll.

Chihuahua is known far and wide for its tiny dogs, the *perros Chihuahuas*. Today they are very rare in the region of their origin, but a few old street-peddlers still try to foist mongrel puppies off on tourists as genuine Chihuahuas!

The Pancho Villa Museum is probably more popular with Americans than with Señor Villa's countryfolk. It was a private undertaking operated by the late Señora de Villa and her numerous family, and the sole support of the tribe. The museum displayed Villa's memorabilia, including six-shooters and the Dodge touring car in which he was assassinated. Since the demise of Señora Villa there is some doubt as to whether the museum will continue in operation.

The museum is located in Calle 10, but since this street has mysterious startings and stoppings, the best way to reach the museum from the bus station is to pick up

Calle 8 and follow it out until it changes its name to Ocampo. Stay on Ocampo until you come to the triangular Parque Lerdo. At the far side of the Parque is the Paseo Bolivar. Turn left on Bolivar and pick up Calle 10, the next street. Turn right and. The Villa Museum is now five blocks more. This sounds like a long way, but it can be walked in half an hour or so from the bus station. Walking is simpler than getting a local bus, which still involves walking about 10 blocks anyway. Better yet, take a cab. It will only set you back about two US dollars.

If you're interested in things 'western', there is a charro outfitting store at the corner of Juárez and Calle 10, and right next door is a shop selling genuine Mexican cowboy boots. The items are not quite the same as their counterparts in the United States, and are lots, lots cheaper. The charro outfitter on the corner of Ocampo and Victoria sells 'cowgirl' clothing – the first I've seen advertised in Mexico.

The vacant lot where Indian women in costume gather on summer afternoons is almost directly across from the Hotel Roma on Calle Libertad, at the corner of Libertad and Calle 12.

Around Chihuahua you will see lots of farmers dressed in plain bib overalls, along with their wives, who are dressed in drab long dresses in the style of 1833. These are Mennonites, members of a Protestant sect founded in Friesland by Menno Simons about 400 years ago. They accept the New Testament as the sole rule of faith, reject infant baptism, the swearing of oaths, military service and holding public office. They lead simple lives and in Mexico are extremely successful farmers. The Mennonites are found as far south as Guadalajara, but they thrive in the states of Chihuahua, Durango and Zacatecas.

There is a bathhouse offering both regular and steam baths, with separate men's and women's facilities – no mixed bathing yet! To get there from the bus station, turn left along Artículo 123 as you leave the front door. It's in the next block.

The showers won't work unless the deadman's treadle is trod upon. Public bathhouses are a tradition in Mexico dating back to pre-conquest times, and a hot bath, even in a warm region, is one of the most relaxing things imaginable.

In addition to the usual post and telegraph offices, the Chihuahua *camionera* has a meat market that sells some groceries. There is also a public accountant, a cowboy outfitter and a drug store which stocks some US magazines (be sure to check the dates unless you're willing to accept back issues).

The *guardaria* in the bus station is only open from 9 am to 8 pm – short hours that have been known to cause considerable bitterness on the part of people who were forced to overnight because they couldn't get their belongings unchecked.

Places to Stay

Chihuahua doesn't get a big play from tourists and as a result there are quite a number of good, economical hotels, most of which are located either near the bus terminal or near the plaza.

Hotel Cayman, on Calle 10 at Juárez, is new, modern and expensive.

Casa de Huéspedes Libertad, on Libertad between Calle 10 and Ocampo, is a small rooming house and is usually full because it is inexpensive.

Hotel Plaza is easy to locate because it is directly behind the Cathedral and only a block from the plaza. It is newish and about the best value for the pesos in town. Moderate.

Hotel Carmen is on Calle 10 at Juárez and advertises air conditioning and heating. In the summer you will need the one; in the winter the other. High moderate.

Hotel Reforma on Victoria between Ocampo and Calle 12 has a huge covered patio-lobby and is a neat, clean house run by an obliging staff. Best of all, it's inexpensive.

Chihuahua is another town that can't make up its mind about street signs. Calle Victoria was also the Calle Guadalupe,

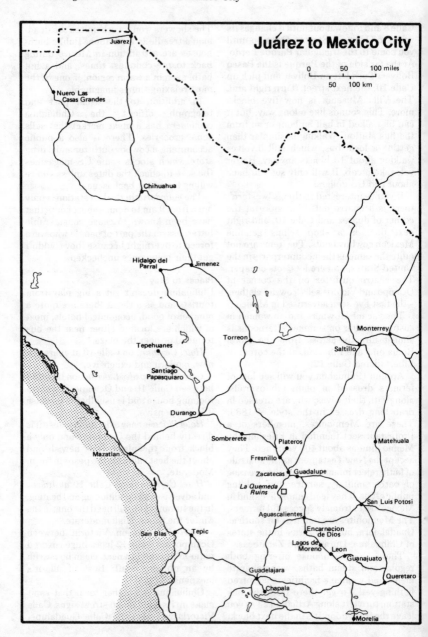

Juárez to Mexico City

0   50   100 miles

0   50   100 km

Juarez

Nuero Las
Casas Grandes

Chihuahua

Hidalgo del
Parral   Jimenez

Tepehuanes

Santiago
Papasquiaro

Durango

Monterrey

Torreon

Saltillo

Sombrerete   Plateros   Matehuala

Mazatlan   Fresnillo

Zacatecas   Guadalupe

La Quemeda
Ruins

San Luis Potosi

Aguascalientes

San Blas   Tepic   Encarnacion
de Dios

Lagos de
Moreno   Leon   Guanajuato

Guadalajara   Queretaro

Chapala

Morelia

and some of the old street signs are still in place and shown on supposedly up-to-date maps.

About 120 metres north of Ocampo on Victoria is the fairly new *Hotel San Juan*, marked by a huge, fancy electric sign. You enter the hotel through the patio of a former mansion. The elevator has odd markings on its buttons – 'PB-1-2-T' – push 'DO' to open the doors. The San Juan is inexpensive and is my current personal favourite in Ciudad Chihuahua.

Hotel Carrillo, on Calle 14 Vieja between Progreso and Carrillo, is very near the bus station, but is not very ostentatious so it is easy to overlook. Business must be good because they're in the process of adding another story! Moderate.

Hotel El Dorado is on Calle 14 at Progreso, two blocks from the bus station along Progreso on the right. The hotel is a nice place in the modern style, but is very expensive.

Hotel del Cobre is on the left as you leave the bus station. This newish house catering to the commercial traveller makes a successful play for bus passengers and is easily seen from the front door of the terminal. As a result it is one of the first houses in Chihuahua to put up the *lleno* (full) sign. Very expensive.

Places to Eat

Chihuahua isn't a bad eating town, and there are a number of acceptable, reasonably priced restaurants.

La Parilla is one of my long-time favourites. The sign out front says 'tacos', but the Parilla is about as far from a taco joint as you can imagine. Try their barbacoa, the most Mexican of dishes. The Parilla is on Victoria between Ocampo and Calle 4. Moderate.

Hard by the left side of the Central Camionera is the little *Cafeteria Rosevel* – the sign painter ran out of t's – on Calle 10 at Artículo 123. This one is popular with cab drivers and other local workers. Usually good and inexpensive.

If you've been hankering for a taste of real, honest-to-God Mexican food, as contrasted with the US-style Tex-Mex concoctions, there is a *Menudoría y Lonchería* just off Progreso toward the centre of things on Calle 10. Inexpensive.

Turn to the left along Progreso as you leave the bus station and in a couple of blocks you will come to the wholesale produce market, always a place for cheap, filling food, especially during the early morning hours. Restaurants and push-carts are, at most, inexpensive.

To my way of thinking, the nicest little sit-down restaurant in town is off the lobby of the *Hotel Reforma*, on Victoria between Ocampo and Calle 12. Moderate. There is another, similar restaurant in the *Hotel San Juan*.

Getting There & Getting Around

To get to the plaza, turn left on Progreso in front of the bus terminal and follow it until you come to Calle 2. Turn right and in six blocks you will come out on the plaza in front of the cathedral. The walk is about 14 minutes.

The Chihuahua al Pacifico has its own railroad station in Chihuahua, just as it does in Los Mochis. To get to the station from the plaza, go out Calle 2 to the Paseo Bolivar, which is a road, not a 'walk' as indicated by the name. Turn right and follow Bolivar to Díaz Ordaz, and turn left, This is for dedicated walkers only. I'm a dedicated walker myself, but I always take a cab – the walk takes over an hour.

The trains for sightseers leave in the morning around 8 am; the train for travellers-only pulls out for Mochis around 9 pm. Buy your ticket and make reservations at the station – not through a travel agent. This will help avoid foul-ups. And check schedules; they are subject to change without notice and in Mexico are sometimes disregarded entirely.

JIMÉNEZ, Chihuahua

Here the high road splits, the western branch going through Parral and the eastern branch going through the triplet cities of Torreón, Gomez Palacio and Lerdo.

TORREÓN, Coahuila
GOMEZ PALACIO & LERDO, Durango
(elevation 1155 metres, population 600,000)
These three are relatively new agricultural towns. Except for political boundaries, they could be considered one city. When you are crossing between Monterrey-Saltillo and the high road, you might find it necessary to stop here. Although there are hotels, I have not had to overnight and have no first-hand recommendations as a result.

James Norman, in his 1972 revision of *Terry's Guide to Mexico*, writes: 'All the hotels in Torreón tend to be pretentious and modern or elegant, but look as though they are patronized by salesmen in ill-fitting tuxedos.' I have, however, heard good things about the *Hotel Galicia* and its funky ambience. An older house, it was recommended by Norman. The Galicia is centrally located on the main plaza, and is inexpensive. If you try it, I'd appreciate a current report.

PAILA, Coahuila
From Paila, on the Torreón-Saltillo road about halfway between the two cities, the distance is 26 km to Parras over a good paved road. Not shown by name on most maps, Paila is a tiny town that sprang up at the junction of the Torreón-Saltillo road and the branch that leads to Parras. Shuttle buses connect with the east-west buses on the main road, meeting their passengers at the little bus station-cum-restaurant. In early 1985 the fare down to Parras was M$80.

SAN LORENZO, Coahuila
About 20 km south of Paila the road leads through hundreds of hectares of vineyards. Soon you come to the huge, white-walled Casa Madero winery and distillery at the wide spot in the road called San Lorenzo. This was one of the first places to grow

vinifera grapes in North America. The winery was actually founded in 1626, making it one of the oldest commercial enterprises in North America. For more information, see Leon Adams' authoritative *The Wines of America* (McGraw-Hill, 1984). Casa Madero turns out a number of brandies and several really good red wines.

PARRAS, Coahuila
(elevation 1535 metres, population 30,000)
Parras is the northernmost and most accessible colonial town in Mexico. Founded in 1598, the agricultural centre is also one of the oldest communities in northern Mexico.

Most of the buildings are left over from colonial days. You will see many charmingly wrought rejas and old, hand-carved doors. The Palacio Municipal (city hall) on the plaza is recent, but the city fathers had the rare good sense to build it along colonial lines – which they promptly spoiled by hanging cheap, window-mounted air-conditioners and roof-top television antennas here and there. A new statue on a marble plinth stands in the official plaza. It is not of local boy and ex-president Madero as you might suppose, but of Father Hidalgo holding aloft the banner of Our Lady of Guadalupe. The market is down the hill from Arizpe on Reforma. The truncated tower on the big main church in the plaza gives it a circumcised appearance, something on the order of a Methodist church in Noblesville, Indiana, USA.

Parras is a much better place to overnight than either Torreón or Saltillo. It is cheaper, too, which is really the primary reason I have never stayed in a Torreón hotel. The *Hotel Plaza* in Parras is a typical, small-town hotel – clean, but unfortunately with parking in the patio. (Small hotels all over Mexico use the same arrangement.) To get there from the bus station, go out the front door and turn right. Walk three long blocks to Reforma, and turn left up the hill. About halfway up the block you will see the hotel's sign on your right.

If, however, you turn left when you leave the bus station, you will be on Arizpe. Turn left again at the end of the block, and you will be on Acuna. About halfway down the block you will find the *Hotel la Fiesta*. I've never stayed at the Fiesta, primarily because it is well away from the centre of things, which lies in the opposite direction. The hotel looks neat, clean and well-kept. The clerk tells me it is inexpensive.

Places to Eat

Parras is by no means a gastronomic centre, but the intrepid travellers who manage to reach it will by no means be faced with starvation.

Travellers usually arrive in Parras after dark, and those who elect to head uptown to the plaza for the night will see, about a block ahead of them when they reach Reforma, a small, triangular restaurant with no name. The *Restaurante sin Nombre* serves local food to local people at locally appealing prices. Try one of their lean-meat hamburgers. Although the hamburger doesn't look like something you'd expect to get under McDonald's golden arches, it holds its own quite well and is inexpensive.

Unusual for country towns, Parras doesn't get up very early in the morning. As I prefer to get an early start, I find that almost everything is closed when I start putting sole to pavement. All is not lost, however, for continuing down Reforma past Arizpe after leaving the plaza, I come to the *Café America*, where I have my matutinal *café con leche* before embarking on the day's travels.

PARRAL, Chihuahua

(elevation 1661 metres, population 75,000)

Most travellers will elect to take the more interesting west branch of the high road, the one that leads through Parral, although the roads differ in distance by only one km. Hidalgo de Parral, usually called Parral, is another old silver-mining town. In the early 1600s, over 7000 men were working in the local mines. Since that time the mines in Parral have closed down one by one until now there are only three or four working in the town itself. The area is rugged, the scenery is spectacular, and some of the small towns in the region are popular with dablers in the western film genre.

The only reason most foreigners ever hear of Parral at all is because a cattle rustler named Doroteo Arrango decided to change his name to 'Pancho' (not to be confused with Francisco Villa, the revolutionary general). This course of action eventually led to Arrango's disastrous end after he retired in Parral. Last I heard, Arrango's old home was being used as a grocery store while the well-known Pancho Villa Museum is in Chihuahua city (described earlier).

There is a recently opened 'Francisco Villa Museum' a short distance from the centre of things. If you arrive from the south you will probably pass it on your way in. Keep an eye open; it will be on your left.

The most interesting building in town is the Palacio de Pedro Alvarado, built by a miner who struck it very rich indeed with the La Palmilla mine. The outside is stunning, with columns fit for a midwestern US post office built around 1880. Inside there is an onyx stairway and a private chapel.

The church of Nuestra Senora de Fatima is much newer and a rockhound's delight. It includes ore samples from the various local mines, making it unique in Mexican ecclesiastical construction.

To get downtown from the Estrella Blanca bus station, go out on the street in front and turn left – the plaza is about three blocks along. From the Omnibus de Mexico station, turn left along the triangular plaza. The Plaza Principal is about two blocks more.

Places to Stay & Eat

Hotel San José is about a block from the plaza and a block from the Omnibus de Mexico bus station. The design is unfortunately Mexican Modern, but it's quiet. Moderate.

Hotel Turista is an older and cheaper house facing the Omnibus bus station across a tiny plaza. Also moderate.

My favourite hotel in Parral is the rather modern *Hotel Moreira*. Unusual for small hotels in Mexico, it has an operating elevator. Best of all, I find no fault with the restaurant off the lobby. The Moreira is on Via Dolores at G Victoria.

Because it is essentially a working-person's town, Parral has an abundance of restaurants with low prices, and one of the better bets is the white-tablecloth house next door to the Estrella Blanca bus station, but not a part of it. Another good choice, and quite popular with the local gentry, is the *Restaurante Turista* in the hotel of the same name by the Omnibus de Mexico bus station. Both are moderate.

Getting Around

Parral is easily the most confusing city in Mexico. Located in a gulch like Zacatecas, it contains many streets that are less than a standard city block long. Rather than fight your way through this maze on foot I suggest you take a cab to any destination you might have in mind, at least until you get oriented. I've been visiting Parral for more years than I can remember, and I still get mixed up fairly often.

Side Trips to San Francisco del Oro & Santa Barbara

These two ancient mining towns were founded by Spanish prospectors about 50 years before the Pilgrims hit Plymouth Rock. Although Parral's mines have pretty well been exhausted, these two old camps are still going great guns. If you want to see what a real old-time mining camp looks like, get on a long-nose bus in Parral and ride the 40-odd km out to either Santa Barbara or San Francisco.

DURANGO, Durango

(elevation 1889 metres, population 200,000)

Over 20 years ago the very knowledgeable writer James Norman described Durango as a 'fair overnight stop for travellers. The city has almost no other attractions.' To make himself abundantly clear, he also said, 'Sightseeing attractions in the city are limited.' This is still apposite.

A lot of travellers wind up in Durango today because it is now a transport hub and the starting point for the road that winds down through the Sierras and ends up in the coastal hot country at Mazatlán. It is also a popular place for rail fans waiting to begin their once-in-a-lifetime trip into the back-of-beyond.

It used to seem that Hollywood or Churubusco were always shooting films here, and signs here and there still proclaim that Durango is 'The Western Movie Capital of the World'. Actually the signs refer to the state rather than to the city. But Durango, being the only place with enough hotels rooms to house a movie-making company, always seemed to have a production outfit in residence. I use the past tense because there aren't all that many 'shoot-'em-ups' being made any more. But there are still a few, and you might very well arrive in time to be part of a crowd scene.

Durango was originally and still is a mining centre, but it is a far cry from the usual mining community such as San Francisco del Oro or La Paz. There is still large-scale mining practically within the city limits. If you stand on the track side of the railroad station you will see a large black hill rising abruptly out of the plain. This is the Cerro Mercado, a mountain of iron ore named for an old-time prospector, Gines Vasquez de Mercado, who was killed by Indians before reaching his home base in Sombrerete. Although the Cerro del Mercado has been mined steadily for decades, the real wealth of Durango was based on silver mining, of which not a trace remains in the city.

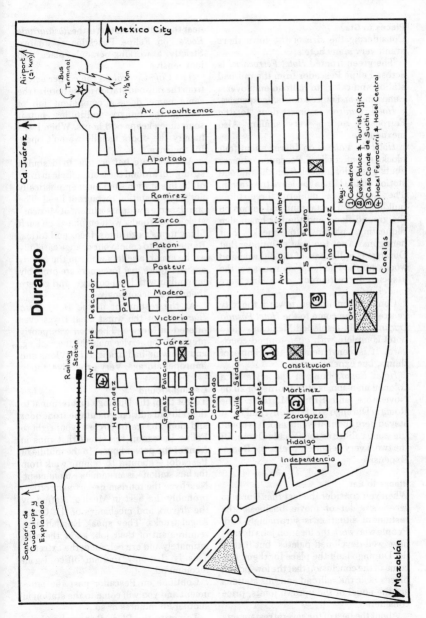

Durango

Mexico City

Airport (21 km)

Bus Terminal

~1½ Km

Cd. Juárez

Av. Cuauhtemoc

Apartado

Ramirez

Zarco

Patoni

Pasteur

Madero

Victoria

Juárez

Constitucion

Martinez

Zaragoza

Hidalgo

Independencia

Av. Felipe Pescador

Pereira

Hernandez

Gomez Palacio

Barreda

Coronado

Aquile Serdan

Negrete

Av. 20 de Noviembre

5 de Febrero

Pino Suarez

Ortix

Canelas

Railway Station

Santuario de Guadalupe y Explanada

Mazatlán

Key:-
① Cathedral
② Govt. Palace ⚥ Tourist Office
③ Casa Conde de Suchil
✦ Hotel Ferrocarril ✦ Hotel Central

Places to Stay

Considering the size of the town there aren't very many hotels.

The green-fronted *Hotel Ferrocarril* is across Felipe Pescador from the railroad station and caters to railroad employees, campesinos and other workers. Inexpensive.

Hotel Central is next door to the Ferrocarril and is very similar. Also inexpensive.

Hotel del Valle is on Juárez about four blocks from Felipe Pescador. Juárez abuts Pescador a block from the railroad station on the left as you leave the station. The hotel is a modern three-storey building with a restaurant and saloon on the ground floor, and the bar has a sign requesting patrons to check their handguns – a not-too-subtle reminder that Durango is still a part of the old wild and woolly north. The hotel is expensive; the associated restaurant and bar are moderate.

Continue on Juárez toward the city centre and you come to the *Hotel Posada Durán*, an old-fashioned Mexican viajero hotel complete with open-topped courtyard. It is convenient to the centre of things, but expensive.

Hotel Roma, built in the style of a colonial mansion, is at the corner of 20 de Noviembre and Bruno Martinez. The Roma is Durango's old standby, and I first stayed here about 40 years ago. It is about the same calibre as the Posada Durán. Of the two, I very definitely prefer the Roma. Expensive.

Places to Eat

When you consider the fact that Durango receives a lot of movie business, the restaurant situation is surprisingly bad. People who work the location jobs usually have well-developed palates, but if they do, Durango isn't the place for them! I've come to the conclusion that the low-priced places near the railroad and bus stations are the equal of the uptown joints, price considered.

About the best of the several restaurants near the railroad station is the *Restaurante Rocio*, on Felipe Pescador at Juárez. Strictly a working-person's place and inexpensive.

The *Café Central* on the corner across from the railroad station in the hotel of the same name does a competent job of feeding the hungry multitudes, but it sometimes keeps odd hours. When I was hungry the doors usually weren't open. Inexpensive.

Another safe bet are the food stands strung out around the traffic circle in front of the bus station – but most emphatically not the bus station restaurant itself. The stands serve a wide assortment of Mexican-style quick foods, with emphasis on such filling items as gorditas, tacos and tortas. Remember to count your change carefully as the amiable sellers who run the stands are well aware that foreigners are probably unfamiliar with local coinage, and govern themselves accordingly.

At the restaurant in the *Hotel Casa Blanca* I got the worst meal I was ever offered in Mexico. The food was poorly prepared, the service matched the cooking, and the wine had oxidized from long and improper storage. Very expensive, too.

Getting Around

To get from the Durango bus terminal to the railroad station, go out the front door and along the traffic circle to your right to Felipe Pescador, the street that runs in front of the power house. In the middle of Pescador – about a 15-minute walk from the bus station – is an immense monument. Nearby is the tourism department office, probably the best in Mexico, staffed by the drivers and mechanics of the Green Angel trucks. They speak English as a requirement of their job, know the area intimately and are helpful in the extreme. This is the only tourism office I can recommend.

Continue on Pescador past the monument and you will come to the station in another 20 minutes or so.

To get to the Plaza Principal and the

Cathedral, cut across the traffic circle and pick up the heavily-travelled street that angles off slightly to the left. About three blocks from the circle is a motel with a large red-and-white sign. The street is 20 de Noviembre and it leads to the plaza in about 40-45 minutes of walking.

To get from the railroad station to the plaza, go to the left one block to Constitución and follow it downtown, about 12 blocks and 20 minutes by foot.

If you want a ride to the railroad station from the bus terminal, catch a red 'Estación' bus on the traffic circle. If you want to go downtown instead, then catch a Centro, or Centro Camionera, or Camionera. The same markings will bring you back to the bus terminal along essentially the same routes.

Tepehuanes & Other Trips

There are a number of branch lines fanning out from the Durango railroad station. The train that leaves for Tepehuanes every Monday, Wednesday and Friday at 7.30 attracts rail fans from all over the world.

Most travellers to Tepehuanes plan on returning to Durango via bus that same evening, but the train is often so late that they miss the last bus. Staying over at Tepehuanes is no problem because there are several inexpensive hotels in town, but it can be a confounded nuisance for those with little time to spare. If you are on short time, get off the train at Santiago Papasquiaro, about 50 km before Tepehuanes, and catch a bus back to Durango. Santiago is a busy town served by several bus lines with many buses to Durango every day, whereas Tepehuanes is essentially an end-of-the-line small town. A local bus meets all trains in Tepehuanes and hauls passengers from the station across the river to town, about 1½ km.

You may hear stories from travellers about the unfriendliness of the people in Tepehuanes but I've always been treated with kindness, consideration and the usual Mexican small-town courtesy.

There are other train trips to be made from Durango. You can catch a turnaround local for Aserraderos (Sawmills) at 7.30 am or a train for Regocijo (the name means joy or pleasure) at 6.30 am. Either of these little-known trains provide more interesting scenery and more trackside activity than the famous Tepehuanes trip which mostly travels through plains country.

On any of these side trips be sure to pack a lunch. There are so few trains – and passengers – that there generally is no food for sale along the tracks, and of course dining cars are unheard-of in these parts.

SOMBRERETE, Zacatecas

(elevation 1800 meters, population 30,000)

Years and years ago Sombrerete was a rich mining town. Though mining in the area never ceased completely as it has in much of Mexico over the years, the town's days of past glory have fled forever. The divided main street, a number of quite nice old Spanish-built stone homes and one out-and-out mansion are reminders of yesterday's bonanza.

Many Mexican travellers prefer the small-town ambience of Sombrerete to the hustle and bustle of larger communities, and stop over here on their way to or from Durango.

Sombrerete is also the starting point for a trip to Chalchihuites, another venerable mining town out in the middle of nowhere which has two current claims to fame: the nearby ruins (not fully excavated and closed to visitors from time to time) and the Instituto Fenix. The latter is a language school using the immersion method whereby the students hear only the language under study. The Instituto has established two separate schools, one in Cuernavaca for absolute beginners, and another in Chalchihuites where the students live with Mexican families and acquire a working knowledge of Norteño Spanish. If interested, write to them at:

Instituto Fenix, Chalchihuites, Zacatecas, Mexico.

Places to Stay & Eat

Hotel Hidalgo is on the main street and a block or two uphill from the bus stations. It is a converted two-storey colonial mansion so large that guests park their automobiles in the patio. The hotel is a fine example of 16th-century Spanish architecture, with large rooms and thick walls that act as heat sinks so the rooms are cool in summer and warm in winter. For practical purposes it is the only hotel in town. Moderate.

The Hidalgo doesn't have a restaurant, and most people take their meals in the restaurant under the portales (down the hill from the Hidalgo and the bus stations), toward the plaza. A glass partition separates the dining room from a shoe store. The food is pretty good, prices moderate.

There is another restaurant in Sombrerete. Go up the hill toward the Hidalgo from the bus station and turn left just before you reach the hotel. The *Restaurante Sin Nombre* (restaurant with no name) is in the first block on the right side of the street. I've eaten breakfast there several times when I wanted peace and quiet with my *huevos con chorizo*. Inexpensive.

Getting There

Sombrerete is 125 km south of Durango on Highway 45 and a stop on all the second-class buses running north and south, but if you arrive via first-class coach you just might wind up getting off on the highway by the turnoff, entailing a walk of about a km to the centre of town.

FRESNILLO, Zacatecas

(elevation 2245 metres, population 125,000)
Not many travellers stop at Fresnillo, and many guidebooks don't even mention it. It is a dead-level city barely in the tropics, high enough to have cool nights in summer and be bitterly cold in winter. Fresnillo is a good place to break the long journey down from Juárez, 1350 km to the north.

The Plaza Principal has an unusual monument giving latitude, longitude, altitude and other geographical information. Odder still, a plaque on the monument is dedicated to General Santa Ana, many times president of Mexico and the man who lost Texas to Mexico by dint of poor generalship. He then surpassed this feat by losing a third of Mexico to the US in the Mexican-American war.

Places to Stay & Eat

About 12 minutes' walk from the central bus terminal is the *Hotel Familiar*, made noteworthy by its red facade and inexpensive rates. To get there from the bus station, cross the little plaza and turn right at the far side on the paved street.

If the Familiar doesn't appeal to you, continue for about five minutes more, past the little plaza with the singular hemicycle monument, and at the end of the street you will come to three small hotels practically side by side: *Hotel Cosmolita*, *Hotel Guerrero* and *Hotel Maya*. All are moderate, and I can't recommend one over the others, as they're all chips off the same block. Whichever you pick, make sure you have enough blankets if you're in Fresnillo during the cold half of the year.

Back in the little park with the grand monument is *Hotel del Fresno*, quite a fancy establishment for a town like this, and with a fancy price, too. Very expensive.

Continuing down the street that passes the del Fresno will bring you to the market. Turn right when you have done your shopping, and take the street that narrows to a paseo impassable to automobiles. You will come out on a little plaza by a church. Across the plaza is the *Hotel Plaza*. It's quieter than the trio mentioned above, but also a bit farther away from activities. Inexpensive.

The street fronting the del Fresno also fronts the *Café Excelente*, my favourite for

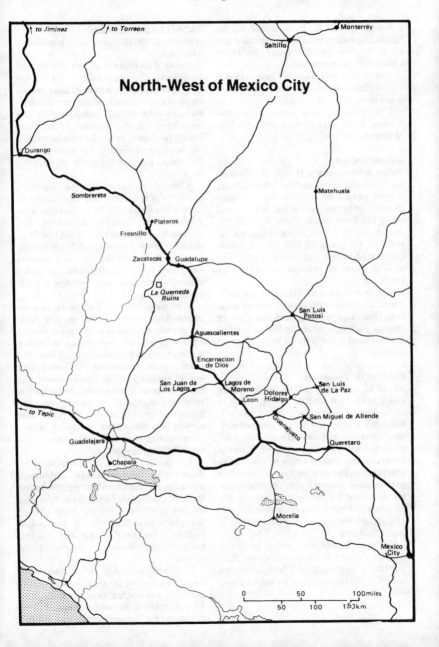

North-West of Mexico City

to Jiminez

to Torreon

Monterrey

Saltillo

Durango

Sombrerete

Matehuala

Plateros

Fresnillo

Zacatecas   Guadalupe

La Quemeda Ruins

San Luis
Potosi

Aguascalientes

Encarnacion
de Dios

to Tepic

San Juan de
Los Lagos

Lagos de
Moreno

Leon

Dolores
Hidalgo

San Luis
de La Paz

San Miguel de Allende

Guanajuato

Queretaro

Guadelajara

Chapala

Morelia

Mexico
City

0   50   100 miles

50   100   150km

a low-priced meal. It is owned by an English-speaking man who made his stake as a *bracero* in the grape fields of California. Inexpensive.

The restaurant in the *Del Fresno Hotel* is a good choice for a US-style breakfast, but it is expensive.

The sunken dining room in the bus station is a better-than-average bet. Moderate.

Getting Around

To get to the centre of things, exit through the front of the bus station – don't laugh, lots of people go out the rear entrance directly onto the paved highway! – and cross the little plaza. Turn right on the paved street. The Plaza Principal is reached by going to the trio of hotels mentioned above and turning right. The walk is about 20 minutes, or M$150 by taxi.

The bus station at Fresnillo is a little jewel, complete with sunken dining area. It is clean and shining, and has a set of murals that sure beat the hell out of the institutional paint jobs on most Mexican bus stations.

PLATEROS, Zacatecas

About 11 km from Fresnillo is Plateros, a small town that started out as a silver camp (the name means 'silver workers'), but after a while the mines petered out. New silver veins were discovered, and these too were worked out, until Plateros became a ghost town with a few residents who hung on because they could commute to the mines around Fresnillo. Today the big source of income is the image in the church which attracts countless thousands of pilgrims each year in their devotional peregrinations.

If you're a seeker of quaint places, I suggest you catch a bus over there. You will find a sign reading 'Plateros' in the corner of the bus terminal on the highway side.

ZACATECAS, Zacatecas

(elevation 2442 metres, population 160,000)

Because Zacatecas is among the highest cities in Mexico and is so far north, it is the last place on earth you would imagine as a tropical city – which it is. Zacatecas can be bitingly cold during winter nights and mornings, but the summer climate can hardly be improved on. Even mosquitoes, the scourge of Mexico, are not severe in Zacatecas because the city is surrounded by desert.

A large billboard on the northern outskirts of town proclaims Zacatecas as 'The Most Colonial City in Mexico'. This statement is open to argument, but Zacatecas does have a lot of old buildings dating from the days of Spanish domination. It also has narrow, crooked streets designed by their builders for pack animals and carts, and perhaps a diligencia or two.

The cathedral in Zacatecas has an interesting exterior and at one time apparently contained a very great deal of silver and gold ornamentation, as befits a wealthy mining community. Over the years, with revolutions, reforms and miscellaneous civil disturbances, it has been pretty well gutted and the interior is relatively drab now, but most people are impressed by the front which is elaborately carved and decorated in sundry styles. There is also a notable side entrance in a totally different motif.

The ancient market in Zacatecas up by the cathedral has been evicted and turned into a small collection of rather interesting and chic boutiques. To reach the relocated market, continue along the lower side of the plaza past the side of the police station. Last time I saw the market, however, there were no *restaurantes a la mesas*.

You will probably have noted the Zacatecas tourist posters showing a tiny cableway car soaring over the cathedral. This is really a masterful piece of trick photography; the aerial tramway doesn't

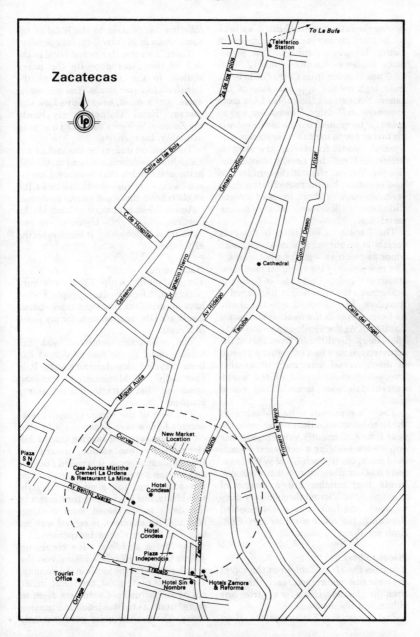

go over the cathedral at all! But it is a heck of a trip anyway and recommended. Catnip for photographers. The Swiss-made cableway operates from 12.30 to 5.30 pm, running from Cerro Grillo to La Bufa high on the opposite side of the cañon. You can see the cables from most anywhere on Hidalgo. The easiest way to get to the terminus from the town centre is via taxi either to the cable car station (the Spanish word for aerial tramway is 'teleferico') or the nearby Motel del Bosque. You can climb to the terminus on foot, of course, but the route lies through a veritable maze of short, crooked streets. Ride up, walk down, is my recom-mendation.

The Zacatecas teleferico is the only vehicle in public service in Mexico with windows clean enough for photography! The movement of the cable car is so slow, steady and sedate that it doesn't seem to bother even the most height-frightened of travellers. The destination to the south, La Bufa, serves as the weather station for Zacatecas. As the weather up on top of the hill is markedly different from that of the actual city, it may be a contributing factor in the universal inaccuracy of weather forecasting in that part of the world. Current teleferico fare: M$150 round trip.

There is supposed to be a Museum of the Revolution at La Bufa sometime in the near future. Currently you will only see outside the building a Schneider 75 mm field piece, the 'French 75' of WW I fame, and a small sandbagged imitation revetment. Inside the building are a couple of machine guns. Viewed through very dirty windows, one looks like a water-cooled Browning, the other a rather rare Colt. Both are about 70 years old.

Places to Stay
You pass the *Hotel Zamora* at the top of the walk just before you reach the plaza from the plazuela. It is a far cry from any Hilton, but it's inexpensive.

Just above the Zamora is the *Hotel Reforma*, no relation to the hotel of the same name in Mexico City. Inexpensive.

There is a recently opened hotel at the end of the plaza opposite the police station, in the same building as the Papeleria Independencia. You will see no name, just a small, easy-to-overlook sign that says 'Hotel'. The hotel is very close to the Zamora/Reforma and a half a step up in quality. Inexpensive.

Turn left on Juárez at the end of the Plaza Independencia and head up the hill. In the next block is the *Posada del Condes*, somewhat less expensive than it looks. It's an old reliable that's still merely moderate.

Across the street from the Condes is the *Condesa*, with slightly higher prices and more reliable hot water. It borders on the expensive.

Places to Eat
The restaurant in the *Condesa* is very popular with local businesspeople. I often have an excellent breakfast there. Other meals are OK, but too dear for my peso. Moderate.

The restaurant decorated with the taurine motif at the foot of Juárez has been recycled into *Armond's* (sic). It is essentially a Mexicanized fast-food operation that attracts lots of young couples.

The best of the economy-model rest-aurants I know of in Zacatecas is located on the narrow street leading up the hill alongside the bus station, toward the Plaza Independencia. It is called *Pavidon* and you can see it from the bus stalls. The Pavidon is not too good for US-style breakfasts, but is a bargain for the rest of the day's meals. Good local cooking. Menudo, for example, is served with no less than five garnishes. Inexpensive.

The *Meson de Mina*, a few metres up Juárez from the Hotel Condes, is now the popular place for the locals in the evening. The food is quite good, the stereo music not at all obtrusive. Customers seem to prefer neckties to blue jeans and running shoes. The food is quite good – mostly local selections. This restaurant is my favourite place in Zacatecas for dinner. Moderate.

Zacatecas tends to sleep in of a morning, and the restaurant in the *Hotel Victoria* on the tiny Plaza Constitución is the first place to open on Sunday morning. They specialize in *rico menudo*, the universal hangover specific, and serve gallons of the stuff every Sunday. Inexpensive.

The restaurant upstairs in the bus station is very definitely not recommended except as a last resort when faced with acute hunger cramps. Moderate.

The *Casa Jaquez* on Hidalgo is about 100 metres toward the cathedral from Juárez, where the new market straggles into view. This is a sort of miniature supermarket running heavily to potables, both alcoholic and temperance.

Just up Juárez from the Hotel Condes is the *Auto Servicio Cremeri la Ordena*, another grocery store. It runs very heavy to cheese and other creamery products. Between here and the Casa Jaquez you can get all you need for an *al fresco* meal which can be eaten up the hill on Juárez, at the end of the next (long) block, in either the little green plaza on the right or in the Alameda a bit further along. Dining this way is very inexpensive and enjoyable.

Getting Around

For a city of around 160,000 people, Zacatecas is remarkably compact, even by Mexican standards, and a sturdy-legged sightseer can pretty well cover the whole area in a couple of hours or so. From the bus terminal in the bottom of the *barranca* (ravine), not much can be seen of the town except a few modern-looking buildings. But amble out of the waiting room and turn right, then right again into the narrow street that goes up alongside the bus arrival area, then uphill for about five minutes, and you will come out on a plazuela. Bear right again and continue straight ahead. In another two or three minutes you will come out on the Plaza

Independencia, too small by far for the present size of the city. The walk from the bus station to Independencia will take about 10-12 minutes at most.

To get to the cathedral and various government buildings, go up Juárez – the unmarked street at the end of the Plaza Independencia that runs in front of the police station – and turn right on Hidalgo, about the second street above the hotels Condes/Condesa. If you turn left on Hidalgo you will wind up in a little park among the few remaining arches of the famous Zacatecas aqueduct.

Getting There

Zacatecas is the intersection for a number of bus routes, and there are direct buses to and from Mexico City, San Luis Potosí, Monterrey, Guadalajara, Juárez and Torreón, to name but a few.

There is domestic air service and a railroad, although I have yet to meet anyone who travelled by rail to Zacatecas – or by air, for that matter.

GUADALUPE, Zacatecas

Three km south of Zacatecas, the ex-Convento de Guadalupe is being converted into a tourist centre by the government. The old convent was actually a seminary for much of its functional life. Somehow the gold ornamentation of the Capilla de Napoles has managed to survive over the centuries and is as stunning today as it was hundreds of years ago when its beauty could only be enjoyed by religious professionals. Guadalupe can be reached by bus from the Central Camionera, by walking (45 minutes down CN-45) or by taxi. It is the big, new-looking project on the east side of the road leading to Aguascalientes and San Luis Potosí.

La Quemada (Ruinas Chicomoztoc), Zacatecas

Unlike the better-publicized ruins in the south-eastern part of the country, such as Palenque and Chichén Itzá, La Quemada ('The Burned') was not damaged by plant growth and heavy-handed 'restoration'. The original structures have been preserved by the dry air. The ruins spread over several hundred hectares and are made up of well-constructed buildings of stone and lime-based mortar. The ruins were abandoned for some reason long before the arrival of the Spanish. I feel that if you are only going to see one set of ruins in Mexico, it should be La Quemada. These ruins can be seen largely as the first Spanish explorers saw them, whereas the 'tourist' ruins are mostly restorations, and not necessarily accurate.

La Quemada is on the Zacatecas-Guadalajara road about 50 km from Zacatecas. There is regular and frequent bus service, although the ticket clerk may not be willing to sell tickets to La Quemada. Another name for the ruins is Ruinas Chicomoztoc – try that. If the clerk still won't sell a ticket, then buy one for Villanueva, about 12 km south, and get off at the side road leading about four km to the ruins. This tactic may be applied if coming from Guadalajara, except you may have to buy a ticket to Zacatecas. In that case, make sure you get on a bus that goes via Juchipila and Jalpa. The ruins are east of the highway, and are marked.

AGUASCALIENTES, Aguascalientes
(elevation 1870 metres, population 325,000)
Aguascalientes ('hot waters') is 128 km south of Zacatecas, and has one of the most salubrious climates in all of Mexico. Its most noteworthy feature is one that the average tourist can't see: the maze of tunnels excavated by some long-forgotten tribe for as yet unknown reasons. The city fathers have long since sealed off the tunnels to keep inquisitive boys from perishing in them, and to the casual traveller there is no evidence of their existence. You'll just have to take my word for it that they're down there.

There are now several shops on Juárez, toward 5 de Mayo, that specialize in selling 95-96% alcohol. That's percent,

not proof! A fine opportunity to make your own cut-price vodka.

Considering its size, 'Aguas' is rather an indolent town. It has an enviable reputation for fine embroidery and knitted garments, but the finest example of this industry seems to be 572 km away in the store in the bus station at San Luis Potosí!

Places to Stay
There are lots of economical hotels in Aguas because there aren't enough tourists or business travellers to warrant building new ones, and in Mexico the older hotels are generally cheaper than new.

Hard by the left end of the bus station as you leave by the front door is the *Hotel Continental*. It is convenient and clean, but noisy because of the proximity of the bus station across the street. Moderate.

Right downtown on the plaza is the *Hotel Imperial*, which was in slow decline 28 years ago. Little has been done to upgrade it since, except to convert the lobby first into a pool hall, and, more recently, into a branch bank. Located downtown, it's expensive.

Also on the plaza is the *Hotel Francia*, easily the best and most expensive hostelry in town. It's a nice place, but ridiculously expensive.

Juárez is a peculiar street. It runs past the deluxe Hotel Francia on one side of the plaza, goes past the new market and winds up at the Calle 5 de Mayo. The Calle Mayo in turn runs back through the plaza in front of the Imperial.

Hotel Don Jesús is on Juárez between Obregón and Larreategui. Don't be discouraged by the violently green patio – the Don Jesús is good value and inexpensive.

Hotel Colonial is misnamed, for it's not colonial at all. It is on 5 de Mayo between San Ignacio and Zaragoza, across from the park. Expensive, but barely so.

Hotel Zaragoza, on 5 de Mayo and La Mora, is another hotel that just barely slips over into the expensive classification, while the nearby *Hotel Roble*, on 5 de Mayo at the end of Juárez, is moderate.

Places to Eat

I must confess I haven't had occasion to eat very often in downtown Aguascalientes, but I have dined several times at the *Paris*, on the plaza by the Hotel Imperial. My only complaint there concerned the prices, which were high.

Absolutely the best place in town to eat is the restaurant in the *Hotel Francia*, with its white, white tablecloths. The dinner table settings include four wine glasses per plate, and they're not all the same size either. Ridiculously expensive.

But there is a bright light at the end of the tunnel. It is the cafeteria in the selfsame *Hotel Francia*. The cafeteria features approximately the same cooking but is more in my range, at merely expensive. Not so many wine glasses, either!

The street market that used to block Juárez is gone. In its place is the *Centro Commercial Jesús Terán* – sparkling clean and well lighted. It is about the nicest little market I've seen in Mexico. Unfortunately, it is short on restaurant stands, although one of the women who used to have a street stand told me she had high hopes of opening another restaurant in the new market. *Quien sabe?*

Opposite the new market is the *Lonchería El Mono*, which seems to be a worthy successor to the market. Try it and give me a report.

Stand in the plaza across the street from the Francia, facing the hotel. The street that leaves the market to the left is Juárez. You will be able to see a 'Tres Hermanos' shoe store sign. Right next to it is a tiny cafe featuring an excellent *menu turistico* at moderate prices.

Across the street from the left end of the bus station as you leave is the restaurant *Hermanos Gomez*. This is probably the busiest restaurant in Aguascalientes – one of my favourites, and the reason I haven't eaten in too many other places. It serves strictly Mexican items, everything from tortas to flan. The cook does a good job with the chilis rellenos. Inexpensive.

Getting Around

The bus station is too far from the plaza for practical walking, but city bus service is frequent and cheap. To get downtown, catch a C Macias Arellano or Jesus María going from left to right at the left side of the terminal by the Hermanos Gomez restaurant. To get back, catch the same bus on 5 de Mayo or at the plaza.

ENCARNACIÓN DE DÍAZ, Guanajuato

(elevation 1800 metres, population 30,000)

Halfway between Lagos de Moreno and Aguascalientes, Encarnación de Díaz is one of hundreds of nice small towns that never receive a second glance from the average traveller.

The plaza looks almost the same as the one in Lagos down the road, but the town itself is much smaller. However, it does have one thing going for it that Lagos doesn't – the trees adorning the plaza are carved into one of the most spectacular topiary displays imaginable. Everything from crows (or eagles?) to lions have been carved from the living trees with utmost patience by a deaf artist.

If you have to overnight, as I once did, there isn't much choice in hotels. I was very comfortable in the *Hotel Casa Blanca,* up the street from the Estrella Blanca bus station. The hotel has an acceptable restaurant; both are run by an English-speaking family, formerly California residents.

LEÓN, Guanajuato

(elevation 1885 metres, population 400,000)

León is the industrial city of Guanajuato, with shoes and leather goods the principal products. On the outskirts in any direction you pass shoe factory after shoe factory. There are not enough colonial buildings to say grace over due to a flood in 1888 that flushed over 2000 structures down the valley. The city is a handy place to branch off the north-south route and catch a bus for Guanajuato and San Miguel de Allende.

Because León has so many hotels convenient to the central bus terminal, a small sampling follows. León is a fine place to stay over in case your schedule puts you in Guanajuato or San Miguel de Allende in the late afternoon. These two destinations are so popular that they often fill all their hotel rooms by 3 pm.

León has had a central bus terminal long enough to allow a number of hotels to spring up in the vicinity. I've stayed several times at the *Hotel León,* the first time while the smell of drying plaster permeated the air. The León is one of several hotels across the street and to the left from the bus station. Moderate.

A couple of other hotels that can be spotted easily from the station are the *Hotel de los Reyes,* 'Especially for Families and Travellers', and the *Hotel Abraham.* These are the newest and very convenient for travellers by bus, but expensive.

A good place to eat is the *Restaurant-Cafeteria Raúl,* on the corner up the street from the Los Reyes and almost directly across the street from the bus station. Moderate.

The restaurant in the bus station itself isn't bad, either. Moderate.

The Eastern Route via Monterrey

This route has the advantage over the east coast route in that the weather is more bearable due to the greater altitude, and there are more interesting things to do and see than there are on the route along the coast itself, which is long on sugar-cane fields.

NUEVO LAREDO, Tamaulipas

(elevation 128 meters, population 500,000)

The new bus station in this border community is located on the southern outskirts of town – an expensive taxi ride out into the country. The most economical way to get to the station is via a Mexican commuter bus from the American bus stations to the Laredo, Texas side of the border.

The bus stops at the immigration office so you can pick up the required documentation. A taxi will stop, too, on request, but will charge for waiting.

MONTERREY, Nuevo León

(elevation 537 meters, population 1,500,000)

Although Monterrey was founded over 400 years ago, it wasn't until 1596 that it became La Ciudad Metropolitano de Nuestra Señora de Monterey. Somehow over the years the spelling has changed; nobody knows why today.

The city did not really amount to much until the arrival of the railroads and modern highways, whereupon it really got busy and soon became the country's centre of industry. Steel mills, a gigantic brewery, a huge bottleworks to supply the brewery, electric motor and bicycle factories – you name it and if it is made in any quantity in Mexico, it is made in Monterrey.

The city was always prosperous, but became even more so with the arrival of industrialization. Today it is one of the wealthiest cities in the country. A few years back Monterrey, which then had less than one percent of the population, contributed 10% of Mexico's total federal taxes.

With this background information you could reasonably expect Monterrey to be a beautiful city, with wide and handsome boulevards and gushing fountains at every intersection, but you would be sorely disappointed upon viewing it for the first time. Monterrey is a grimy, hustling, bustling factory town about equally divided between light and heavy industry, with no environmental laws worthy of mention, and with a street system planned several hundred years ago.

There are several things worth seeing, and quite a bit of historical interest. The new Palacio Municipal, a stunning example of the best of current Mexican architectural thinking, takes up the southern end of the Plaza Zaragoza, thereby eliminating much of the city's badly needed open space. In the middle of the plaza is the usual man-on-horseback statue, this one of General Zaragoza. The new building is perched on stilts above the ground floor, with a couple of escalators to reach the first floor from ground level. I have yet to see both of the escalators working at the same time.

Monterrey was the scene of one of the bloodiest battles of the Mexican-American war. The Mexicans fortified the town well, using the walls that extended above the flat roofs on the traditional buildings as ramparts. When the battle began, these rooftop sharpshooters held the city until the Americans began tunnelling through the walls with sledgehammers. The Americans then threw grenades through the hole, after which they considered it safe to go ahead and enlarge the hole and begin the process all over again.

Most of the city that Zachary Taylor

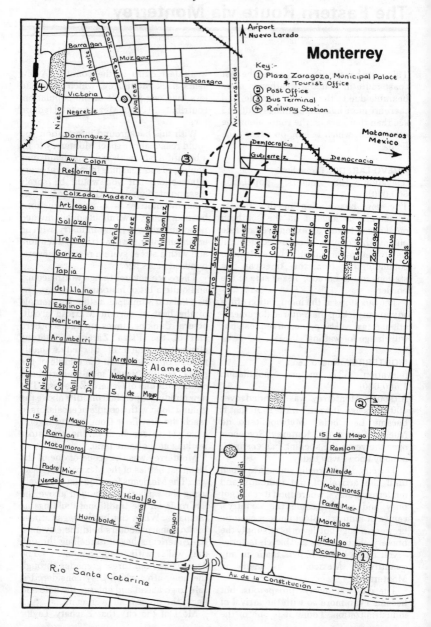

took is no more, but the history buff will be interested in visiting the Bishop's Palace, then a fort but now a museum and in somewhat better shape than when the Americans took it by assault. To reach it go out Matamoros until it crosses Benitez. The Palace is on a hill overlooking the city, and on a rare clear day affords a fine view of the city. Taxi fare is M$200.

Places to Stay

The hotels in downtown Monterrey are vastly overpriced and no more convenient for the traveller than staying out near the bus station. After all, you can see everything in central Monterrey, including the Bishop's Palace, in about three hours, so running back and forth sightseeing doesn't present a problem. It's unlikely that any free spirit in good health will spend more than a single day in Monterrey before moving on. I prefer to get a room in Saltillo (90 km away) and visit on a day-trip basis; but if you have to stay in Monterrey some hotels reasonably near the bus station are:

Hotel Regis, Jiménez at Reforma. Don't be put off by the cavelike lobby or the garish modesty panels on the balconies. Moderate.

Hotel Norte, Democracia at Mendez. Only a block from the market, but quiet withal. Little traffic. Expensive.

Hotel Habana, Cuauhtémoc between Madero and Reforma. No extra charge for the Art Deco facade. Moderate.

Hotel Pino Suarez, on Pino Suarez between Colón and Reforma. Moderate.

Hotel America, Cuauhtémoc between Reforma and Colón. Don't let the rock-group posters plastered in the windows daunt you. All rooms are equipped with fans. Very convenient to the bus station and often full. Inexpensive.

Hotel Reforma is next door to the America and often full. This speaks well for its low rates. Inexpensive.

Places to Eat

Economical eating is a problem in Monterrey, but if you go out the front of the bus station and turn right, and then make another right onto the first street you come to, you will see a number of small restaurants ahead, the very worst of which will beat bus station food in both price and quality. Inexpensive.

If you're heading downtown these are somewhat out of your way, so turn left on leaving the station, then right on the next street, Pino Suarez. On your way downtown watch for the little *Café Galis* on the right side of the street. The Galis serves typical country food – the kind intended to fuel someone enough to swing a machete or drive a 26-wheel truck hour in, hour out – and serves it inexpensively.

There is a *VIPs* restaurant close to the bus station. Turn left as you leave the station, then left at the next corner. The VIPs is at the end of the long block, well worth the five-minute walk for its sparkling sanitary facilities, especially after taking a look at the filthy bus station restrooms. It's air-conditioned, too. Expensive.

Sanborn's, on Morelos between Escobedo and Zaragoza, serves up the usual expensive North American foods and is the prime source for US magazines and English-language books.

The *City Market* is on Colón to the left as you leave the bus station. Madero, near Juárez, is a market in itself with sidewalk vendors purveying everything from wedding rings to switchblade knives.

For the benefit of those who prefer to build their own meals picnic fashion, there is a *Super 7* supermarket across the street from the bus station.

Getting Around

The bus station at Monterrey is huge. In addition to the usual post and telegraph offices, it contains a movie theatre, fruit stands, bathhouse, keymaker, liquor store, copy centre and even a vendor of herb medicines. Be warned of its low, dingy ceilings and complete absence of fans. The left luggage (guardaria) is in Waiting Room Five.

To get to the Plaza Zaragoza – Monterrey's main plaza – catch a Ruta 1 bus at the shelter outside the bus station and ride downtown. The same bus will bring you back by a different route – central Monterrey is all one-way streets. If you want to hoof it, go out of the bus station and turn left, then right at Pino Suarez, the next street. Follow it through the famous arch about 19 blocks to Humboldt and turn left. The plaza is seven more blocks. I walk it in about 45 minutes.

To get to the railroad station, go out of the bus station and turn right, then right again onto the next street, which will be Villagran. Follow it four blocks to Victoria and turn left. The railroad station is now three more blocks.

Monterrey has a busy international airport, but I have never met a traveller-for-pleasure who flew into Monterrey; they prefer to fly deeper into Mexico to more interesting places.

SALTILLO, Coahuila
(elevation 1568 metres, population 300,000)
Monterrey's choking industrial smog often extends 90 km, all the way to Saltillo. For practical purposes the whole distance is one gigantic factory estate, producing everything from auto parts and phosphoric acid to brandy.

Saltillo is noted for its ponchos and serapes of cotton and wool, but they are no cheaper here than anywhere else in Mexico, so unless you are on your way north when you stop, or have come here especially to purchase woven goods, it makes no sense at all to carry the bulky material over the country. If you buy on your trip north you will have the advantage of having your eye sharpened by seeing the products of the rest of the country. This can be important because there has been a marked drop in quality in locally-made goods in recent years.

If you're a student of Mexican architecture you will be interested in the cathedral on what is technically the main plaza by the government buildings. It is the northernmost example of the Churrigueresque style of decoration. The inside has been systematically pillaged over the centuries.

Saltillo figured in the international financial news in 1981 when the governor of the State of Coahuila and his cohorts, mostly members of his immediate family, were dismissed after they stole over US$80 million. The governor was not prosecuted because President Lopez Portillo figured that being removed from access to the treasury was punishment enough.

Places to Stay
The low-price hotel situation is much better in Saltillo than it is in Monterrey, so if you really have a reason to visit Monterrey, get a room in Saltillo and visit Monterrey on a day-trip basis. This is especially convenient in summer because with its greater altitude Saltillo almost always has cool nights, whereas Monterrey in summer is a sweltering mess. And the air, summer or winter, is much cleaner in Saltillo than it is in smoggy Monterrey.

I usually stay in the *Hotel Hidalgo*, an older house less than a block from the plaza where the local buses stop. I've always had hot water. Inexpensive.

The *Hotel Conde* on Treviño at Acuna is a very poor second on all counts to the Hidalgo. Inexpensive.

The *Hotel Saade*, on Aldama near the bus plaza, is not quite up to the promise of the lobby with its wood panelling, marble floors and trim. The experienced, over-stuffed furniture is being recovered. Moderate.

Since the previous edition of this book the two hotels across the way from the bus terminal have been completed. Essentially similar, both are on the low end of moderate.

Places to Eat
The best economical eating in Saltillo is at

the *Victoria*, next door to the Hotel Hidalgo. The first time I entered its doors was to use the long-distance telephone and I ate to pass the time while the call went through. After that I went to the Victoria just for the eating itself. Moderate.

The market is just off the bus plaza on the opposite side from the Hotels San Luis and Hidalgo and is the place to get a really cheap, no-frills meal. It is also the place to shop for a poncho, serape or blanket. Meals inexpensive.

Getting Around
The new bus terminal is way out at the edge of town – and Saltillo is a large town. There is excellent bus service to anywhere in the northern part of Mexico, and a pretty fair restaurant on the premises. The station is too new to have attracted very many food-stall operators, but I expect that will change soon, and the two new hotels opposite the station will logically have a restaurant or two.

The green-and-yellow micro-buses marked either 'Ruta 9' or 'Central-Centro' will take you to downtown Saltillo if you don't mind some crowding. I've seen 24 adults, plus God knows how many little kids, in one of the Ford or Chevy vans. It may be easier on your dignity if you take one of the many cabs into town for M$200 or so.

There is an airport and scheduled air service, but I can't imagine anyone flying to Saltillo except on business.

MATEHUALA, San Luis Potosí
(elevation 1534, population 55,000)
Matehuala is easy to identify from afar: a huge concrete church, shaped like a 200-litre steel drum split lengthwise and laid on its side, looms over the town. The bell-supporting structure is built of bits and pieces of scrap iron. The town is a pleasant place to break the journey for a day or two, or a month if you have the time. It is quiet and peaceful, as befits one of the rare cities in Mexico with about the same number of people today that it had in 1960.

Most foreign travellers who stop over in Matehuala do so not because of the ambience but for the trip up the hill to Real de Catorce, an old mining town that looks pretty much as Taxco must have looked a half-century ago, before Bill Spratling showed it the way to prosperity.

Places to Stay
The hotel situation in Matehuala is good because of the *Matehuala Hotel*, one of the best values for the peso in Mexico. It is an old, buff-painted two-storey barn of a building constructed around a red-tiled patio studded with old-fashioned bridge tables and upholstered chairs with unique designs formed by holes. Inexpensive.

The relatively new *Hotel Monterrey* is almost straight across the street from the long-haul bus station. It has a brown brick front and an electric sign that's usually working. Inexpensive.

Places to Eat
For a good restaurant try the *Domi* on the small plaza behind the Matehuala Hotel. It offers a large assortment of typical Mexican dishes and is open from early in the morning until late at night. Inexpensive.

Around the corner to the left of the Matehuala Hotel is the *Restaurant Fontella*. The place is nicely decorated with blue overcloths on white tablecloths; no oilcloth here. Chairs are red-bottomed colonial replicas. There's a big, electronic bug-killer over the cash register, greatly appreciated during the spring, summer and fall. And believe it or not, the Fontella is inexpensive.

The *Bar Quijote* is right across a narrow street from the Hotel Matehuala. This has to be one of the nicest little neighbourhood bars in Mexico. It doesn't stick its customers up – a bottle of Superior is only M$150 including a *bocado* (morsel). This is a fine place to while away the time when you've missed the bus up to Catorce.

Go out the front of the long-haul bus station and turn left, and left again at the corner. You will soon come to several restaurants and a casa de huespedes that have replaced the old street market here. Everything is inexpensive.

Getting There & Getting Around

Essentially, Matehuala is laid out along one main street, and to get to the Matehuala Hotel from the long-haul bus station, simply go out the front door and turn left – it's a 15-minute walk.

Matehuala is on the main bus route between Saltillo-Monterrey and San Luis Potosí. There is also a smaller line that leaves from another station by the Hotel Matehuala and goes to Cedral and Real de Catorce.

REAL DE CATORCE, San Luis Potosí

(elevation 2755 metres, population 700) There is a persistent, and probably apocryphal, story that Real de Catorce, which means 'Mining Camp of the 14', refers to the 14 bandits who supposedly made their headquarters in the canyon. One was known as 'The Frito Bandido!' I have also heard it said that the town got its name from the 14 coins – Spanish *reales* – discovered in the remains of an abandoned building several centuries ago. Take your choice.

Today Real de Catorce is almost a ghost town; its population has gone from an estimated 30,000 or so down to somewhere around 600 or 700. Most of the present residents cluster around the plaza and church. Their homes are surrounded by hundreds of skeleton houses lacking roofs and rejas, most of them with front doors securely locked and awaiting the reopening of the mines and the return of their long-dead owners. Spooky.

In all likelihood the mines will open again eventually because they didn't close down from lack of values but because the town had the bad luck to be located in a canyon. When the revolution came along all it took was one man with a 7 mm

Mauser and a couple of clips of cartridges on the side hill to stop all activity by an occasional shot at anything below.

This happened now and then and it eventually halted the mining operations. During the years the mines were closed the drawings of the diggings were lost, the machinery was carted off, the rails through the tunnel were pulled up, and the once-thriving community of Real de Catorce became a mere shell of its former vigorous self. Nevertheless it is always possible for a few hungry and determined people to make a few pesos now and then by livestock raising or small-scale mining. Recently the mining has been for antimony although the original mines were primarily a silver proposition. There is some interest in reopening the mines, and a Swiss firm was retained to make a survey of the old workings extending deep into the mountains that surround the town on three sides. There is also an attempt to turn it into a craft centre, a la Taxco. Humberto Hernandez is acting as Catorce's Bill Spratling, and already a few of the old buildings have been repaired and restored.

A small museum under the church has a few items on display that date from the town's heyday, among them papers signed by the original Lopez Portillo, a young Spanish mining engineer and the ancestor of the man who eventually became Mexico's president. There are also hundreds of *retablos* (little pictures) in the church – some sophisticated, some naive – celebrating and giving thanks for the miraculous intercession of the saint who saved the donor's life from fire, flood, dynamite blast, irritated bull or what have you. The caretaker will allow you to climb the tower, the best place to view street after street of roofless houses. In the tower take a good look at the chicken ladders, made of logs with notches chopped along one side. These were used for climbing up and down the mine shafts, often with murderously heavy baskets of ore. Imagine the result of the slightest misstep in the pitch darkness.

The Casa de Moneda is across the street from the church and at one time contained minting machinery for the manufacture of silver coins. The equipment has long since been scrapped, and part of the big old building is currently being used for a private residence.

The rails have been taken out of the railroad tunnel and it has been turned into a one-way vehicular road. If two vehicles happen to meet in the hole one of them would have to back out, so there is a telephone at each end connected to a 'dispatcher' who lives in a shack at the Catorce end.

Deep within the mountain a mining tunnel bisects the vehicle tunnel, and in the drift the miners have built an altar, a common practice in Latin mines, but the only one I know of that can be seen from a bus. Watch for it on the right side – you'll see the candles.

A short distance past the Abundancia Hotel, and on the opposite side of the street, is Hector Alonso's Gift & Curio Shop, worthy of a visit even if you have no pressing need for a gift, handicraft or curio. Señor Alonso speaks English and is a very amiable person. Knowledgeable, too – he is a native of Catorce. Among other unusual items he carries are ore samples from the local mines. Some of them, such as galena crystals, are quite spectacular.

Continue along what passes for a main street in Catorce, past the Casa de Moneda and the Hotel Abundancia, until you reach the tiny plaza. Turn right uphill at the far end of the plaza and in about a half a km you will see an old bridge, and just past that, another church. This one is surrounded by the community graveyard. To the left of the entrance is a tiny chapel, now in the throes of restoration.

Places to Stay

There are two hotels and a huespedes in Catorce. The road from the tunnel leads 'downtown' past the side of the church. Just below the church is the *Casa de Huespedes La Providencia*. This small, family-run operation is very inexpensive.

Continuing past the church for a block or so, the cobblestoned street passes the *Mesón de Abundancia*, a hotel created by combining several old buildings. It's a fine job of conversion, with huge, high-ceilinged rooms and hot, hot water. A bargain with moderate prices.

Hard as it is to believe, Humberto has finally gotten some signs up and his place up the hill from the Abundancia is identified quite well now: *Hotel el Real, Restaurant*. Beneath the above is a little sign that says 'Cocina Italiana' – complete with the Italian national colours. Moderate.

Places to Eat

Catorce is not much of a restaurant town, and hotels are the places to eat.

I've never eaten there, but I understand the *Providencia* puts out home-cooked meals – you eat in the kitchen – at inexpensive rates.

I have eaten very well at the *Abundancia*. The big, stone-walled old dining room serves good food at reasonable prices. Try the *asado de boda* – I recommend it. The name translates as 'marriage roast'; the dish is a close relative of the Philippines' *adobo*. The meals are easily the equivalent in quality and quantity to those in most very expensive places but the Abundancia is moderate.

The *Hotel de Real* used to put out standard Mexican fare of excellent quality. I missed the opportunity to try the Cocina Italiana, but will the next time I'm in town. Moderate.

Getting There

There are two ways of getting to Real de Catorce. The less common is by railroad, which is even more inconvenient than it is for the rest of Mexico and involves catching the train in Nuevo Laredo, Saltillo or San Luis Potosí, getting off at Estación Catorce and perhaps hiking over the trail some 14 km into town. A man with a jeep is supposed to meet all trains, but the possibility of having to hike must not be overlooked.

The other way is by the bus that runs from Matehuala at about 90-minute intervals. The first trip up is around 7 or 8 am and the last bus leaves Catorce around 4.30 pm. Running time is approximately an hour and 20 minutes.

Although it is possible to go to Catorce during the afternoon, take a quick look around and return to Matehuala that same day; most people either make the trip up in the early morning or stay overnight in Catorce.

The buses are specially made, 37-seat affairs on standard truck chassis – the last 25 km or so of the trip is over a cobblestone road. They are woefully short on baggage room. The bus company has a posted limit of 20 kg per passenger, a rule that is honoured mostly in the breach. To reach the Turismos de Altaplano bus station, simply go left as you leave the Matehuala Hotel; it's in the middle of the next block. While getting your ticket look at the 11-by-14-inch colour prints on the wall. In case you've forgotten what it looks like, that white stuff in the pictures is snow.

SAN LUIS POTOSÍ, San Luis Potosí

(elevation 1917 metres, population 325,000)

Most of Mexico's old mining towns owe their existence to a silver strike, but San Luis Potosí got its start when gold was discovered in the San Pedro Hills, about 20 km from the present city. Prior to this the region was the site of several missions. The early miners, being natural optimists, decided to name their town after the fabulously wealthy mining camp of Potosí, Bolivia, in the hope that some of the luck would spread. It didn't, much.

Although the Mexican operations turned out well, they never achieved the wealth of their South American namesake. In a few years the growth of the community, coupled with the shortage of drinking water, caused the officials to move the town to its present location. In addition to the gold of the original discovery, silver, lead and some copper were later found at San Pedro, and the future of the fledgling city was assured.

Today San Luis Potosí makes its living from mining, transportation and commerce. Although it is not a national monument, San Luis cherishes quite a number of handsome colonial buildings, mostly clustered near the heart of the city.

The life of most Mexican cities is concentrated on the plaza, and this is even more true of Potosí than most. Four plazas are worthy of mention.

First is the Plaza de San Francisco, at Universidad and Aldama. The Franciscan order built the monastery on the south side of the plaza and gave it the present name. Next to the church on the west side is the Museo Regional de Arte Popular, specializing in the handicrafts of the state of San Luis Potosí. Incorporated in the museum operation is the Fonda Típica Potosina. Unless a rock group is performing, the area is quiet and peaceable – the ideal place for a picnic.

The Plazuela del Carmen at Escobedo and Othón contains the Templo de Nuestra Señora del Carmen – the most interesting of the city's churches and probably the best surviving example of Baroque construction in Mexico. Among the interior decorations is a *reredo* (religious painting) attributed to that Mexican Renaissance man, Tresguerras.

The Jardín Hidalgo, at Othón and Zaragoza, isn't a garden at all, it's really the Plaza Principal. At one time it was called the Plaza de Armas, or parade ground. This is where you will find the Palacio del Gobierno, originally erected in 1770 but reconstructed and extensively repaired time and time again. It was here that Juárez, ignoring petitions for clemency from most of the countries and important personages in Europe, signed Maximilian's writ of execution. The Palacio Municipal was built as a private residence and has been the city hall for a little over 50 years.

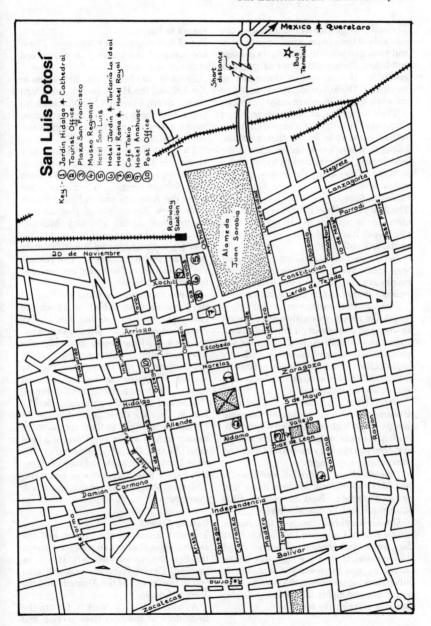

San Luis Potosí

Key:-
1. Jardín Hidalgo + Cathedral
2. Tourist Office
3. Plaza San Francisco
4. Museo Regional
5. Hotel San Luis
6. Hotel Jardín + Tortaría La Ideal
7. Hotel Roma + Hotel Royal
8. Cafe Tokio
9. Hotel Anahuac
10. Post Office

The cathedral, formerly Parroquia, on the east side of the square, was begun in 1670 and took 240 years to bring to its present condition. Perhaps because of the long gestation, the interior is decorated in Byzantine, Doric, Gothic, Baroque and so on, while the exterior is (mostly) Baroque.

The Alameda, at Universidad and Constitución, is the city's largest and most restful park. It is so big that a person lolling on a bench near the fountain in the middle isn't bothered unduly by the traffic honking its way along the busy streets on either side.

Places to Stay

The fairly new *Hotel del Río* is across the street to the right of the railroad station as you face it. It is the closest moderate hotel to the railroad station.

Hotel San Luis is old, but a long, long way from being picturesque. Its best points are its location next door to the railroad station and its inexpensive prices.

Hotel Jardín, on Bravos at Xochitl, is about the nicest reasonably priced hotel in town and only about 30 minutes on foot from the bus station. Best value for the pesos. Moderate and recommended.

Hotel Roma, on Constitución at Bravos, is in an old, thick-walled private home. It is run-down but inexpensive.

Hotel Royal, on Constitución between Bravos and Othon, is another antique building with high ceilings and windows to match. It needs restoration, but when it's restored you can bet your boots it won't be inexpensive any longer.

Hotel Anahuac, on Xochitl near Bravos, has Mexican Miracle Modern decor and secured parking. Best bargain in SLP after the Hotel Jardín. Moderate.

On Universidad, just on the Juárez Circle side of Calle San Luis and not too far from the overpass, is the *Hotel Universidad*. It is on the right side of the street as you go toward downtown. It advertises 'agua caliente día y noche' (hot water day and night). This I rather doubt, but it is inexpensive for now.

Places to Eat

Potosí has oodles of restaurants. These are some of the places I've patronized over the years:

Tortaría la Ideal, on Bravos near Xochitl and the Hotel Jardín, has a sign saying 'Service Day and Night', and I have yet to find them closed. They are quick, have a wide assortment of sandwiches and are inexpensive.

The *Café Tokio* has moved to a new location at 415 Othón, near Constitución on the opposite side of the block from their former location. Their new place faces the Alameda and is highly visible from there. Regardless of the name, it serves good-quality ordinary Mexican workers' food and does it in a hurry. It is also a good place for an American-style breakfast such as 'hot kakes'. The Tokio is the busiest joint in town and my personal favourite. Moderate.

The restaurant in the *Hotel San Luis*, 20 de Noviembre at Othon, is about the cheapest place to eat, but the quality pretty well matches the price. Inexpensive.

I once tried the restaurant under the new and ridiculously expensive *Hotel Arizona* across the street from the bus station. Weary of the local corn-based cuisine, I wanted a simple meal of bread, cheese and wine and a white tablecloth to match. This is a difficult combination in Mexico because places that serve wine are usually aghast at the very idea of a light meal like this. But here I received exactly what I ordered, dispatched with courtesy and nary a raised eyebrow or comment. The meal was very expensive and worth every peso.

Getting Around

To catch a bus for the centro, exit the second-class station and wait for a bus at the first corner on your left. It will be marked 'Centro-Retorno' and will take you to the far end of the Alameda and the Jardín Hidalgo.

An alternative is to walk it. Go out the front door of the first-class section and turn left. At the traffic circle swing around to your left and get off at the street directly behind the statue of Juárez. This is Universidad, and the Alameda is now about 20 minutes of steady walking.

The bus station at San Luis is divided into separate first-and second-class sections, in the form of an 'L', with the restaurant at the junction serving both halfs. The terminal is unusual for the variety of merchandise and services offered. In addition to the usual telegraph and post offices it also has a local and long-distance phone store, a pharmacy, sweets stands, a bookstore, two restaurants, a watch and clock shop and a leather-goods store selling everything from martingales to surcingles. There is even a store in the first-class section near the restaurant stocking a fine collection of price-marked Aguascalientes needle goods, such as shawls and other practical things. These are rather difficult to find in their home town.

The railroad station is opposite the middle of the Alameda on the Othon side. It is sometimes shown at the end of the Alameda by the overpass but that station has been largely abandoned for years.

There is an airport, but only business people and locals use it.

DOLORES HIDALGO, Guanajuato

(elevation 1929 metres, population 90,000)

Dolores Hidalgo is the perfect example of a small, peaceful country town, a place where a dog chases a cat – and they both walk. But as an historical site it combines for Mexico the attributes of Concord, Boston, Philadelphia and Mount Vernon rolled into one, for it was here, in 1810, that the parish priest, Miguel Hidalgo, issued his ringing cry for freedom, the grito repeated by politicians major and minor all over the republic each 16 September.

Today Dolores derives most of its income ·from the fabrication of hand-painted ceramic tableware which is shipped all over Mexico, and from the streams of patriotic Mexicans who arrive by chartered bus, automobile and bus from all parts of the country. Unfortunately for the patriots, the church is often locked tighter than a drum; it is still in use as a parish church in spite of its status as an unofficial national monument.

Hidalgo's residence has been turned into a museum containing many of his personal possessions, including, I am told, a peculiar chair with a concealed chamber pot. This is hearsay to me because although I've tried to visit the museum on several occasions I have yet to find the door unlocked. There is a sign on the door saying that the admission is M\$15, and also giving the hours of operation, but the latter is to be taken with a gram of salt. I've had the same bad luck with the famous Tamayo Museum in Oaxaca.

If you leave the Flecha Amarilla bus station and turn left you will be on Hidalgo, and in a couple of blocks you will come to the Museo Hidalgo complete with identification plaque installed under the direction of the luckless Maximilian.

Across the street is the Artesanias en Piel shop which has a good selection of personal leather goods such as belts, purses and billfolds. On the same corner is the Mercado de Artesanias, an old house converted into a sales room for the local ceramicists' work, mostly tableware. This is far and away the best assortment under one roof in Dolores, and is worth a visit even if you're perfectly satisfied with the Balleek you use at home.

If the Mercado de Artesanias doesn't have enough pottery for your taste, turn right as you leave the Flecha Amarilla station and cross the Río Laja, and you will see wholesaler after jobber, most of whom sell retail, too.

In the same neighbourhood are several huaracherías that still hand-make the old-style country footwear, comfortable, long-lasting and cheap – far superior to the stuff sold in tourist meccas such as Taxco and Cancún. It's also cheaper.

The street names, incidentally, have all been changed a number of times and most streets have at least two different street signs. The only street names that haven't been changed over the past century or so are Hidalgo and Morelos.

Places to Stay & Eat

The hotel situation in Dolores is good in that I have never had any trouble walking in off the street and getting a room, and bad in that there isn't a lot of choice.

The best hotel in town is the *Posada Cocomacán*, on the right corner of the plaza facing the Parroquia. It has a good restaurant (when it's open) and is quite popular during the fall duck season with nimrods up from Mexico City. Both the hotel and restaurant are moderate.

Along the same street as the Cocomacán and up the hill beside the church is the *Hotel el Caudillo*. There is a restaurant in the Caudillo where I've had both good and bad meals, depending on who is stirring the cazuelas back in the kitchen. Inexpensive.

The *Restaurante Plaza* on the plaza opposite Hidalgo's old church is very popular with local business people from the shops around the square. It also has long-distance phone service. Moderate.

Or you may prefer to take your chances at the market. Go along Hidalgo from the Flecha Amarilla bus station and turn left at the plaza. The market is then a block or two further. Walking time: 15 minutes.

Getting There & Getting Around

As Dolores Hidalgo is about halfway between Guanajuato and San Miguel de Allende it is a good base when visiting either of those popular destinations – it is much more likely to have economical hotel rooms available when everything in San Miguel and Guanajuato is full to overflowing.

Bus service is excellent, with buses from Mexico City, Guadalajara, San Luis Potosí, and such out-of-the-way places as San Felipe and San Luis de la Paz. Flecha Amarilla has the best service and its own terminal with baggage checking and so on.

Omnibus de Mexico and Estrella Blanca buses stop along the plaza.

POZOS, Guanajuato

(elevation 1850 metres, population 2500)
Pozos is another ghost town similar to Real de Catorce or an unrestored Taxco. It's unusual in that some of the buildings around the miniscule plaza have been refurbished, but the treatment is only facade deep – there is nothing but air behind some of the imposing fronts.

The old mines were mainly strung out along a ridge – go uphill from the little zócalo and keep working your way up and to your left. There are hundreds of roofless houses; at one time Pozos was a city with 40-50,000 people, fine homes, cobbled streets, piped water and its own generating plant but the revolution put an end to prosperity, and today Pozos is slowly turning into rubble with that charming decrepitude that only Mexico can muster.

To get to Pozos, first go to San Luis de la Paz, which is located 116 km south of San Luis Potosí on the Querétaro road, 86 km north of Querétaro, and about 40 km east of Dolores Hidalgo. There is fairly frequent bus service to and from all these points.

Pozos itself is about 15 km from San Luis de la Paz, and there are several buses a day from the little central terminal in San Luis. The return trip is even easier because an enterprising taxi driver runs a shuttle service, parking in the little plaza in Pozos until he gets a full load for the return trip. Costs about M$150.

GUANAJUATO, Guanajuato

(elevation 2090 metres, population 75,000)
Guanajuato is one of the most popular destinations in Mexico, and deservedly so. It has a superb site, a great deal of colonial charm and a rich and entertaining

history. Plus it has the facilities to handle a large number of visitors.

Guanajuato is an old silver-mining town, the first discovery having been made back in 1548, followed by strike after strike. These were not nickel-and-dime prospect holes, either. The Conde de Rul, owner of the bonanza Valenciana mine, was supposed to have spent a thousand pesos a month on incidentals, yet he had enough left over to pay for churches and monuments.

Because the town is high among rugged mountains where flat ground is at a premium, the city has very little room for streets and one is so narrow it's called 'The Little Street of the Kiss' – post cards show how people can lean out of their balconies and kiss their neighbours across the way. The narrow, crooked streets contribute a good deal to the attraction of Guanajuato, but also make it extremely vexing to get around on wheels. Guanajuato is probably the only city in the world where Americans habitually choose to walk.

The incredible traffic problems persist, even though most traffic now goes underground along the old riverbed. This practical state of affairs actually happened almost by accident. The community had always been plagued by flash floods; finally, after an especially severe flusher in 1905, the government built the Túnel Porfirio Díaz to bypass the river, whereupon all that remained was to construct a few entrances and exits and the city had a ready-made underground roadway.

No city in Mexico has as many points of interest in as small an area as Guanajuato, and there are guidebooks in English and Spanish wholly devoted to the city, although I have never seen any mention of the Túnel Díaz that makes it practical.

Sightseeing in Guanajuato proper is simple because the town is located at the bottom of a narrow canyon with essentially just one street, Juárez, which becomes Sopena, which becomes Paseo de la Prensa. In this case, Prensa refers to the

two dams, built in the late 1700s, from which the city draws its water. Guanajuato had piped water before the United States was incorporated.

Guanajuato has blossomed out in a bunch of attractive white-on-green direction signs. These are for the benefit of drivers, not pedestrians. I talked to several walkers who made the mistake of following one of the signs and wound up doing extensive backtracking.

Last, but by no means least, the *sanitarios publicos* are on the top floor of the restaurant building next door to the Mercado Juárez.

Mercado Hidalgo

The iron-framed Mercado Hidalgo is a couple of blocks up the street from the bus station, a remarkably well-stocked market for a town of this size. The main floor is the food section selling fruit, vegetables, meat, fish, bread and anything else a family is likely to eat, but the interesting feature for the traveller is the balcony encircling the main floor where clothing, copper cookware, cazuelas, toys, shoes, purses and seemingly everything available

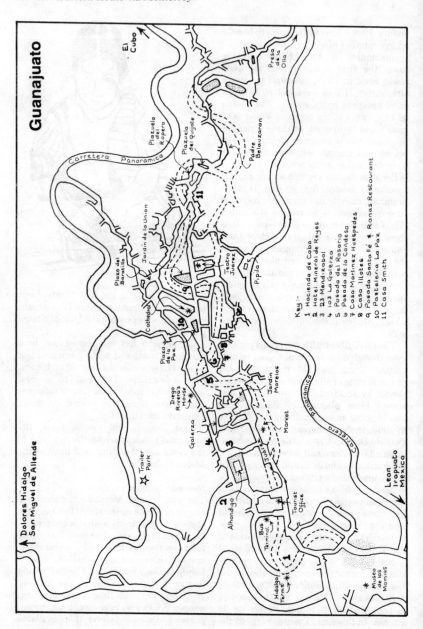

Guanajuato

Dolores Hidalgo
San Miguel de Allende

Carretera Panoramica

El Cubo

Plazuela del Ropero

Plazuela del Quijote

Padre Belauzaron

Presa de la Olla

Plaza del Baratillo

Jardin de la Union

Cathedral

Teatro Juarez

Pipila

Diego Rivera's House

Plaza de la Paz

Galerza

Trailer Park

Alhondiga

Bus Terminal

Hidalgo Terminal

Jardin Morelos

Market

Tourist Office

Carretera Panoramica

Museo de las Momias

Leon
Irapuato
Mexico

Key :-

1 Hacienda de Cobo
2 Hotel Mineral de Reyes
3 23 Mendizabal
4 103 La Galerza
5 Posada del Rosario
6 Posada de la Condesa
7 Casa Martinez Huespedes
8 Casa Illotes
9 Posada Santa Fé ✦ Ranas Restaurant
10 Pastelería La Paz
11 Casa Smith

in Mexico for the consumer is sold. Some people spend hours on the balcony and leave insisting they haven't had time to see everything.

When the Mercado was built in 1911 they left the marble floor and entrance columns of the original market and turned it into a tiny paved plaza, the Jardín Morelos, a totally delightful place where oldsters nod the afternoon away and children play.

Plaza de la Paz

Next on Sopena (née Juárez) is the Plaza de la Paz, surrounded by handsome, imposing buildings. The one with the plaque stating that Humboldt stayed here is the former residence of the Conde de Rul and is another of the excellent designs of that Mexican of many parts, Tresguerras.

Jardín de la Unión

Almost next door to the Plaza de la Paz is the lovely Jardín de la Unión, which could well be considered the Plaza Principal of Guanajuato. On the left of the Jardín, at the upper end, is the newish El Agora de Baratillo, a wonderful place to read away a lazy afternoon at one of the white-painted, cast-iron tables.

Plaza del Baratillo

Walk through the Agora and you will be on yet another of the secluded plazuelas the Latins do so well, the Plaza del Baratillo. It is also called the Plaza Gral Manuel Gonzales, and has several other names. It has a beautiful fountain, which would be improved no end if the water were turned on. 'Baratillo' means 'second-hand' in Spanish, but I have never been able to find anyone in Guanajuato who could explain how it became attached to a quiet little plazuela.

Teatro Juárez

Across Sopena from the Jardín Union is the celebrated Teatro Juárez, another of the efforts of the late President Díaz. A typical colonnaded classical design, the Teatro is no longer much used, although for the usual small admission fee you can wander around and gawk at the elegant interior. The foyer alone is worth the trifling price of admission. Adorning the front roofline of the Teatro are statues depicting the Muses – the work of W H Mullen, of Salem, Ohio. There are nine Muses, of course, but the Juárez only has eight. Question: Who was left out?

Paseo de la Prensa

Keep going uphill on Sopena and eventually it turns into the Paseo de la Prensa. Keep on and you will reach the dams. There are several parks up here, and it is a wonderful place to dine al fresco. The 45-minute walk there from the bus station takes you through Guanajuato's better residential district, past the Palacio de Gobierno, itself a former private home.

University of Guanajuato

If this uphill walking doesn't appeal to you, go through the Jardín de la Unión and turn left on Cantarramas. This leads you back toward the lower end of town, past the imposing University of Guanajuato with its steps that seem to reach the sky.

Residence of Diego Rivera

Next, Cantarramas changes its name to Positos after a slight jog. The boyhood residence of Diego Rivera at No 47 has been turned into the usual museum. Sketches for some of his famous murals are on display, as are a number of easel paintings. Guanajuato is one of the most reactionary cities in Mexico, an even match for San Miguel de Allende and Guadalajara, and during his lifetime Rivera was a non-person in his old home town.

Alhóndiga de Granaditas

Stay on Positos and you will come to the Alhóndiga de Granaditas, the old granary with a bloody history. During the early stages of Mexico's revolt against Spain the Spaniards forted up in the Alhóndiga which was then a new building constructed to store grain against years of poor harvests. The walls were thick and the doors were sturdy, and the rebels were having no luck at all in their siege until a young miner named José Barajas volunteered to set fire to the massive portals. Barajas' nickname was 'Pipilia', which means hen-turkey, but nobody remembers today whether he got it because of his high-pitched voice or the way he walked.

Pipilia had a slab of sandstone tied to his back as a sort of early-day flak vest. He braved the hail of bullets and destroyed the doors, opening the way for the insurgents to take the warehouse. His deed is commemorated by the huge statue on the hill overlooking the town from the south-west. The rebels had to fight every inch of the way when they took the Alhóndiga after Pipilia breached the door, and the last Spaniard died on the roof with a sword in his hand. Later a number of Royalists were taken prisoner and incarcerated in the Alhóndiga. The incensed people of Guanajuato broke into the place and murdered nearly 250 defenseless men.

But the fortunes of war always favour first one side and then the other, and it was soon the Spaniards' turn to capture Guanajuato. They set out to inflict the usual Draconian justice. Royalist General Calleja made it his first order of business to order everyone in Guanajuato to be executed, including women and children. A number of men had been killed when a priest, José María de Jesús Belaunzarán, interposed himself between the executioners and their victims and stopped the slaughter by the force of his personality and the cross he held on high.

Later the Spanish captured and executed Hidalgo, Allende, Aldama and Jiménez and their heads were returned to Guanajuato and hung from hooks at the four corners of the Alhóndiga, hooks which are there to this day. Now the Alhóndiga is a peaceful museum showing paintings and odds and ends pertaining to the history of Guanajuato.

The Panteón

The best-known tourist attraction in Guanajuato is the Panteón, a collection of mummies that are exhibited in a gruesome museum of their own. When the corpses are put into niches in the graveyard they shrivel and dry, rather than disintegrate. At the end of five years the bodies are evicted from their cubbyholes unless their relatives come up with additional rent. Most of the bodies are put in a common grave, but the more interesting are put in cases in the museum. Among the 'interesting' mummies are a miner still in boots and overalls, and a woman who died in childbirth, complete with half-delivered fetus. I saw it years ago before the exhibit was moved to a new building, and that was more that enough for me.

To get to the Panteón, turn right on leaving the bus station and follow the street uphill past the railroad station. There are signs and it would take a good deal of effort to get lost. The walk takes about an hour; the return downhill considerably less. Non-walkers can get a cab from the rank in front of the Central de Autobuses. Expect to pay M$300-400 for the ride, depending on how well you haggle.

Entremeses Cervantinos

Another don't-miss are the Entremeses Cervantinos put on during the spring by the university students. They are mostly in mime, so a lack of Spanish is no bar to their enjoyment. They are performed outdoors as was intended.

A recent development is the annual two-week International Cervantes Festival, sponsored by the State of Guanajuato. This is a major cultural event with internationally-known dance companies, singers and other performing artists. It is usually held in April or May, months when the weather is especially fine.

La Valenciana

The Iglesia de San Cayetano, on the road to Dolores Hidalgo and about the same distance from the bus station as the Panteón, is better known as La Valenciana. To the best of my knowledge this is the only church named after a mine.

The Valenciana was built by the Conde de Rule and the cost was divided between the Count and the miners working at the La Valenciana mine across the road. The name of the architect is long forgotten, but the church is one of the best, and best-preserved, examples of Churrigueresque decoration. In my opinion it is one of the most beautiful exercises in Colonial church-building in the country. The interior matches and justifies the exterior. There are three Churrigueresque altars, in marked contrast to the usual Mexican church which is a medley of periods, styles and techniques. Pay close attention to the pulpit, one of the best demonstrations of the woodworker's art I ever laid eyes on.

Even allowing for the fact that the church is slightly lopsided and out of balance because the planned second tower was never built – apparently local church politics prevented – this is the church to inspect in Mexico.

The Valenciana mine that paid for it all, one way or another, is directly across the road from the church. It was shut down about 50 years ago after several hundred years of continuous operation. The machinery was removed but within a few years new hoisting gear was installed and operations resumed, albeit on a much smaller scale. It is a fascinating place with the huge patio formerly used in the ore-dressing process, many old buildings, most of them roofless, and some old, old Ingersoll air compressors and bit sharpeners. I wandered around at will, with nary a word from anyone, probably because the miners couldn't conceive of anybody except another miner being interested in their activities, but I don't guarantee you will have the same good fortune. Try it anyway.

Marfil

If you are interested in the rehabilitation of old buildings, then visit Marfil, about five km from town toward Silao. Marfil was originally the suburb where the better-off mine people lived, and was severely damaged by the same flood that led to the construction of the Túnel Díaz in Guanajuato. By the end of WW II it was practically a deserted ghost town and in very bad condition. In common with Alamos, Taxco and San Miguel, Marfil has been largely rebuilt through the efforts of well-to-do Americans who have retired in the area. As with Taxco, the restoration of Marfil is largely the result of the inspiration of a single individual, an American named Belloli. He is to be commended.

Places to Stay

Guanajuato has lots of hotels to take care of its burgeoning tourist business, but even so it occasionally fills up with nary a room to be had. During the Entremeses it always fills to the rafters on weekends. If that happens I suggest you try Dolores Hidalgo or León. León is a large city with lots of hotels convenient to the bus station, while Dolores is more interesting but with only three small hotels. If you have no luck in these places I suggest you simply give up the whole idea and plan on returning the next year with advance, money-down reservations. Or plan on staying in Leon or Dolores and commuting, a practical ploy because the distances are not very great and there are lots and lots of buses.

The *Posada la Condesa*, a block down Juárez from the Plaza de la Paz, has a sort of impressive lobby, what with suits of plate armour and all, but don't be fooled; it's not nearly as expensive as it looks. Moderate, and usually full.

The *Hotel Mineral de Reyes* is on 5 de Mayo past the Alhóndiga, a five-storey cream building with balconies on the left side of the street. Red flowerpots on the individual balconies are a thoughtful touch. I've enjoyed several sojourns here once I learned to duck the concrete beam above the last steps as I came down the narrow front stairs. Best value in Guanajuato. Moderate.

The *Hotel Murillo*, on the second street behind the bus terminal, off 5 de Mayo, looks like a nice hotel for a wayfarer but it really caters to the large-family trade. If there are two or three couples in your group this is a good choice and quite cheap when the tab is split four or more ways. Expensive.

The *Hotel Alhóndiga*, across the street from the Murillo, seems to function at about the same level as the Reyes, and I've had good reports from its guests, but I have never been able to catch it with the desk staffed, so I can't say so myself.

Another good bet, although a bit more expensive, is the *Hacienda de Cobo*. As you cross the bridge in front of the Central de Autobuses look down the old creekbed to your right and you will see a white, igloo-like structure with 'Hacienda de Cobo' painted thereon. To reach it, turn right on Juárez and continue until the sidewalk jogs to the left around a store. Just before the jog you should find an inconspicuous iron gate opening on a sloping driveway. This is the pedestrian entrance to the Hacienda. It is more motel than hotel, and the automobile entrance is on the other side on the road coming in from Silao. The hotel has lots of thoughtful little touches, such as a couple of bottles of Electropuro bottled water, crown-sealed, in each room. Expensive, but good value for the money.

There are a number of hotels practically side by side on Juárez after it crosses 5 de Mayo a block or two up the hill from the bus station. They used to be inexpensive, but recently they have jacked up their prices. Now some are high/moderate and others expensive. They are far from worth their prices but they are among the first in town to rent all their rooms.

Guanajuato is such a popular destination that nearly all the hotels have not only raised their rates but have also been able to keep pretty well filled in spite of it. The only inexpensive place to stay I know of is the *Casa Martinez Huéspedes* on Alonso, a short street that branches to the right from Juárez near the Jardín Morelos and returns to Sopena a few blocks farther up. I've never stayed there because it always seems to be full when I try to register but it looks like a rather nice casa de huéspedes. Inexpensive.

Places to Eat

For a quick *comida*, washed down with a bottle of Negra Modelo, it is hard to beat the little *El Cedro* restaurant near the tourist information booth on Juárez and only a short block or so from the bus station. It is heavily patronized by country families in for a day in the big city, but they somehow have always managed to fit me in at one of their six tables. Inexpensive.

A little farther up the street there is a three-storey, open-sided building next to the Mercado Hidalgo. This is a sort of restaurant/department store where the sellers who used to operate on the sidewalk on the opposite side of the market now have their permanent stalls. No two of them serve exactly the same thing, and I've had everything from pozole to blood-sausage sandwiches there at one time or another. This is the best value in town for a very wide assortment of basic dishes. Restrooms are on the top floor. Inexpensive.

Do-it-yourselfers will enjoy the *Pastelería Santa Fe* on the Plaza de la Paz across from the Basilica de Nuestra Señora de Guanajuato. It is both a bakery and a pastry-shop and a good place to pick up some of the ingredients for a picnic. Inexpensive.

The last time I checked the best place to eat in downtown Guanajuato was the restaurant/sidewalk cafe of the Posada Santa Fe in the Jardín de Unión. This is recommended only if the price is no problem, for both the restaurant and the hotel are ridiculously expensive.

The 4 *Ranas* (Four Frogs) restaurant, overlooking the Jardín de la Unión and the Teatro Juárez, is actually the dining room of the Hotel San Diego and is located on the second floor thereof. It has good food, albeit with a rather limited menu, and I've never been served a bad bottle of the red. It's the only place in town to buy frogs' legs – naturally – and a place to be saved for those special occasions because it is ridiculously expensive.

The restaurants in the little bus station are a good choice for breakfast, especially the one that costs a peso to visit. Inexpensive.

There is a *simpático* sit-down bar on the Jardín Unión opposite the Agora. With lots of atmosphere and heavy, dark-polished wood, it's more like a better private club than the average Mexican saloon. The bar has a brick-red paint job and a sign reading 'La Ronda Bar y Carnes'. I've had a healing glass there from time to time, but have never eaten. Expensive.

Considering that Guanajuato is not on the main road to anywhere, it has exceptionally good bus service, and you can catch a bus to Guanajuato from the Central del Norte in Mexico City, or San Luis Potosí, or Guadalajara, or even Matamoros, but don't waste much time waiting for a direct connection. It may only run once or twice a day. Get a bus to León or Querétaro and then get another bus from there. Querétaro, especially, is a good shot. One bus company or another has a bus every half-hour or so. Forget the railroad, and the air service is poor.

SAN MIGUEL DE ALLENDE, Guanajuato
(elevation 1950 metres, population 40,000)

San Miguel de Allende is one of the four most photogenic and picturesque cities in Mexico. Its only peers are Guanajuato, Pátzcuaro and Taxco. Of the four, San Miguel is the one with the largest and most visible foreign colony.

As a retirement community San Miguel has a number of advantages. First off, until a very few years ago run-down buildings were dirt cheap and could be rehabilitated very economically. The weather is superb, unlike at Alamos where somewhat the same situation prevails but where the weather is hot as blue blazes in summer. San Miguel is rather more intellectual than the other three, due largely to the Instituto. Perhaps most important of all, there are so many English-speaking people around town that a retiree can get along just dandy without learning more than half a dozen words of the national language.

The town was founded by a Spanish priest, Juan de San Miguel. For many years it was called San Miguel el Grande to distinguish it from the numerous smaller San Miguels that clutter the map of Mexico.

One of the original conspirators in the revolution against Spain was a young man from San Miguel el Grande named Ignacio Allende. For his efforts he was executed by the Crown and his head wound up on a hook at one corner of the Alhóndiga in neighbouring Guanajuato. Immediately upon throwing off Spanish rule the town of San Miguel decided to honour its favourite son by adding his name to the town's existing name, a very common Mexican practice. The locals call it 'San Miguel' and let it go at that.

San Miguel owes its present-day beauty to the wealthy people of Guanajuato, who build their homes away from Guanajuato – always a rather difficult place to live, although nice to visit. And, although San Miguel was eclipsed by its neighbours up the road at Pozos and Guanajuato, it was once the centre of a prosperous mining district in its own right.

For San Miguel is one of the most handsome towns in Mexico, with fairly wide streets and quite moderate grades for a mountain community. Lots of the streets are cobblestoned, which makes it unwise to wear high heels. Many of the old buildings were occupied throughout their existence by families with the resources to keep them in good repair, and the town is full of beautiful unrestored structures. San Miguel is another monument town where plastic-fronted movie theatres and dirty Pemex stations are forbidden in the central city. For years it was a popular movie set for Hollywood and Churubusco filmmakers. *The Brave Bulls, Serenade*, and other major pictures were shot here.

The town's most distinctive landmark is the Parroquia. It started out in life as a nondescript Franciscan church, but the town wanted something unique to grace its plaza, and during the late 1800s it was rebuilt under the direction of an Indian stonecutter named Ceferino Gutierrez who in turn apparently received his inspiration from a postcard view of one of Europe's great cathedrals – stories disagree as to which one. The official name of the church, in case you're asked, is Parroquia y Santa Escuela de Cristo.

The Instituto Allende, just 'Instituto' to the residents, is the entity that can fairly take the credit for the renaissance of San Miguel. The Instituto is housed in a former convent and when it was started San Miguel was just another semi-ghost town sitting on the side of a hill and listening to its roofs cave in. The Instituto attracted well-off Americans who fell in love with the place and later returned to rehabilitate the then-cheap old houses and make San Miguel their homes. Even without the history it is entertaining to wander around the extensive grounds of the Instituto. To give some idea of the size of the place, there is a hotel with a parking lot located on the premises that is fairly well separated from the enclosing structures.

The Instituto has some competition nowadays from the Academia Hispano Americana, located at Reloj and Insurgentes in an old mansion complete with the usual beguiling patio. The Academia emphasizes its Spanish-language classes and is one of the better schools of its type in the Republic. Students are encouraged to take board and room with a local Mexican family and thereby entirely avoid hearing and using English. This 'immersion system' of language instruction is probably the most efficient technique going and I'm told the Academia has excellent results overall.

Essentially, however, San Miguel is a Mexican town that has been around for hundreds of years, with its own traditional enterprises that have nothing whatsoever to do with battening on the foreign visitors. For instance, San Miguel is the principal supplier of the 'colonial' lamps seen all over Mexico.

On your way out Calle Zacateros (street of the coffinmakers) for your inspection of the Instituto and its grounds, there are several factories and shops selling lamps and kindred items, such as candle-holders, vases, table lamps, salvers and so on. The goods in the shop of H Llamas, mostly brass, are of a particularly high order of craftsmanship. Other stores along the calle sell items made of sheet iron, tin plate, brass, silver, aluminum and even gold. Unlike the shops in Taxco, these largely provide items of a utilitarian, or quasi-utilitarian, nature.

On the plaza, to the right as you face the Parroquia, is the Colibri, a book and art supplies store that stocks Mexico's most extensive selection of English-language paperbacks and also selected magazines from the US. The two amiable, English-speaking women who run the Colibri have been around San Miguel for many years and are a priceless source of information about the place.

There is a library in San Miguel, run by the American colony, that specializes in English-language books. If interested, inquire at the Colibri for the address.

There is a Laundromat on Canal below the arch, diagonally across the street from the Posada de las Monjas. Recommended.

The grocery store with the best stock in town is located under the same set of portales as the Colibri. It has a large selection of things Americans are likely to

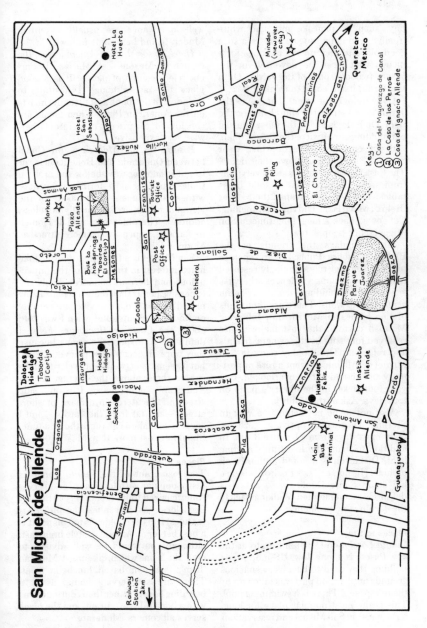

San Miguel de Allende

Key:-
① Casa del Mayorazgo de Canal
② La Casa de los Perros
③ Casa de Ignacio Allende

buy, such as pancake mix and white (really) granulated sugar, and is also a good place to pick up the makings for a picnic, which can be devoured in the *bosque* (woods) south of the Jardín. Or in the Jardín itself, come to think of it.

Calle Reloj is the street that leaves the Jardín' across from the church and on the right. On Reloj is one of the most unusual old buildings in Mexico, the Casa Cohen, with six entrances, five of which wear Stars of David carved above their doors. The Casa Cohen nowadays sells everything from spray paint in cans to solid brass tables. The Cohens still spell their street 'Relox', which is the Old Spanish spelling. Cohens go back a long, long time in San Miguel. Nice people, too.

Most Sundays the friends of the Biblioteca Publica (Public Library) sponsor tours of some of the stunningly restored mansions – fabulous residences otherwise sequestered behind massive doors set in centuries-old walls. There are thousands of fine homes in Mexico but, following Moorish custom, the vast majority are reserved for visits by the owners' friends and relatives. The Sunday tours in San Miguel de Allende present a rare opportunity and should not be overlooked. Buy your tour ticket in the library's patio on tour days. Ask at the Colibri.

Also not to be neglected is a visit to Sterling Dickinson's private gardens, open most days from 11 am to 3 pm. In addition to being the Instituto's guiding light, Dickinson is a noted authority on orchids. His home – 'Los Positos' – is on a hill at 38 Santo Domingo, so a taxi is definitely recommended. Walking back to the Jardín is no problem.

Places to Stay

Quinta Loreto, on Callejon Loreto at the new Paseo, is a long, low, US-motel-type building that used to have very spacious grounds until a good part was taken up by the new paseo. There is a swimming pool. This is the most popular place for long-term guests in San Miguel and reservations

well in advance are usually essential. Moderate and best value in town.

Hotel Mesón de San Antonio is at the corner of Mesones at Macias. Rooms encircle a couple of patios. It is a good place to stay, although I hesitate to include it in this book as it (usually) insists on the American Plan. When meals are considered, the price is moderate. Otherwise very expensive.

Posada de las Monjas is on Canal between Quebrada and Beneficencia, or to put it another way, below the arch on Calle Canal. It is a former convent – witness the name – that has been the victim of a new, architecturally tasteless, addition. The older part, which I much prefer, is less expensive and more attractive. Moderate.

San Miguel is a town that doesn't take much interest in the plight of the impecunious, and there are far more ridiculously expensive hotels than there are reasonably priced houses. I'd about given up entirely on finding a cheap hotel when I was told about the *Casa de Huéspedes Felix*. I didn't get to inspect the rooms because they were all occupied whenever I tried, but it seems neat, well kept, well run and a cut or three above the average Latin-American rooming house. It is on a side street off Zacateros in a maze of short streets – not far from the Jardín – and I suggest you take a cab there the first time. Shouldn't cost more than M$75-100.

Places to Eat

The restaurant at the *Quinta Loreto* is justly popular with foreigners and serves Americanized food. It gets very little play from locals as a result – the *indígenas* (natives) feel the cooking is too bland. It is a best bet for an American-style breakfast, although you would be well advised to omit the ham, which, like most Mexican 'ham', is a ham-based luncheon meat. There are set serving hours, as at a boarding house, rather than continuous as with a bona fide restaurant, and the place serves all comers. Moderate.

After the Loreto, the next-best breakfast spot is the *Carrusel* on Canal between Macias and Hidalgo, less than a block from the Jardín. The Carrusel serves American, Mexican and 'Continental'-style breakfasts until high noon. It's an odd place, a padded-seat saloon by night which uses the restaurant entrance, and a short-order joint during the day, dispensing hamburgers, hot cakes, bacon and eggs and so on. Expensive.

On the corner of the plaza by the Parroquia is the all-new *Terraza* restaurant. The Terraza was one of the oldest restaurants in San Miguel, but it was forced to close a few years back to make room for a religious equipment store. Now it has moved a few doors toward the post office from its previous location and some of the tables are out in the open on the terrace – hence its name. It is the best place in town for people-watching and sidewalk-café-ing. The Terraza is more popular with foreigners than residents, probably because of the prices. Expensive.

A very popular spot in the evening is the *Posada la Fuente – Mama Mia's*. Obviously aimed at the younger set in that the menu runs heavy to hamburgers and pizza, it appeals to just about all ages. Service is fairly prompt and unfailingly cheerful. This is a pleasant place of an evening, say around 10 pm. Moderate.

A place exceedingly popular with the foreign set is the *Bugambillas*, on Meson at he corner of Reloj. Food is quite good and the atmosphere is fairly authentic colonial, with the tables in the patio of an old mansion. Expensive.

If cost is no object then the best place in town is on Zacateros on the way out to the Instituto. It's called *Genios* and is located in a dowdy storefront on the right side of the street. The plain, rustic sign doesn't shout its message and it's easy to overlook. Unpretentious or not, Genios can come up with such things as tripe a la mode de Caen and oysters Rockefeller. Ridiculously expensive and worth it.

The restaurant in the *Las Monjas* hotel is only open for breakfast and lunch; for some reason it elects not to serve dinner. It makes a respectable job of the meals it does. As the residents of the Las Monjas, especially the long-term snowbirds, tend to be older North Americans, the food tends to be bland. Otherwise recommended. Moderate.

Getting There

There are several buses a day from the Central del Norte in Mexico City, and frequent service to Querétaro, Guanajuato, Celaya and so on. There is one problem: for some reason San Miguel has not seen fit to erect a central bus terminal, and the bus 'station' moves from time to time. It is now in its fourth location in less than a decade. Currently the buses stop down the hill in the middle of nowhere, about 10 blocks from the Jardín. For what it's worth, the stop is near the Jardín de San Juan de Dios, more or less at the corner of Los Organos and Beneficencia. Although it is not too far to walk, I suggest you catch a cab the first time – the maze of streets is confusing. If you elect to walk, the simplest way to get uptown is just to head uphill, meanwhile keeping a sharp eye out for the big churches in the neighbourhood of the plaza. Don't try it at night.

Trains haven't stopped at San Miguel in years, and there is no airport.

Mexico City (elevation 2207 metres, population 18,000,000)

The Mexicans simply say 'Mexico' when referring to their capital, but on some maps it is called La Ciudad de Mexico. The English-speaking call it Mexico City, but by any name it ranks as one of the great cities of the world.

It was laid out by the Spanish to their standard pattern in the early 16th century and has been the subject of improvements and alterations on an almost annual basis, the most notable of which was Maximilian's Paseo de la Reforma. A cosmopolitan, cultured individual, Maximilian wanted his capital to have a wide boulevard suitable for strolling ladies and gentlemen, the equal of Paris' Champs Elysees. In this undertaking, at least, he succeeded admirably. Today his Reforma is the centrepiece of the city and one of the world's great boulevards. When first built it ran only to Calle Hidalgo, but during the past few years it has been extended all the way out to Gonzalez.

The Spanish founders intended that the zócalo would be the heart of their city as it is in most of Mexico, and they took advantage of the flat terrain to lay out a huge plaza, one of the largest in the country. Around the zócalo are the National Cathedral, the City Hall, Capitol and the President's office. The national pawnshop is an afterthought.

The Spanish are also responsible for the Alameda, the expansive park a few blocks away; but in their day it was used for burning those unlucky enough to fall afoul of the Inquisition, and it was not until the reign of President Díaz that it began to take on the pleasing aspect it has today.

Mexico City has been the capital of Mexico since the days of the Aztecs. Cortés and his allies took it from the Aztecs by force of arms and made it their own capital in part, I suspect, because it provided a large selection of ready-cut building stones from the pyramids dotting the region.

From time immemorial Mexico City offered financial opportunity. First to the old Conquistadores, who became enormously wealthy men if they survived, and more recently to millions of the wretched and impoverished poor who automatically turned their faces to the capital as they were starved out of their home villages. Currently it is estimated that about 300,000 people a year move to the capital; and this, coupled with the natural increase in a population that translates 'the pill' as 'la aspirina', has strained the city's finite resources to the breaking point. To the foreigner the best evidence of this is the eye-watering, throat-searing, all-pervasive smog that blankets the city for weeks on end. On days when the smog is about average it can put Los Angeles to shame, and it poses a real problem for travellers with respiratory difficulties.

The population explosion has caused public transport to be all but unusable during certain hours of the day, has made the downtown sidewalks nearly unwalkable, and has created theatre lines that routinely stretch for blocks. Foreign travellers would be well advised to do as the more affluent natives do – to stay in Cuernavaca or one of the other outlying towns and commute to the city on one of the excellent bus lines.

The above remarks notwithstanding, Mexico City is one of the most fantastic communities in the world, and one I've enjoyed for years.

Street Names

Mexico City has the most confusing street-naming 'system' this side of Tokyo. With a few exceptions – notably Reforma and Insurgentes – every street has several names. For instance, one of the most important streets is the one that begins as Mexico Tacuba, changes its name first to Rivera de San Cosme, switches to Alvarado as it approaches the Reforma, changes again to Hidalgo on the opposite side of Reforma, and then when it gets to the other end of the Alameda changes to just plain Tacuba. Then it runs for a while and changes to Guatemala. And so on. For this reason I occasionally refer to a street as Alvarado/Hidalgo to try to simplify things.

Basically the system was very logical back in the days when Mexico City was, like Los Angeles, a number of suburbs in search of a city, and it caused no confusion at all to have a 'Hidalgo' in three or four little towns, but with the burgeoning population the small towns merged. As an indication of the magnitude of the problem, there are over 60 streets named Morelos in Mexico City.

So if you want to go anywhere, make sure you know the district in which your address is to be found. Otherwise your cab driver will be justified in picking the one that sounds logical to him, and in charging you for driving to the next street on the list if his first guess doesn't suit.

The Reforma

The Reforma was designed to be – and is – one of the great avenues of the world. I would recommend that you set aside one morning, preferably a Saturday or Sunday when the weekday crowds are absent, to stroll from the National Lottery Building at Hidalgo/Alvarado along the avenue to Chapultepec Park. This is the original length of the Reforma as conceived by Maximilian's architect. The addition extending beyond Alvarado is a recent afterthought, occasionally called La Reforma Nueva, and is rather dreary. This goes for the western end, beyond Chapultepec Park, as well.

Make this a stroll, not a heel-and-toe walk, so you can gawk unashamedly at the new buildings that spring up every year, window-shop, or gaze at the few great residences that still survive.

An impressive example of late 19th-century construction is the multi-tiered, towered brownstone at the corner of Reforma and Guadalquivir. It sits on some of the most expensive real estate in the world, where land sells for pesos per square cm, and each time I make this stroll I pause and admire and wonder how long before simple economics cause it to be replaced by a 22-storey example of Bauhaus Mexican Modern design.

Another fine old home houses the University Club at Lucerna. It has been fitted out with a black-and-white canvas marquee, but this doesn't detract from the elegance of the basic structure.

The Japanese Embassy at Rio Nilo strikes me as probably the premier example of restrained contemporary design in Mexico.

Chapultepec Park

My stroll ends at Chapultepec Park and its seven museums, lakes, amusement park complete with scary roller coaster, and the old battlefield of Molino del Rey.

The internationally renowned Museum of Anthropology is here, but you really need a whole day to devote to touring it, or better yet, two or three.

National Museum of History

In Chapultepec Castle itself is the National Museum of History. This museum contains a large amount of memorabilia pertaining to the country's history, and also the residence of Maximilian and Carlotta, including Carlotta's beautifully refurbished quarters. The formal gardens were designed by Carlotta herself.

The main museum has a grand assemblage of such artifacts as a whole room full of pianos, the largest collection of horological instruments this side of the British Museum, and a carriage collection that rates a building of its own. It is worthwhile to spend several hours wandering around the History Museum alone. More time is needed to see the other museums.

Molino del Rey

When you stroll back along the Reforma, this time on the opposite side of the street, the Molino del Rey is on the far side of the

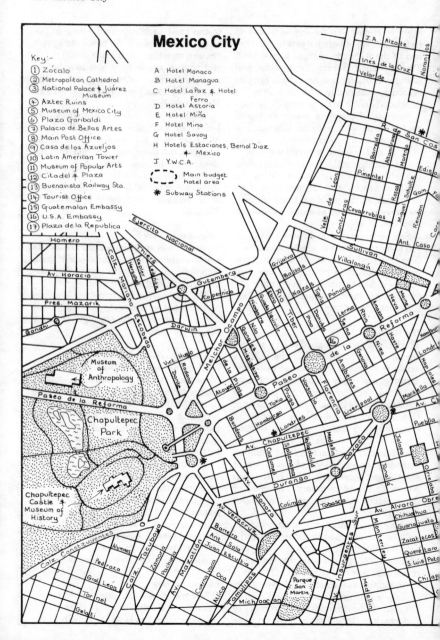

Mexico City

Key:-
1. Zócalo
2. Metropolitan Cathedral
3. National Palace & Juárez Museum
4. Aztec Ruins
5. Museum of Mexico City
6. Plaza Garibaldi
7. Palacio de Bellas Artes
8. Main Post Office
9. Casa de los Azueljos
10. Latin American Tower
11. Museum of Popular Arts
12. Citadel & Plaza
13. Buenavista Railway Sta.
14. Tourist Office
15. Guatemalan Embassy
16. U.S.A. Embassy
17. Plaza de la Republica

A. Hotel Monaco
B. Hotel Managua
C. Hotel La Paz & Hotel Ferro
D. Hotel Astoria
E. Hotel Miña
F. Hotel Mina
G. Hotel Savoy
H. Hotels Estaciones, Bernal Diaz & Mexico
J. Y.W.C.A.

Main budget hotel area

Subway Stations

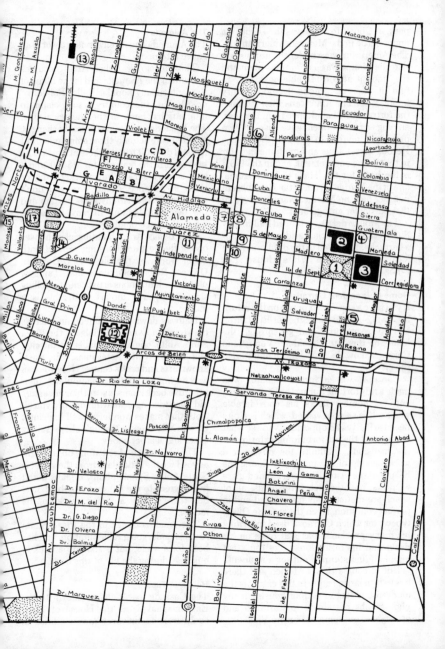

park, at Chivatito. This was the scene of a major battle in the Mexican-American war. The Americans were under the impression that the Molino was a munitions plant and they took it at considerable cost, only to find it was of practically no military importance. The Americans then stormed the fortress of Chapultepec from the rear, an engagement which gave rise to two persistent myths: In Mexico the 'Ninos Heroes' street signs and monuments refer to that losing engagement, and in the US it is the basis for the 'Halls of Montezuma' line in the Marine Hymn of the Republic. In point of fact, no Marines were involved in that particular engagement.

The Molino del Rey is the red building by the President's official residence. It is now a barracks and closed to the public, as is the local version of the White House, Los Pinos.

Home of President Carranza

If you have a spare hour or two on the return leg, swing over to the corner of Río Lerma and Río Amazonas and go through the home of the late President Venustiano Carranza, now the least-known museum in the city.

Carranza was a former senator who made a tidy fortune during the Díaz regime, and his home reflects his considerable wealth. It is seldom visited, which is a pity because it gives an opportunity to see what lies behind the oft-forbidding exteriors of the mansions. I admire the design and workmanship of the parquetry floors, the beauty of the tastefully-done stained-glass windows, and the rich furnishings, all of which are meticulously maintained and in perfect condition. Even the antique Oliver typewriter which Carranza used in writing his many proclamations still rests on his desk, and his office looks like the great man had just stepped out for a moment.

But of course this is Mexico and there has to be a jarring note. In this case it is the modern building next door housing many photographs pertaining to Carranza and his regime, but none of Pancho Villa.

The Alameda

The Alameda and its environs are worth an entire afternoon.

The Palacio de Bellas Artes occupies one end of the Alameda and is the home of the fantastically popular Ballet Folklorico de Mexico, the country's sole claim to international fame in the theatrical line. The Folklorico program constantly changes, and there are actually three companies, but it is still difficult to get tickets at times. The best seats in the house go for M$300, and it may be necessary to buy a ticket a day or three in advance. Make sure you don't arrive late – the Tiffany glass curtain and the beautiful lighting display alone are worth the price of admission.

The Bellas Artes building also houses one of the best art museums around, with major works by the big five: O'Gorman, Orozco, Rivera, Siquerios and Tamayo, plus other indigenous artists and travelling shows. If you're an art buff, this is a must.

Halfway down the Alameda and across the street on Avenida Hidalgo is the Plaza Santa Anita, one of the smallest in the city, and the Mercado Artesanias, the least-known arts and crafts centre. Here you can watch women deftly manipulate their primitive back looms just as their ancestors did centuries ago, weaving *típico* (typical) cloth that makes wonderful wall hangings. Or you can browse through shops selling silver and leather goods.

The old church of red stone on the right as you face the little plaza from the street is Santa Anita. Spanish-built, it leans about five degrees to the left due to subsidence, but there's nary a major crack in the facade.

The small complex in the Plaza Santa Anita is undergoing rehabilitation, and has been for a while, but it should be back in business during the life of this book.

House of Tiles

The Casa de los Azulejos, known to the English-speaking as the House of Tiles, could well be the best-known edifice in

Mexico, and one of the best extant examples of Mudejar decoration. It was built in 1596 without the tiles. These were added by one of the descendants of the Count of the Valley of Orizaba who had married a wealthy woman. The house has had a varied history, often bloody. One of the former owners was murdered on the grand staircase, above today's dining room, and at one time it was the home of the Jockey Club. It is now owned by the Sanborn chain, with the usual shops on the ground floor, and the company's general offices on the second. The restaurant is located in the original patio. The feature that contributes so much to the attractiveness of the House of Tiles is that it began as a private home and Messrs Sanborn did not make any changes so the house essentially remains as it did back in the days when grand balls were held in the patio. A definite must. It is reached by passing the Alameda on Juárez, which then changes its name to Madero.

Main Post Office

While in the neighbourhood step into the Main Post Office, at the corner of Cárdenas and Tacuba/Hidalgo. It is one of the best instances of spare-no-expense imitation colonial designs in Mexico City. It was completed under the Díaz regime, about 1907. The inside lives up to the promise of the exterior, with the beautiful bronze and woodwork you might find in a profitable private bank of the day. For philatelists the stamp collection displayed on the first floor is a pleasure and a delight.

Torre Latinoamericana

Another point of interest in the same vicinity is the 44-storey Torre Latinoamericana at Juárez and Cárdenas near the end of the Alameda. Its construction was a major engineering accomplishment because of the softness of the ground and the continuing subsidence. The very best view of the city is from the observation deck, or – better yet – from the tower on top of the building. Buy a ticket in the lobby – the

elevator from the ground floor only goes part way. At the top end of the elevator trip you can either admire the view or climb some stairs to the flat roof. And if you're still game – I'm not – it is possible to climb even higher into the tower proper, some 150 metres or so above the street. The gigantic city is fantastic at any time of day, but it's absolutely breathtaking after dark when it seems as if the whole valley lights up. The view is best immediately after a rain when the ever-present smog is at a minimum.

The Zócalo

Proceed along Juarez/Madero away from the Alameda five blocks from the Tower and you come to the zócalo. Its official title is the Plaza de Constitucion. Originally, the zócalo had a fine collection of greenery, but it interfered with the aim of some cannoneers who were bombarding the Palacio Nacional during some revolution or other, and the trees fell victim to the gods of war. Naturally the government never quite got around to replacing them.

Later, most of the streetcar lines converged on the zócalo, and when the trams were phased out – a great mistake as later events proved – the square was concreted. The Metro is beneath it now, and there is an underground walkway running diagonally under the zócalo to the Pino Suarez Metro station, built so that pedestrians could avoid some of the intolerable congestion of the weekday downtown sidewalks.

The best time to see the zócalo is at night, not during the day when the jostling multitudes interfere with contemplation. At night, too, the well-planned lighting system enhances the buildings surrounding the plaza – something the hazy sunlight doesn't do.

National Cathedral

The National Cathedral that occupies most of one side of the zócalo is worth an hour or two. The cathedral is built on the site of an earlier church which was razed in 1573; it had also been constructed on another building. The cathedral was pretty well finished in 1667, but it took another 130 years to add the towers, and the building still isn't quite complete. As it now stands, the cathedral is a mismatch of different styles and designs and technically speaking the whole thing doesn't work very well. The lantern and dome are by Tolsa, for instance, and are not really appropriate for the edifice. The end result of all this combining of assorted bits and pieces is a huge building that manages to dominate the zócalo by sheer size.

The cathedral was seriously damaged by a fire in 1967. The fire was supposedly started by faulty wiring, and the repair work is still underway. (Mexican wiring today is the same invitation to disaster as the installation that nearly destroyed the interior of the cathedral.)

The small church to the right of the cathedral as you face it looks like a part of the cathedral, but it isn't. It's the Sagario Metropolitano, a separate church, both physically and politically, in its own right. It is in a different parish entirely and serves as the local church.

Palacio Nacional

The Palacio Nacional is another building that was accumulated rather than built, a process that took 235 years. It is a veritable treasure trove of salons, ballrooms and beautiful halls, and much of it is open to the public. Over the centre entrance hangs the bell that Fray Hidalgo rang when he called for Mexican Independence. It is rung each year on 15 September at 11 am by the President who then recites the words of the original Grito. This always brings an immense throng to the zócalo. On any other day tourists by the thousands enter to view the vast murals by Diego Rivera, murals that occupied the last quarter century of his life. The murals were unfinished because the master died during the project. His sketches exist and, though it would be a simple matter to complete the work as designed, it was decided to leave them as they are as a monument to Mexico's greatest wall painter.

Entrance is by the centre door. The right-hand entrance as you face the building is reserved for El Presidente, and the left leads to the Juárez Museum, mostly of interest to Mexican patriots and the few foreign Mexican history buffs.

A pre-Cortés site is being excavated on the side of the Sagario and on the opposite side of the street. First discovered in 1913, work has been underway most of the time since, and new and interesting discoveries are still being made. Most of the objects taken from the hole have wound up in the Museum of Anthropology in Chapultepec Park, but there is still enough to warrant a look-see.

Monte de Piedad

Some bargain hunters are more interested in the Monte de Piedad than in all the rest of the buildings in the zócalo put together. The Monte de Piedad is the national pawnshop, with branches all over Mexico. It was started by the Conde de Regla, a miner who made a huge fortune around Pachuca, in 1775. The building itself was built by Cortés as a vice-regal palace. The pawnshop is operated by the government in the public benefit and makes loans on almost anything, except livestock, that can be brought through the door. There aren't that many bargains, but every now and then there is a sleeper.

Museum of the City of Mexico

Another old home, now converted into a museum, is at the corner of Pino Suarez and El Salvador. Originally called La Casa de Conde de Santiago de Calimaya, it was built in 1598 and until 1964 was occupied by descendants of the builder. It has now become the Museum of the City of Mexico and should be on the must-see list of any visitor who desires an overview of the history of the area, from the pre-Aztecs to Villa and Zapata. Even for those with a total and complete lack of interest in things historical it should be included in any reconnaissance of the area, just for the building itself.

Monumento de la Revolución

On the other side of the Reforma from the zócalo is the Monumento de la Revolución.

Located at the end of Juarez, it started out as a new capitol building, the last major effort of the Díaz era. It was no more than underway when Díaz was deposed, whereupon all work stopped. When things quieted down there wasn't enough money left to complete the structure, so someone had the happy idea of converting it into a monument to the just-ended Revolución. The two wings that had been partially built were demolished, and the bodies of Villa, Zapata, Carranza, Calles, Madero and Cárdenas were interred there so the building became a monument. Mexicans often refer to it as 'El Elefante'. In keeping with its nickname, the building is huge – 62 metres high – with other dimensions to match.

Museo de San Carlos

The Museo de San Carlos is on Alvarado opposite Aldama, but for some reason some guidebooks and maps show it on the opposite side of the Reforma. Locally it is sometimes known as La Casa de Buenavista because for many years it was the home of the family of that name. The building itself is superb. Designed by the same Tolsa who did the dome of the Cathedral, it is a much better feat. The San Carlos Museum houses the best collection of European paintings in Latin America and continually presents travelling shows. On the first floor of the semicircular mezzanine is an interesting collection of sculpture by Mexican artists.

Plaza Garibaldi

The Plaza Garibaldi comes alive at night. Garibaldi is also referred to as the Plaza de los Mariachis, which pretty well sums up its after-dark attractions. There are lots of nightclubs in the neighbourhood, including some of the city's raunchiest. Not generally recommended at night for unescorted ladies – young, old, liberated or otherwise. The plaza has quite a few cheap restaurants, including a number of *restaurantes a la mesa* – restaurants on the table – said table placed on the sidewalk. The plaza is on Avenida Lázaro Cárdenas at Avenida Republica de Honduras, about a 15-minute walk from the Alameda.

Markets

Mexico City is so large that it has a number of good-sized markets. They are fairly well arranged as a general rule, with different types of merchandise segregated into different areas. My favourite is the Lagunilla, on Allende at Rayon. Not as big as some of the others, it has two fairly large buildings and is really more of a bazaar than a market. A fine place for shopping for such practical items as comales, huaraches, belts, lamps and so on. The easiest way to get there is by Metro. Go out to the Allende station and walk north on Allende.

Near here is the Sunday Market, an incredible open-air market specializing in the widest assortment of new, slightly used and used-up merchandise under the sun, displayed on stands, on the pavement, on sidewalks, on trays and even pinned to merchants' suit jackets. The market is only for experienced hagglers, because here you are dealing with people more concerned with the worth of the customer than the value of the merchandise. Nevertheless, someone told me about a valuable antique porcelain tray purchased here for a pittance. It was later sold for enough to underwrite the lucky purchaser's trip to Mexico.

Places to Stay

The hotel situation in Mexico City has been getting worse year by year. Part of it is due to the rampant inflation that has the Republic by the purse strings, and the rest is caused by the merciless application of the law of demand and supply. There have been no low-price hotels built in the capital for years, and every year a few more are torn down to make way for new office buildings. This has created a sellers' market in economical housing unequalled outside of London.

This is not to say that there are no reasonably priced hotels left, but those that survive are in 'less desirable' neighbourhoods and very definitely aren't in the Zona Rosa, where the imitation-Gucci shop is located, where the super-expensive spas have their town offices, and where the majority of the fancy restaurants and some of the very best hotels do business. But surprisingly, there are low-priced hotels within four or five blocks of the Alameda, and one or two not too far from the Zona Rosa, which is generally agreed to be around the Sheraton Hotel on the Reforma.

The vicinity of the Plaza San Fernando, at Guerrero and Alvarado, used to be laced with economical hostels but these days they are nearly all expensive, to say the least. For years I used to stop at the *Hotel Monaco*. I liked the house, the location, and the comfortable little tree-shaded plaza across the street, but during the past few years the rates have become very expensive.

Similarly, the *Hotel Managua* across the plaza from the Monaco, the *Hotel La Paz* and the *Hotel Ferro* on Mina, and the *Hotel Astoria* on Zarco off Mina have all elevated themselves into the very expensive class, or are planning on doing so very shortly.

The *Hotel Mina* at Salgado and Mina is a quiet, well-run hotel with a mosaic facade and was happy to be inexpensive a few years ago. Now it is very expensive, too.

But things get better as you go along Alvarado away from the Reforma. The last street before reaching Insurgentes Norte is Bernal Díaz and in the first block on Díaz there are the *Hotel Estaciones*, the *Hotel Díaz* and the *Hotel Mexico*. This is an industrial neighbourhood, mostly devoted to the express package departments of the various bus companies and very congested during weekdays, but deserted after nightfall and weekends. All these hotels are moderate, but have been known to drop into the inexpensive bracket because of an expression of dismay on the face of the prospective guest.

The *Hotel Savoy*, on Zaragoza right off Alvarado, is a newish hotel conveniently located but without a centavo wasted on ambience. Expensive.

A bit farther along Zaragoza is the green-fronted *Hotel Miña* (not Mina), even less attractive from the street than its neighbours. A glance through the front door tends to dishearten those with too much luggage – there are no less than 34 steps up to the first-floor lobby. But once the heights are scaled the Miña turns out to be quite comfortable, with large rooms and firm, lump-free mattresses. Moderate.

The aged *Hotel Cortez*, on Hidalgo a few steps off the Reforma, looks from the outside like a genuine inexpensive find, but it is a part of the Best Western chain of motels and hotels and is ridiculously expensive.

A good hotel for walkers is the *Hotel Marin* at the corner of Caso and León. León intersects the Reforma near the Colon monument and the Sanborn store. Don't be misled by the three styles and types of brickwork in the front. Over the years a couple of additions have been grafted on the peculiar half-hexagonal building. The Marin gets almost no tourist play and so is little affected by the vagaries of that volatile trade. It often has rooms available when everything else in town is full. Moderate.

There are quite a few small hotels between Alvarado and the Buena Vista station. If you walk out on Insurgentes Norte you can see a number of them. Because they are rather off the beaten path they get very few foreign travellers. They quite often have rooms when all else is full, but there are entirely too many to list here. They are, however, a defense against sleeping on the railroad station floor.

The *Asociación Cristiana Femenina*, the Mexican YWCA, is on Humboldt and Articulo 123, three blocks from the Alameda and one block from the Juarez Metro station. Reports recommend it highly as a safe and economical place for women to stay right downtown. Moderate.

A practical alternative to actually staying overnight in Mexico City is to get a hotel room in Cuernavaca. This can be a necessity at times, especially in summer, when it is practically impossible to rent a hotel room in the capital. Also you'll avoid the smog, which can be extremely irritating. If you do decide this is the way to go, get a room well ahead of time, say about noon. Cuernavaca can fill up too.

Places to Eat

One of the best *VIPs* restaurants is just one block off the Reforma on Ramirez. Chain operations make every effort to standardize their branches, but the fact remains that they aren't equal. VIPs is a businesslike outfit and although it is definitely US-oriented the majority of the customers are from the local community. In the case of the VIPs on Ramirez many of the customers are editorial staff of the area's several newspapers. There is another VIPs not too far away, on the corner of Insurgentes and the Reforma, but I definitely prefer the one on Ramirez, with its spotless johns. Expensive.

The *Parillada Zurich*, on the Reforma down the street from Sanborn's Lafragua and Reforma branch, is a restaurant specializing in *queso al carbón* – charcoal-grilled cheese. The Reforma today is about evenly divided between Burger Boys and super-expensive hotel dining rooms, and the Zurich falls somewhere in between. Although primarily a place to grab a quick snack, it does pretty well in the meal department. Ideal for Saturday afternoon when it is fairly uncrowded. Inexpensive.

About as close as you can get to a genuine American hamburger will set you back around M$300, or as much as the average comida corrida. And even for $300 you can't seriously expect to receive a Big Mac. The Mexican version resembles a British Wimpy more than it does its US counterpart.

The largest assortment of low to medium-priced restaurants is located at *Insurgentes Plaza*, the Metro station three blocks off

the Reforma on Genova. The plaza is about 200 metres across and lined with everything from a *Burger King* to a restaurant accepting every known credit card. It also has book shops, a natural food store, a record outlet and even a Conasupo supermarket. The plaza offers the widest assortment of everything and is not too far from Chapultepec Park.

The *Centro Cultural Librerías Reforma*, on the Reforma between Lafragua and Juarez, is a combination coffee house and bookstore. This is not too unusual in Europe, but is a rare combination on this side of the ocean, north or south. Only Spanish-language books are sold, but I've seen customers reading English, German, French, Dutch and a couple of languages I couldn't identify, along with their *café con leche* or Cerveza Corona. This is a hangout for readers, writers, scholars and print-media professionals, and I have yet to see anyone reading one of the ubiquitous comic books. Moderate.

When Guerrero crosses Alvarado it becomes Rosales and on this short street are located two of the handiest and most economical restaurants to the Alameda. First is the *Restaurante Nacional*. The Nacional serves almost the same traditional Mexican food as a small-town restaurant in Michoacan. Inexpensive.

Or you can go a few metres up the street to the *Cafe Rosales* and have a go at that internationally famous Canadian delicacy, chop suey. If your taste buds don't lust for ersatz Chinese, try their pastry with a cup of coffee. In any event the tab will be inexpensive.

Sanborn's House of Tiles serves American-oriented food with Mexican overtones. The soda fountain is the place for a quick snack or a chocolate sundae. For a main meal I definitely recommend eating in the old patio, two floors high and glassed over. The soda fountain is expensive, the restaurant ridiculously expensive, but it's worth it at least once.

The little arts and crafts market off the Plaza Santa Anita, halfway along the

Alameda on Hidalgo, contains a couple of 'típico' restaurants, and I make it a point to eat in one of them, the *Restaurante Fonda Santa Anita Alameda*, at least one afternoon each time I visit Mexico City. Inexpensive.

Getting There

Air The vast majority of travellers arrive in Mexico City by air, and Mexico City International is, and always has been, the crossroads of Latin-American air travel. There are so many airlines flying to Mexico City that it seems there is always an excursion or special promotional fare available. See the Getting There chapter for more details.

There is a departure tax, usually around US$10 (payable in local currency), and Mexican airlines charge 15% for late cancellations and 50% of the fare for no-shows unless the seat happens to be sold to someone who was on standby.

Bus Things get a little more complicated for those arriving by bus as there are no less than four intercity bus stations. The largest and most popular is the huge Terminal del Norte, which handles almost all of the buses going to and from the northern part of the country, including some services to Veracruz and Manzanillo. As you enter the concourse you will see ticket booths selling taxi tickets. If you want a taxi, tell the ticket seller where you are going, buy your ticket, and find a taxi going in your direction. This is another *colectivo* arrangement – ride-sharing, that is.

If you don't want a taxi, keep right on going past the ticket booth and look for a city bus marked 'Terminal Norte – Plaza Insurgentes' which will take you to the heart of town, turning around at the Insurgentes Metro Station.

Somewhat cheaper is to take the Metro, and there is a new station right in front of the Terminal. Just walk over, look at the system maps on the wall, figure out how you are going to get to your destination, buy a ticket (five tickets for five pesos) and set

out. But be warned that rush hour on the Mexico City Metro is like no other public transportation rush hour in the world. You will be turned back if you have too much baggage (another advantage of the tote bag system), but during the rush hour you will probably be turned back even with a tote bag.

If you don't intend to stop over in Mexico City and plan on continuing immediately to Cuernavaca and Acapulco, you will need to change bus stations to the Central del Sur. There is a shuttle bus running between these two popular stations marked 'Centro Médico – Hospital la Raza', or perhaps 'Central del Norte'. To go downtown, catch a No 7D.

The Central del Sur is hard by the Taxquena Metro station. Go out the front door of the bus station and turn right and follow the crowd. The Metro will take you direct to Hidalgo and the Reforma.

The Terminal de Autobuses de Pasajeros de Oriente handles most of the passengers to Veracruz, Puebla, Yucatán, Oaxaca and Guatemala. It is located at the Lázaro Metro station for the benefit of those with a reasonable amount of luggage. You can also take a Ruta 100 bus to the Alameda and the Reforma. Most of the buses continue on to the western terminal, the Terminal Poniente de Autobuses. It is the smallest of the lot and essentially handles Toluca traffic.

The Metro stop for the Terminal Poniente bus station is Observatoria.

Rail There is only one railroad station in Mexico City now that the narrow-gauge railroad is a thing of the past. Officially it is the Terminal de Ferrocarriles de Mexico, but it is called Estación Buena Vista by the locals after one of the leading families. Trains to all parts of Mexico, from Mérida to Mexicali, arrive and depart here, although it is impossible to buy a ticket for a trip passing through Mexico City – in this respect trains are like buses.

Because train fares are lower than bus fares, except sleepers, the trains tend to be crowded with people to whom a couple of pesos is important money. The second-class cars become littered as soon as a train leaves the station, and the first-class is only slightly better. If for some reason you elect to take a train, by all means go Pullman, even if it is a day trip and you will be unable to use the berth.

The Buena Vista station is on Insurgentes Norte a short distance from Alvarado. It takes about 15 to 20 minutes to walk there from Alvarado/Hidalgo and Reforma. Or you can catch a bus at Plaza Insurgentes headed for the Terminal del Norte bus station and unload as you pass the railroad depot.

To get downtown from the railroad station by bus, go out the front door, turn right and cross Insurgentes Norte and catch the first bus that comes along. All things considered, I prefer to walk.

While you're at the Buena Vista, take a gander at the locomotive on display near the front door – it's a Shay. As with all Mexico's display steamers, it looks as if it is ready to be fired up and driven off under its own steam. Vandalism is not a problem in Mexico.

Getting Around

Airport Transport Expect the airport to be undergoing repairs and/or alterations. Like San Francisco International, it has been under construction for 20 years that I know of and no sooner do they finish one project than they commence another.

The airport is not too far from the centre of things and the most popular way to get downtown is via one of the VW vans they call *colectivos*. They take off as soon as they are loaded, and if you let the driver know you aren't in any hurry you will probably wind up with a grand tour of the central part of the city. Price: around M$500.

There are also special city buses that stop in front of the terminal and run to the Alameda. They have luggage space, charge around M$150, and display a destination sign that says 'Centro' or 'Alameda' or the like.

The all-out cheapest way to get downtown is to get a Metro subway train in front of the terminal. You are bound for the Hidalgo station, which is on the corner of Hidalgo/Alvarado and the Reforma, and will have to transfer. Maps are posted in all the Metro stations, so it is easy to figure out how to get around. Tickets cost a peso each in blocks of five. One at a time, a peso and a half.

Don't try the Metro during the rush hours in the morning and afternoon, and note that hand-carried luggage is definitely not permitted. During the rush hour even tote bags may be turned back.

Public Transport Transport in Mexico City is a disaster during the rush hours, which are essentially the same as rush hours in any city, except they seem to last longer. Cabs are unavailable except perhaps at the terminals; buses are jammed and pass by customers at every stop. And these remarks go triple for the Metro which has gotten so bad – 6,000,000 passengers a day – that there are separate lanes at many stations for women and children to save the children from being crushed and women from being fondled.

I've found it best to skip public transportation entirely for these periods, which is not as bad as it sounds because downtown Mexico City's points of interest are mostly within walking distance of each other.

Guards are posted at the Metro stations during the rush hours to turn back people with bulky packages, suitcases and whatnot. I've even seen a few well-dressed gentlemen refused admittance because they carried ordinary briefcases. Outside of the rush hours I have never had any problems riding the Metro with my small shoulder tote bag.

For some obscure reason, many Europeans like to travel with huge framed packsacks and I've seen them turned back even during the late evening hours when the cars were running with about a dozen passengers apiece.

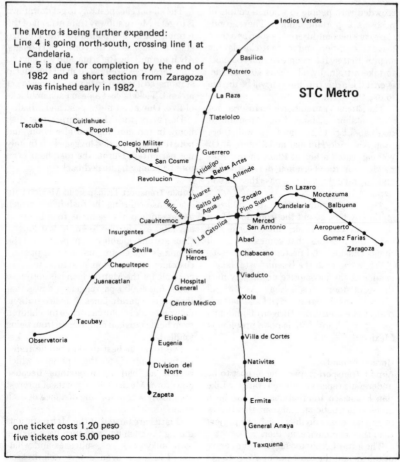

The Metro is being further expanded:
Line 4 is going north-south, crossing line 1 at Candelaria.
Line 5 is due for completion by the end of 1982 and a short section from Zaragoza was finished early in 1982.

STC Metro

Indios Verdes
Basilica
Potrero
La Raza
Tlatelolco
Tacuba
Cuitlahuac
Popotla
Colegio Militar Normal
San Cosme
Guerrero
Hidalgo
Bellas Artes
Revolucion
Allende
Juarez
Zocalo
Sn Lazaro
Moctezuma
Salto del Agua
Pino Suarez
Candelaria
Balbuena
Balderas
Cuauhtemoc
I La Catolica
Merced
San Antonio
Aeropuerto
Insurgentes
Abad
Gomez Farias
Sevilla
Ninos Heroes
Chabacano
Zaragoza
Chapultepec
Juanacatlan
Hospital General
Viaducto
Centro Medico
Xola
Tacubay
Etiopia
Observatoria
Eugenia
Villa de Cortes
Division del Norte
Nativitas
Zapata
Portales
Ermita
one ticket costs 1.20 peso
five tickets cost 5.00 peso
General Anaya
Taxquena

AROUND MEXICO CITY
Guadalupe

The Virgin of Guadalupe is the most venerated saint in Mexico. The story has it she appeared to an Indian named Juan Diego and told him that a church should be built at the place where they met. The bishop didn't believe Diego's story and requested additional proof. The Virgin appeared to Diego a second time and instructed him to pick some flowers on a hill where no flowers had ever grown. He picked the flowers and carried them in a cloth to the bishop. When the bishop unwrapped the flowers the image of the Virgin was imprinted on the cloth. Now the cloth hangs over the the altar in the Basilica of Guadalupe in a gold frame.

Annual pilgrimages to the church grew to involve so many people that there was not enough room to accommodate the multitude. At present a gigantic basilica is being built, designed by the same architect who did the fine Museum of Anthropology.

Many of the pilgrims to Guadalupe still follow the ancient practice of approaching the Basilica on their hands and knees, sometimes crawling for several km. This is an ongoing practice, but from 3-12 December it reaches a degree of frenzy that astonishes foreigners. So many people come to visit the Virgin that they wind up sleeping on the streets in the area around the church because the hotels are full. There is another, somewhat less well-attended, pilgrimage during Easter Holy Week.

Guadalupe will take the better part of a day, assuming you start around 9.30 am and return in the late afternoon.

Twenty-five years ago Guadalupe was out in the countryside, and the fashion was to walk out to Sunday mass from the town centre, but now the city has engulfed the little village and the walk is no longer very popular. Most people take the Metro and get off at the Basilica station.

Floating Gardens of Xochimilco
In the opposite direction are the Floating Gardens of Xochimilco, which were once just that. In the beginning, twigs were woven into rafts capable of supporting a thin layer of earth. Flowers and vegetables were planted and eventually their roots grew through the floats and anchored the rafts. Eventually the rafts became small islands. Today the term 'floating garden' usually refers to the boatloads of flowers picked for the Mexico City market.

Xochimilco is extremely popular with the locals as a picnic site, and hundreds of families spend Saturday and Sunday here, eating, drinking beer and enjoying the domestic scene. They load up with picnic supplies at the supermarket at Taxquena and then take one of the red PCC tram cars that stop outside the door of the Metro station.

To hire a boat and a poler to propel it costs around M$2000 an hour, a lot more than it is worth for one or two people. I'd say skip it unless you can get up a group to split the cost.

Xochimilco is a city in its own right, with about 125,000 inhabitants. The easiest way to get there is to take the Metro to the end of the line at Taxquena station and change to one of the red PCC trams that stop right outside the door of the Metro station.

Pyramids of San Juan Teotihuacán
The pyramids of San Juan Teotihuacán are among the most striking in Mexico. At one time the pyramids were the centrepiece of a thriving community of something like 100,000 people. They were abandoned around 700 AD; nobody knows why. Today they are well-manicured relics, maintained as a tourist magnet by the government.

If you're a ruins buff these are among the most convenient, spectacular and economical to visit in Mexico. To get there, go out to the Terminal del Norte and buy a ticket from one of the ticket counters to the far left as you enter the terminal. The trip takes about an hour, and the bus will drop you off at the gate. Pack a lunch – commercial feeding facilities are unreliable. There is a small entrance fee. To return, catch a bus where you got off and pay the driver's assistant. There are lots of buses going both ways.

Tula
Tula is another abandoned city a little farther out than Teotihuacán. Here are located the famous Pyramids of the Sun and Moon that you see on so many tourist-oriented advertisements and brochures. It is one of the most popular pre-Colombian sites in Mexico, and justly so.

Tula is not quite as easy to reach as Teotihuacan because the bus stops about a half-hour's walk from the entrance. I suggest you take a cheap taxi out from town and pack a lunch. Get your bus tickets for Tula at the left end of the concourse in the Terminal del Norte. There are actually several bus lines serving both sites – watch the signs in the back of the ticket offices. The bus takes about two hours. Again, catch the return bus where you got off.

South & East of Mexico City

Places east of Mexico City, including Veracruz, Oaxaca, San Cristóbal las Casas and the Yucatán, can all be reached by bus from the Terminal de Autobuses de Pasajeros de Oriente. The terminal is hard by the San Lazaro Metro station, and is also accessible by the Ruta 100 bus that you can pick up on the Reforma downtown. The leading bus lines, first class, are the ADO (Autobuses de Oriente) and the Cristóbal Colón (which runs all the way to the Guatemalan border by Comitan). Service is frequent and good, and is only slightly higher in price than second class.

Trains for Veracruz, Mérida and Oaxaca leave from the Estación Buena Vista on Insurgentes Norte.

The region also has excellent air service provided by Aeromexico (formerly Aeronaves) and Mexicana, plus a host of local airlines.

PUEBLA, Puebla

(elevation 2149 metres, population 1,000,000)

Many cities in Mexico can, with justification, lay claim to a rich and lusty history, but Puebla has been involved in almost everything that has happened in and to the country since Cortés first tramped through on his way to take on the Aztecs.

Puebla is also involved in the USA's history. Back in 1847 the city was captured quite easily by General Winfield Scott, who was on his way to take Mexico City and win the Mexican-American war. He had fought several pitched battles on his way up the hill from Veracruz, most notably the battle of Cerro Gordo, and he decided to leave Colonel Thomas Childs behind in Puebla with about 400 sick and wounded men who were unfit for service.

Scott anticipated no particular difficulties, believing that General Santa Ana would busy himself with readying for the eventual defense of Mexico City. Things didn't work out precisely as anticipated, and Santa Ana, who badly needed a fresh victory after a series of defeats brought on mostly by his own ineptitude, elected to recapture Puebla instead of concentrating on the main issue at the capital.

Childs got wind of the impending attack and collected a number of cattle, a few hundred sheep and some military equipment, forting up in the zócalo. Santa Ana, because he had 2500 men, expected a repeat of the Alamo episode and a 'great victory' that would fuel propaganda. Things didn't go as Santa Ana planned – they seldom did! – and the Americans refused to surrender. They held out for about a month, after which time Santa Ana was forced to withdraw when Colonel James Lane arrived with reinforcements from Veracruz.

A few years later, during what the Mexicans call the 'French Intervention', the troops of Napoleon II were soundly defeated by a Mexican force under the command of General Ignacio Zaragoza. The date of the battle, 5 May 1862, accounts for celebrations on that date every year, as well as for all the streets named '5 de Mayo'. In 1863 the French besieged Puebla and took it in two months, a date that is not commemorated. And then on 2 April 1867, General Porfirio Diaz retook the battered city.

Since those bloody days, Puebla has been fairly peaceful, not to mention prosperous. Today Puebla derives the bulk of its income from manufacturing, and the original city is surrounded by factories manufacturing cement, glass, cloth, bricks and the colourful Puebla tiles which are shipped all over North America.

Puebla tile is made by the same process as the famous Talavera polychrome tile in Spain and was one of the first manufacturing operations in the New World. It resists weathering and ageing remarkably well, and its application to the domes of countless Mexican churches and building facades contributes greatly to Mexico's unique appearance.

The best example in Puebla of the use of the native tile is on the building called 'La Casa de Alfeñique' ('The Wedding Cake House'). Located at Avenida 4 Oriente and Calle 6 Norte, it now houses the Regional Museum. *Alfeñique* means 'almond cake' – the building's name reflects the ornamentation plus the generous use of white Puebla tile that makes it look like an outsize frosted cake. Even if museums generally leave you cold as a margarita, the place is worth a visit.

Another museum is now located in the ex-Convento de Santa Rosa, on Avenida 4 Oriente at Calle 3 Norte. This was at one time a huge operation of the Dominican Order, and today it is mainly interesting for the kitchen. Known locally as La Cocina de Santa Rosa, it is a fantastically well-preserved tiled kitchen that was used for hundreds of years. In conjunction with the kitchen is a crafts museum and salesroom, but the kitchen is the attraction both for tourists and locals, and it is worth a visit by anyone interested in cooking and/or eating.

The Capilla del Rosario, also known as the Templo de Santo Domingo, is on 5 de Mayo at Avenida 4 Poniente. It is also noted for its beautiful and decorative tilework. The Templo gets its informal name from the Rosary Chapel, the most thoroughly decorated ecclesiastical building in the city. The walls, ceilings, supporting columns and even the portales are covered with gold, figures and bas-relief carvings; the image of the Virgin on the altar is jewelled. A visit to the chapel will give you some idea of what the great churches were like before the Reform Laws and assorted revolutions and martial disturbances stripped most of them of their riches. I don't know why this particular chapel was spared.

Another place that shouldn't be overlooked is Convento de Santa Monica, often called the Secret Convent. On Avenida 18 Poniente at 5 de Mayo, it is another place with a long and fascinating history. The building was originally built in 1606 as a sort of halfway house for respectable women whose husbands were out of town, an idea that failed either because the respectable women of Puebla refused to cooperate or their husbands took them along. The building was then used by the church as a convent and reformatory for prostitutes. There is no record of whether this scheme worked any better than the previous effort, but it had a longer run. When the Reform Laws abolished convents in 1857 the establishment went underground, and in 1862 the still visible part became a women's college, Santa Monica.

The secret convent lasted until 1934, when it was closed by the government. Today the convent is a museum and anyone with the paltry price of an admission ticket can enter through an apartment by way of a door disguised as a china cabinet. Quite fascinating.

Those interested in military artifacts can go out to the forts of Guadalupe and Loreto. This is where Zaragoza put his name on street signs all over Mexico by soundly defeating the French. In addition to being rather interesting in their own right, the forts are on a hill and offer a commanding view of the city and the surrounding countryside. To get there, catch a bus marked 'Fuertes' by the zócalo, or walk there in about 40-45 minutes from the zona centro. Go out 5 de Mayo to Avenida 38 Oriente and turn right and go to 2 Norte. Turn left, then right on Calzada de los Fuertes.

Places to Stay

The economy hotel situation is fairly good, but bear in mind that the first hotels to fill during the summer are the cheaper places, and that Puebla is popular with history-minded Mexicans as well as tourists from far away parts. Most of Puebla's hotels are designated by large white plastic signs bearing big 'H's in red, with the hotel's

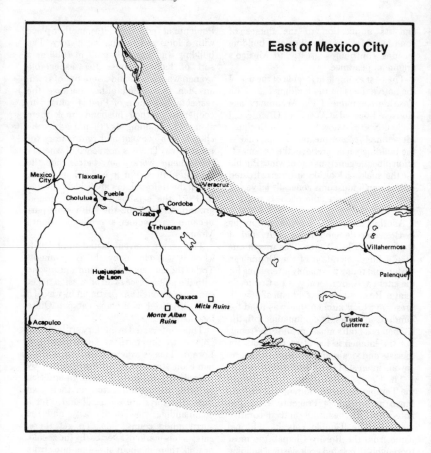

East of Mexico City

name beneath the letter in black as a sort of afterthought.

The *Hotel Ritz*, on Calle 2 Norte between Avenida 4 Oriente and Avenida 2 Oriente, is no relation whatsoever to the caravanserai in Paris. The institutional buff lobby has seen about two decades since a touch-up on the paint job, and the kitchen exhaust fan from the restaurant next door discharges into the foyer, but let's not knock it too hard because Puebla doesn't have much leeway when it comes to hotels in the inexpensive classification.

There are two *Palacio* hotels in town,

both on Avenida 2 Oriente near Calle 2 Norte, and both pretentious and costly. Ridiculously expensive.

The *Hotel Embajadores* is on 5 de Mayo between Avenida 4 Oriente and Avenida 6 Oriente. The patio shows a marked Moorish influence, and the rooms are large. All rooms used to have two or more beds, which made them very expensive, not to mention crowded, but the management has seen the light at last and most rooms now have one bed. Prices are now more moderate.

The *Hotel España* is on Avenida 6

Poniente between Calle 3 Norte and 5 de Mayo. This is a small, working-person's house, at least as interested in peddling lottery tickets as in renting rooms. Inexpensive.

Posada Los Angeles is on Calle 4 Norte near Avenida 2 Oriente. In the beginning this *posada* (hotel) was a casa de huéspedes, but a few years back it was promoted to a posada when the owners got enough money to buy a neon sign. It is close to the bus station and a good value. Moderate.

The *Hotel Latino* on Calle 6 Norte at Avenida 2 Oriente is in the same block as the ADO bus station. It offers a brown-and-white-tiled lobby and fairly large rooms. The hotel is usually full, but is worth a try. Moderate.

Places to Eat

The *China Poblana* restaurant, across the street from the entrance of the ADO bus station, is very attractively decorated. It serves such local specialties as *adobo, carne asada a la Poblana* and, of course, the inevitable *mole Poblano*. This is a new place, very attractive, and they don't charge IVA. Moderate.

There are a couple other *auténtico* restaurants in the same block, but I've so far had no opportunity to try them.

Sanborn's is on Avenida 2 Oriente

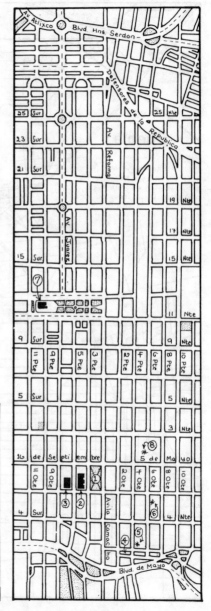

Puebla Central

1 Plaza de Armas
2 Cathedral
3 Post Office, Tourist Office & Casa de la Cultura
4 Mercado El Parian & ADO Bus Terminal
5 Museo del Estado 'Casa del Alfeñique'
6 Museo de la Revolución 'Casa de los Serdán'
7 Museo de Historia Natural (Acuario Municipal)
8 Capilla de Rosario (Templo de Santo Domingo)

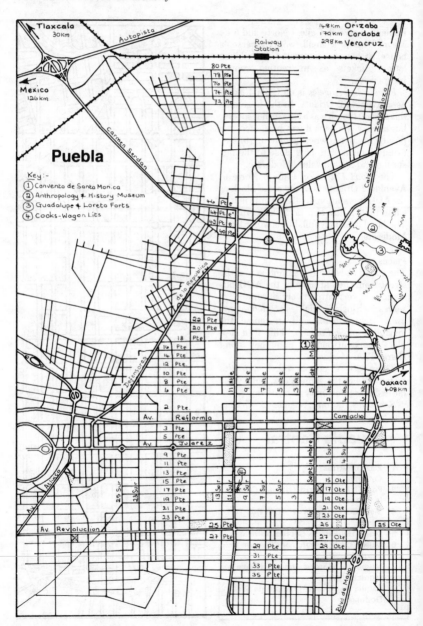

between 5 de Mayo and Calle 2 Norte. The store offers books and magazines in English, along with American and Mexican food and a good photography department. Spotless restrooms. Expensive.

Restaurante la Princesa, on Calle 3 Norte just off the Reforma, has tablecloths and domestic wines such as Los Reyes. It also has the other characteristics of a very expensive restaurant, though prices are moderate.

Super Tortas Angel, on Calle 2 Sur at Avenida 5 Oriente, is another of Mexico's many misnamed businesses. Although it sells quite good tortas, the Angel is the place where everybody buys Bismarks (jelly doughnuts). A couple of these, a litre of pasteurized milk and a seat on a bench in the zócalo will make a very inexpensive lunch.

Vittorio's, a bar-cum-pizza joint on the plaza opposite the Princesa, serves real pizza, with more filling than crust. Vittorio's uses Machego cheese from Chiapas (instead of the Mafia-made mozzarella employed in the US) with outstanding results. Beer and wine are available. There are two happy hours a day when two drinks go for the price of one. The service is good, so Vittorio's is my first stop in Puebla. Expensive.

There are sidewalk cafés under the portales around the Plaza de la Constitución. They are very popular with the locals as a relaxing place to solve the problems of the day or just to watch the people weaving their way among the tables. It has been said that if you sit at one of these tables it won't be long until everyone in Puebla passes in parade, and I can well believe it. Moderate.

Getting There & Getting Around

Puebla is a transportation hub, and buses leave for San Lázaro station in Mexico City every few minutes. ADO is a first-class bus line and is the preferred method of travel in this part of the world.

To get downtown from the ADO first-class station, go out the front door and turn right. The plaza is a couple of blocks away. Walking time is about six minutes.

ADO has the habit of putting the sanitarios on the second floor, and the stairway leading to the toilets is hidden behind the snack-and-postcard counter.

Be careful about taking a second-class bus to Puebla unless it is well-nigh unavoidable, as might be the case if you are coming in from Tlaxcala. Second-class buses have no permanent station and are likely to drop you out in the middle of a depressed neighbourhood a M$250 cab ride from the plaza.

CHOLULA, Puebla

About 15 km from Puebla, Cholula makes a convenient side trip. It is the current location of the University of the Americas, usually listed as being in Mexico City. This is an institution of higher learning that has a large American enrollment. Not only is the institution a great place to acquire a working knowledge of Spanish, it is also the only US-accredited college in Mexico.

The average traveller visits Cholula because it is said that there is a church for each day of the year, a story I've heard all my life. I've never met anyone who had conducted an inventory. But I will agree that Cholula is a perfect example of conspicuous consumption when it comes to churches – there are enough of them to stock another Mexico City. The most noteworthy of the churches is the little Sanctuario de los Remidios built on top of the Tepanapa Pyramid a few blocks east of the plaza. It was the largest of all the Mexican pyramids, so large that over eight km of tunnels have been explored within the structure. The pyramid itself is now a museum, and some of the tunnels have been illuminated for the benefit of the visitor. Warning: be sure to take a small flashlight. Light goes off in the tunnels now and then, and there is nothing on earth darker than the inside of a crooked tunnel.

Cholula's history has been bloody. Cortés was invited to Cholula by the Indians; while he was there, he got word of a conspiracy on the part of Moctezuma to murder him and his men. The Spanish were never ones to turn the other cheek, and Cortés nipped the plot in the bud by slaughtering some 6000 Aztecs during the course of a single night.

TLAXCALA, Tlaxcala

(elevation 2285 metres, population 40,000)

This is another enjoyable side trip. About 30 km from Puebla, Tlaxcala is the capital of the tiny state of the same name. Due to its high, fairly isolated location, the capital has air that is crystal clear and smog-free.

Tlaxcala gives an overall impression of cleanliness, and the ample plaza is well maintained. As in Puebla, there is a sidewalk cafe under the portales; otherwise the two places have nothing at all in common. The Iglesia de San Francisco, about one km along the road to Puebla, is claimed to be the oldest church in the New World (a title disputed by another little church near Veracruz). On the pulpit of the adjacent chapel is the hard-to-decipher inscription, 'Aqui tubo principio al Santo Evangelio en este nuevo mundo'. (Here the Holy Gospel had its beginning in this new world.)

For old-building buffs, I recommend the Sanctuario de Octlán. Unusual for Mexico, the facade is white plaster, elaborately carved. The towers have bases covered with red tiles and the elevated parts are covered with more white plaster. Also a rarity in Mexico, the interior is as spectacular as the outside, with lots of carved wood and polychromed and gold-leafed figures. The Sanctuario is about 750 metres from the plaza – ask any local for precise directions.

Tlaxcala is a good place to buy hand-woven cloth, although very little of the actual weaving is done there. Much of it is done in nearby Santa Ana, where the Sunday Market is probably the best in Mexico for blankets, serapes and so on.

Places to Stay

Tlaxcala gets almost no visits from foreigners, and very little from locals, so the hotel situation is rough. The only hotel I can recommend is the Albergue de la Loma Restaurante y Hotel, the best place in town. As the name implies, the fairly new hotel is located on a hillside. It isn't far from the new bus terminal, but cab fares are cheap so I suggest you take a cab, at least for the first time. Very expensive.

Places to Eat

There are quite a number of restaurants, but I recommend the sidewalk café under the portales on the plaza. The food is fair, the ambience excellent. Moderate.

If that doesn't suit, my other recommendation is to go up the hill to the Albergue de la Loma Restaurante y Hotel, where both food and ambience are good. Expensive.

TEHUACÁN, Puebla

(elevation 1679 metres, population 100,000)

Tehuacán is the supreme example of the quiet, peaceful, utterly charming Mexican town where nothing much ever happens and never has. It has an almost-perfect climate, too. The area abounds in mineralized springs, and for centuries before the arrival of Cortés and his hard-bitten crew the Indians came great distances to bathe in the healing waters.

During the 19th century the springs were operated as spas, and Tehuacán was to Mexico as Baden-Baden, Bad Gasswasser and Bath were to Europe. The businesspeople of Tehuacan felt deeply that the water's benefits should not be confined to Mexico's wealthy, and began bottling and shipping it all over North America. Then it was discovered that a lot of people denied themselves the benefits of the mineral springs because they disliked the taste, so the astute entrepreneurs began to add sugar and flavourings to conceal the mineral taste, a practice that continues to this day.

Top: Museum of Regional Art in Patzuano — inlaid floor of dried cattle bones.
Bottom: One of the 11 patios in *La Casa de Once Patios*, a showcase for local craftspeople in Patzcuaro.

Top: The balcony of the restaurant in the Gran Hotel, Taxco.
Left: Campesino in Taxco.
Right: Taxco shows more Spanish influence than almost any other Mexican town.

Although 'Tehuacan' is a brand name and there are a number of water bottlers in the area, it is better to ask for 'agua Tehuacán' in most of Mexico, rather than 'agua mineral'. Ordering agua Tehuacán anywhere in Mexico will get you a bottle of mineral water, even if the actual brand stocked is Garci Crespi or other brands.

Tehuacán has one of the most captivating plazas in Mexico, with wide sidewalks, handsome shade trees and cool concrete benches. The plaza is partially surrounded by portales, and under the arches are sidewalk cafes.

As with any country town, there is no nightlife and no old forts – apparently the old-timers never figured a few mineral-water outcroppings were worth fighting over. The only industry is bottling, and although visitors are welcomed in some of the plants, they look like Coke or Pepsi bottling works anywhere – same machinery, same smell.

You could spend half an hour inspecting the Templo del Carmen, easily visible from the plaza. It has some unusual tilework on the dome and is more interesting on the outside than the inside.

Next to the church is the Museo del Valle de Tehuacan, in perfect tune with the peaceful tenor of the community.

The little Palacio Municipal is a multi-tiled jewel of a building on the plaza that looks as if it has been standing there since Juárez was a cigar roller, but it was only constructed in 1959, the local authorities having had the good taste to construct it along ultra-traditional lines.

Places to Stay

The *Hotel Spa Peñafiel* was one of the deluxe hotels where the rich came to take the waters during the 1800s, but it has fallen on bad times because the wealthy don't go to spas in droves anymore. It still costs an arm and a leg to stay here, and the staff can be very insistent about the clients taking their meals on the so-called American plan. Still, the place is definitely worth visiting. Maybe you can have a

cold bottle of brew if you don't want to drink any of the mineral water running out of the 'cave' next door. The Spa Peñafiel is located on the way in from the Puebla-Orizaba highway, on the right side. Overly expensive.

On your way downtown from the ADO bus station you will pass the *Hotel Mexico*, a time-honoured establishment and a rarity in Mexico – it boasts that it accepts American Express cards. Wander in through the lobby as if you were a guest, and take a look at the patio with its Spanish-styled fountain. All is colonial style – bar, restaurant, and so on. Pleasant, but ridiculously expensive.

Continue on Independencia – the street you're on – past the plaza, and in the next block you'll find the *Hotel Hibernia*, reconstructed from one of the early great houses. Only two floors surround the unusual patio, but the first floor is a good seven metres above the ground floor. Moderate.

Turn right off Independencia on to the next street after the plaza and you will be on Calle 3 Sur, although there probably won't be a street sign in sight. In about 35 metres you will come to the *Casa de Huéspedes Veracruz*. The sign says, 'Hot Water All Day'. Inexpensive.

If you continue along Calle 3 Sur to the corner of Avenida 12 Oriente, the next street, you will see the weather-beaten sign and the peeling paint of the *Hotel Madrid*. The Madrid has a pleasing patio with concrete benches surrounding a sunken fountain, caged birds a-singing and leaded-glass windows separating the lobby and the patio. There are also quite large rooms, lots and lots of ambience, and all this for about a third of what you would expect. Inexpensive.

Places to Eat

The place to eat in Tehuacán is the *Restaurant Peñafiel* on the plaza. Take your choice and eat indoors or out on the sidewalk beneath the portales. The restaurant has a widely varied menu, mostly 'international food', although a few Mexican dishes are included for the more traditional-minded customers. There's a good selection of wine, mostly domestic, some imported, but only one brand of beer. The Peñafiel is an excellent choice for those who can afford to fork over M$2000 for a lunch with wine. Wildly expensive.

The little *Café Lupita*, across the zócalo from the fancy Peñafiel, is both good and reasonably priced, a welcome combination. Big Humphrey Bogart fans churn the air on the occasional hot day and chase the insects away. Enjoy the red tablecloths and that rarest of all amenities in Mexico – attentive service that is prompt and caring. And wonder of wonders, there's an espresso machine that works and is used. Try the *queso fundido*, which loosely translates as cheese fondue, though this is not quite the stuff ski lodges serve as an *après*-ski snack. Instead of toast, you get lovely, fresh little flour tortillas. Inexpensive.

For a splurge at dinnertime, I suggest you hike back up to the *Hotel Mexico*. It will be ridiculously expensive, but the food will be as good as any in town.

Getting There & Getting Around

Getting to Tehuacán is extremely easy. It is on the Puebla-Oaxaca route, and also on one of the Mexico City-Veracruz routes. There are lots of buses you can take.

You may also take the train from Mexico City or Puebla, although I definitely do not recommend it.

To get downtown from the ADO bus station, turn right as you leave the front door and the plaza is only about a five-minute walk away.

ORIZABA, Veracruz
(elevation 1228 metres, population 225,000)
Orizaba is an industrial centre, specializing in the industries that delight in erecting tall smokestacks and belching evil smells high into the air. But not quite high

enough; the pollution laws in Mexico are more a joke than a deterrent. The most interesting feature of Orizaba that I could discover is the retired juice jack, No 1002, on display in the street divider on the way from the highway to the ADO bus station.

Orizaba has signs reading, 'Orizaba Desires a New Image – Help Us!'

The trip down the hill from Tehuacán should be made at night for those with a low tolerance for heights. There are a few places where it is a very long way down.

CÓRDOBA, Veracruz
(elevation 929 metres, population 135,000)
The high point of Córdoba's history was the occasion when General Agustín Iturbide, soon to be Emperor, and Viceroy Don Juan de O'Donoju, soon to be unemployed, signed the Pact of Córdoba which made Mexico free of Spanish domination and an independent nation.

The building on the plaza in which the treaty was signed eventually became the Hotel Zevallo, which by means of systematic lack of care gradually became a ruin. Recently the rear part of it collapsed under the accumulation of dry rot and years, and the building is no longer in business as a hotel, although a few old-timers still pass their time playing chess and dominoes in the relatively safe front area of the patio.

As Mexican cities go, Córdoba isn't very old, having been founded under the direction of Viceroy Fernandez de Córdoba in 1618. The Church of the Immaculate Conception on the plaza reflects this relative newness, being considerably more modern in appearance than most plaza churches. The building is painted a peculiar light green with white trim and seems to change colour with changes in the weather. It is the only church I have ever seen with medallions of palm trees mounted on the facade.

Córdoba is close enough to the Atlantic coast to attract strolling marimba bands, and you can enjoy spending a few hours at one of the cafes under the portales on the north side of the plaza, drinking some of the famous local coffee, chewing the fat and encouraging the musicians now and then with a few pesos.

Places to Stay

On your way downtown from the ADO station, in half a block and on the same side of the street, is the *Posada Nast*, with 'cuartos economicos'. This clean, neat-looking establishment is a former private home built in 1912. Inexpensive.

As you enter the plaza from the direction of the bus station, you will see a huge, dark, new-looking building diagonally across the square. This is the *Hotel Mansur*, not nearly as new as it appears. This is a fairly good hotel. Every imaginable credit card is accepted, though the rooms are ridiculously expensive.

A little farther along to the right of the Mansur, and facing the far side of the church, is the *Hotel Virreynal*, an older house with a clean, tiled lobby containing comfortable old-fashioned chairs where both guests and strangers are free to take five as the mood strikes them. The rooms are large and well-equipped for a hotel of today – there is a spittoon in every room. Moderate.

If you leave the plaza just before the Mansur, on the street that used to continue across the plaza by the church before it became a paseo, you will see the *Hotel Los Reyes*, Córdoba's answer to the old problem of lodgings for the moderately unrich. To get to the desk you climb a wainscoted stairway. The rooms are not overly small, unless you plan on giving ballet lessons. Moderate.

To find really cheap places, continue past the Virreynal and turn left at the corner. About three squares away you will see an ancient church that apparently blocks the street. If you go to the church and turn right onto the cross street you will find several economical casas de huéspedes. Inexpensive.

Places to Eat

Directly across the street from the ADO station, and in plain view therefrom, is a small restaurant. I've lost the name, but I remember specifically that it beat the hell out of the eatery in the bus station. Inexpensive, too.

On down the street toward the Posada Nast there are a number of inexpensive and moderate restaurants.

One of the best places to eat, if not the best, is the restaurant off the lobby of the *Hotel Virreynal*. Enter either from the lobby or from the street. Aged wood, tables with clean white tablecloths, and highly professional waiters are in the restaurant's favour. Espresso coffee, excellent cafe con leche and quite an extensive menu of both Mexican and international items are served. Naturally a place like this is expensive, but worth it.

The *Restaurante Parroquia* is on the plaza beneath the portales on the north side, up the street from the Mansur. Mainly because of the similarity of names, Córdoba regards the late Manuel Benitez, El Córdobes, as one of its own, and there must be 20 fine Spanish bullfight posters on the walls. This is another place with competent waiters, and is the ideal place to meet the local gentry. Expensive.

Between the Mansur and the Virreynal is a passage leading through the centre of the block to the *Restaurante Los Brujos* (Restaurant of the Sorcerors). The passage is only a short block long, but that's enough to remove the Brujos from the high rent district, and far enough from the plaza to eliminate overcrowding. Nobody seems to know how the Brujos got its name, and there is certainly nothing supernatural about the place. The food is above average for small towns, and is inexpensive.

For really economical eating, turn left on the street just past the Virreynal. This is a sort of open-air restaurant district, with about a dozen restaurant barrows. Inexpensive.

For a treat, go along this street to the church. Often parked in front is a cart selling deep-fried *churros* (fritters) and plantains. The latter are delicious and the former require the digestion of a billy goat. Very inexpensive.

If all this walking, eating and drinking is catching up with you, on the side of the church on the plaza (facing the Hotel Virreynal) there are five public toilets behind the candle shop. There is a slight charge, but it can be well worth it.

VERACRUZ, Veracruz

(elevation two metres, population 500,000)

Veracruz is the principal seaport for central Mexico, and the Atlantic-side port for Mexico City. It is rich in history, and its modern history really starts with Grijalva in 1518, followed a year later by Cortés. It was near here that Cortés burned his ships and formally launched the conquest of Mexico.

Since those days every invader attempting to take Mexico has found it necessary to first take Veracruz, which although well fortified has never presented any vexing problems. The French took Veracruz easily in 1838, and it was here that the infamous Santa Ana lost his leg in repelling the bill-collecting expedition.

The French were back, in company with the British and Spanish, in 1862. For political reasons England and Spain withdrew, and France went at Mexico alone. Today this operation is known in Mexico as the 'French Intervention'.

The Americans also took their chances at Veracruz, and captured the city in 1847 on their way up to Mexico City. In 1914 the Americans once more overcame the town, an action that was roundly denounced in both Mexico and the US, although it did not lead to a declaration of war. This action still rankles the thoughts of patriotic Mexicans although it took place before most of them were born.

The Veracruz battle under General Winfield Scott in 1847 is still of interest to military historians, as it was a first in so many spheres of war. This was the first genuine combined operation in which soldiers, sailors and marines operated together on land. Heretofore the soldiers had fought on land and sailors at sea, but in this battle Scott had the cooperation of the naval commander, who supplied both the heavy naval guns for use ashore and the trained gunners to fire them. In addition, Scott engineered an amphibious landing that is a textbook operation to this day. He built hundreds of lightweight, compact lighters (flat-bottomed boats used for loading and unloading ships) and ferried several thousand men and their equipment ashore from the massed troop transports.

The Spanish spent a fortune in 1746 and 1771, fortifying Ulúa on Gallega Island about one km from Veracruz. They regarded this fort as as impregnable. Among other things, it had over 250 cannon of various calibres, metres-thick stone walls, and a built-in moat.

The Americans elected to take the city first and turn their attentions to Ulúa later. They landed their naval guns on the dunes a few km south of the city and manhandled them overland, with a surprising lack of resistance on the part of the defenders, the first of many Mexican blunders.

The Americans began the siege of the walled city by spending a little over a week consolidating their positions. They surrounded the city on the dry side, set up their heavy naval guns and called on the authorities to surrender. The Mexicans were told that once the shooting started no one would be allowed in or out. Naturally, the Mexicans refused to lay down their arms, and the Yanks began to systematically demolish Veracruz building by building, block by block, using both ordinary land field pieces and the much larger naval ordnance.

After two days of merciless around-the-clock shelling, the Mexicans pleaded with Scott to allow the women and children to leave, but he pointed out that he had offered them their chance and it had been refused, and continued the bombardment. Scott also reiterated that there would be no truce, only surrender.

The shooting had commenced on 22 March, and the city capitulated on 27 March, whereupon Scott began preparations to attack the 'impregnable' Ulúa. But it turned out to be unnecessary. Ulúa's commander had closely observed the American technique in taking the fortified city and had seen the terrible havoc wreaked by heavy naval ordnance on stone-built structures. He wanted no part of it for himself, his men and his rock fort. He surrendered without firing a shot and abandoned Ulúa without destroying the huge stock of military stores. The munitions came in very handy in the American advance on Mexico City because they were at the tail end of a supply line thousands of km long.

General Santa Ana seriously considered shooting the commander who surrendered the country's most prestigious fort and thus opened the road to Mexico City, but it's not known if this was done.

San Juan Ulúa was more successful as a prison than as a fort, operating as a prison under the Spaniards, Mexicans and French. Latins have never been high on prisons as reformatories, and a prisoner in Ulúa was there to be punished. A popular attraction for the modern tourist is the oubliettes, in which extremely high tides actually came up into the cells. It was said that anything over six months in one of these jugs was tantamount to a life sentence.

The ancient fort is one of the best-preserved examples of Spanish military construction extant and is well worth visiting, aside from the macabre aspects. The walls are so thick that guardrooms and stairs were built within them. The tops of the walls were made wide and smooth to facilitate the heavy guns mounted along their outer edges. Semi-circular iron tracks were set in the stone to facilitate traversing the heavy artillery. There were also high observation towers for spotting, and several drawbridges that could isolate the firing points. No wonder the Spanish, and later the Mexicans, regarded Ulúa as an invulnerable bastion guarding guaranteeing the safety of the country's second-most vital city. Unfortunately, this faith in fixed positions has never been justified.

Ulúa is Veracruz's most interesting feature. Allow yourself at least three hours to absorb the fine points of the magnificently useless old pile. To get there, catch a S J Ulúa bus going from right to left in the second street seaward from the plaza. Or you can walk there in 40 interesting minutes. Go straight through the plaza to Zaragoza and turn left. Cross the overpass over the railroad yards and turn right by the old stone electrical substation. Continue on through the container yards, the largest in Mexico, pass beneath the Conasupo grain conveyors and follow the signs. The S J Ulúa bus back to the plaza waits by the ticket office.

The tourist office doesn't spend any of the 10-peso admission charge on lighting, so it is definitely advisable to take a small flashlight along.

Ulúa has a number of guides, mostly monolinguals, who cope with the tours of Mexican adults and school children. Be suspicious of these people – I heard one telling an awe-struck group of the 'heroic resistance' put up by the fort during the American intervention.

During the summer Veracruz is hot, sultry and downright uncomfortable, with millions of mosquitoes and hungry little flies. Have lots of DEET. During the winter the weather is about like Miami's (Florida, USA), but now and then a 'norther' will strike with no warning whatsoever.

The infamous norther is a cold wind that starts up around the North Pole and picks up speed. It gets colder and more powerful crossing the US Great Plains, with nothing but a few windmills and barbed-wire fences to impede its progress. When it finally hits Veracruz it will cause the temperature to drop 20°C in a matter of minutes, and with an astronomical chill factor. So if you're going to be away from your hotel for any length of time, take a coat.

On your way out to the Paseo de Malecón and the waterfront from the plaza, you will

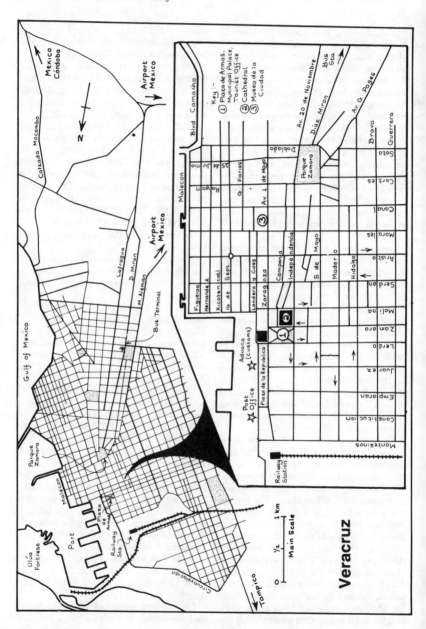

Veracruz

pass a considerable number of concrete stands selling such goodies as turtle-shell combs, miniature lighthouses and other items specifically intended for the tourist trade. If any of this tempts you, remember that bargaining is the name of the game.

Stand in front of the Hotel Vigo at the corner of Molina and Coss to view an odd building. Apparently the designer set out to plan a conventional pyramid, thought better of it, and made two parallel cuts from top to bottom, ending with a sort of semi-pyramid with two vertical and two slanted sides.

The newsstand under the portico on Independencia at Zamora stocks a few US magazines and also the English-language *Mexico City News*.

Places to Stay

Considering that Veracruz has some grand hostelries intended for wealthy customers awaiting the arrival or departure of steamships, the town has a remarkably large assortment of economical hotels.

Right next door to the ADO bus station is the *Hotel Central*, misnamed because there is nothing central about it, though it is quite convenient for travellers by bus who feel a need for a night's rest after the long run down the hill from Mexico City. Expensive.

The bus station is on Díaz Mirón at Orizaba, and if you pass the Hotel Central on your way downtown at about the third intersection you come to the *Hotel Tabasco*, two floors with a cream topside and a light blue lunch stand on the ground floor. Moderate.

In the next block after the Tabasco is the tile-fronted *Hotel La Paz*, actually more a motel than a hotel, with off-street parking, which always tends to raise the rate. Expensive.

Farther in on Díaz Mirón, about a dozen blocks from the bus station, is the *Hotel Avenida*, four floors with the Café Noche y Día restaurant on the ground floor. The hotel is fairly new and so large that it takes longer to fill than most in the area. Moderate.

Things generally are more expensive downtown, and hotels are no exception.

Hotel Rias, on Zaragoza near Lerdo across from the Aduana Maritima, has a couple of great advantages. It is just far enough from the plaza to avoid the strolling orchestras that tend to play all night in the plaza, usually several at the same time sawing different things. And it is somewhat cheaper than it would be if it were directly on the plaza. Still, it's expensive.

Another place far enough from the plaza to avoid the worst of the noise is the *Hotel Vigo* on the corner of Molina and Coss. This is an older house, but not as run-down as many of the older hotels in Veracruz that gave up trying when people switched from ships to planes. Expensive.

The cheapest place to stay in downtown Veracruz is the *Casa de Huéspedes* near the Hotel Rias. This little rooming house caters to countryfolk, and your fellow guests will likely as not include a few Indians in white outfits with Zouave pants. Make sure the fan works, if only to drive the mosquitoes away. Inexpensive.

Places to Eat

The restaurants around the Plaza de Armas are intended for drinking beer, listening to marimba bands, spitting shrimp hulls on the tiles, and conversation – not for serious eating.

A popular way to spend a languid Saturday afternoon in Veracruz is to gather a few friends, book a table in front of the *Bar Santiago*, order a few bottles of Agua Tehuacán mineral water, a fresh bottle of Viejo Virgil or San Marcos brandy and a bucket of ice, and tell stories while watching the level in the bottle sink with the sun.

Come right down to it, Veracruz is not really a very good eating town, probably due to the hot, muggy climate. Even *pescado Veracruzana*, the fish stew that can give bouillabaisse a fair run for its money, was better up north at Guaymas than in its home town.

The above remarks notwithstanding,

there are a few places I've been patronizing for years.

The *Gran Café Parroquia*, across the street from the church, is about the closest place to eat well near the Plaza de Armas. A large place, it copes with the crowds very well. Moderate.

By the fish market, a block to seaward from Coss, is a solid string of little restaurant stands, most specializing in seafood. The tables at the *Día de la Marina* are on the opposite side from the plaza, and the restaurant gets almost no play at all from tourists, but I'm of the opinion it is better in almost all respects – except seeing and being seen – than anything except the *La Paella* on the zócalo. The Marina is popular with dining-out local families. Inexpensive.

One of the best places to eat in Veracruz, and the best on the plaza, is the *Restaurante la Paella* behind the church. This is the only restaurant on the plaza itself that concentrates on feeding the public rather than on serving drinks. The name, again, is not to be taken too seriously, although I've had an excellent paella Valenciana or two there. It isn't a spartan establishment and neither is it too Spanish. Expensive, but usually well worth the price.

Just past the Hotel Avenida, to the right of the bus station, at Díaz Mirón and Aragon, is the gigantic supermarket *Chedraui*, part of a chain operation. It sells everything from baked goods (such as the morning *pan dulces*) to the latest Beatles reissues. Fresh fruit, though, is handled by the barrows lining the curb out front. The supermarket is about a 15-minute walk from the ADO station.

Getting There & Getting Around

Veracruz is a transportation centre, so there are buses north and south along the East Coast, and to Mexico City. These leave constantly. This makes it very easy to catch a bus up to Córdoba which, with its greater altitude, is a much better place to stay than Veracruz.

ADO stations almost never have baggage checking service, but the station at Veracruz is an exception. There are a number of lockers against the wall toward the restaurant. Anywhere else they would be coin-operated, but in Veracruz a *ficha* (ticket or token, not to be confused with a *flecha* or *fecha*) is required. There is no sign indicating where to purchase a ficha, but you get one from the combination soda fountain and magazine store on the bus side of the waiting room. Ask the cashier – there's no sign here either. And be sure to remember the locker you used because the numbers on the keys don't correspond to anything in particular.

To get downtown from the Central Camionera, catch a bus running along Díaz Mirón from left to right in front of the bus station and stay with it until you reach the business district. If you elect to walk, go out the front door and turn right on Díaz Mirón. There is a confusing set of intersections at the Parque Zamora, but continue straight ahead past the park, and then angle slightly to your left at Rayon and you will wind up on Independencia. The Plaza de Armas, also known as the Plaza de la Constitución, is seven blocks more. Walking time: 45 minutes.

There is scheduled air service to Veracruz by local airlines.

There is also more-or-less regular train service to Mexico City.

PAPANTLA, Veracruz

(elevation 300 metres, population 150,000)

Nestled among lush green hills, Papantla is blessed with a beautiful location. The weather is better than that of Veracruz in winter and about the same in summer. There are also quite a number of interesting colonial buildings. However, the town's fame doesn't rest on these notable attributes.

Papantla is famous for its vanilla, and at times the town is permeated with the delicious smell of drying vanilla 'beans'. (Vanilla isn't really a bean at all, but a green-bean-shaped product of a variety of

orchid.) I definitely advise the visitor to skip the usual practice of buying several bottles of 'pure vanilla extract' to take home. Some bottles may contain an economical adulterant which happens to be a deadly poison. This has become a problem for the government's pure food department, and as the word gets out, it bids fair to kill Mexico's vanilla industry.

Papantla's other claim to fame is a unique performance by some of the Indians. They erect a high pole and then suspend themselves from ropes wound around the pole. At a signal, they cast off and spin around the pole as their ropes unwind. As they descend, the non-twirling member of the quintet does a fast heel-and-toe on a platform atop the pole. To say this practice is dangerous is to put it mildly. It used to be done only on Corpus Cristi Day, but lately performers have taken to twirling almost every Sunday, or whenever there are enough foreigners in town to make it worthwhile. Regardless of the circumstances, the trick is probably the most spectacular in Mexico, right up there with the boy divers of Acapulco.

Getting There
Papantla is a stop for the majority of the buses making the trip between Veracruz and Tampico/Poza Rica, so getting there is absolutely no problem.

Side Trip from Papantla
Tajín, a rare Totonac ruin, is about 12 km from Papantla. The place would be neglected if not for the pole spinners. If you're interested in ruins, I would recommend the ones in Yucatán, Campeche and Chiapas instead, especially because the Tajín area is infested with tiny chiggers that lie in wait for the unwary in grassy areas. The local Indians tie the bottom of their pants tightly at the ankle, and I suggest you do likewise. DEET will discourage the pests, but won't stop them from biting if they're hungry enough. The little *bichos* taught me to never, but never, wear pants with cuffs anywhere.

HUAJUAPÁN DE LEON, Oaxaca
During the winter of 1980-81 a severe earthquake struck the State of Oaxaca. The epicentre was near the crossroads city of Huajuapán, where the earthquake caused considerable damage and a large number of fatalities. Only a few months later, little evidence remained of the disaster. Approximately halfway between

Puebla and Oaxaca, Huajuapán is by no means a garden spot, but if you have to stay over, there is an economy-model hotel not too far from where the buses stop. It is on the east side of the main stem – you'll see it as you come south – dressed in a coat of dark green paint. Moderate.

OAXACA, Oaxaca

(elevation 1545 metres, population 195,000)

Oaxaca is, with justification, one of the most popular tourist destinations in Mexico. In addition to a wonderful year-round climate, travellers come for the ancient Zapotec and Mixtec ruins, the museum in the former convent, the band concerts in the plaza, and the relaxed atmosphere.

Each year more and more tourists arrive, until at times it seems there are more foreigners in the plazas than there are locals. There are quantities of tourist-oriented shops, but part of Oaxaca's charm comes from the local people, who pursue their way of life with little or no contact with outsiders. Oaxaca is one of the few large communities where numbers of people still converse in pre-conquest languages, and Zapotec and Zapotec-accented Spanish are everywhere in evidence.

The State of Oaxaca has well over a million non-Spanish-speaking citizens, a severe problem to a government that is attempting to impart a knowledge of rudimentary birth control techniques, and families with a half dozen children led by a pregnant, nursing mother are not at all uncommon.

One of the most popular stops on the tourist round of inspection is the Church of Santo Domingo at Gurrion/Constitución and 5 de Mayo/Armentia y Lopez, to me the most impressively decorated church in the country. To step inside the front doors when the sun is just at the right angle is to be dazzled by the gold leaf which covers the whole altar end of the interior. It is a big place, with walls as thick as six metres in places. When construction started in 1575, churches were expected to double as

fortresses. There is a popular story to the effect that the church was started with a bankroll of M$2.50, but this I doubt. When construction was finished, it had cost in excess of M$2,000,000, and this I don't doubt.

The exterior is Baroque, with niches occupied by statues. The splendid chapel on the right as you enter is the Capella de la Virgen del Rosario, in itself as large as some churches and far more elaborately decorated than most.

As you enter, look up toward the choir loft. The odd tree with all the figures growing on the branches is actually the family tree of the Guzman family, Señor Guzman being the instigator of the church.

For many years the convent attached to the church was a military post, but recently it has been converted into a regional museum, with heavy emphasis on artifacts recovered from the nearby ruins of Mitla and Monte Albán, including gold jewellery recovered from the tombs. Pretty as they are, I am somewhat more impressed by the superb design, and construction to match, of the old building itself. It survived 300 years of convent use, topped off by a century or so of abuse by the various Mexican army detachments, and still survives in almost the same condition as when the masons finished their work.

I have read much about the Rufino Tamayo Museum, on Morelos between Tinoco y Palacios and Porfirio Díaz, and all reports have been enthusiastic. However, when I'm there it is never open, and I've been there at least a dozen times when the sign says the museum is open to the public. The museum is supposed to contain a superlative collection of pre-conquest art amassed by Tamayo (not a collection of the master's own output).

Mexico's beloved Juárez, the promulgator of the Laws of Reform and the man who signed the order for Maximilian's execution, was a Zapotec Indian who had the great good fortune to be adopted and raised by a wealthy family in Oaxaca. His home is on Garcia Vigil between Carranza and Quetzalcoatl. Maintained as a museum, of course, it affords an interesting glimpse of life as enjoyed by the upper classes during the middle of the 19th century.

Except for a street name, there is no mention of another local boy who made good in a big way, Porfirio Díaz. A good case can be made that he did more to drag Mexico into the modern world than any other individual since Cortés. Statues of Juárez are everywhere; Díaz · is all but forgotten.

Oaxaca has a lending library with English-language books on Piño Suarez across the street from the Alameda. The books are mostly for the long-term resident, rather than for the itinerant. The Universitario bookstore, on Guerrero just off the zócalo, stocks a few English-language paperbacks, both new and used.

Oaxaca has a reputation as a knife-making centre, which in past decades was well deserved. But of recent years the quality of the Oaxaca knives has deteriorated. Formerly they were hammered out of high-carbon steel from springs, files and other high-carbon items, shaped, oil-tempered and ground, but in recent years some knives sold in Oaxaca (still etched with traditional designs, including an eagle on the handle) have been absolutely useless except as mantle decorations.

There are lots of useful and practical native handicrafts for sale at the markets: lightweight braziers for cooking over charcoal; slightly permeable water jugs (ollas) that allow water to dampen the outside surface, evaporate and keep the contents cool; hand-woven cloth with alluring típico designs, ideal for winter-weight skirts; wooden chocolate beaters, intended to be twirled between the palms to give the layer of rich foam so essential to the enjoyment of Mexican chocolate; huaraches of several designs with tough-as-a-hog's-nose soles hand-carved from old tires; beautifully decorated belts and the buckles to go with them; lamps of wood, onyx, glass, brass and clay; and clay figurines similar to those found in the ruins,

made by descendants of the original artists.

The market where all these goodies are available, along with everything you can possibly imagine, is by no means a secret, although there are no signs and little evidence of market activity from the street. Across the street from the second-class bus station, the market is largely ignored by tourists, many of whom believe the market in Oaxaca is the poor affair downtown that nowadays confines its efforts mostly to non-prepared food.

The nicest time to visit Oaxaca is during the latter part of December. The Fiesta de la Virgen de la Soledad gets underway on the 16th, and from then until after the new year there is something doing almost every day. Especially interesting is the Noche de Rabanos. On that night wonderfully carved radishes – rabanos – are sold in the plaza, as well as little bañuelos, a sort of deep-fat-fried pan dulce. The latter are served on clay plates which are smashed with great ceremony after the bañuelos are eaten.

The whole town blossoms with nativity scenes which, since snow is largely unknown, are constructed with Spanish moss as a base. These are built in windows facing the street, or in one corner of a front room where the street window is left uncovered, so the passers-by as well as the family may enjoy. On Christmas Eve elaborately decorated trucks and handcarts parade through the downtown section.

It is hard to beat Oaxaca in December. Best of all, the weather is the kind one associates with Mexico: cool mornings, warm sunny days, followed by cooling evenings. The air is invigorating and the townspeople seem even happier than usual. Poinsettia plants are to be seen everywhere as Indian women pack them through the streets. The country people bring in huge, grey-green bundles of Spanish moss and pile them along the little Alameda de León. There is a feeling of happy Christmas anticipation, easily transmitted even to the first-time, English-only visitors.

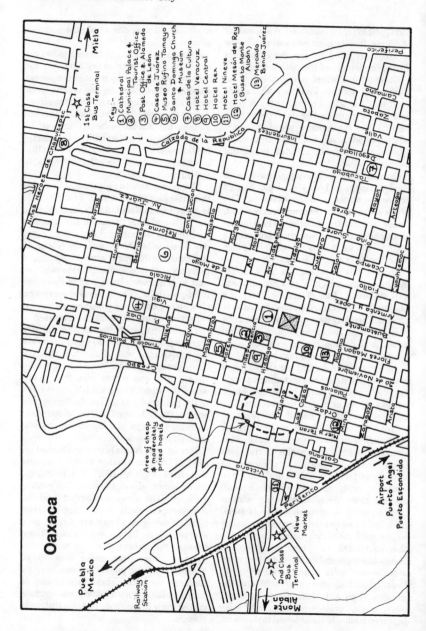

Oaxaca

Key:—
1. Cathedral
2. Municipal Palace + Tourist Office
3. Post Office + Alameda de León
4. Casa de Juárez
5. Museo Rufino Tamayo
6. Santo Domingo Church + Museum
7. Casa de la Cultura
8. Hotel Veracruz
9. Hotel Central
10. Hotel Rex
11. Hotel Nineve
12. Hotel Mesón del Rey (Buses to Monte Albán)
13. Mercado Benito Juárez

1st Class Bus Terminal

Mitla

Calzada de la República

Niños Heroes de Chapultepec

Av Juárez

Reforma
Constitución
Abasolo
Av Morelos
Av Independencia
Av Hidalgo

5 de Mayo
Alcala
Vigil
Diaz
Alianza
Bravo
Matamoros
Morelos
Independencia
Hidalgo

Tinoco y Palacios
Crespo

G Forja
Humboldt
Berriozabal

Area of cheap + moderately priced hotels

Las Casas
Tinoco

Mier y Teran
Galeana
Ordaz
Victoria
Periferico

New Market

Railway Station

Puebla Mexico

2nd Class Bus Terminal

Monte Albán

Airport Puerto Angel Puerto Escondido

Armenta y López
Bustamante
Fiallo
Ocampo
Cauhtemoc
Pino Suarez
Reforma
Libres
Rayon
Arteaga
Xicotencatl

Flores Magon
Aldama
20 de Noviembre
Zaragoza

Guerrero
Cabrera

Periferico
Camacho
Zapata
Valle
Degollado
Tacuboa
Insurgentes

Ruins of Monte Albán & Mitla

Part of Oaxaca's attraction for travellers is those great nearby ruins. Monte Albán is closest to town, and the one most often visited by foreigners. It is a gigantic place, occupying something over 40 square km. The plaza is 200 by 300 metres – six hectares – which compares very favourably with big-city plazas in modern Mexico.

Zapotec Monte Albán thrived for over 20 centuries and then, for unknown reasons, was abandoned and turned into a vast necropolis by its neighbours. Shortly thereafter the site was occupied by the Mixtecs. No builders they; the Mixtecs simply moved into old Zapotec buildings. In those days the area was very densely populated, as indicated by over 260 sites discovered so far. Archaeological invest-igations at Monte Albán have been under way for over half a century. A great deal has been learned about the lives and and history of the early inhabitants, and a number of excellent guidebooks to the ruins have been written in English, Spanish, French and German – available both in Oaxaca and the little museum at Monte Albán. If you obtain one of these books, and spend some time reading up on the subject before you make the trip out there, it will greatly enhance the pleasure of the visit.

Plan to spend a little time. Monte Albán will take several days to tour; anything less won't really do it justice.

Monte Albán is only about nine km from Oaxaca. Many visitors take a cab from the plaza, which is an expensive way to go unless there is a full load to split the tab. Most arrive by bus. The bus stop for the Monte Albán coach changes from time to time, but at present it is at the Hotel Mesón de Angel, on Mina between Mier y Terran and Díaz Ordaz. Buses run throughout the day, so it is possible to go out early and return late. Check the schedules – as with the station location they are subject to whimsical change. And be sure to pack a picnic lunch. Although there are usually food stands, neither the stands themselves nor the quality of their food is reliable.

Mitla, Oaxaca's other major ruin, is approximately 45 km from the Plaza de la Constitución, and it is not nearly as extensive or as interesting as Monte Albán, so it is the least-visited of the two sites. But if you have only a single day to spend, I'd suggest Mitla. It can be fairly well examined in two or three hours, whereas a short visit to Albán doesn't allow much more than a quick glimpse of the ball court or the Danzantes.

Getting to Mitla is simplicity itself. Hike out Trujano to the second-class bus station and board the Mitla bus at gate 15. The buses run every half-hour or so and the trip takes about an hour and a half. Fare is approximately M$250.

Places to Stay

Although Oaxaca has hotels by the dozen, it has visitors by the hundreds, with the predictable result that the hotels get filled quite often, and a few make the most of this golden opportunity to overcharge.

Hotel Veracruz, two blocks to the left as you leave the first-class bus station, is newish and would be extremely convenient for the person who arrives late at night via first-class bus, except that it tends to fill up early. But if you are lucky enough to get a room, you will have one of the better buys in largely overpriced Oaxaca. Expensive.

Hotel Santo Tomás, Abosolo near Juárez, is an older motel-like place displaying the oval logo of the Mexican Hotel Association which has always seemed to me – perhaps unfairly – to be a good indication of an overpriced house. The Santo Tomás makes a considerable effort to give value with an accommodating staff and efficient maid service. Expensive.

Most of the economy hotels are between the zócalo and the second-class bus station.

Hotel Central, on 20 de Noviembre between Hidalgo and Independencia, was the low-priced standby in Oaxaca, but grew sloppy and careless. Recently management has got its act together and the Central is again worthy of mention, and a good choice for those who feel they just have to be close to the plaza. Expensive.

If you go to the corner of Trujano and Díaz Ordáz you can see seven hotels. The thing to do is make a personal inspection trip and take your choice – Mexican room clerks are used to showing prospective customers their rooms. Prices range from low-moderate to expensive.

Maison del Rey, on Trujano between Díaz Ordáz and Mier y Terran, is hard to overlook. It has a cream-and-yellow front with brown grilles around the balconies. Moderate and recommended.

Hotel Jiménez, on Mier y Terran between Trujano and Hidalgo, is more an economy-model motel than a hotel. There is parking in the courtyard for a few vehicles. Moderate.

Hotel Paris, a fairly new house at Trujano and Galeana, has a beige facade, comfortable beds, hot water, small rooms and a price about 20% higher than it should be. Even with the addition of enclosed parking it's expensive.

Hotel del Pacifico, at Mier y Terran and Trujano, is also fairly new and offers the same amenities as the Paris but at a somewhat more reasonable price. Moderate.

Hotel Ninive is another newish hotel at Perifico and Las Casas, which is the next street south of Trujano at the stoplight by the railroad tracks. You can watch for it as you leave the second-class bus station and start toward the centre of town. It is so far from the plaza that the price is moderate.

There is a real, up-front *Casa de Huéspedes* in the first block of Trujano after you leave the traffic light by the railroad tracks. The place is not otherwise identified by name. Inexpensive.

Back uptown, the *Hotel El Presidente* on 5 de Mayo between Abosolo and Murgui is in the tastefully rebuilt former Convento de Santa Catalina. This is a really first-rate job of conversion and worthy of an inspection, but I feel their rates border on the outrageous. Ridiculously expensive.

Places to Eat

Oaxaca is a fair eating town, with most of the lower-priced restaurants serving Oaxacan regional items as well as standard Mexican fare. Mexican is better. But first I'll mention a couple of places to avoid.

One is the restaurant in the ADO bus station. ADO operates its own restaurants, which are definitely not up to the standards of its buses. Among other objectionable habits, they show a distressing tendency to serve reconstituted orange juice, and Bimbo sliced bread – the ultimate insult in a land that makes *bolillos*. And because of the low standards of ADO food, they don't do too much business, which in turn means that food spends too much time in the steam table. These remarks definitely apply to the Oaxaca first-class terminal.

The other restaurant to avoid is right on the Plaza Constitución. It calls itself the *Fuente de Sodas el Tule*. It has the best restaurant setting in town and traps a few unwary travellers with its rather elaborate menu. If you go there, stick to beer and/or soda fountain items and take a table overlooking the square. It's in the same block as the Señorial. Ridiculously expensive, too.

Eating anywhere around the plaza in sidewalk cafés turns out to be expensive and not very good, but try the *Café el Cazador*, only a block from the plaza on Trujano. The Cazador features both Mexican and regional dishes, and is moderately priced.

Prices drop as you get farther away from the zócalo, and the *Super-Cosino Kosinto* is no exception. Located on Hidalgo between Díaz Ordáz and J P Garcia, it is larger than it looks from the sidewalk. Really a room and a half in size, the restaurant has featured standard Mexican fare for a long time. Moderate.

As you go out Trujano toward the second-class bus station, the restaurants gradually get smaller and cheaper, and the Kosinto is situated in the midst of an area thick with inexpensive restaurants.

For the real peoples' restaurant at

peoples' prices, keep walking out Trujano until you come to the railroad tracks. The long, low brick buildings to the left of the big Central Commercial Popular building are the new market. Skip the first building and try the second and third, entering from the bus station end. There are at least a dozen food stalls serving both Oaxacan and Mexican specialties. These are well-prepared and generally inexpensive.

If the yen for snow-white tablecloths overcomes you, then try one of the hotels around the plaza, especially the *Monte Albán* on the plaza. The patio has become the dining room. This is a very spacious establishment with clean restrooms. Their wines have proven dependable so far, though the menu is singularly unimaginative. I make this my standard breakfast stop. For breakfast it's moderate; other meals are expensive.

Getting There & Getting Around

Oaxaca has excellent first and second-class bus service, and there are buses for Puerto Escondido, Puerto Angel, San Cristóbal las Casas, Mexico City, Veracruz, Villahermosa, the Guatemalan border, and dozens of little backwoodsy towns that don't even appear on maps.

To get uptown from the second-class bus station, turn left as you come out on the broad divided avenue. Go past the big Centro Comercial Popular store and cross over the railroad tracks and the Perifico at the traffic light. Then take the street that angles off to the left. Eventually this street bends to the right to become Trujano, which leads you to the plaza. Walking time: 15 minutes.

To get from the first-class bus station to the centre of town, turn left on leaving the station. Go three blocks and turn left again on the well-traveled Avenida Juárez and follow it 11 or 12 blocks, then turn right on Independencia or Hidalgo – either one will take you to the Plaza de la Constitución in three more blocks. Walking time is 20 minutes.

There is city bus service, but it is not worth the trouble to get to or from the bus station by a city bus. If walking is inconvenient, then catch a taxi.

There is railroad service to Oaxaca from Mexico City via Puebla and Tehuacán. It takes about 15 hours when the trains run on time, and running on time is not a universal trait among Mexican trains. There are two trains, a day train and a night train. Both are slow.

Oaxaca has excellent air service, with both Mexicana and Aeromexico having several flights a day to Mérida, Veracruz, Mexico City, Villahermosa and so on. A local airline, Oaxaqueños, serves Puerto Angel and Puerto Escondido. Arriving passengers can take a colectivo to town at around US$2. Theoretically a colectivo may be taken to the airport, but this is often more trouble than it's worth.

TUXTLA GUITERREZ, Chiapas

(elevation 550 metres, population 210,000)

Twenty-five years ago, Tuxtla was a small, modern town dedicated to making money by supplying necessities to a large part of Mexico. Since then, nothing has changed except the town's size. Tuxtla is the transport centre of the State of Chiapas, with bus service to Villahermosa, Mexico City, Oaxaca, San Cristóbal las Casas and Guatemala.

The first and second-class bus stations are some distance apart, and the streets are a little confusing, so if for some reason you find it necessary to transfer between the stations, take a taxi. Fare is about M$200.

The airport offers service to Mexico City and way points.

There is no railroad.

Places to Stay

For those who must overnight, there are several hotels near the second-class bus station. Go out the front door and turn right, then left at the end of the street – about 50 metres. Turn right where the street appears to end, and the *Hotel*

Ricamar is about a half block away. This is a modern, box-style construction, fairly new. Moderate.

Lone female travellers may prefer the *Casa de Huéspedes San Roque,* located just before the Ricamar. Their sign says 'We accept only Misses' (in Spanish). Inexpensive.

If, instead of turning right for the Ricamar, you jog left and continue for another block, you will see on your right the rather bedraggled *Hotel Los Leones.* It is a small hotel that has suffered a fire in the recent past. The electric sign has long since bitten the dust, but the angle-iron frame is still there. Inexpensive.

Almost directly across the street from the first-class station are two hotels offering similar accommodation: the *Hotel Santo Domingo* and the *Hotel María Teresa.* They have the habit of filling early because they are highly visible from the station and are moderate in price.

If those two hotels are filled, pass them and turn right at the next intersection. In the next block are three more hotels that are unlikely to be filled, as they are all either expensive or very expensive.

Make sure that the fan or air-conditioning is operating – low-altitude Tuxtla can get mighty hot during the summer.

Places to Eat

Go out the front door of the second-class bus station and turn right. At the end of the street is a cross-street lined with restaurant stands. The vendors who run them serve better food than that at most bus station restaurants. Inexpensive.

Inasmuch as the first-class bus station is right downtown, the restaurant situation there is somewhat better, and more expensive. Go past the hotels María Teresa and the Santo Domingo to the left of the door as you leave the station. Turn right at the next corner. In a block or so, you will come to the Esponda Hotel, and across the street from the Esponda is the *Restaurant Cesar's.* This Cesar's doesn't claim to have invented any salads, but it puts out a pretty fair meal. Moderate.

Right across the street from the station is a small restaurant. The name escapes me, but it is fairly good and inexpensive.

SAN CRISTÓBAL LAS CASAS, Chiapas
(elevation 2165 metres, population 45,000)
It is but a short 43 km from Tuxtla to San Cristóbal las Casas, but in that distance the elevation increases over 1600 metres, with an infinite increase in colonial atmosphere and ambience in general.

San Cristóbal las Casas is one of the unspoilt jewels among Mexican cities, and one of the most determinedly colonial towns in the Republic. It is also the only city where large numbers of Indians from the surrounding countryside continue to wear the traditional costumes unique to each village. It is common to see Zinatecáns in their beribboned hats, Chamulas in white or black tunics with coloured sleeves and men from Huistán in 'diaper' pants.

During the last 50 years San Cristóbal las Casas has been a magnet for both Americans and Europeans who appreciate the small-town way of life, as well as for scholars studying the numerous tribes. Some are attracted, too, by the superb climate, which is much like Guadalajara's.

Recently the ready availability of low-cost air fares from Europe, plus an increasing awareness of Mexico's unique qualities, has brought ever-increasing numbers of French, Swiss, German, British and other Europeans to San Cristóbal las Casas, and today the place is a veritable Babel. An increasing number of signs are going up stating that the businesspeople can speak French, German and English, whereas a few years ago you were fortunate to find a shopkeeper who spoke unaccented Spanish.

The city was founded in 1528 by Diego Mazariegos, a compassionate man who was soon replaced by a heartless individual named Juan Enrique de Guzman, every

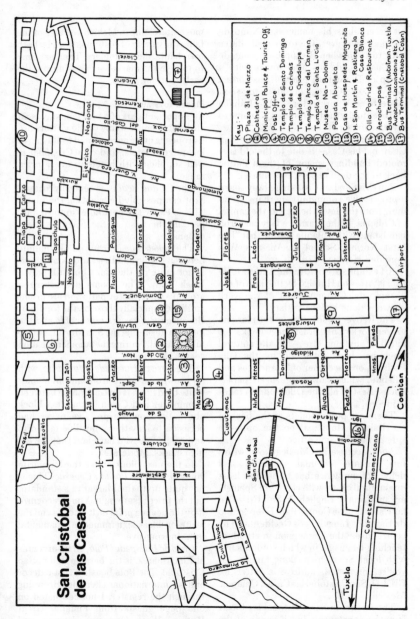

San Cristóbal de las Casas

Key:-
① Plaza 31 de Marzo
② Cathedral
③ Municipal Palace & Tourist Off
④ Post Office
⑤ Templo de Santo Domingo
⑥ Templo de Caribas
⑦ Templo de Guadalupe
⑧ Templo y Arco del Carmen
⑨ Templo de Santa Lucia
⑩ Museo Na - Bolom
⑪ Posada Abuelita
⑫ Casa de Huespedes Margarita
⑬ H. San Martín & Rostícería la
        Casa Blanca
⑭ Olla Podrida Restaurant
⑮ Aerochiapas
⑯ Bus Terminal (Autobran Tuxtla.
        Autotran Lacandonia, etc.)
⑰ Bus Terminal (Cristobal Colon)

bit as cruel as his namesake, Nuño de Guzman. However, the town really dates back to 1545 when Bishop Bartolome de las Casas made his appearance with a group of Dominican priests. Las Casas, like Vasco de Quiroga in Pátzcuaro, soon made himself 'protector' of the Indians and eventually the town added his name to the existing Cristóbal.

Most of the architectural charm of San Cristóbal las Casas is due to the old tile-roofed buildings, many of them dating back to the days of las Casas himself.

San Cristóbal las Casas has always been a progressive community, perhaps stemming from the days when it was the capital of Chiapas. In the plaza is a lacy cast-iron bandstand with a plaque stating that 'The First Normal School in America Was Founded Here in 1828'.

Art exhibits are held in the Auditorio de Bellas Artes on Hidalgo by the arch of the Templo del Carmen. Most of the work shown is done by local artists.

The Reoveco bookstore on the plaza no longer stocks English-language books – or much of anything else – but the cultural slack has been taken up by the Olla Podrida, on the corner of Mazariegos and Allende, which now offers used paperbacks. Best of all, the Olla Podrida takes trade-ins.

There are public toilets at the back of the Palacio Municipal on the opposite side of the Turismo office.

And, of course, any Mexican town with a fine climate, colonial buildings and delightful ambience has to have at least one cultural centre with classes in Spanish, art and usually English. In San Cristóbal las Casas it's the Centro Para Intercambio de Estudios Linguisticos Occidental. The centre uses the immersion method of teaching language, in which students live with local Spanish-speaking families. If you're interested, address a letter to: CIELO, San Cristóbal las Casas, Chiapas, Mexico.

The market in San Cristóbal las Casas is not very extensive but it is one of the most interesting in Mexico because of the fantastic variety of costumes worn by both merchants and customers. The best time to take in the market scene is during the early morning hours.

Places to Stay

An important part of a pleasant stay is an affordable hotel. Many of the visitors are Europeans quite accustomed to staying in low-priced hotels, and San Cristóbal is well supplied with hotels in every price range.

The *Ciudad Real* is as centrally located as it can possibly be, right on the plaza. This is easily the best hotel in town and, partially because of the plaza location, expensive.

The *Hotel San Martín*, on Guadalupe between Utrillo and Belesario Dominguez, is not quite on the plaza but still only a block away. The rooms are arranged around a three-storey patio and are bright and airy, especially those on the top floor. Because the rates are reasonable and the location desirable, the San Martín is often full, especially during the summer vacation season. Moderate.

The *Casa de Huéspedes Margarita*, with its brown-and-white front and blue-and-white tiled floor, is on Guadalupe between Dominguez and Colón in the next block above the San Martín. I've never had occasion to stay there, but I've talked to several people who have and they gave it high marks. Moderate.

In the next block above the Margarita you will find the *Posada Cepeyac*. This is not quite up to the Margarita's standard, but the price is sure right. You'll recognize it by the peeling paint on its facade and the white-on-black sign framed in ornamental iron. Inexpensive.

Casa de Huéspedes Pola, on Insurgentes at Piño Suarez, is the bargain find of San Cristóbal. The Pola boasts a rustic decor and an international clientele. Browsing through the register, I noticed listed on one page guests from Finland, Great Britain, West Germany, France and

Spain. It is close to both bus stations and only about 10 minutes from the plaza. Inexpensive.

Up Insurgentes from the Pola is the *Posada Insurgentes* and the *Posada Lupita*; both are convenient to the bus stations and are very inexpensive.

The French-speaking traveller will feel right at home at the *Casa de Huéspedes Chamula*, whose owner makes quite a point of his ability to speak French. Inexpensive.

The *Posada Abuelita*, on Tapachula near Tuxtla, has to be the cheapest place to stay in San Cristóbal las Casas, especially for those with their own sleeping gear. It is a sort of cross between a casa de huéspedes and a youth hostel where people can save around M$150 a night by bedding down in the dormitory. With or without sleeping gear, it's inexpensive.

Finally, two travellers from London told me they stayed in the *Hotel Santa Clara* on the zócalo, which wasn't nearly as expensive as it looked.

Places to Eat
The *Rostícería la Casa Blanca Restaurant,* on Guadalupe between Utrillo and Dominguez opposite the Hotel San Martin, is exactly what it says on the sign – a place that sells roasted chickens, and a restaurant as well. Bigger than it appears from the sidewalk, the Blanca does a booming business with both locals and foreigners in the morning with café con leche and pan dulce. Good service. Moderate.

Los Arcos, a block off the plaza on Madero, doesn't get much business from visitors although it is popular with local residents. Food is strictly Mexican and good; they do liver especially well. This is another place a lot larger inside than it appears from the outside. Inexpensive.

Hotel Ciudad Real has a small, white-tablecloth restaurant in the patio. The quality of the food has come up immensely during the past couple of years. This is another place more popular with local people than with foreigners. Expensive.

Olla Podrida, on the corner of Mazariegos and Allende, gets a lot of beard-and-sandal customers who know a good thing when they taste it. Their bread is home-made, and is also sold to the public. Moderate.

On Avenida Juárez, near Madero and only a block from the plaza, is the *Salchichería Die Freunde.* Here you will find the best assortment of sausage outside of Mexico City. Cheese, too. This is a good place to get the cold cuts and cheese to go with the bread from the Olla Podrida; this combination, together with a couple of bottles of sweating-cold beer, is the cheapest meal you can have in San Cristóbal las Casas. Inexpensive.

Admittedly it is quite a walk, but the vendors up at the market do the cheapest and about the best meals for the peso. I've been eating with them almost from the time the concrete was poured, and I'm of the opinion that the extra walk out from the centre of town is worthwhile. Very inexpensive.

There is a restaurant called *El Triangulo* across the Carretera Panamerica from the Cristóbal Colón bus station. You can actually see it through the big plate-glass window in front of the waiting room. It does a good business with truck drivers heading down Guatemala way. Inexpensive.

Getting There & Getting Around
Almost everybody arrives in San Cristóbal las Casas by bus from Tuxtla. There are quite a number of buses every day, and the distance – 80 km – is too small to warrant bothering with airplanes.

I said almost everybody. A few hardy souls arrive on the daily second-class bus that makes the trip through the hills from Palenque – one of the more scenic runs in Mexico.

To get downtown from the second-class bus station, go out the front door and turn left, then right at the first street. Go two blocks and turn left on Hidalgo – you will be able to see the arch a couple of blocks in front of you. Continue on Hidalgo until you reach the plaza three blocks beyond the arch. Walking time is about 15 minutes.

To get downtown from the Cristóbal Colón first-class bus station, leave the waiting room and turn right on Insurgentes; the plaza is just seven blocks. Walking time: 12 minutes.

Guard your valuables! The economic situation is so desperate for the locals that pickpockets have even started working the second-class buses at San Cristóbal las Casas, and travellers are a natural prey for *rateros*.

I learned this the hard way.

PALENQUE, Chiapas

(elevation 30 metres, population 35,000) 'Palenque' means 'palisade' in Spanish; the town takes its modern name from the nearby cliffs. The original name was Santo Domingo – why it was changed no one can tell me. Although cattle raising is the local specialty – you'll see herds of lop-eared, humpbacked cattle along the road, accompanied by cattle egrets – Palenque makes most of its money through travellers who come to gawk at the nearby ruins. There are well over a dozen hotels and at least an equal number of restaurants for the comfort and sustenance of the wayfarer, both in the village itself and along the road to the ruins. There are also a number of gimcrack shops and peddlers eager to sell you their wares.

Guidebooks to the ruins are available in Palenque Village – can you imagine a 'village' with over 30,000 inhabitants? – in Spanish, English and usually in French and German. These will go far toward explaining the ruins, which are entirely too large to be covered well in a general guidebook of this nature. However, I will mention the Tree of the Foliated Cross, unique in the Americas, but with a nearly identical duplicate at Angkor Wat in Cambodia. Also to be found at the ruins are sculpted figures holding flowers; they, too, have their counterparts in a Buddhist temple in India.

Travellers coming to Palenque, particularly in the hot, humid summer months, will be well advised to have plenty of DEET (see Sources section in Facts for the Visitor) for protection from Palenque's voracious insects. The insects are especially plentiful wherever there is grass and shrubs. DEET won't eliminate the problem, but it will at least make it bearable.

Places to Stay

Since visitors to the ruins constitute the major source of income for Palenque's townsfolk, it logically follows that there are numerous motels, most of which are entirely too dear for dedicated Scots penny-pinchers like myself. There are also a number of hotels, motels and trailer camps on the dead-end road leading from the Palenque to the ruins, but I feel it is much better to be located in town where there is a wider assortment of restaurants and other facilities aimed at bettering the existence of the independent traveller.

When I'm in Palenque I tend to stay right on the Parque Central at the *Hotel Palenque*. This is an older house that endeavours to stick the guest for the double room rate regardless of the number in the party. At either the single or double rate, it is moderate. If there has been a paucity of guests, the establishment has been known to haggle, but if the town is full you're sure to pay the aforementioned double rate. The hotel is reported to have yet another, lower, rate for travellers who carry their own hammocks, but as I don't go this route I can't speak from personal experience. There is also a hefty extra charge for air-conditioning, which I feel doesn't work nearly as well as a ceiling-mounted paddle fan for which there is currently no extra charge. Even with all the 'extras', however, the Palenque is still moderate.

If the Hotel Palenque happens to be full, I walk toward the setting sun on Juárez, about a block from the Plaza, and check in at the *Hotel Misol Ha*, smaller than the antique Palenque and another place with a dual rate. The charge for air-conditioning is exactly double the un-cooled rate. I still prefer the fan for which there is (usually) no charge. Inexpensive/moderate.

Hotel Avenida is across the street from the second-class bus station. As a rule there are no buses after midnight or before 7 am but I still suggest trying for a room in the back of the house, away from the street noise. There are double beds. Although I've not done so, I would not hesitate to stay here. Best of all, it is somewhat less expensive than the houses up in the centre of things by the Parque Central. Inexpensive.

Places to Eat

It's hard to beat the *Restaurante Nicte-Ha* on the Parque Central. It serves both Mexican and Yucatecan specialties: *mole poblano, chicken pibil.* I was in the Nicte-Ha one evening when a Frenchman mistook the bottle of *salsa Habanero* on the table for the milder Tabasco of the United States, and applied it accordingly. It took him about three bites to discover he'd made an awful mistake. Not only is the Habanero one of the hottest peppers in Mexico, it tends to get hotter and hotter with the passage of time. It is locally famous for this quality. Moderate and recommended.

Restaurante Maya, right next door to the Nicte-Ha, has beautiful, well-done menus and prices that border on the ridiculous. Both food and prices have been better at the Nicte-Ha for years. There are persistent rumours around town that the Maya is about to be taken over by new owners, which will probably change things. For now, all it's got going for it is the location. Expensive.

You can always beat the relatively high prices in the uptown restaurants by strolling the few blocks to the market. This is extremely practical for breakfast but doesn't work at all for dinner because the market vendors go home early. They

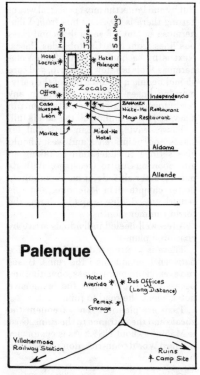

all serve about the same dishes, and I remember with affection the fine *sopa de chicharrones* I had here a few years back and have never been able to locate again in Palenque. Generally inexpensive.

Another reason for staying in town rather than in the midst of the jungle on the way to the ruins is that it is simple to obtain the makings for a picnic lunch, a practical necessity for those intending to spend a full day at the ruins. Pickings there are mighty scanty.

Getting There & Getting Around

Palenque is one of the very few places in Mexico where there are many arrivals by rail, usually from Mérida or Campeche on their way back to the US after flying to one of the international airports in Yucatán.

But by and large, the most practical way of getting there is by ADO bus from Villahermosa or any of several second-class bus lines from San Cristóbal las Casas. Next is by second-class bus from Villahermosa. This is a slow, slow trip, and care should be taken to catch one of the early-morning buses – those arriving in any resort town in Mexico much after 4 pm run a severe risk of finding all the hotels full.

Those leaving for San Cristóbal las Casas and points east and west should give serious consideration to taking an afternoon bus up to Ocosingo. With its much greater altitude, it has an infinitely better climate than Palenque, and this remark goes double in spades during the torrid summer months.

A few well-heeled individuals arrive by chartered plane.

There is pretty good local bus service between Palenque and the ruins. Buses run every hour, more or less, obviating any necessity to patronize the expensive hotels along the road to ruin.

Taxis are plentiful. They frequent the zócalo and the entrance to the ruins. Cost is M$500 – about US$2. As is customary in Third World countries, don't hesitate to bargain.

OCOSINGO, Chiapas

(elevation 2000 metres, population 15,000)

Until relatively recent times, Ocosingo was inaccessible to ordinary vehicular traffic. It was at the end of a dead-end road that has been upgraded into a through highway. Because of the paucity of traffic, the charming old colonial town has suffered less from galloping modernization than almost any municipality you could care to name, short of being declared a monument city.

Ocosingo is the ideal place to break a trip to or from Palenque or San Cristóbal, as it is about halfway – timewise – between the two. Palenque is low, humid, almost unbearably hot in the summer, and infested with the hungriest insects short

of Puerto Vallarta's, whereas Ocosingo with its much higher altitude has none of these problems. In addition, Ocosingo has a number of quite reasonably priced hotels and restaurants, and a charming plaza surrounded by shade-giving *portales*. The fountain in the centre of the plaza sometimes works. Also in contrast to Palenque, Ocosingo does not depend on travellers for the bulk of its income. The main business is cheese-making, and the locally produced *machego* cheese is relished all over Mexico.

Places to Stay

Right on the plaza itself is my favourite stopping place, the *Hotel Central* with all the amenities – tiled bathrooms, well-furnished rooms and fans. This last is not really required for most of the year but I'd rather have a fan and not use it than really need one that turns out to be unavailable. Best of all, the hotel is at the low end of inexpensive.

Not too far away, less than a block off the plaza to the north and on the same street, is the *Hotel Margarita*. It is similar to the Central in price and ambience, but I much prefer the Central because of its central location. The hotel is also inexpensive, but almost M$100 dearer than the Central.

For those who are really pinching centavos, there is the *Hospedaje San José*, about a block from the plaza on Calle 1 Oeste. It is cleaner by far than you would expect of an establishment in this price range. The hospedaje is about M$300 less than the Central and the Margarita, which makes it very inexpensive indeed.

Places to Eat

Right on the plaza is the *Restaurante la Montera*, which serves typical Mexican food, well prepared. It is somewhat inclined to serve chewing-gum white bread to foreigners in the well-founded belief that they must prefer it since so many of them eat it at home. Inexpensive.

The *Paladino* is also on the plaza, along

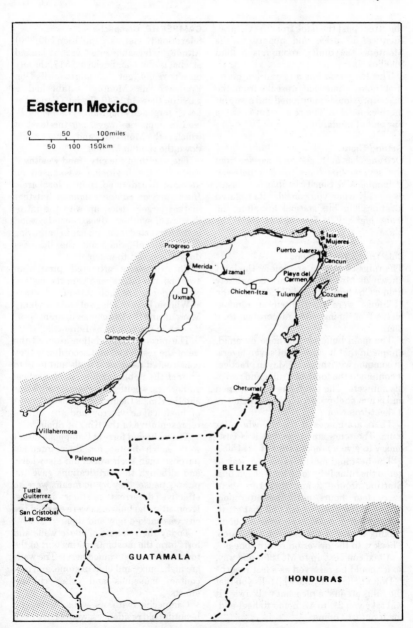

Eastern Mexico

0   50   100 miles
  50   100 150 km

Progreso

Merida
Izamal

Uxmal

Chichen-Itza

Campeche

Isla Mujeres
Puerto Juarez
Cancun
Playa del Carmen
Tulum
Cozumel

N

Chetumal

Villahermosa

Palenque

BELIZE

Tustla
Guiterrez

San Cristobal
Las Casas

GUATAMALA

HONDURAS

the street past the bank from the Central. Identical in price and quality to the Montera, the dining room has a loud jukebox. Inexpensive.

The *Margarita* has a restaurant on its first floor, somewhat upscale from the places previously mentioned and a wee bit more expensive. The restaurant is at the low end of moderate.

Getting There

Ocosingo has quite good bus service from the several bus lines running between Palenque and San Cristóbal las Casas, especially when you consider its isolated location. The bus stations are along the main highway a few blocks from the plaza.

Side Trip to Toniná Ruins

The ruins of Toniná are among the least known in Mexico. They are completely unlike Chichén-Itzá and Tikal in that the buildings were distributed at random instead of being sited according to a plan.

The main building is a huge pyramid, unique in that it consists of seven layers. In common with the usual Mayan practice, it contained the tomb of a ruler and two of his subjects. The tomb has been opened and is now sheltered from the elements by a sheet-iron roof.

There are guides at the site who offer tours. The tours are gratis, but it is customary to give a *propina* (tip) of M$150.

The best and most inexpensive way to get to the ruins is by local long-nosed bus. Starting around 3 am, they run about every four hours until mid-afternoon. Although the distance isn't all that great, the trip often takes well over an hour, making it one of the slowest in Mexico. Check with the driver on return times.

A taxi can cost up to M$1800 one way, so it should be reserved as a last resort.

Don't believe anyone who tells you that the ruins are just a pleasant walk away. It will take you 3½ to 4½ hours to heel-and-toe it out to Tonina.

CAMPECHE, Campeche

(elevation 13 metres, population 100,000)

Although Hernández de Córdoba landed at what is now Campeche in 1517, the city didn't really get its start until Don Francisco de Montejo established a garrison there in 1540. Today Córdoba is largely forgotten while Montejo is memorialized in numerous ways, not the least of which is the Montejo brand of beer made down the road in Mérida.

The wealth of the city – and wealthy it was – in the beginning was based on logwood dye derived from a local tree, *Hoematoxylon campeachianum*, but that market largely dried up with the introduction of synthetic dyes. Some logwood is still harvested today for use in improving the colour of wine, but the business doesn't amount to much.

The rich city attracted pirates in swarms, and interwoven with the history of Campeche are such noted freebooters as William Parker, Diego el Mulato, Henry Morgan, and the Dutchman Laurent Graff (known in Campeche as Lorencillo).

The pirates' depredation aroused the ire of the residents, and accordingly they constructed a series of walls and forts to protect the noble families, ecclesiastical authorities, wealthy merchants, politicians and the King's Lieutenant – this last a sort of bush-league viceroy and the official representative of the King of Spain.

The walls and forts at Campeche didn't work much better for their intended purpose than such works did elsewhere, and although the fortifications gave the pirates pause, they by no means were an effective deterrent to their activities. Even after the bulwarks were erected the city was sacked now and then.

Today the remains of those walls and forts form the most interesting part of the town and its most valued asset. The walls are high, bulky and built of stone, and now contain museums and other cultural efforts.

Campeche, with its walls, forts and beautiful old residences, would have been a logical contender for a place on Mexico's list of national monuments, so that its handsome works could have been preserved, but it never made the list and as a result has been afflicted with some examples of Mexican Modern Miracle architecture. The Palacio Gobierno and the hotels Baluartes (Ramparts) and El Presidente are outstanding examples of this, especially as they were built between the old city and the ocean.

A definite plus for both Campeche and Mérida is their system of street numbering, with the odd-numbered streets going one way and the even-numbered streets intersecting them at right angles. There are also street signs at every intersection. Contrast this with the usual haphazard Mexican method of naming streets two or more times with no system and no street signs.

The little Museo de Historia at Calle 57 and Calle 8 emphasizes weapons used by the early Colonials. There are also lots of other items, mostly with a marine orientation, such as a figurehead, rudder and tiller.

The King's Lieutenant had an important position, and lived accordingly. If you stroll up Calle 14 you will find La Casa de Teniente del Rey between Calles 59 and 61. Admire the Baroque facade and iron-studded door, and inspect the interior if you get a chance.

Campeche is loaded with odds and ends made of turtle shells. Be advised that sea turtles are on the endangered species list, and combs, pearl-inlaid model pistols and such are liable to be confiscated at the border of any country.

Places to Stay

The arm-and-a-leg expensive *Hotel El Presidente* is a typically overpriced installation on the waterfront below the Water Gate at the foot of Calle 59. Go through the gate and angle through the parking lot on your right. I never seem to have very good luck with the Presidente hotels, and the one in Campeche is no exception. My

room came with two 'F' (*frio* or 'cold') faucets in the shower, the door to the hall could only be opened part way, and condensation from the air-conditioning pipes dripped down the back of my neck as I opened the door. All in all, this was not the sort of service anyone would reasonably expect, but I was staying there for the very best of reasons: arriving there rather late in the day in mid-summer, I found everything else in town full. Ridiculously expensive.

Facing the Presidente is the *Hotel Baluartes*, in the same price range but older and better managed. I've stayed at the Baluartes several times over the years and my only criticism is of the price: ridiculously expensive.

The *Hotel Campeche*, on the plaza opposite the church at Calle 57 and Calle 8, is inexpensive.

The *Hotel Reforma*, on Calle 8 near Calle 57, is an old-fashioned viajero-style house that sometimes hangs its washing in the patio to dry, a homey touch. The Reforma is usually full of country people, perhaps because the rates are so reasonable. This is the cheapest you can do downtown, which may not be too much of an advantage considering the size of walled Campeche. Inexpensive.

It seems as if the elderly *Hotel Castlemar*, on the corner of Calles 8 and 61, has always been a part of the Campeche scene with its large rooms, thick walls and high windows that swing wide to catch the cooling trades of an evening, but nowadays there is a huge, modernistic building blocking the view to seaward – though not quite all the breeze. The Castlemar is another hotel built on the bones of an old mansion. It's an excellent value, and I recommend it. Moderate.

Hotel Cuauhtémoc has been turned into a business boarding house.

Out on Gobernadores at Calle 45 (also Chile), directly across the street from the bus station, is the *Hotel Central*. A fairly new building with furnishings to match,

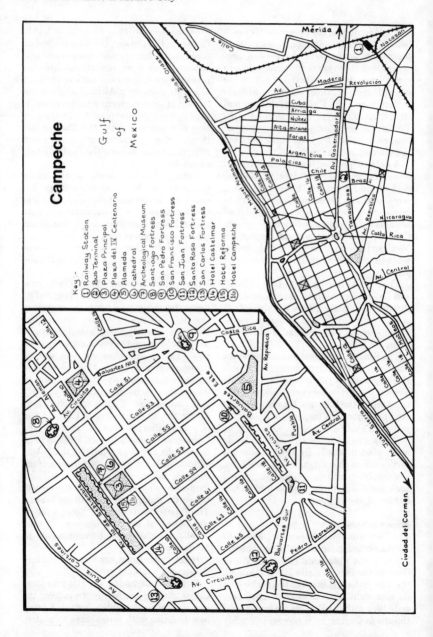

Campeche

Gulf of Mexico

Key :-
1. Railway Station
2. Bus Terminal
3. Plaza Principal
4. Plaza del IV Centenario
5. Alameda
6. Cathedral
7. Archeological Museum
8. Santiago Fortress
9. San Pedro Fortress
10. San Francisco Fortress
11. San Juan Fortress
12. Santa Rosa Fortress
13. San Carlos Fortress
14. Hotel Castelmar
15. Hotel Reforma
16. Hotel Campeche

Mérida

Ciudad del Carmen

the Central tends to fill up sooner than other hotels in town. It is popular with bus and truck drivers, for Gobernadores is the road to Mérida once it leaves the Campeche city limits. Expensive.

Places to Eat

The best place to eat in Campeche, by popular agreement, is the *Restaurant Miramar* at Calle 61 and Calle 8. Like the neighbouring Castlemar, it seems to have always been a part of Campeche. It has waiters who know their business and it offers a good, professionally prepared meal. The Miramar advertises 'All Brands Of Beer', and I believe it. The wine, however, is overpriced and I have seen fellow diners return bottles that had sat too long upright in a tropical climate. The return was accepted in good grace. During the afternoon the Miramar fills with affluent locals. Expensive, but well worth it.

The *Café Continental*, on Calle 61 and 8, opposite the Miramar, is a smallish coffee-shop-type operation that does good business with the bureaucrats working across the street. It is much cheaper than the Miramar, but has considerably less panache. Moderate.

The restaurant on the ground floor of the *Hotel Campeche*, Calle 57 at Calle 8, facing the plaza, is heavily patronized by working-class local people, which means it gives good value. Inexpensive.

Both the *Baluarte* and the *Presidente* have restaurants serving standard Mexican/international fare. If you have a choice, take the Baluarte. Very expensive.

The market is located just outside the old city wall on the opposite side of town from the ocean, at the ends of Calles 57 and 59. Because this is a seaside city, many of the food stalls specialize in seafood, and make a good job of it. Here you can find the cheapest eating in town short of buying the ingredients and doing it all yourself *al fresco*. Very inexpensive.

Getting There & Getting Around

Unless you fly into Campeche, you will approach and leave through low, flat fields studded with strange-looking tropical breeds of cattle. The cattle will be accompanied by cattle egrets, which live on the insects stirred up by the animals' huge hooves. Sometimes I think the egrets like to ride on the cattle to keep their feet dry. Originally an Old World bird, the egret has adapted very well to the Mexican and Central American lowlands. I've watched them for hours on end.

Campeche is on the main bus line to and from Yucatán, and a large number of buses going to and from Mérida stop here. However, during the tourist season many of them are full and the ticket agents won't sell tickets until the coach arrives and the number of seats available is ascertained.

Campeche also has air service, so if you can't get on a bus you might decide to fly. It is only 176 km by road to Mérida, and I have known several people who, failing to get on a bus in reasonable time, pooled their assets and took an air taxi. Contact Viajes Campeche, on Calle 10 between 57 and 59, half a block from the plaza.

Campeche has railroad service to Mérida and Mexico City. This is a practical way of getting to Palenque station and quite popular with wayfarers, as it eliminates going into Villahermosa and doubling back.

To get from the bus station to the Plaza Principal, go out on the heavily travelled Avenida Gobernadores and turn left. At the first baluarte it changes its name to Calle 18. Stay with it past the market to either Calle 55 or 57. Turn right and the plaza is four blocks away. Walking time is 25 minutes.

The railroad station is out beyond the bus station. Take a cab.

MÉRIDA, Yucatán

As with so many of the cities the Spanish built during the early years of the conquest, Mérida is constructed on the remains of a much older Indian city. The plaza is supposedly laid out on the remains of the pyramid torn down to provide building material for the conquerors' homes. This may very well be. The plaza is extraordinarily attractive and of a size appropriate to the size of the city – about 200 metres square. The story goes that a ship carrying Indian laurel seedlings intended to grace the Prado in Habana was wrecked off the Yucatán coast, and some of the trees wound up in Mérida where they still enhance the plaza.

For some reason the plaza in Mérida has more names than any square in Mexico, some of them being Plaza Principal, Plaza de la Constitución, Plaza de Armas, and even, on some present-day maps, simply Jardín.

The cathedral, aside from its size, is not unusual either in design or decoration. The main reason to visit it is to see the wooden figure called 'El Cristo de las Ampollas' (the Christ of the Blisters). Apparently it was carved in the village of Ichmul from the wood of an extraordinary tree. The story goes that this tree was seen mysteriously aflame on several occasions, yet when examined the following morning it was unharmed. A few years later the church that sheltered the Cristo burned, but the statue was undamaged except for some blisters. It was brought to its present resting place in 1645. A rip-roaring fiesta is held 28 September-13 October to honour the Christ of the Blisters.

The most interesting of the colonial dwellings is the Casa de Montejo, built by the son of the original Montejo. Located on Calle 63 across from the plaza, it was built before anyone thought of such foolishness as equality, and among the decorations are carved figures of caballeros, each with a foot on the bowed head of an Indian. The building is now open to the public for the usual few pesos admission fee. It should not be overlooked.

Mérida became a very wealthy city through henequén, a fibre product mainly used to make cordage. As in any prosperous city, the rich built large and imposing homes for their families. The best collection of these mansions is on and around Paseo de Montejo. To reach the Paseo from the plaza, go out Calle 60 to Calle 47 and turn left. The Paseo is between 56 and 58, number 56A under Mérida's street numbering system – about a dozen blocks or so from the plaza.

One of the pleasures of Mérida for locals and tourists alike is to load into a *calesa* (chaise) drawn by a placid nag and tour the town in dignity and comfort. This is a very enjoyable way to take in the Paseo de Montejo. The calesas also double as taxis, and it is not uncommon to see a country family carrying innumerable bundles get out of a calesa at the railroad station or at one of the bus stations.

Mérida has dozens and dozens of stores, stands and vendors selling handicrafts and locally manufactured goods. The guayabara shirts sold all over Mexico are mostly made in tiny back-room factories in the city, although they are just as expensive – or as cheap – in Guadalajara as they are in Yucatán. In Mérida it seems there is a shirt factory in every block, and sometimes two or three. One that I like and that marks its prices (most don't) is the Jarana on Calle 62 between Calles 59 and 61.

Fine leatherwork is done locally, too. One good leather shop with reasonable – and marked – prices is Casa Rubio, on Calle 56A between Calles 63A and 65, across from the post office. This has about everything imaginable in the leather line, including covers for Bic lighters, dozens of wallets and billfolds, passport cases and belts.

The Casa de las Artesanías del Gobierno del Estado de Yucatán, on Calle 63 between Calles 66 and 64, is entered via the patio of the school. This apparently discourages those few foreigners who have heard of it. A handicraft salesroom that's practically a museum of contemporary Yucatecan handmade goods, it has everything you can think of: handmade kitchen chairs, mortar and pestle sets, real clay piggy banks, turquoise rings, 'Panama' hats, and beautiful *huipiles* (a traditional Mayan blouse) like those the women in the market have been wearing for hundreds of years. All merchandise is price-tagged and is generally of better quality and lower price than the wares in the stores and stands around town. The bulk of the customers are local people rather than tourists.

While you're visiting the Casa de Las Artesanias spare a few minutes for a stroll around the building housing the shop. It is an art school with interesting displays of the students' and instructors' work. The beautiful old building has been tastefully converted.

So-called 'Panama hats' are woven around Mérida out of henequén fibre. This is the fibre used to make sisal ropes, and it is extremely tough and durable. The hats are so flexible that they can be rolled up for packing and will still recover nicely.

The Spanish word for 'Panama hat' is *jipijapa*, locally shortened to *jipi*. The pochismo for 'hippy' is also jipi, pronounced identically, which can cause confusion and occasional ill feelings when someone touting for a store walks up to a neatly-bearded gentleman and says, 'Jipi? Jipi?'

Anyone who looks at all like a foreigner will be invited to visit shirt factories, jewellery shops, jipi warehouses – you name it. It is best to ignore such invitations because they are often motivated by commissions on every sale, which are added to the price of the merchandise. This is another good reason to avoid shops without price tags.

A popular item with travellers are Yucatán hammocks. These are actually used for sleeping by a good percentage of the residents of the peninsula, both Indian and otherwise. They are the ideal hot-weather sleeping arrangement, as they allow free circulation of cooling air all around the body.

The hammock, widely thought of as originating in Yucatán, is an import from Haiti. Before hammocks were introduced, people slept on straw mats, and many still do. In Yucatán today, hammock-making occupies whole families. Hammocks come in three general sizes: single, double and matrimonial. Inspect all three sizes so you will be able to tell the difference at a glance. Although hammocks are sold in many stores and on the street, the best place to buy them is in the big market, or at the Casa de Artesanias. If you shop in the market, compare the workmanship, sizes and prices because all three vary from stand to stand. Remember that in these hammocks you lie diagonally, not fore-and-aft as people do in the United States.

The bulk of the hammocks you see are made of henequén and are what the countryfolk – and a lot of city people, too – use every night of their lives.

The best hammocks, however, are made with linen strings, and you can bet that if you locate a flax-strung hammock the workmanship will be of the very highest quality.

If you need photographic-sized batteries, the Foto-Mercado on Calle 67 Between Calles 58 and 56 has the best stock in town. These are rather hard to find in Mérida.

Places to Stay

Despite the influx of well-off tourists who automatically opt for the expensive hotels, restaurants and so on, Mérida is well supplied with more modestly priced establishments.

Hotel España is on the little Plaza Hidalgo (also known as the Parque Cepeda Peraza and the Parque de Jesús) on Calle 60 between Calles 59 and 61. It is a grand, unrestored house definitely worth viewing as a prime example of Yucatán's past glory. With its spacious rooms, grand staircase and fine old doors, it would be an ideal place to spend a month or two some winter. Expensive.

Mérida

Key:-

① Bus Terminal
② Railway Station
③ Govt. Palace & Tourist Office
④ Cathedral
⑤ Post Office
⑥ Market
⑦ Casa de Montejo
⑧ Archeology Museum
A Plaza Hidalgo, Gran Hotel,
   Hotel Caribe & Hotel España
B Hotel America
C Hotels Cayre & San Pablo
D Hotels San Jorge & San Fernando
E Hotels Oviedo & La Paz
F Hotel Maria del Carmen
G Hotel San Luis
H Hotel Latino
I Hotel Margarita

Hotel Posada Central, Calle 55 at Calle 58, is across the street from the railroad station and is an oddity in this age of highway and air travel. It is admittedly quite some distance from the plaza, but this could be an advantage under crowded conditions that can quickly fill all the easily visible hotels in town. Regard the Central as an ace-in-the-hole. Moderate.

Hotel D'Farahon, on Calle 65 between Calles 56 and 54, is a climb-one-flight-to-the-lobby sort of place with the redeeming virtues of low rents and convenience. The other buildings on the block are being rebuilt one at a time, but it looks as if it will be a long time before they get around to the D'Farahon. Until that happens, it is a low-budget hotel where I've never seen the 'completo' sign up. Inexpensive.

Hotel America, on Calle 67 between Calles 58 and 60, is a few blocks off the plaza, but not far enough to take the glow from the economical price. There is a restaurant on the premises. Inexpensive.

Hotel La Paz, Calle 62 between Calles 65 and 67, is a big old barn of a converted town house. It's about the same vintage as the ridiculously expensive Colón a few blocks up the street, though there the similarities end. The Paz is essentially a family hotel for the people from Progreso who arrive by bus, and is a rarity this close to downtown because it is inexpensive.

Hotel Oviedo, on Calle 62 between Calles 65 and 67 in the same block as the Paz, is a little fancier and a bit more expensive as well. It is popular with European travellers. Moderate.

Hotel Hernández, on Calle 67 between Calles 58 and 60, has been serving the impecunious traveller for a long time. The tile-trimmed marquee bears a coat of peeling Neptune green paint. Within the front door the place is laid out like a typical motel, except nothing larger than a moped can be brought into the courtyard. Inexpensive.

The *Casa de Huespedes,* just up the street from the moderately priced Hotel Sevilla on Calle 62, a block from the plaza, is too easy to overlook. It has a small, homemade white-on-black sign hanging in the doorway, and a huge lobby/patio. As casas de huéspedes go, this is a nice place. Watch for it very carefully because it is easy to overlook. Inexpensive.

A number of small hotels have accumulated around the main bus station in Mérida.

Turn right as you leave the station, and the *Hotel Alamo* is at the end of the block. During the summer vacation rush the Alamo is very likely to be full, but it is always worth a try. Moderate.

Across from the entrance to the bus station on Calle 69 is the *Hotel San Jorge,* all new and blue-tiled. It looks expensive to say the least, but surprisingly it isn't. I recommend it, but if you're bothered by noise select a back room. (Calle 69 carries most of Mérida's heavy bus traffic, although there are no late-night buses and the station closes up tightly during the wee hours.) Moderate.

Also across the street from the entrance to the Central de Autobuses is the tiny lobby of the *Hotel San Fernando,* easy to overlook in spite of the coating of blue and white paint on the facade. It's usually full, but like the Alamo, is worth a try. Moderate.

On the corner to the left of the bus station entrance is the *Hotel San Pablo.* It prefers family rentals, but during the slack season occasionally rents both singles and doubles. For groups, it is inexpensive.

Places to Eat

The best shot for an economical breakfast for early-risers are the two bakeries near the plaza. The one on the plaza itself at the corner of Calle 63 and Calle 62 is better known and has a larger assortment of goodies, but the other one, on Calle 61 between Calles 58 and 60 , has a refresco machine so that their customers can buy a bottle of Coca, to wash down their pan dulces. Very inexpensive.

As always, the market is the place to go for really low-cost eating. There are two markets in Mérida. The one fronting Calle 60 is called a 'bazaar' and sells clothing, shoes, hardware and other items, and very little in the way of food.

The other market is behind the bazaar and handles the food items. Walk over on Calle 67 and continue straight up a ramp and into the market building. At the head of the incline turn left and you will find a row of food stalls selling both Mexican and Yucatecan dishes. This is a good place for arroz con pollo, liver and onions, eggs ranch style and so on. Inexpensive. At the top of the ramp you will encounter another well-stocked artesanias complex, this one mostly specializing in silver, watches and other costly gift items.

The *Restaurante Les Balcons Health Foods Comida Vegetarian,* on Calle 60 between Calles 57 and 59, has upgraded itself. It is in the same place, but it is now more or less a part of the Hotel del Parque, a newish moderate hotel. I have yet to try the hotel; the Balcons is still a good bet provided you skip the red wine, a remark that applies to the rest of the places on the peninsula. The restaurant is upstairs and is rather more interestingly furnished than the usual Mexican hash house. It is also slightly more expensive than most vegetarian restaurants, and sells beer and wine, plus some meat dishes for the omnivorous. The menu is in English and Spanish. Moderate.

The *Plaza Hidalgo* has been improved by paving the street so it's level with the curbs and by barring all motor vehicles except taxis supposedly delivering passengers to one of the hotels on the plaza. The paved-over space has been converted into a sidewalk cafe sans sidewalk. Currently food and drinks are brought to the cast iron tables from the Hotel Caribe. As with all setups along these lines in Mexico, it is more a place for chatting, smoking, talking and drinking than it is for serious eating, but is a very enjoyable place to idle away a few evening hours. Expensive.

Los Almedros, located out toward the railroad station on Calle 59 between Calles 50 and 52, is easily the best-known restaurant in Mérida. The famous local specialty, *poc-chuc* (a Mayan pork chop), originated here. If you like poc-chuc, this is the place for you. The dish is just one of the things the Almedros does well. The restaurant also has atmosphere in abundance and isn't all that expensive – it's much cheaper, in fact, than dozens of other places around town that give you less and charge more. Expensive and worth every peso of it.

Mexican cities with extensive bus traffic and centralized bus stations ordinarily sprout small eating houses like porcupines sprout quills, but Mérida has relatively few restaurants in the bus station area.

The best place anywhere near the station, and a pretty good working person's restaurant in any league, is the *Restaurante y Coctelería la Terminal* to the right and across the street as you leave the station. It is only about 75 metres away but can't be seen from the station exit proper. The 'Cocteleria' part of the name refers to seafood cocktails, not the martini variety. The Terminal is one of the few restaurants that cling to the fine old Latin-American custom of giving the customer a snack with his or her bottle of beer. Most of the Terminal's customers are local residents, and not necessarily bus passengers. Inexpensive and recommended.

For economical eating during the evening, a good bet is *Las Mil Tortas,* on Calle 62 between Calles 65 and 67, across the street from the Progreso bus station. There were only 15 tortas at last count, and not 1000 as indicated by the name, but they are real whoppers with piping-hot filling on a heated bolillo. Very inexpensive.

The little restaurant on the ground floor of the *Hotel America,* on Calle 67 between Calles 60 and 58, is another place to have a reasonably economical evening meal. It will cost a bit more than Las Mil Tortas, but the menu is somewhat more extensive.

Top: Patio of the Hotel San Francisco in El Fuerte, Sinaloa.
Left: Most of Mexico's older Moorish style homes are built around a patio.
Right: 'Los Balcons Pizzerua y Restaurants and Health Food Place' in Merida.

Top: Market scene in Oaxaca.
Bottom: In another market.

This is another place that does liver well, and I have had excellent *huevos motulenos* several times. Inexpensive.

Getting There & Getting Around
To get downtown from the main bus station, turn left as you leave the building's exit on the left side, then right at the corner, on Calle 69. In four blocks turn left on Calle 62 and follow it three blocks to the plaza. Walking time: 15 minutes.

If you happen to arrive for the first time from Progreso on a bus, simply turn right as you leave the station and the plaza is a couple of blocks straight ahead. Walking time: five minutes.

Arriving in Mérida by air is increasingly popular, especially from Miami and other southern US cities. The regular fares are relatively economical because of the short distances involved, and discount fares bring the price down even more. From Yucatán the flight to Oaxaca avoids a long and often uncomfortable bus ride, and Mexico City is only a couple of hours away by jet, whereas the trip by bus or train can eat up the best part of a couple of days. Consult your travel agent for latest schedules and fares.

Rail fans will enjoy the train trip between Mérida and Mexico City; most people won't. Pullman is five times as expensive as second-class, and first-class is more than twice as expensive. If you must cut expenses to the bone, and have survived the trains of Turkey, India or Indonesia, you might cope with second-class quite nicely, but at the end you'll have to agree that this is a hard way to travel. Regardless of where you ride on the train, be sure to pack a good-sized lunch that will hold you for a couple of days. There is no dining car on the train and the hawkers who swarm aboard now and then never seem to be around when the hunger pangs strike. The schedule calls for a 37-hour trip, but I have never heard of the train arriving in Mexico City on time, and five to eight hours off the advertised is about par for the course.

To get to the plaza from the railroad station, go out the front of the building and through the gate on your right. Keep going on Calle 55 to Calle 60. Turn left on 60, and three more blocks will bring you to the plaza. Walking time: 20 minutes.

PROGRESO, Yucatán
(elevation two metres, population 31,000)
Very few visitors to Mérida make the short 33-km trip down to Progreso. In fact, not too many travellers have heard of the place, which is too bad because it makes an enjoyable side trip for people who have seen too many ruins and are tired of loafing around the Plaza Hidalgo. Progreso was, up until the late 1940s, a wealthy and thriving community, its economy based on henequén, one of the most profitable and least labour-intensive of all agricultural crops. Because the slope of the sandy beach is so gradual, one of the last things Progreso did before the town's demise was construct a two-km concrete finger pier that can handle several of the largest ocean-going freighters at a time. Today it is a fine, lonely place to fish.

The henequén industry was killed by the development of synthetic fibres, but not before it had made dollar millionaires by the dozen. Many of these wealthy families built palatial homes on Progreso's Malecón, along the shore to the right of the main street as you approach the ocean. Although a few casual travellers wind up in Progreso, they rarely discover these beautiful old mansions. Most take one look up and down the unimpressive main drag and head back to Mérida.

For the beach enthusiast Progreso has many km of fabulous South Sea island-type beach, with palm trees that sway in the tradewinds, smooth sand, and a sloping shore that allows you to wade about 300 metres in some places before the water reaches your shoulders. The best of the beaches are found out toward Chicxulub, five or six km along the beach to the east of Progreso. A good road parallels the beach. I learned about Progreso from two young travellers who come to Progreso every winter and spend three or four months camping on the beach. They went into town every few days for supplies, which didn't cost them very much because they were both enthusiastic fishermen.

Places to Eat

Most people don't spend enough time in Progreso to discover the really good restaurant on the zócalo. The *Córdobes* is famous among the better-heeled locals. Most seaside restaurants specialize in seafood and neglect everything else, but the Córdobes has a rather extensive menu and prices are surprisingly reasonable. Moderate.

On the main stem as you come in from Mérida, on the right side, is a new-looking seafood restaurant with lots of plastic in the decor. This is *Soberanis,* part of the chain of seafood restaurants that started in Mérida and now includes a resort hotel or two. The Soberanis is higher in price and a little lower in quality than the Córdobes down on the square, but appeals to people more satisfied with Denny's and Howard Johnson's than funky Mexican restaurants. Expensive.

Getting There

Most people get to Progreso on the shuttle buses that leave Mérida from their own station on Calle 62 between Calles 65 and 67. Several buses make the 30 or 40-minute run each hour.

Rail fans occasionally catch a local train from the station on Calle 55 at Calle 48 in Mérida. This is a slow, charming train ride, usually taking a couple of hours or more.

CHICHÉN-ITZÁ, Yucatán

This is one of the best known, most popular, and attractive ruins in Mexico. Chichén-Itzá's popularity contributes greatly to its attraction because the site is such a money-maker for Mexico that a good deal of money is expended in maintaining the grounds, thus making it even more attractive to visitors.

Chichén-Itzá is one of the premier Mayan – and Toltec – ruins, and if you are only going to see one ruin in south-eastern Mexico, then by all means make it Chichén.

Guidebooks on Chichén in Spanish, English, French and German are available both in Mérida and at the site itself. They go into a great deal of detail and are heartily recommended, but in case you don't get one, here are a few 'must see' highlights:

El Castillo The largest building in the complex, built atop still another pyramid containing rooms. The Castillo was, among other things, important in astronomical calculations.

Chichén-Chob Hieroglyphics inside the upper chamber are thought to be pure Mayan. At present, they are illegible.

Temple of the Warriors A complex in itself, with courtyards, colonnades, pyramids and so forth.

Ball Court You'll see two walls 83 metres long, and stone rings approximately 7.3 metres above the ground with inner diameters of 46 cm. The object of the game was to drive a ball through the ring using only the elbows, feet and knees. The captain of the losing team sometimes lost his head as well.

Cenote Of great interest to the modern tourist, for in order to propitiate the gods all sorts of valuable items were thrown into this well's depths, including gold, silver and jade jewellery, and young virgins. One Edward Thompson, who bought the entire well for US$75 in 1885, dredged the Sacred Well and brought up buckets of skeletons, medals, gold bells and a huge quantity of jade. He shipped the bulk of his finds to the Peabody Museum in Boston; not too long ago the Peabody sent some of the treasure back to Mexico.

Places to Stay

There are a number of hotels in the area because Chichén is a fantastic people magnet, but they are entirely too expensive for my taste.

I prefer to get a bus to Piste, check into the *Posada Novelo* and use it as my base of operation, rather than commute from Mérida every day. The Novelo is certainly no Rodeway Inn, but it is only about 3.5 km from the site – less than an hour's walk. Moderate.

Several wayfarers have recommended booking a room in Valladolid and commuting the 30 km to the ruins by bus. There are lots of hotels in Valladolid, but the handiest for those essaying this ploy is the *Bar y Restaurante Mendoza*. You can see it from the front door of the bus station; it's only about 50 metres away. Inexpensive.

Getting There

Chichén-Itzá is about 122 km east of Mérida on the heavily travelled road to Valladolid and Cancún, a route with considerable bus traffic, so ordinarily getting out to the site from Mérida is not a problem. When things are crowded, as can happen during the summer and winter 'seasons', taking a more expensive tour out from town may be preferable to standing and sweltering for several hours in the non-air-conditioned bus station.

UXMAL, Yucatán

Uxmal, about 60 km south of Mérida, is much smaller than Chichén-Itzá, and a great deal more has been done to make it attractive to the visitor. For instance, there are two light-and-sound shows every evening, the first at 7 pm in Spanish, the second at 9 pm in English. Because Uxmal covers such a small area, about 1000 by 700 metres, it is easy to take in the town in a single day, and if I had only a day to spend I'd choose Uxmal and see all of it, rather than go out to Chichén-Itzá and see only a small part.

Uxmal is somewhat harder to reach than Chichén, as it is not on a main road. There are buses, but not many. From Mérida, catch a bus bound for Hopelchen or Campeche, or a Campeche bus that goes down Highway 180. Buy a ticket to Uxmal if they will sell it to you, or one to Santa Elena 14 km beyond, and unload at the ruins.

Most of the buses that ply this part of the world don't adhere to any particular schedule, so you may have quite a wait on the return leg. Alternatively, you can continue on to Campeche after you've finished ruin-seeing.

There is no nearby town to Uxmal (such as Piste, near Chichén), and though hotels have have sprung up over the years to milk the tourist traffic they have all been extremely dear. The restaurant situation isn't much better; this is another place where a well-planned brown-bag lunch is definitely in order.

Because of the transport problems, Uxmal is one of the few places where I would recommend you take a tour at any time of the year, mostly for the transportation end of the deal. I try to avoid getting a tour with lunch included, preferring to take my own. There are lots of tour companies in Mérida, so shop around. I've had the best luck with Yucatán Travel Service, which has an office up on the Paseo de Montejo 475-C, Suite 12. The Uxmal tour from Mérida costs around US$20, without lunch.

IZAMAL, Yucatán

(elevation six metres, population 25,000)
Izamal is about 70 km by road from Mérida, but it might just as well be on the other side of Mars as far as the average traveller is concerned. It appears in few guidebooks, which is a great shame, because Izamal has a good deal to offer.

The principal item of interest is the Great Convent of Izamal, built on a huge Mayan pyramid on the theory that the existence of a Christian church would discourage the Indians from their 'devil worship'.

The convent has a huge open patio surrounded with portales, and has a restful calm reflecting its great age – it was built in the mid-1500s and is one of the oldest convents in the Americas. It's located along one side of the plaza. Some distance across the plaza from the convent is an unrestored pyramid called Kinch-Kama.

There are lots of pyramids in the area – there are thousands on the Yucatán Peninsula – and if you can persuade the sexton to permit you to climb up in the tower of the church you will be able to see mound after mound, each covered with lush jungle growth. Every one of them represents a Mayan pyramid or other structure.

There is a park beside the convent, and the new marketplace is on the street that runs between the convent and the park.

Getting There

The best way to get to Izamal is by the mixed train that leaves from Mérida station at Calles 55 and 48. You don't have to be a rail fan to enjoy this little narrow-gauge *lechero* as it winds through flat henequén fields, stopping at such places as Tixkob, Cacalchen and Tekanto to load and unload freight and country people bearing immense bundles of henequén fibre, hats, or huipiles, with now and then a live turkey or a few fighting cocks thrown in.

Unless you'd like to repeat the trip, I suggest you make the return leg by bus. You can catch one direct to Mérida, or if the wait happens to be too long, catch a bus by the plaza for Hoctun.

Hoctun is on the Mérida-Valladolid road and catches a lot of traffic. The buses to Hoctun from Izamal go two different routes, either 23 km via Kimbila, or 32 km via Kantunil.

CANCÚN, Quintana Roo

(elevation three metres, population 45,000)

Cancún is really two places. The resort area is a sandy island called the Zona Hotelería, extending into the clear waters of the Caribbean. The other Cancún is the Zona Comercial (or Comercio), which is the business and residential area for employees of the big hotels. It includes a huge number of stores selling duty-free merchandise and items appealing to travellers.

Some years back, the Mexican government commissioned a computer study to determine the ideal locations for some all-new resorts, and Cancún came up heads. Since then construction has gone on apace, and today there is practically a solid line of huge, expensive hotels along the Zona Hoteleria. The fancy hotels start at around M$4000 a day and go up – way up. They are kept full by an astute, never-ending publicity campaign. Witness the Third World conferences held there in late 1981. To accommodate these conferences, the regular paying guests were evicted, regardless of their reservations.

If you go left out of the bus station and left around the end of the building, then cross the heavily travelled street and turn left again, you will be on a shopping street where everything from otoscopes to Crescent wrenches are available at about 50-100% over Stateside prices. This is a free zone and the merchandise is intended for consumption by Mexicans who often come great distances to do their shopping here. Many US citizens on package tours really lap all this up, apparently under the misconception that they're getting a bargain. They aren't!

Places to Stay & Eat

The vast majority of the mainland hotels are almost as costly as the ones out on the sandy island. I could only locate one reasonably priced place in the overpriced Cancún area. It is the small, brown-fronted *Hotel Azteca*. To reach it, go along Tulum, the street that runs the length of the Zona Comercial, as if going to Puerto Juárez. It is less than a km on the seaward side of the road. Moderate.

The eating situation is somewhat rosier because, although the local people never stay in hotels, they do eat in reasonably priced restaurants.

The bus station restaurant is usually overcrowded with *refresco* (refreshment) drinkers. As a place for anything else it is definitely not recommended.

If you go left out of the station, around the side, and look across the busy street (technically it is Uxmal, but Cancún has no street signs so far) you will see a store called *El Triunfo*. The restaurant *Leonardo* is on the other side of the Triunfo, a ray of hope for travellers who need a fairly quick meal. Leonardo's specializes in such Yucatecan delicacies as *cocinata de la plancha* and *poc-chuc*. Best of all, the Casablanca fans under the *palapa* (thatched) lean-to not only stir up a much-needed breeze but also manage to hold the ever-present flies at bay. A restaurant with class aspirations, Leonardo's even has custom-made ashtrays emblazoned with its name. Moderate.

If you go right from the bus station instead of left, and then turn left on the boulevard, you will be on Avenida Tulum. Go along Tulum about two blocks and you will come to a big bakery that has everything you can imagine in the way of baked goods, from bread to exquisite pan dulces, for reasonable prices. Inexpensive.

A few doors beyond the bakery is the *Restaurante Veracruz*, which rarely ever sees a tourist. This is strictly a local place for locals, and more Mexican than Yucatecan. It's the kind of place where the cook will emerge from the kitchen if he or she suspects you didn't enjoy your order. I consider it the best go in Cancún Comercial. There is a clean unisex toilet – bring your own paper, of course. Moderate.

If you continue walking for about 10 minutes along Tulum toward Puerto Juárez, you will arrive at the crossroads where the Juárez road branches right. Here you will find the *Centro Comercial del Crucero*, a small public market. At the far end of the complex there are a number of typical marketplace food stalls. I like the *Restaurante Iciatel*, though it doesn't sell beer. There is a gigantic jukebox on prominent display. Inexpensive.

Getting There & Getting Around

Cancún has a busy international airport, with flights to various places in the US and Europe, as well as to Mexico City and other spots in Mexico. Local carriers also fly to Cozumel, which can be a great time-saver over taking a bus down to Playa del Carmen some 70 km away, and then waiting on the ferry to Cozumel before finally embarking on the 50-minute voyage out to the island.

Cancún is the terminus for buses from Mérida on the east and Chetumal on the south, and there are regular buses for Mexico City. Persons intending to stop off at Palenque or Oaxaca on their return leg are best advised to buy a ticket to Villahermosa and catch another bus to their destination. Or to go to Campeche and take a train up to Estación Palenque.

At the end of the curve that brings Uxmal into Tulum, near the Mexicana office, there is a shop renting small, fat-tired Honda 90 motorcycles. This is the economical and time-saving way to explore Cancún, Cozumel and the surrounding country. But bear in mind that motorcycles are designed to carry one person, not to be ridden two-up. If there are two of you, rent two scooters – the additional safety factor is well worth the slight extra cost.

PUERTO JUÁREZ, Quintana Roo

(elevation two metres, population 1500)
Because of tourist development, Cancún has greatly outstripped Puerto Juárez in size, and it will probably surprise many visitors to discover that Puerto Juárez is by far the older of the two. The town is about five km from the intersection of Uxmal and Tulum, and is the place to get the ferry to Isla Mujeres.

Places to Stay

The *Motel Isabel* is the type of business that springs up to take advantage of people in a bind. The customers are unfortunate travellers who miss the last ferry to Isla Mujeres and have to overnight on the mainland. The Isabel charges Cancún Comercial hotel rates and gives as little as legally possible in return: no towels, no hot water, no pillow slips, inefficient maid service and ridiculously expensive rates.

Slightly better, although not much, is *Los Faroles*, which at least has hot water most of the time. Both the Isabel and the Faroles are hard by the ferry landing. Expensive.

The moral of the story: don't miss the last boat, which leaves for Mujeres slightly before dusk – they supposedly don't run at night.

Getting There

There is city bus service from Cancún direct to the ferry landing. To get there from Cancún, catch a Ruta 3 bus on Avenida Tulum or Avenida Cobá, the road that runs along the sandy island among the fancy and expensive hotels. To get into Cancún from Juárez, catch a Ruta 3 Hotelería bus where it turns around in the parking lot by the ferry landing. Tell the driver when you board whether you are going out to the Zona Hotelería or just into Cancún Comercial – the trip out to the hotels calls for an extra fare.

Puerto Juárez is the end of the line for many long-haul buses coming from Valladolid, Chetumal and Mérida, rather than Cancún proper, so getting there is no problem at all.

When arriving at the Cancún bus terminal, you must go out one of the front doors and turn right across the divided boulevard to catch a local bus. The buses only pull up at designated stops (*paradas*).

The lightly laden might enjoy the walk out to Puerto Juárez after being cooped up in a bus for some hours. Turn left along the abovementioned boulevard and go out to the El Crucero intersection. Turn right on the road that parallels the Caribbean. Distance is about five km, walking time about an hour.

ISLA MUJERES, Qunitana Roo

(elevation two metres, population 10,000)

There are two stories about how the island got its name, both apocryphal. The first tale has it that when the Spaniards arrived on the scene they found a number of terra-cotta figurines, most emphatically feminine. The second relates how old-time pirates used to leave their women on the island while they went to sea. I lean toward the first version, but vouch for neither.

Isla Mujeres is a small island, only about eight km long, less than half that wide and shaped a bit like a lacrosse racquet. It is surrounded by beaches. Though the town and the island carry the same name, this never seems to cause any confusion.

From the average traveller's point of view, Isla Mujeres is the nicest place on the Yucatán Peninsula. Progreso is superior in many ways, but in Progreso you have to speak Spanish, be a loner or import a companion. In Mujeres you can always find someone to talk to in your native language, no matter what that may be.

One of Mujeres' attractions is that although it has allowed itself to succumb to the lure of the Yankee dollar – and the Swiss franc, British pound, French franc and what have you – it still derives its primary income from the sea. Aquatic-minded visitors find the fantastically clear surrounding waters the ideal place for skin diving. And Mujeres is a compact place, with sandy beaches within easy walking distance of the low-priced hotels grouped near the ferry landing.

A popular excursion is to the 'fort', supposedly built by a slaver named Mundaca. The story is a romantic one. When the US abolished slavery and the black ivory trade consequently toppled, Mundaca retired to Isla Mujeres and built himself an elaborate home. Following the custom of the times, Mundaca considered his house his castle, and built it as one. He is said to have fallen in love with a woman who married another man, and shortly thereafter Mundaca died in Mérida, though of a fever rather than of unrequited love. Eventually the original purpose of his abandoned hacienda was forgotten and people began calling it a fort. Today the place sits in isolated splendour on the opposite end of the island from the town, and Fermín Mundaca de Marechaja, in accordance with his wishes, lies in the little graveyard on the island.

A bit beyond the so-called fort, at the southern tip of the island, there is a lighthouse and a small Mayan ruin. The ruin is said to have outlasted no fewer than four lighthouses. Just before the lighthouse is a fairly secluded beach, Garrafón.

The town has a plaza, but differs from most Mexican communities in that this plaza is is not the focus of the town. The ferry dock is; it is possible to just spend an enjoyable week on Mujeres itself.

Reading is a popular pastime on Mujeres, but I couldn't find a bookstore stocking foreign-language books. Taking up the slack somewhat is the practice of some innkeepers. They collect books left behind by departing guests and use them as lending libraries for later arrivals.

A blight has attacked Mujeres' beautiful palms, requiring many of them to be destroyed. A goodly share of those remaining display dead leaves and look to be candidates for the axe.

Mujeres has a dive shop complete with air compressor and water tank for the benefit of the scuba-diving fraternity.

Places to Stay

Because the Mujeres airport is too small to accommodate the larger planes, the island is not afflicted with too many wealthy travellers or package tour operators. As a result, Mujeres has a nice supply of reasonably priced housing – in marked contrast to Cozumel and Cancún.

Almost straight ahead as you leave the passenger ferry is the *Hotel El Paso*. It has no electric sign, so it might be a bit difficult to locate in the dark if you happen to catch the late last ferry, but during the day the hotel's white front and red trim will help you locate it. The man who runs the El Paso also operates day trips for nature-lovers to Isla Contoy, a national park and bird refuge north of Mujeres. The El Paso is moderate.

The bulk of the viajero hotels are close together, reached by going to the left along the Malecón as you leave the ferry dock, then right up the next street, Madero.

The *Motel Ma José*, called 'María' by the islanders, is about 15 metres up Madero. Don't be discouraged by all the weary bicycles in the lobby and out front. They are for rent and don't belong to the guests. Almost all the rooms have individual balconies. The hotel is a concrete block construction, beige with white trim. Moderate.

A few metres beyond the María is the *Hotel Martinez*, with a pale green front and brown-and-yellow tiled patio perimeter. It makes a point of saving books left by customers, for the use of future customers. A nice feature of the Martinez is that the owners are thoughtful enough to string a few clotheslines in the patio for the convenience of the wash-it-yourselfers. However, they charge the doubles rate for singles when the hotels on the island begin to fill up, which makes the hotel very expensive.

On the corner above the Martinez is the *Hotel Osario*, the best hotel in the immediate area. The Osario is well maintained, and therefore looks newer than it is. Moderate.

Up Madero beyond the Osario is a place on the corner that looks like an old-time motel. It used to be the *Hotel Luis*. Turn left here and you will shortly come to the corner occupied by Ciro's restaurant. Diagonally across the street is the *Hotel Zorro*, a small peoples' hotel that rents the ubiquitous little nifty-fifty Honda step-through cycles. Inexpensive.

If you pass the Zorro and turn right up the hill by Ciro's, you will find the *Poc-na* on the right side of the street at the end of the block. This is a hostel-type operation, extremely popular with European travellers who are more inclined to pack sleeping equipment than are Americans and Canadians. There is a pleasant palapa-shaded patio for eating, drinking, and making new friends. Meals, beer and wine are available. For those with their own sleeping gear, the Poc-na is inexpensive. Otherwise it's moderate.

Places to Eat

As you amble off the ferry dock you will see the restaurant *Villa del Mar* on the corner of the Malecón in front of you. This is a good spot for a cooling draught taken in air-conditioned comfort, but other than this, I'd skip the del Mar as the service is slow and the food overpriced. Expensive.

If you turn right as you leave the ferry, at the end of the block on the Malecón you come to the *Restaurante Tropicana.* This is a true-blue seafood house that doesn't even list that Mexican standard, enchiladas, on its menu. Most of the patrons are local working people, fishermen and boatmen. Moderate.

The *Restaurante-Bar Gomar* up the hill off Madero, at the plaza, is the place where everybody goes of an evening. Here you will find a larger proportion of beards and a smaller ratio of brassieres than anywhere in Mexico short of Puerto Vallarta. The decorations are well thought out, the ambience is fine, and the food is OK. My only complaint is the acute shortage of sanitarios, especially for a place that dispenses a lot of beer. Expensive, but worth it.

If you feel in the mood to put on the dog, *Ciro's Lobster House* is a good choice. The food and service are the best in town short of what is available at the few fancy hotels. Ciro's is convenient to the economical hotels. Expensive.

Also on Madero, in the next block above the Osario, is the miniscule *Panadería la Reina,* a bakery popular with wanderers and residents alike for reasonably priced bakery items and for the tables and chairs where customers can have coffee and consume their purchases on the premises – the nearest Mujeres can come to a coffeehouse. Very inexpensive.

If you continue past the Zorro and Ciro's for a block or so, you will come to the city market. Not a very big market, but then Mujeres isn't a very big town. Fish is naturally a big item with the lunch stands. The *Juguería Margarita* makes its orange juice from chilled oranges, a pleasant treat in the tropics where juice is usually squeezed from *al tiempo* (room temperature) fruit. Very inexpensive.

Across the street from the market is the sit-down restaurant *Lonchería Chely.* Like the rest of Mujeres' restaurants, this is primarily a seafood establishment, but they also do a prime job with their breakfast eggs. Unusual for this leisurely end of Mexico, the Chely opens bright and early. Inexpensive.

Turn right between the Zorro and Ciro's, and up the hill a short distance is the *Poc-na*, a sort of hostel that feeds its residents at inexpensive rates.

Getting There

It is possible to fly to Isla Mujeres by air taxi, though I must admit I have yet to meet anyone who has done so. It is more practical to fly to Mujeres from Cozumel, because both are islands and getting from one to the other will take a minimum of about four hours by surface transport. Again, however, I've never met anyone who has done so. The carrier is Aerocaribe.

Several passenger ferries and one car ferry haul thousands of passengers a day from Puerto Juárez to Isla Mujeres. The trip over the clear blue water of the Canal de Yucatán takes 45 to 55 minutes.

Passenger ferries run about every hour. The fare in 1983 was about US 60c.

The US-made auto ferry doesn't actually leave from Puerto Juárez – it docks at Punta Sam, a few km farther along the beach. The car ferry hauls passengers at a lower rate than do the passenger ferries, but the dock is rather hard to reach and the ferry sails only about three times a day. This strikes me as a rather hard way to save M$25 or so.

Although Isla Mujeres isn't very big, lots of visitors rent bicycles to visit the fort, Garrafón or the lighthouse. The bicycles don't cost too much on a per-day basis, but if one will be needed for any great length of time it is advisable to buy it used and resell it when parting time comes.

A couple of locals rent Honda step-through motorcycles.

COZUMEL, Quintana Roo

(elevation six metres, population 30,000)
The third of Mexico's Caribbean resorts is located on the Isla Cozumel, a fairly large island about the same distance from the mainland as Isla Mujeres. Isla Cozumel is Mexico's largest island and was occupied by a few fishermen and a small military and air force detachment until it was 'discovered' by *Holiday* magazine.

The island was originally discovered by the Spaniard Juan de Grijalva in 1518 and was at that time occupied by a few Mayas. There are many ruins on the island, indicating that there was at one time a fairly large population. During WW II the US built an airfield on the island – Mexico was one of the Allied nations – and the same field, somewhat enlarged, is in use today.

Prior to its relatively recent popularity, the town of Cozumel was known as San Miguel, or San Miguel de Cozumel. You will still hear the old name once in a while, but the town is mainly known as Cozumel by natives and foreigners alike. The plaza is straight up the street from the dock and isn't up to the town's prosperity.

As with the rest of Quintana Roo, the island is a free zone insofar as customs duties go, even though Quintana has been a state for several years now. There are a number of 'Importaciones' shops that do a thriving business with the package tour customers, but Mexican nationals rarely make the trip out to the island as everything there is available three times over in Cancún Comercial with a lot less hassle.

The waters around Cozumel teem with marine life, and the water is warm and crystal clear. Diving is excellent, and scuba and other equipment can be rented. The government has conservation laws prohibiting the taking of certain marine animals, and these laws are enforced. Find out what is permitted before you put a spear through a fish or break off a coral branch. Mexico doesn't believe in rehabilitating an offender, but they do believe in punishment as a deterrent. A foreigner who runs afoul of the conservation law is unlikely to repeat the error upon hitting the street again some time later.

Cozumel has km after km of white-sand beach, and by federal law the beaches are public property. Some of the most attractive beaches are quite isolated, and many foreigners are tempted to try nude bathing. My advice: don't. The same thing that happened to the party of foreigners in Puerto Penasco can happen in Cozumel, although I will agree that the islanders are somewhat more blasé about the antics of gringos than most Mexicans.

Places to Stay

You might expect Cozumel to have lots of economy facilities, but such is far from the case. The few hotels with people's prices are often full. Isla Mujeres is better for the independent traveller from every standpoint than is Cozumel. However, on my last visit I was able to locate a few places that didn't cater to the package tour business.

The new *Hotel Mesón de San Miguel* faces the plaza, and is about as central as a hotel can be. Because it is not a 'resort hotel', it doesn't fill up all at once.

Ridiculously expensive, which in Cozumel counts as pretty reasonable.

To the right of the ferry landing, and plainly visible therefrom, is the *Hotel López*. It is another ridiculously expensive house, which roughly corresponds to moderate anywhere else insofar as amenities are concerned.

To reach the *Hotel Mary Carmen,* go up on the plaza from the ferry slip and turn right on the street that parallels the plaza on the bay side. Continue past the Hotel Lopez, and turn right at the Banco Atlantico. The hotel is just up the street from one of the Pepe's Grills. Convenient and moderate.

The *Hotel Flores* is on Calle Rosado Salas, off the Malecon to the right of the ferry landing and halfway up the first block. It stands out because of its marine green paint. If you can get a room it will be moderate.

Just before you reach the Flores you will pass the *Hotel Suites Elizabeth.* This is a good deal only for those who share accommodations. Expensive.

Some travellers are tempted to camp on the beaches to beat the high price of accommodations, but I don't believe this is practical. The impoverished local sees even the poorest of wayfarers as enormously rich, and now and then someone camping on the sandy shore gets attacked or robbed of everything he or she has.

In these respects Cozumel is like Acapulco, and for the same reasons.

Places to Eat

Las Palmeres, across the Malecón from the ferry landing, is Cozumel's counterpart of Mujeres' Gomar, except the customers are older, richer, more dignified and look like they're having less fun. The place is large and the service is good.

The best restaurant in Cozumel used to be called *Pepe's;* now there are three of 'em. I don't know which is the original Pepe's Grill, but I like the one that's down the street from the Hotel Flores. Moderate.

There is a 'world famoso' *Carlos & Charlie's & Jiminy Kitchen's Since 1800* eating house on the Malecón a few blocks to the left as you leave the ferry dock. This one is upstairs in a brown-painted building decorated with retired merry-go-round horses. Expensive.

Getting There

The independent traveller normally gets to Cozumel by way of the passenger ferry from Playa del Carmen. Business is so good that ferries now leave approximately once an hour, starting at dawn. The ferries are much better than those on the Puerto Juárez-Isla Mujeres run. The trip out to the island takes about 50 to 55 minutes. Twenty-five years ago the ferry to Cozumel made only one trip a week, sailing from Puerto Morelos, which is still the port for the automobile ferry. In those days the trip out to the island took a good three hours.

There is a small shuttle plane at the little Carmen airport that will enable you to 'do' Cozumel in a single day and do it thoroughly. It leaves every half hour or so.

I recommend spending only part of a day in Cozumel, even if this means indulging in an airplane ride – not that expensive because of the short distance involved.

Some of the buses down from Cancún are scheduled to connect with the passenger ferries, and often do.

There is scheduled jet service both to Mexico City and the United States.

TULUM, COBÁ & XEL-HA

Tulum differs from the usual Mayan ruin because it was built as a fort on the coast rather than a ceremonial city. It is about 115 km south of Cancún on the road to Chetumal, and is readily accessible from either city.

The side road to Tulum is well marked, and the ruins are about a km off the main highway.

Pack a lunch before starting out. Food

and drink are available around the entrance to the site and along the road to the highway, but the choices are limited.

A detailed description of Tulum would take too much space for a book of this nature, so I suggest you get one of the guidebooks sold at the ruins and in Cancún Comercial.

Cobá is probably the least visited ruin in Mexico that is actually on a paved road. The turnoff is about one km south of the Tulum junction, but whereas the ruins of Tulum are only about one km from the main road, Coba is something on the order of 50 km. Most people who reach the site do so through their own efforts, because there are almost no buses and not enough traffic to make hitch-hiking practical. There are some tours from Cancún and Playa del Carmen. I would advise visiting Tulum, which is in the open and close to the ocean, and has fairly frequent bus service. Cobá is surrounded by breeze-stopping scrub jungle and is hot, muggy and buggy. It is also not very big and I

regret both trips I made there. If you do go to Cobá, pack a lunch. The one or two little stores along the side road are not reliable.

Xel-ha (shell-ha) is a swimming hole located about 15 km north of Tulum, and is the regular cooling-off place on the way back for people who have visited either Tulum or Cobá.

Getting There

If you go down to Tulum by bus from Cancún, take a second-class bus. They run much more frequently than the first-class buses, and could save you considerable time.

Returning to Cancún presents more of a problem. During the afternoon, which is when you'll probably return, the buses often run with capacity loads and may not stop to pick you up. Expect the bus that does stop to be crowded.

There are almost no buses to Cobá.

The turnoff to Xel-ha from the Cancún-Chetumal highway is signed, and theoretically Xel-ha should be easy to visit by bus from Tulum, but in fact this is impractical. Hitch-hiking in this part of the world is difficult because of the paucity of private vehicular traffic. It is cheap and easy to visit either Xel-ha or Tulum by bus from Cancún, but not both on the same day.

I get out from Cancún on a rented 90cc Honda motorbike, but it is common for groups of intrepid ruin examiners to pool their resources and drive down in a rented automobile.

The little Hondas plug along at an easy 50 kph or so and I ride down to Tulum in about 2½ hours, which compares very favourably with the bus when allowance is made for waiting time and wayside halts. The bike beats the bus hollow on the return. If you go by motorcycle, remember it must have its little tank filled at the Tulum intersection Pemex station.

With your own wheels, stopping at Xel-ha is no problem.

CHETUMAL, Quintana Roo

(elevation four metres, population 60,000) Chetumal is one of those out-of-the-way places most people visit on their way to somewhere else, in this case Belize, which is not to say anything against the town itself. It is a nice place that looks clean due to a series of hurricanes (the most recent in 1945) that almost destroyed the town.

Back in the days when Quintana was a territory, it was a free port to encourage commerce, and now that it has become a state the government hasn't thought to change the rules. There are dozens of shops carrying everything under the sun that can be manufactured in far-away places: canned hams from Denmark and Poland, Scotch shortbread, socket wrenches from West Germany. All this and a great deal more in a single shop – stores in this part of the world don't specialize.

This merchandise is considerably more expensive than in the US and really isn't intended for tourist consumption. Mexicans and Belizians buy most of it and in turn smuggle it back into their own countries. I

expect that the government will put a stop to this free port business any year now.

Chetumal is a prosperous town, as are most border cities in Mexico. Such things as portable radio/cassette players (ghetto blasters) for M\$134,400 and scuba outfits for M\$300,000 are not all that uncommon.

Chetumal is not the place for sightseeing. For practical purposes it is a one-street city, with most of the businesses, including hotels, restaurants and the bus station, clustered along the Avenida de los Heroes – which for the traveller starts at the CFE generating plant and ends at a monument on the shore of the Mar del Caribe, about one km.

Places to Stay

Considering how much money is at large in Chetumal, it is surprising to find as many low-priced hotels as there are. The problem is that they are usually full by the end of the day. Since many people going to Belize have to stay overnight, it is wise to nail down a room as soon as possible. Failing this, I've wound up sleeping several times on a concrete bench across from the bus station on Heroes. This wasn't too uncomfortable. The weather is warm and things get quiet when the bus station closes sometime before midnight.

Most of the hotels are to the right of the bus station as you leave, but there is one to the left. To reach it, turn left as you leave the station, then right at the first cross street. It is then about a block to the hotel with the fascinating name, the *Ucum*. It is actually more a motel than a conventional hotel, with lots and lots of guarded parking space. The Ucum often has rooms after other hotels have been filled, because many casual travellers never find out about it. Expensive.

Directly across from the Terminal de Autobuses on Heroes is the strictly deluxe *Hotel Continental*, a shining example of modern design. The plain brown front gives no clue at all to the size of the house. You almost need a map or a guide to find the bar, let alone the Restaurante la

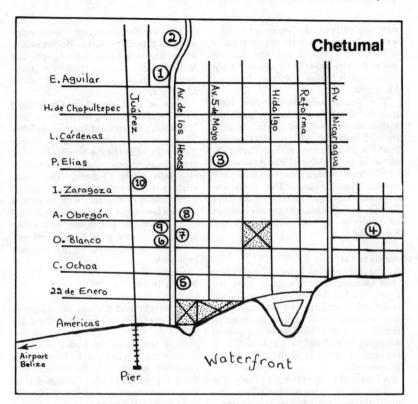

Chetumal

E. Aguilar

H. de Chapultepec

L. Cárdenas

P. Elias

I. Zaragoza

A. Obregón

O. Blanco

C. Ochoa

22 de Enero

Américas

Juárez

Av. de los Heroes

Av. 5 de Mayo

Hidalgo

Reforma

Av. Nicaragua

← Airport Belize

Pier

Waterfront

Cascada. The hotel has everything from an outdoor short-order stand to a disco complete with auto-triggering strobe lights. The disco goes like gang-busters hours after the Presidente up the street locks up. One bar has an intriguing name, the Switch Bar. Ridiculously expensive.

The *Hotel Tulum* is actually above the Terminal de Autobuses, but noise should not be too serious a consideration here because the bus business begins to slow down about 9 pm and by midnight the station is locked. This is always among the first hotels in town to fill. Moderate.

To the right as you leave the bus station and across the street is the *Hotel Brazilia*. It is actually on Aguilar, but easily visible from the front of the bus station across the little plaza. Moderate.

On down Heroes and to the left on Quintana Roo is the little *Hotel Quintana Roo*, small, inconspicuous and easy to overlook, as the sign merely says 'Hotel', and not very loudly at that. Moderate.

On the same street is the three-storey *Hotel Barod*. It gives a good first impression with its tiled lobby and clean floor. Fairly new and expensive.

Further down Heroes is the *Hotel Doris*. I stayed there some years back and there seem to have been no changes at all except in the additions and the price. Moderate.

The *Hotel Big Ben* is another hotel on Heroes. It is a newish, three-storey structure without an elevator and with a walk-up lobby. I figure the reason it looms so high over its neighbours is to allow the owner to sell advertising space on the highly-visible sides of the building. Moderate.

The *Azteca* is a hard-to-find hotel roughly behind the bus station. Leave the station and turn left, and turn left again by the CFE powerhouse. If it's dark you will hear the powerhouse rumble. Turn right at the first cross street. The Azteca is in another new building painted a bright and shining cream colour. The main disadvantage here is that it is above the Chez Farook, an establishment greatly inclined to loudness as the night wears on. Expensive.

Places to Eat

Eating in Chetumal is less of a problem than sleeping. Again starting from the front of the bus station, the first restaurant is *La Japonesa*, right by the door. The Japonesa earns most of its money through the sale of soft drinks, but is capable of whipping up a filling late-night snack for a reasonable price. It is open 24 hours. Moderate.

A little to the left on Heroes is the public market, quite a bit different from the usual Mexican market. Can you picture a public market selling hand-painted silk-and-ivory fans from Spain, Korean ginseng, Dutch gouda cheeses and canned iced tea from Hayward, California, USA? This is a good place to get a meal that's both tasty and cheap, but you won't enjoy it unless you eat at a stall with a big paddle fan to chase the flies away. Very inexpensive.

Restaurante Grijalva, to the right on Heroes as you leave the bus station, then left on the Avenida Cardenes, is recognizable by its colour scheme – an orange front, cream walls, red-bottomed chairs and international orange tablecloths. The cuisine is more Mexican than Yucatecan. Inexpensive.

Along Heroes past Avenida Cardenes, the *Restaurant Baalbek* has such odd

dishes – for Mexico, anyway – as tabouleh and pita bread. It also has Bogart ceiling fans to discourage flies and is a good place to find a late evening domino or backgammon game. Unexpectedly good. Moderate.

Once when I stayed in Chetumal I awoke with a burning desire for a good breakfast, preferably of *huevos moteleños*. This is a Yucatecan specialty usually made with refried beans, tortillas tostadas, green peas, various chilis and whatever else falls ready to hand. The whole mixture is then topped with fried eggs. I tried various restaurants with no luck at all. As a last resort, I ambled down the hill to *El Presidente* and ended with a fine breakfast, cooked to perfection and with service to match, but the price was very expensive.

Getting There

Chetumal is an eight-hour ride on the bus from Mérida, and it takes just about as long to get to Puerto Juárez at the other end of the state. As I said, it is the last place in the world one would pick for a destination. You can also fly from Mérida but this is seldom done by tourists since the main reason to visit Chetumal is to stop over on the way to Belize. It is easier to fly to Belize direct.

To get from Chetumal to Belize City, catch the direct bus, which usually runs several times a week, or take a cab the six km to the border crossing, enter Belize and depend on local transport in that country. There are usually rattle-trap buses and trucks fitted with plank seats, from the border to Corozal Town and from Corozal to Belize City. The fare from the Mexican border crossing to Belize City should run around $3 or $4 Belize.

Sometimes you can catch a ride on a produce truck. If you're fortunate enough to be offered a ride, expect to pay. In Belize there is no free lunch and no free rides, either, as a general rule.

An interesting side trip for wayfarers going from Yucatán to San Cristóbal las

Casas or Oaxaca is to cross into Belize, exit at Melchor, Guatemala, and visit Tikal, that most magnificent of ruins. Exit Guatemala via Huehuetenango and El Tapón, entering Mexico via El Tapón and Comitán. If possible, check this out with the Guatemalan Consul when you get your visa. The last time I tried this trip, the Guatemalans in a sudden fit of pique had closed the border.

Cuernavaca, Morelia & the Mexican Riviera

CUERNAVACA, Morelos

(elevation 1542 metres, population 300,000)

Cuernavaca has always been a haven for the wealthy, who preferred it to Mexico City. First came the Aztec rulers, then the Spanish beginning with Cortés himself, and after independence came rich Mexicans and their families. Of recent years Cuernavaca has become the home-away-from-home for a number of Americans, and it is generally conceded that Cuernavaca has the second largest American colony in Mexico after Guadalajara/Chapala.

A factor contributing to Cuernavaca's present popularity as a retreat is its closeness to Mexico City. It doesn't take very long to drive 75 km on a divided highway. And due to the ridge surrounding Mexico City, very little of the obnoxious smog for which the capital is infamous manages to waft down to Cuernavaca.

The Borda Gardens are Cuernavaca's best-known feature. These were built by José de la Borda, the French miner and prospector, with some of his Taxco-derived riches. The huge park is a prime example of a very rich, self-made man's open-handed generosity toward his adopted land. One pool, for example, is about 120 metres long, and there are winding paved walks, fountains and more fountains. This is one of the very few public old-world-type formal gardens open in Mexico.

The gardens supposedly cost a million or so pesos, and originally were absolutely magnificent, but like many Mexican operations they were allowed to deteriorate. At one time they were all but abandoned, and the premises were occupied by squatters' shacks and families with no visible income and an appreciation of a good downtown location.

Of recent years the gardens are being rehabilitated, a process marred by incredibly poor workmanship far below the original standard. The electrical work is especially poor.

Considering how short of green recreational areas Cuernavaca is, use of the gardens is comparatively low. Probably this is accounted for by the M\$10 admission fee, a high price for a stroll in a public park, but it does make the gardens the ideal place for a lazy, fairly private afternoon picnic.

The Jardínes de Borda are on Morelos at the end of Hidalgo; entrance is by way of a standard flat-fronted building that could be the home of a tyre repair shop, and then through two patios. The tourist office is in one of the rooms in the double-patioed entrance structure.

Contributing to the incidence of Americans in Cuernavaca are the language schools teaching Spanish by the immersion method, wherein students board with local families and hear only Spanish. This system seems to work extremely well. Information is available from the tourist office. (For a ripping good read, I recommend John D MacDonald's *Please Write for Details,* a story describing the founding of a summer art school in Cuernavaca.)

Cortés' Palace is now the Museo de Cuauhtémoc, and well worth the small admission fee. It is much more diversified than most local museums, and not too crowded with pictures of bygone politicians, although there is an excellent Diego Rivera. The bill for the museum was footed by Charles A Lindbergh's father-in-law when he was ambassador to Mexico. It is heavy on the nuts and bolts of daily colonial life, such as sugar-cane squeezers, ox bows, stills, weapons, armour, diligencias and tools. Anyone with a modicum of curiosity will spend at least three hours here, and probably a whole day. The museum is on the plaza which in Cuernavaca is called the Jardín Juárez.

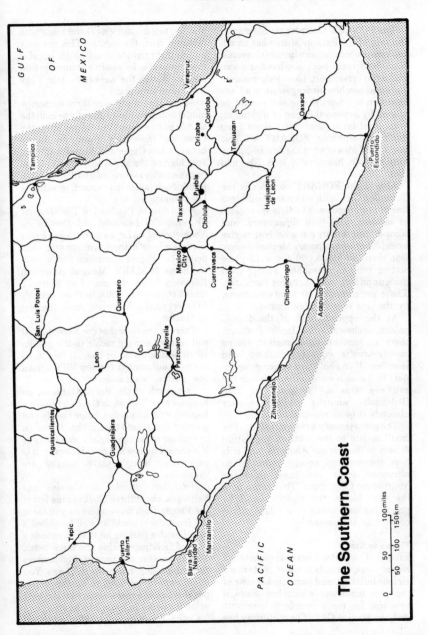

The Southern Coast

The FONART Complex on Salazar by the side of the Palacio/Museo has an all-too-rare preoccupation with useful ceramic household items, but it also has some non-utilitarian ceramic art, plus cloth, wooden-ware and bamboo birdcages. All in all, the selection is a worthy one and should be visited by anyone thinking of picking up some local native handicrafts. Even if you don't buy anything, FONART will give you a good idea of what the better-quality locally-made handicrafts look like and cost.

Also in the FONART complex is the Ceramica Gris, with an entirely different line of merchandise. The Gris specializes in modern, high-tech dinnerware, and some of their sets are remarkably attractive examples of contemporary Mexican design. But then, at M$25,000 for a 12-place setting you can reasonably expect good design and high manufacturing standards. These are intended for local customers, for the Gris sees very few tourists.

At the opposite end of the Cortés palace, technically the Jardín Pacheco, there is another small market selling mostly crafts, quality clothing and jewellery. If you hold that wearing copper next to the skin wards off arthritis or the evil eye, this is the place for you. Beautifully wrought copper jewellery abounds at quite reasonable prices.

The plaza is really a two-part affair. The small square to the north of the Jardín Juárez is the Parque Alameda, and it is here the mariachi groups gather of an afternoon across the street from the Multibanco Comermex. They often pass the time before the nightly round by practicing new tunes – in effect a free concert for the passersby.

Places to Stay

Prices in Cuernavaca have skyrocketed of recent years, partially because of Mexico's vicious inflation, and partially because of the new motorway which has made it practical for many people to commute daily to Mexico City. The motorway has also led to a booming weekend trade with refugees from the capital. This not only means that prices tend to be high, but also that it is next to impossible at times to find a room during the weekends. Don't say you weren't warned.

At one time there were three economy-model hotels on Leyva directly behind the Cortés palace. Now the only one left is the Casa de Huéspedes Dora, on Leyva between Las Casas and Abosolo. It's not very high on the social scale, but you can be reasonably assured of a bath – there is a public bath house in conjunction with the Dora. Inexpensive.

According to Pat Noel of The Mexican Traveler, the beautiful old Posada de Xochiquetzal, on Leyva at Abosolo – easily the nicest hotel in the downtown area – has done a 180-degree about-face and become the home of MARV (Mexican-American Recovery Villa), the site of an alcoholic treatment centre. I will miss those delight-fully wet sunday brunches, easily the best in Mexico.

There is a rumour that the Xochiquetzal will resume serving meals to the public, albeit without wine or beer. If this turns out to be unfounded, the new VIPs is but a few minutes' walk away.

Just north of the Borda Gardens, on Morrow near Tejeda, is the Hotel Colón y España with its peeling beige facade and painted imitation stone lobby. It has an overall air of benign neglect, and looks as if it should be low in price. However, it is expensive, though there usually are vacancies.

Hotel los Canarios at Morelos and Fabregas, about three blocks to the left of the Flecha Roja bus station as you leave the front door, could as well be called a motel, with a parking lot that surrounds a core of buildings within the huge patio. This is another instance of appearances being deceiving, but in the right way. You might expect the hotel to be expensive, but this one is a real sleeper and the best value for pesos in town. Moderate.

Casa de Huéspedes Marilu, Hotel

America and the *Posada San José* are within 50 metres of each other on Aragon y León between Morelos and Matamoros. They differ in detail, but not much. The Hotel America, for instance, has two floors and may clutter up its patio with a few guests' cars. The Marilu has a cheerful two-storey patio with full-sized trees growing in crimson oil drums. Both the America and the Marilu are moderate. The San José is a European-type pension that serves meals, and is a favourite with hucksters and buskers. Inexpensive.

Hotel Penalba is on Matamoros between Degollado and Aragon y León. This hotel is famous for the menagerie in its patio, but the last time I was there they were down to a single chicken in a cage. The Penalba is hard to miss, with its smooth-plastered lower floor and red-brick upper. Moderate.

Laundry There is a laundromat on Morrow just down the hill from Morelos, but it is not a coin-op as it would be in the US. Here they use household-type washing machines. The service is quick and gentle on clothes.

Places to Eat

Eating is a better proposition in Cuernavaca than sleeping; the hotels are easily filled, while there is always a place to get an economical meal. Start with the *Tacos Caballero* in the Flecha Roja second-class bus station, a bit above most Mexican bus station operations in quality and a good place for a snack on the run. Inexpensive.

Downtown on Rayón near Galeana are a couple of worthwhile restaurants. The one closest to the Jardín Juárez (with the small-tiled front) is the *Restaurante Bar Acuario,* and a little further along and on the other side of the street is *El Tepa.* On first glance El Tepa could easily be mistaken for a torta joint because of the tacos-al-carbon set-up in the front, but it is a full-fledged restaurant. Both rely to a considerable degree on the patronage of government employees and are quite

similar in most respects. Perhaps the Acuario does have a shade more class, but then the Tepa has service that's a little better, as a rule, and the Tepa is very slightly cheaper most days. Moderate.

Vegetarian restaurants in Mexico are usually a good go – reasonable in price, with better-than-average cooking, but the *Vegetariano* on Salazar near the Cortés palace is an exception. It is a very pleasant, shady patio beneath the FONART handicrafts emporium, but the prices are high.

Restaurante Vienes, on Tejeda at Comonfort, has a multicultural selection of food – French, English, Spanish and German – with an emphasis on Austrian entrees. If the place appears full from the sidewalk, you will probably find a table in the upstairs dining room, except around 3 pm. Expensive, but worth the price.

Café la Cueva, on Obregón below Rayón, is my favourite for breakfast. It is much larger than it appears from the street, with a back dining room. As well as breakfast, the Cueva has a complete midday menu, often including such Norteño items as *cabrito al horno* and *barbacoa,* both rare this far south. Moderate.

Practically next door to the Cueva is a large bakery with a small supermarket as part of the overall operation. Meat, bread, cheese, wine – you'll find all the classic ingredients for a picnic under one roof, and the Borda Gardens are only four blocks away. Inexpensive.

For a really grand assortment of things edible and otherwise, try the *Aurrera,* below the Flecha Roja bus station. Just turn right as you leave the station and it is in the next block. The Aurrera is a unit in a supermarket chain and the most general of stores. There you can have a Yale key duplicated, buy a pair of jeans, get wine, bread and cheese for a picnic in the Borda Gardens or have a hamburger with a malt chaser right in the store.

VIPs is a restaurant chain with outlets that look pretty much like Denny's in the United States, but there is a new and

Cuernavaca

shining exception in Cuernavaca. It's located near the Xochiquetzal on Juárez between Abosolo and Las Casas, and is worth visiting for the architecture alone. Fountains, lighting and the building itself make this one of the best examples of recent Mexican design in the country. Expensive.

Getting There & Getting Around

Bus service to Cuernavaca from Mexico City is fantastic. All the bus companies leave from the Terminal del Sur, but they arrive at three different bus stations in Cuernavaca.

I prefer to catch a Flecha Roja bus from Mexico City because it stops in the middle of the low-rent district. Autobuses Pullman de Morelos' station is at the corner of Abosolo and Netzahualcoyotl, which is about the same distance from the plaza as the Flecha Roja station, but in the opposite direction. The Estrella de Oro stops way down south on Morelos about a km from the center of things. This is a first-class operation and the way to go for those heading down to Acapulco or Zihuatanejo. Taxco is such a short distance away – only about 100 km – that it doesn't make much difference whether you go first or second-class. Generally the extra convenience of the Flecha Roja station tips the balance in its favour.

Although there are city buses, downtown Cuernavaca is so compact that walking is the preferred way to travel, unless you have the misfortune to be lumbered with an excessive amount of dunnage. If this is the case, M$150 and a cab will take you to any of the hotels or restaurants mentioned above.

TAXCO, Guerrero

(elevation 1676 metres, population 61,000)

Taxco is another of Mexico's colonial monument cities where all new construction must be in the colonial style, and permits for any building at all are very difficult to obtain.

The beauty of the old buildings, coupled with their picturesque setting, make Taxco a photographer's paradise. In my opinion, it's superior in this respect to Guanajuato or San Miguel, both of which have to a certain extent the same history and setting.

Taxco actually isn't very old, nowhere near as old as it appears. Although silver mining in the modern sense began in the days of Cortés, the town really dates from the arrival of José de la Borda, a French prospector and miner. He had previously had more financial ups and downs than a roller coaster, but at Taxco he had a magic touch. He located one rich silver vein after another and wound up one of the richest

men in a country where the rich were – and are – very rich indeed.

Taxco owes a large part of its attraction to the hills on which it is built, and it does seem at times as if there are only two directions, uphill and downhill.

The wealthy miners built as grandly as the limited amount of land available would permit, and their homes have been tastefully restored in recent years to their original aspect, giving the town a colonial look unmatched anywhere in Mexico. The old-world appearance is enhanced by cobblestoned streets, far and away the best cobble-laying I have ever seen. Taxco is the only place I know where the streets routinely have two-tone designs inbuilt.

The mines began to play out during the early years of the 20th century, and the finishing touches to Taxco's prosperity came when the country lapsed into anarchy about the time of the revolution. Today there is one active mine, across the Carretera from the town – you can see it from the Estrella de Oro station. Using all new and modern equipment and techniques, it doesn't look much like the usual Mexican mine, which tends to date back several hundred years and shows it.

With the failure of the mining industry, Taxco began to lose population as families were starved out. The abandoned buildings became more and more decrepit until the town began to take on the aspect of a ghost town like Real de Catorce or Pozos.

This was the situation when a young Yale University student, William Spratling, came to town to write a book. He fell in love with the place and eventually settled there. Recognizing that something must be done to provide an economic base if Taxco was not to wind up a pile of rubble, he hit upon the happy idea of making silverware and jewellery. He also began to train the young men of the area in silversmithing. At one time his operation, the Taller de Delicias employed several hundred barefoot apprentices, many of whom went on to become today's wealthy businesspeople.

Fifty years after that modest start in the mind of a single gifted person, the silver business has come to dominate the city. Silver shops stand shoulder to shoulder, with sometimes as many as five or six in one block. The silver does not come from Taxco's mines; perhaps at one time this might have been possible, but today Taxco is no longer a major silver producer and the metal is bought on the open market.

Spratling had the ill fortune to be a better teacher, designer, inspirer and dreamer than he was a businessman, and he eventually lost control of the business he had founded. He died in an automobile accident in the late 1960s.

Borda had a pet saying, 'God gives to Borda; Borda gives to God.' He put his money where his mouth was by under-writing the Church of Santa Prisca on the tiny Plaza Principal to the tune of around M$7 million – a huge amount at the time. Borda insisted on overseeing the actual construction of the church, giving it a unity of design rare in Mexican churches of this size, which often take a hundred years or more to finish. Santa Prisca took a mere seven years.

Today the view of the church is blocked somewhat by the ubiquitous Indian laurels on the plaza, but the structure is still an impressive one. Its proper name is the Iglesia de San Sebastian y Santa Prisca. It is often miscalled a cathedral on the basis of its size and beauty.

The Museo de Guillermo Spratling is directly behind the church and is easily identified by the plaque on the wall. It has some excellent examples of pre-Columbian art, along with considerable Taxco memorabilia and artifacts pertaining to its recent history. The Museo also mounts shows on its own, such as the exhibition of bark paintings I was privileged to view on my last visit to Taxco.

It is almost a necessity to prowl around Taxco on foot. For one thing, finding a parking spot is well-nigh impossible. For another, the narrow streets were laid out for pack trains and horses, and for some years wheeled vehicles were not even permitted in town, which would be a good idea today. The streets are mostly one-way, confusing, and seem to spiral off in all directions. Between stone walls about 4½ metres apart, they sometimes carry two-way traffic plus pedestrians on both sides, with no curbs or sidewalks on most of the streets.

Taxco has a peculiar method of installing water pipes on hilly pedestrian walkways. Instead of being run to one side, or buried well out of the way, the pipes are placed in the centre of the walkways, often on the surface. This means that a person coming downhill can easily put a heel on an exposed pipe instead of the expected rough cobble and take a header, and on Taxco's steep hills a fall is deadly serious.

Cobblestones and high heels don't mix. The most practical footgear is flats, with made-for-work huaraches a close second. The soles should be stiff because cobblestones are noted for inflicting painful stone bruises on tender feet. Some local women like to wear spike heels, even while pregnant or carrying a baby, but now and then they fall, too.

A fleet of Volkswagen minibuses now roams some of the wider streets. The buses don't hold many passengers, but there are lots of them, and they give good service. It's been said that Mexico was made for the VW, and nowhere is this more true than Taxco. The locals call their small buses *burritos*.

Visiting the silver shops is the big thing to do in Taxco – after all, it's famous throughout the western world for hand-made silver. Most of the shoppers who scurry from one store to another are convinced they will somehow get a bargain if they buy from the 'factory', but that isn't the way it works. The only advantage shopping in Taxco has over buying Mexican silver in Mexico City or Tijuana is the fantastic assortment from which to choose, and the prices are actually

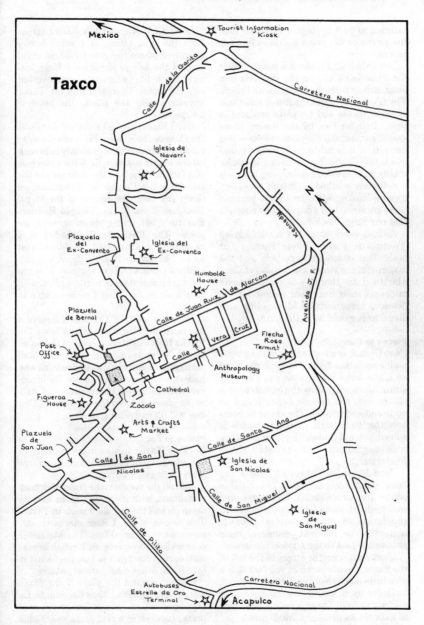

Taxco

inclined to be a bit higher in Taxco than the prices of the same goods in faraway places.

Nevertheless, I make it a point to visit the Platería Gloria, on the Plazuela San Juan, across from the Hotel Santa Prisca. The Gloria has about the finest collection of silver, brass and tin-plate artifacts in town. Belt buckles by the dozen, brass vases, gargantuan tin-plate masks – you name it, if it is made from flat or round stock the Gloria has it. Even if you're totally disinterested in shopping, the shop is definitely worthwhile. It isn't necessary to stop looking with the Gloria because there are about half a dozen silver shops in that one short block.

Almost every shop has a sign saying 'Fábrica de Plata', 'Silver Factory', or both. This is mostly hyperbole and the majority of the stores are simply retailers who tend to charge exactly the same prices as their next-door neighbour, by previous agreement. In Mexico this isn't illegal as it would be in the USA.

Places to Stay

Casa Grande is an old and confusing hotel on Plazuela San Juan. The problem is not with the hotel itself, which is perfectly straightforward, but with the entrance it shares with the cinema beneath and an odds-and-ends dealer. The entrance bears only the 'Cine' sign. Once the puzzle is solved, you will find still another hotel in a once-magnificent old private home. Moderate.

Casa Melendez, between Plazuela San Juan and the zócalo, is an old, reliable house for experienced foreigners and well-to-do Mexican families. As the third generation of the Melendez tribe is currently the resident manager, close attention is paid to the service. Moderate.

Hotel Jardín, on the street to the left of the Santa Prisca church as you face it, is a nice little place that may not get as much business as it would like because it is difficult to find. There is only a small sign to indicate its presence. Moderate.

Hotel del Monte, on Calle Juárez across from the post office, is a small family operation where the grandchildren crawl around the lobby. Rooms are large and airy as befits a mostly unconverted colonial home. A real rarity in Taxco anywhere near the plaza, the hotel is inexpensive.

Even harder to find than the Jardín is the *Casa de Huéspedes.* The easiest way to reach it the first time is probably to branch off the zócalo to the right of the church as you face it. Watch on the right side of the street for the Centro de Artesanias; go down and continue past it to the steps. Continue down to the Templo Bautista and turn left, going down some more steps. The Casa de Huéspedes is a rambling, multi-storied building that looks like an illustration from a 19th-century edition of Don Quijote. It is the most economical place to stay in Taxco – if they have room – that I've been able to locate.

Recently another *Casa de Huéspedes* has opened to the right as you leave the Flecha Roja bus station, next to the water works. It appears well kept and well managed. I was unable to find anyone who had stayed there. Except for its inconvenient location – a 15-minute uphill walk to the plaza – it looks like a good bet. This one will fill early. Inexpensive.

Places to Eat

Because Taxco has so many tourists, it has a large number of restaurants, one or more to fit every purse.

Just off the zócalo is the *Hotel Melendez* restaurant, with its dining room looking down on half the red-tiled roofs in Taxco. This is one of the better places to eat, particularly for breakfast. The Melendez comes close to serving an English breakfast, except the toast is hot. Breakfast is moderate; other meals are expensive.

Further around the plaza is the *Pizza Dama,* near the Hotel Agua Escondido. La Dama not only serves a wide assortment of pizzas (cooked in a real pizza oven) plus spaghetti and hamburgers, it also has that internationally known Texican delicacy, *chili con carne*. This is the only place in Mexico I have encountered it. There are two varieties: if you look like a New York or California gringo you automatically get the milder, flatter variety; if you look like a Texican or a Mexican you get the real stuff, the kind that will grow and/or curl the hair on your chest. Eat on the balcony during the evening and enjoy the night view of the town. Moderate.

Cielito Lindo, on the plaza a few doors from the Melendez, is my favourite dinner spot. Occupying Spratling's former establishment, it seems as if it has been there forever, but it has only been open about 15 years. The food is Mexican and international. The wine has been dependable so far.

The Cielito Lindo's menu is cast in concrete, which means it can get monotonous as a steady diet, so I often switch to *Los Balcones*. It's a little hard to find, so read carefully: go up to the Bar Paco, off the plaza. Then follow the signs around to your right. Try to get a table on one of the balconies so you can enjoy the plaza scene below. Food quality is almost up to the Cielito's. Expensive.

The market vendors, as always, are the best shot for cheap eats. To reach the market, face the Hotel Melendez and go down the hill on its right side. One whole floor of the market is practically devoted to prepared foods, from pan dulces to restaurant stands. Inexpensive.

There are a couple of worthy saloons in Taxco. The *Bar Paco* overlooks the plaza; decor is colonial. It is essentially next door to the Balcónes, with the same view of the action.

My personal favourite is the *Bar Berta*, famous for having originated the drink of the same name. Berta is long gone, but the bar is well run as a family operation with a funky atmosphere. There are two stories, and the bartender scurries up and down a narrow staircase like a monkey. A low balcony gives a view of the plaza. The bar is located along the plaza. The bar is located along the plaza from the Cielito Lindo.

Getting There & Getting Around

Taxco is well served by both first and second-class buses. Those from Mexico City leave from the Terminal del Sur; those from Acapulco leave from the Flecha Roja and Estrella de Oro stations. From Acapulco on Estrella it is best to get your ticket and bus reservation a day ahead of time because first-class bus companies dislike putting on extra buses to handle the overflow. This means that they often leave passengers for the next bus.

The Estrella de Oro first-class bus station in Taxco is a pseudo-colonial gem of a building with tables and leather-bottomed chairs. Other good things for the passengers, such as a branch of Turismo, make it easily the nicest bus station in Mexico. To get from the station to the plaza, simply go straight across the highway and start up the cobblestoned hill. Keep climbing until you hit a square right-hander, and there is the Plazuela San Juan. If you go straight across in front of the Casa Grande and out the other side, in approximately 100 metres you find yourself on the Plaza Principal. Walking time is about 15 hard minutes.

To get uptown from the second-class Flecha Roja bus station, simply go to the top of the street that runs alongside. This will bring you to the market. Go up the stairs to the next-to-the-top floor, then out the back and into a narrow passageway. This will bring you out on the street beside the Melendez. Turn right and reach the plaza in about 25 metres. Climbing time is 15 sweaty minutes.

A cab from either station will set you back about M\$150 – this will be pesos well spent.

Little VW combi buses, called *burritos*, travel a circular route, eventually winding up at the plaza. These are cheap and often crowded. I recommend walking or taking a taxi.

CHILPANCINGO, Guerrero
(elevation 1158 metres, population 76,000)

Chilpancingo may very well be the most untouristed city in Mexico. Located 133 km and about a three-hour bus ride from Acapulco, its altitude gives it a far superior climate. Some people who take their summer vacations at the beaches in Acapulco spend their last night in Chilpancingo, where it's much cooler, and continue on to their destination the following morning feeling refreshed.

The Hotel Posada Melendez is across the road from the Estrella de Oro bus station. An imitation-colonial house, it isn't as old as it looks. There is a huge, tiled, spic-and-span lobby and some big, olde-time rooms upstairs. The hotel looks as if it's ridiculously expensive, and would be if it were in Acapulco or Oaxaca, but here it is moderate.

MORELIA, Michoacán
(elevation 1900 metres, population 425,000)

Morelia is another city that has become a national monument, which means that it remains much as it was before Morelos became a national hero and the Spaniards called the city Valladolid, after the place in Spain where Fernando of Castile wed Isabela la Católica.

After the revolution, when it became popular to tack the names of the new crop of heroes onto the existing city names, Valladolid went the whole hog and changed its name completely. More than patriotism played a part in the renaming, for Mexico has several Valladolids large and small, notably the one in Yucatán, causing no end of postal confusion.

Enterprising young entrepreneurs peddle maps of Morelia along the sidewalk beneath the portales, alongside the zócalo.

The cathedral facing the Plaza de los Martires is one of the most beautiful in Mexico and one of the few that started out with one unifying style and stuck to it, even though its construction took more than a century. It is made of the usual trachyte, in this case more brownish than pink, in pure Plateresque style, and in excellent proportions.

The interior was originally as impressive as the exterior, and the huge open centre of the building is still striking, but the solid silver communion rail was confiscated by the government when the church refused to pay a war assessment around the time of the Reformation. The interior decorations are in excellent taste, but only go back to about 1900. Enjoy spending an hour or so admiring this beautiful example of the builder's art.

You may be fortunate enough to arrive at the cathedral at a time when they are presenting an instrumental program of sacred music. Oddly enough, although the building is built of stone, the acoustics are quite good. Periodically, and especially during December, these programs are presented by a group about halfway in size between a chamber orchestra and a full-blown symphony. Very enjoyable and definitely worth the while.

The beautifully executed Stations of the Cross in the cathedral should be admired by any visitor to Morelia. These are done in high relief, in contrast to the usual two-dimensional oils. They appear to this untrained observer to be quite ancient.

Hidalgo crosses the plaza and dead-ends at Calle Corregidora, across the street from the side entrance of the ex-Convento de San Agustín. Of particular interest are the 39 misericordias at both sides of the altar. These are ingenious seats made so that the people sitting in them appear to be standing – a great boon during long ceremonies.

The cloisters of the old convent are quite extensive, covering an entire city block. Deviating somewhat from standard practice, they are located in front of the church, sort of like a small, semi-private plaza. The cloisters are deserted during the day; in the evening they are devoted to the Cult of the Taco Vendor.

Turn left as you arrive at the convent and go along Corregidora to what is in effect its back yard. The yard has been restored recently as a pleasant miniature park. At the left rear of the restoration there is a cul-de-sac containing several rough benches – an ideal location for a quiet picnic or bit of meditation. This cul-de-sac is behind the house where local hero Morelos is supposed to have been born. He wasn't, but this was the family home where he was reared. The house is now a museum containing memorabilia relating to the great man, and can be entered or exited from either end. The museum reinforces my long-standing contention that revolutionary leaders then or now do not tend to spring from humble origins.

The Casa de Ochoa, 'Curiosidades y Ropa Típica, Especialidad en Chales de Fiesta y Lana Manteles', carries the best selection of serapes, rebozos, ponchos and such that I have seen in Mexico. Some of them aren't all that practical, but they sure are pretty. The stock is pricemarked unless Señora Josefina Ochoa has over-looked an item or two. The Casa de Ochoa bears no identifying sign, only a small glass-enclosed display case featuring deluxe items like an evening shawl made with silver wire. When I asked Señora Ochoa why no sign identified her shop, she raised her eyebrows, shrugged and replied, 'Because I have been here for over 30 years and all my customers should know where I am by now!' Her shop is located in the Portal Consistoriales between Abosolo and Hidalgo, almost directly across the plaza from the Hotel Casino. I recommend it even if you have no particular interest in wrap-arounds.

There is a more-or-less public library behind the tourist office – really part of the college system – at the end of the Palacio Clavijero facing on Madero, across the street from the College of San Nicolas. For those interested in United States history from another viewpoint, I recommend the *Invasion of the North Americans in Mexico*

in six volumes, Nos 216 through 221. The library also stocks Prescott's *The Conquest of Mexico* in Spanish.

Also in the Clavijero Palace are a number of government offices; the patio is usually filled with lines of citizens waiting to transact business. The interior is worth a look for a view of a former private home on the grand design. Complete with patio, it reminds me somewhat of Salamanca, Spain. This is a fine subject for photos.

The tourist office is in the Palacio Clavijero at the corner of Madero and Galeana and is, in my experience, not a lot of help for the wayfarer.

The Posada de la Soledad is an expensive place to stay, but this should not discourage the wayfarer from stepping inside and savouring the exquisitely done restoration. Around Christmas the children of the employees and guests have their own celebration in the Soledad's patio, complete with blindfolds, clubs and piñatas filled with candy and trinkets – a heart-warming sight and a barrel of fun for the kids.

The Palacio del Artesano, really a part of the old San Francisco Church, is on Frey J de San Miguel one block south of the main drag, Madero. San Miguel changes its name to Dominguez when it crosses Madero. The Church of San Francisco is one of the oldest in Mexico. The Palacio del Artesano more than justifies the six-block walk from the plaza. A fantastic assortment of hand-made Michoacan goods is on display, including lacquerware, copperware, birdcages (sans birds), pottery, clothing and everything used by country people. All is for sale, and every piece is pricemarked. This is a much better place to buy than the public markets, and as a general rule better merchandise is available here than in the villages where the items are actually made. The palacio occupies three large rooms and is quite extensive. Not a place to spend a mere five minutes.

Another crafts market, much handier for independent travellers, is reached by

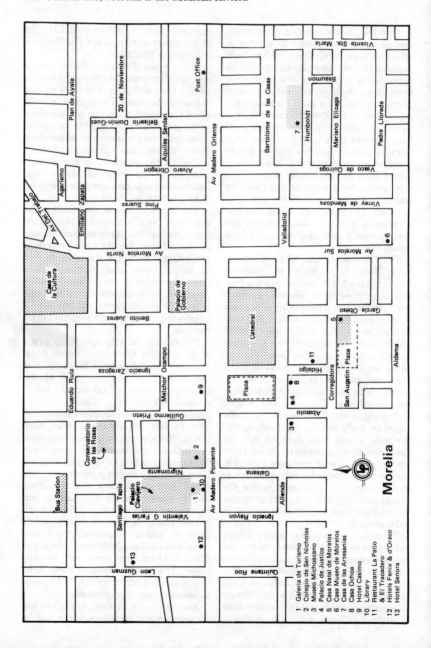

Morelia

1 Galería de Turismo
2 Colegio de San Nicholas
3 Museo Michoacano
4 Palacio de Justica
5 Casa Natal de Morelos
6 Casa Museo de Morelos
7 Casa de las Artesanias
8 Casa Ochoa
9 Hotel Casino
10 Library
11 Restaurant La Patio
   & El Tracadero
12 Hotels Fenix & d'Orzco
13 Hotel Senora

turning left on leaving the bus station, then right at the first street. In the next block is the Mercado Dulces y Artesanias, one of the best markets of its kind going. Here you'll find kg after kg of candy. Haggling is in order; nothing is price-marked.

Morelia's market is called the Mercado Independencia. Market aficionados can reach it by going out Madero to Vasco de Quiroga and turning right, then left on Cardenes – the *mercado* is then two blocks away.

The post office in Morelia is on Madero opposite the corner of Alonso de la Veracruz, or the Calle del Duende – take your pick. It's about five blocks past the cathedral from the plaza, on the opposite side of the street next door to a huge old church. Look carefully for the mailbox on the wall of an old building – the post office is not well signed. The street number, for those inclined to the hard way, is 369.

The cube-like bookstores found on plazas from one end of Mexico to the other – notably the charming Plaza de las Martires, the *plaza principal* of Morelia – are the responsibility of the Secretary of Public Education. Indifferently maintained, they do very little business and do much to alter the ambience of dozens of heretofore pleasant plazas.

Places to Stay

Morelia has lots of economy hotels, although most guidebooks see fit to mention only the Soledad and others of that ilk.

Hotel Allende, on Allende between Cuatla and Bravo, has an unprepossessing, dingy exterior that conceals a two-storey open patio planted with flowers and tropical shrubs. This is a real find in a largely overpriced town. Inexpensive.

Hotel Fenix is on Madero between Guzman and Farias. Its only real disadvantage is an unfortunate habit of using the patio for a parking lot, but it is an extremely rare bird, an inexpensive hotel fairly close to downtown.

Hotel Orozco, almost next door to the Fenix, doesn't use its patio for a parking lot, which may explain why they charge slightly more than the Fenix. Moderate.

The last several times in Morelia I've stopped at the *Hotel Casino* on the plaza. I use a front room, especially during December, where I can stand on the little balcony and take in the sights of an evening. The staff is thoroughly competent. There's a restaurant on the premises. Moderate and recommended.

Stand in front of the bus station and look around. You'll see three medium-budget hotels. My favourite is the *Hotel Plaza.* Like the others in this neighbourhood, it is fairly new and has a good restaurant on the premises. Moderate.

Places to Eat

There are quite a number of reasonably priced restaurants in Morelia.

The *Restaurante Boca Del Río,* on Farias at Tapta, is a seafood place hundreds and hundreds of km from the nearest salt water. Mexicans do wonderful things with fish, especially considering that they are not seafaring people. The kitchen crew dresses like British ward nurses, with white headdresses to keep things sanitary – not generally a consideration in Mexico. However, do not order wine by the glass. The Boca buys its house wines in big jugs and as Mexicans generally aren't big wine drinkers, the jug can sit open on the bar a long time before the last glass is sold. Moderate.

Under the portales facing the plaza are sidewalk cafés intended more for gossiping, beer-drinking and passersby-watching than for serious eating. Invariably these cafés are served by restaurants in the buildings behind them. Quality varies, as do prices, but generally they are moderate to expensive.

The *El Patio* restaurant is a new establishment on Hidalgo near Corregidora and the San Agustín church. Located in the patio of a former private home, it is a very pleasant place for a long afternoon lunch. Unlike the food in most new restaurants, in Mexico or anywhere else, the food here has been good from the opening day on. I hope it survives – the mortality rate for new restaurants in Mexico is about the same as for new computer software outfits in the States. Expensive.

The *Trocadero* is another long-running restaurant a few doors up from the Patio. Very popular, it attracts a wide cross-section of the populace, from businessmen to students from San Nicolas College a few blocks away. The restaurant does considerably more business than it has capacity to handle efficiently. When you do get waited on, the food is surprisingly good, but the slow service at the Trocadero is the reason I was driven to try the more costly El Patio. Moderate and recommended, except for the above *caveat*.

On the left as you leave the bus station is the *Plaza Hotel*. I've eaten there a number of times, and it beats the bus station restaurants hollow. Moderate.

The Morelia bus station restaurants are among the poorest in Mexico. If you step out the front door of the station and look up and down the street, you will see about half a dozen beaneries that will feed you better and cheaper than the places behind you.

There is a small grocery store located at the corner of Abosolo and Corregidora, only a block off the plaza, where most of the bits and pieces that make up a picnic can be purchased. I've supped several times in the little blind passage behind Morelos' house on rainy days – it's roofed over.

Getting There & Getting Around

Morelia is the transport hub of the region, and at the inconvenient little bus station you can catch a direct bus for Pátzcuaro, Manzanillo, Guadalajara, San Luis Potosí – in fact just about anywhere in the northern or western part of Mexico.

It is about 385 km from Morelia to Mexico City, and about six hours by bus,

with a stop at Toluca, so unless you want to get into the capital pretty late it is best to catch an early bus. I try to leave around 7 am or even earlier.

The rest rooms in the Morelia bus station are to the left or right as you enter the building from the bus stalls – easy to overlook, especially if you are in a tearing hurry.

To get downtown from the bus station, turn left as you leave, then right at the next street. The second street will then be Madero. Turn left and the Plaza de Armas will be three blocks more. Walking time: 15 minutes.

PÁTZCUARO, Michoacán

(elevation 2188 metres, population 45,000)

Pátzcuaro is the ideal small Mexican town that has everything: climate, lakeside location, fairly flat site, history and great beauty; yet the burgeoning tourist business hasn't had much influence on the day-to-day life of the inhabitants, perhaps because the bulk of the tourists are Mexican nationals.

The town is unique in that the founders laid the foundations for great growth and provided for it with two plazas, rather than the usual small town's one. The larger plaza, called either the Plaza Principal or the Plaza Grande, is almost the size of the zocalo in Mexico City, while even the minor plaza, the Plaza Chica (officially the Plaza Bocanegra), is still larger than the tiny square at Acapulco, a city about 10 times the size of Pátzcuaro.

The city's life centres on the Plaza Chica. It was here that the buses used to load and unload. The market starts at the Plaza Chica and runs back a couple of blocks or so. Most of the economical hotels and restaurants are nearby. When a local feels like taking a bit of rest, he or she usually does so on one of the benches in the shade of the trees on the Plaza Chica.

On the other hand, the Plaza Principal, at least four times the size of the Plaza

Chica, is essentially a public park. Here there are dozens of ancient ash trees, a lovely fountain and lots of concrete benches. Because it doesn't attract many people – and the few it does attract are simply lost in its immensity – the Plaza Principal is almost always an uncrowded place for reading, napping, courting, picnicking or just plain loafing.

One of my favourite Mexican museums is the Museum of Popular and Regional Arts at the corner of Arciga and Quiroga. More like a large country home than the usual museum, it is located in what was the College of San Nicolas. The college later moved to Morelia. The museum has an entrance that's unusual because it's at the corner rather than in a wall facing the street. Its patio has an operating water well, the old-fashioned kind with a bucket and rope. Among the other exhibits is a replica of a 16th-century kitchen that looks as if it only needs charcoal and a match to begin boiling a *cazuela* of *pozole*.

Another don't-miss is the Casa de Once Patios (House of 11 Courtyards). Once it was a Catherine convent; today it is filled with the clackety-clack of traditional wooden foot-powered looms weaving cloth to be sold at one of the nearby shops. The Casa de Once Patios is not a museum but a small shopping centre, and is occupied by stores selling cloth, lacquerware, beaten-copper cookware and so on. There is even a restaurant which I have yet to find open for business. One of the Turismo offices is here, and I haven't found it open either. But even if you're not in a buying mood, this place is definitely worth a visit simply to enjoy the ambience of a well-constructed building some 400 years old. It's justifiably a favourite locale for amateur painters and photographers.

Beautiful lacquerware is made in and around Pátzcuaro, but of recent years much of it is of inferior quality, on the verified theory that the average tourist for whom the work is intended won't know the difference anyway.

High-quality lacquerware is made by applying numerous coats of different colours to the ware, and ending with a jet-black layer. The design is then made by cutting away the various layers until the desired colour is displayed. This is a tedious and time-consuming operation, and an expensive one. Most of the lacquerware sold now is made by simply laying on a coat of black lacquer, allowing it to dry thoroughly, and then adding the design as if the artisan were painting a teacup or tole painting. Obviously this is a much cheaper process and, if items made this way can be sold for the same price as the quality article, it can be quite profitable.

Another thing to remember about lacquerware is that it is extremely fragile, at least as fragile as the equivalent in porcelain, and it must be packed very carefully to withstand handling by baggage-smashers.

Everywhere you go in Pátzcuaro you will see references to Don Vasco de Quiroga. He was sent from Spain in 1450 to replace another Spaniard named Nuño de Guzman. Guzman was renowned for his cruelty, and this in a hard-nosed land. At one time he was the kingpin of the region centering on Lake Pátzcuaro, and among other things he roasted the chief of the local Tarascan Indians over a slow fire in a vain attempt to force him to divulge the source of his tribe's gold. The official Spanish policy was never one of mis-treatment of the Indians, and when word got back to Spain of Guzman's activities, he was dismissed. Vasco de Quiroga, one of the great men of the Conquest, was delegated to replace him.

Don Vasco started out in life as a lawyer, and a successful one at that. He took religious vows late in life, and although he rose rapidly through the church hierarchy, he was 68 when he became bishop. His wisdom and compassion endeared him to the Indians as much Guzman's activities made him detested. Don Vasco provided Pátzcuaro

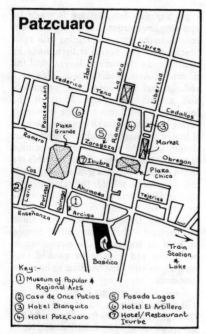

Patzcuaro

Key:-
① Museum of Popular & Regional Arts
② Casa de Once Patios
③ Hotel Blanquita
④ Hotel Patzcuaro
⑤ Posada Lagos
⑥ Hotel El Artillero
⑦ Hotel/Restaurant Iturbe

with a potable water system that served the community well for about 300 years. He also founded the College of San Nicolas, now in Morelia.

Don Vasco's crowning achievement was the construction of the cathedral. The building was begun in 1540, and much is made of the fact that Don Vasco never lived to see it completed. But then, neither has anybody else. It was damaged by an earthquake while under construction, and the planned tremendous dome was never built. The present facade is an afterthought. Though the building never became a cathedral, it was finally raised to colegiata in 1907. Today most local people refer to it as La Basilica, which is as good a name as any.

The Basilica is a focal point for pilgrims, who come for hundreds of km by tour bus to venerate the Virgin made of corn-stalk pith and orchid juice. The story is that she was discovered floating in the lake. The Indians come from the surrounding *aldeas* (villages) to venerate her on the 8th of every month.

Bishop Quiroga's ashes are kept in a safe in a small chapel behind the altar in the Templo de la Compania de Jesus, about two blocks to the south of the Basilica on the opposite side of the street.

Many visitors to Pátzcuaro go out to one of the inhabited islands in the lake, the most interesting of which is Janitzio, more like an island town in the Mediterranean than a Mexican Indian community. Europeans object, though, to its general air of uncleanliness, unusual in a Mexican town. On the top of the Isla de Janitzio is a huge statue of Morelos by Guillermo Ruiz.

Boats for the island leave from the Embarcadero, one km or so from the plazas off the road to Morelia by car or directly down the hill from the Plaza Chica on foot.

Places to Stay

Pátzcuaro is well blessed with low-cost hotels and attracts large numbers of foreign tourists as a result.

Hotel Blanquita must be the best-kept secret in town. Although it is small, clean, quiet, comfortable and convenient, I have yet to see a foreigner there. It is beside the upper, concrete building at the end of the market. Inexpensive.

Hotel Pátzcuaro, less than a block from the Plaza Chica on Ramos between Tena and Zaragoza, has a peculiar lobby with rustic trim and a non-operational fireplace. Except for the slabs tacked up around the lobby, it is a standard small viajero hotel. Inexpensive.

Posada Lagos is on Zaragoza between the two plazas. The low, narrow lobby is really a hall leading to the two-storey patio out back, around which the hotel is constructed. A sign at the rear of lobby says 'Hotel y Restaurante' but there's usually no restaurant. Otherwise, the Lagos is another standard small hotel, but if you share the late W C Fields' dislike of small children, stay away from it. Inexpensive.

Hotel el Artillero, on Quiroga between Zaragoza and Tena, is another hotel in a rebuilt mansion – complete with French doors opening onto iron-railed balconies. Moderate.

Hotel Mesón del Gallo is on Cos off the Plaza Principal. By both location and appearance you would expect 'the Rooster' to be another reasonably priced house, but this establishment caters to package-tour groups travelling high on the hog, and it's ridiculously expensive.

Hotel Posada de la Rosa, Hotel San Agustín and *Hotel Concordia,* on the Plaza Chica alongside the market, are upstairs hotels over stores. All three are about the same quality. These hotels are not a bad deal because you can't find a more central location. Inexpensive to moderate.

Posada de la Basilica, on the corner opposite the Basilica, has a fireplace in most of the rooms and is easily the best bet during late fall, winter and early spring, for Pátzcuaro gets colder than a well-digger's elbow at night. Although I've stayed at the Basilica several times over the years, it took a nudge from Pat Noel to remind me to include it. There's a restaurant and a pleasant patio. Recommended. The Basilica is at the upper end of moderate.

Places to Eat

I swear that every last restaurant in the region, from Morelia to Uruapan, features the *pescado blanco* caught by the Indians with photogenic butterfly nets. The fish are in the order of medium-size herring but not as tasty. Persistent overfishing is depleting the whitefish supply, and they will soon be so expensive that the locals won't be able to afford them. The restaurant in the *Hotel Blanquita,* hard by the concrete market building, is in the hotel building but otherwise has no connection. Because it is by the market and serves well-prepared food at reasonable prices, it does a lot of business with

locals. It is probably too far off the plazas for the floating foreign population to locate; I have yet to see another tourist there. Inexpensive.

The market itself is, of course, a logical place for economy dining. The little market at Pátzcuaro has a number of food stalls that are more a part of the Plaza Chica than of the market itself. Very inexpensive.

The *Gran Hotel* on the Plaza Chica has a restaurant reached by going through the lobby toward the back of the building. Both the hotel and restaurant are moderate, and both offer good value for the money. The chef does especially well with soup.

The restaurant in the *Posada San Rafael* on the Plaza Principal is another excellent choice, especially should you get the urge for an American breakfast, which they do very well. Breakfast is moderate in price; other meals are expensive.

Also on the Plaza Principal, the restaurant in the *Hotel Mesón Iturbide, Servicio de Cafeteria* (on the corner of Calle Iturbide and the Plaza Principal) is a quiet, contemplative place for a leisurely breakfast. This is a pleasant, traditionally decorated restaurant with quite a bit of ambience. It is my favourite Pátzcuaro breakfast spot, and is inexpensive.

If you really want to put on the dog some evening, try the restaurant at the *Hotel Mesón El Gallo,* on Cos near the Plaza Principal. First make sure, though, that there's no tour bus there. Lots of hokey atmosphere and very expensive.

Getting There

Pátzcuaro has direct bus service from such far-flung points as Guadalajara, Querétaro and Mexico City, but don't worry about a direct bus unless one is due to leave right away. Get a ticket to Morelia and catch a bus from there to Pátzcuaro. There are dozens of buses every day and at least half a dozen bus lines.

Flecha Amarilla, Galiano and Tres Estrellas de Oro have a new joint terminal in Pátzcuaro; if at all possible, try to catch one of these three lines. This should present no problem since these companies account for about 95% of the long-haul bus traffic into Pátzcuaro. Buses are no longer permitted to stop along the Plaza Chica, and the other companies, such as Herrandura de Plata, stop at various locations around town.

Pátzcuaro is the originating terminal for buses going to dozens of small isolated places, such as Tacambaro, Pedernales and Ario de Rosales. To get from the new Flecha Amarilla/Galiano/Tres Estrellas terminal to the Plaza Chica, go out the way the buses come in and turn left. Go to the next corner by the Herrandura de Plata (silver horseshoe) station and turn right. The Plaza Chica is now two blocks straight ahead.

There is daily train service to and from Mexico City, the fastest of which is advertised to take 10 hours and the slowest a full day. Only a committed rail fan would consider taking the train. In Pátzcuaro the railroad is a considerable distance from town, requiring most passengers to take a cab.

One final remark: Pátzcuaro regards the Fiesta of the Immaculate Conception with great seriousness, and at that time thousands of pilgrims converge on the little city. Unless you want to sleep in one of the plazas – as a great many families do – I suggest that around 8 December you make a day trip to Pátzcuaro from Morelia or Uruapan. Both are 63 km, and there are lots of buses.

URUAPAN, Michoacán

(elevation 1676 metres, population 180,000)

Uruapan is largely unknown to the tourist trade, and as a result sees almost no foreigners, yet it is one of the nicest cities in Mexico – mostly because of its unique, elongated plaza.

The plaza is, technically speaking, really three plazas laid end-to-end. The one on the western end is Jardín de los Martires, with statuary commemorating military heroes; the one in the middle is the Plaza Principal; and the one on the eastern end is the Plaza Fray San Miguel. I'll simply refer to them collectively as 'the plaza'.

Uruapan is a modern city with progressive merchants. For instance, it is extremely difficult to find stores in Mexico that have even heard of micro-cassettes, let alone stock them. But Mr Sound, on the plaza in Uruapan, not only stocks them, the clerks there know what they are used for.

I'd about given up on patronizing a barber shop in Mexico – Mexican barbers are generally not very adept at trimming beards. But when I saw a black-bearded professorial type getting a trim by a barber a few doors from the Plaza Hotel, I risked my whiskers. And he did a first-rate job.

Uruapan has a sweet tooth, and the portales along one side of the plaza shelter about a dozen candy sellers. The sweets are not a special type, as with Celaya's *cajeta*. Instead, Uruapan has everything from chocolate to candied fruit – I am especially taken with the candied figs and limes.

The market is the handiest in Mexico – it starts at the corner of the plaza by the Hotel Capri and goes, and goes, and goes. It has a larger assortment of the same things sold in the better-known market at Pátzcuaro up the road, with the possible exception of lacquerware. Shapeless and meandering, the market takes hours to explore. It's especially strong in copperware and guitars, both famous regional products.

During the week ending with Palm Sunday, Uruapan throws an old-fashioned fair, a sort of Mexican county fair. Artisans from nearby towns bring their products and compete for prizes. Copperware, clay tableware and figurines, leather goods both decorative and utilitarian, lacquerware, guitars and rebozos from Paracho, reed place mats and statues – you name it, and if it comes under the heading of handicrafts and is made within

200 km or so, it will be exhibited. More social than commercial, the fair is one of the most enjoyable local shindigs in Mexico.

When you come right down to it, Uruapan resembles Tehuacán without the bottling works. A peaceful, charming town with an exceptional climate, it's another good place for a honeymoon, writing a book, or just loafing for the good of one's soul.

Places to Stay

When you consider that Uruapan is virtually unknown to the majority of the people who visit Mexico, it has an amazing number of hotels. Most of the hotels in town are clustered around the plaza, as they should be.

There are three small hotels on the short cross street at the end of the plaza opposite the Plaza Hotel. They are the Hotel Capri, Hotel Moderna and Hotel Oseguera. The only one I've stayed in is the Moderna – I arrived in town late and it was the first hotel I found with a vacancy. I drew a front room without taking into consideration the early starting time of the buses on the plaza, and was awakened about 6 am. All three hotels are inexpensive.

Proceeding up the left side of the long skinny plaza toward the Hotel Plaza, you'll come to the Hotel Hernandez, quite modern, in a four-floor building with an elevator. For some reason, I'd never stayed in the Hernandez, so I decided to try it in late 1984. To say I was pleasantly surprised would be putting it mildly. A real rarity in Mexico, the bath water was hot enough to scald hogs. Moderate and recommended.

Further along the plaza is the Hotel Concordia. It looks to be very old, but it is reasonably well kept. Don't be discouraged by the fact that the hotel has every credit card decal anybody ever heard of, plus a couple of strangers, plastered on the glass. Moderate.

Continuing along the same side of the

plaza, you'll come to the Hotel Regis. It differs from the preceding two in that it doesn't have a free-standing restaurant. The restaurant in the Regis opens off the lobby and is entirely internal. Expensive.

On the end of the plaza is the Hotel Plaza, a deluxe Best Western house. Ridiculously expensive.

Continue to the right along the street at the end of the plaza fronted by the Hotel Plaza, and in a short block you will see the Hotel Tarasco, a brand-new, sparkling clean house. It's very expensive, but quite nice.

Places to Eat

Uruapan is a pretty fair eating town. The Restaurant Emperador under the Hotel Hernandez is one of my favourites. It's very popular with people from the surrounding shops, as well as with country people in for the day. The fare is basically Mexican, but not exclusively. For example, a chef's salad should not be ordered as a light appetizer before a meal. I inventoried one and it consisted of cooked green peas, onions, lettuce, avocado, crisp-fried bacon, Vienna sausage, Cheddar-type cheese and little rolls of processed ham. Plus a pretty fair salad dressing. The only thing lacking was jalapeños en escabeche. Moderate.

Another of my favourites is the Restaurante y Cafeteria la Pergola, right next door to the Hotel Concordia. It is easily the most popular dinner place in town, bar none. I recommend waiting until after 9 pm because it is usually too crowded before that hour. The menu runs to fairly well-prepared international dishes. Try the hamburguesa especial. I guarantee it will be nothing at all like the burgers served by Wendy's or McDonald's. The bartender pours a pretty fair copita. Moderate to expensive and recommended.

Almost directly across the plaza from the Hotel Hernandez is a collection of food stalls, about what you would expect to find scattered through the market anywhere else. Technically, I suppose they are *restaurantes a las mesas*. To reach them, go in alongside the church. Look for a colonial-style sign that says 'Mercado de Antojitos'. Antojitos are usually defined as 'little whims', but in this case they are much more than that. Walk back in this fairly wide paseo until it opens out into a moderately large area chock a block with little restaurants arranged around a sort of sunken patio. There are at least 15 or 20 restaurants serving conventional Mexican dishes. The food is both good and filling – and best of all, inexpensive.

The little *Puesta del Sol Supermercado*, in back of the fancy hotel plaza, does not charge corkage in the restaurant occupying its front end, so the thing to do is place your order and then wander back into the Super and pick out the wine that will match your preferences. The youngish restaurant manager is that oddity in Mexico – a local with an interest in and appreciation for fermented grape juice. His advice is honest, not commercially biased, and in my experience, thoroughly reliable. This method of dining is almost as economical as out-and-out picnicking. On my last visit I picked up a half-bottle of San Juan del Río *vino tinto,* (a blend of Maldec and Cabernet Sauvignon), nine years old, for just M\$246 (about US\$1.17 at the time), which combined with a M\$124 hamburger, produced a veritible travellers' delight.

PARICUTÍN, Michoacán

In 1943 a volcano erupted in the field of one Dionisio Pulido. Eventually the lava engulfed a whole village, and today all that remains are the towers of the church. Craig Gillispie calls the sight 'one of the wonders of the world'. Take a bus from the central bus station to Paricutin and make local arrangements when you arrive. The volcano is about 15 km from Paricutin.

PARACHO, Michoacán

For players of stringed instruments, a trip to Paracho will be of interest. This little town is where most of the better-quality

guitars are made, and from here they are shipped all over North America. You won't necessarily get any bargains in Paracho, but you will have an almost limitless choice as to tone, size, ornamentation, number of strings and so on. On 8 August there is an interesting local celebration. Women in *china poblana* skirts escort a bull through the streets. (The skirt's name comes from a legendary Chinese slave girl shipwrecked on the Mexican coast. Her skirt was the colours of the Mexican flag – red, white and green. She eventually ended up in Puebla.) At the end of the bull's journey, it is turned into *shuripo,* an odd local specialty flavoured with chilis. The celebration is lots of fun, with music, dancing and beer drinking. Paracho is about 40 km north of Uruapan – take a bus from the central bus station.

Because people often come to Paracho to supervise the voicing of their bespoken instruments – a project often entailing several days – there is a nice, small hotel for their convenience. You'll find it at the corner of Bravo and 20 de Noviembre, the main stem, a couple of blocks or so south of the little plaza. It's called the Hotel Hermelinda, and it's at the low end of moderate.

Two shops do a first-rate job of concert guitar-making, and come well recommended by the musicians I've met. One is the shop of José Luis Díaz, who not only makes guitars but is also willing to undertake repairs. He is located at 20 de Noviembre 361.

The other noteworthy shop is Las Michoacanas. The forthright and amiable proprietor will be more than willing to show clippings of famous musicians using his creations. The Michoacanas is at 20 de Noviembre 67.

On the way to Paracho from Uruapan, you'll travel most of the way through copses of piney woods interspersed with small, not-very-productive fields outlined by stone walls.

CAPACUARO, Michoacan

(elevation 1770 metres, population 2500)
Capacuaro is, like Paracho, a community
wresting its living from woodworking, but
unlike Paracho, with its sophisticated
musical instruments, Capacuaro does not
specialize. In fact, just about everything
used in Mexico that can be hand-made
from wood is fabricated in Capacuaro,
including semi-finished furniture that will
later become 'colonial replicas' in expensive
shops; children's toys; chocolate frothers;
and garish combinations of yarn and wood
destined for wall decorations and other
unlikely handicrafts.

The road passes smack-dab through
the centre of town, and on non-rainy days
it is common to see almost every home
decorated with short pine balks leaning
against the walls to season before they are
converted into useful and/or decorative
items for the national market.

Capacuaro is an interesting place in
which to prowl, and you will usually be
welcomed at the little factories. They are
definitely worth a visit if time is not of the
essence.

There is usually a restaurant or two in
operation, although there is no hotel at the
moment.

Capacuaro is easy to get to and from,
located as it is on one of the main north-
south bus routes.

Getting There & Getting Around

Uruapan is served by a number of bus
companies and has a brand-new Central
de Autobuses. Buses come down from
Morelia/Pátzcuaro and up from Cardenes
on the coast.

The bus station is too far to reach by
foot, even if a wayfarer happens to know
the way, but there is city bus service direct
to the plaza. Get a bus marked 'Camionera'
or 'Plaza'. Just about any bus line winds
up at the plaza. Only slightly more
expensive is a taxi – it will cost about
M$150, and is well worth it if you dislike
crowded buses.

PUERTO VALLARTA, Jalisco

(elevation three metres, population
132,000)
Some 20-odd years ago James Norman
described Puerto Vallarta as a 'remote,
charming fishing village' and 'Mexico's
nearest equivalent to a quiet Mediterranean village, even to the tourists who are
beginning to discover it.' This is still true,
except that the tourists have now discovered Puerto Vallarta in a big way.

Modern Puerto Vallarta is an excellent
illustration of what publicity can do for a
community. When Elizabeth Taylor and
Richard Burton were filming *Night of the
Iguana* here, they kept the gossip writers
busy for months, and every story went out
datelined Puerto Vallarta. At the time, the
town was not to be found on most highway
maps.

From that time on, Puerto Vallarta has
had a mystique that has brought tourists
in ever-increasing numbers, and the
town's population has multiplied about 25
times in as many years, making it Mexico's
fastest-growing city. But Vallarta is not
running solely on the momentum generated
by *Night of the Iguana* – it has one of the
most aggressive and able tourism departments in Mexico.

Basically it is a small town, and men still
go out in the small hours to catch the fish
that form one of the staples of the poorer
families' diet. Renting a sport-fishing boat
is no problem at all. Just go down on the
Malecón (Díaz Ordaz) at 31 de Octubre,
by the Hotel Rosales, and make the best
deal you can. These are large cabin
cruisers, but the economy-minded can
usually find a small open outboard boat,
such as the local fishermen use, for about a
quarter of the price.

Because Puerto Vallarta's basic industry
is tourism, it isn't a good place to shop for
handicrafts. It's a fine place, though, to
buy tourist-oriented merchandise, and
there are cowboy shops, onyx stores,
boutiques, and antique shops – Mexico
has lots and lots of antiques. To top them
all is the little shop called Aquí es José,

translated on the sign as 'Here is Joe!'

Joe now has competition. Around the corner is a store calling itself *Acá es Joe* (*Here* is Joe).

Puerto Vallarta is great on diving, and there is a fully equipped dive shop at Díaz Ordáz 770, along the beach from the Casa Blanca.

It seems as though every shop window has a sticker or poster advertising 'Inglés con Lord Twig'. Lord Twig is a branch of an extremely successful Guadalajara-based language school.

Even in tourist towns it is sometimes difficult to find English-language books, but there is a bookstore on Juárez near Acá Joe's with a stock of paperbacks and a few periodicals.

The Laundrymat Nelly, on Hidalgo between Guerrero and Libertad, gives good service. Recommended.

The most popular beach is the Playa del Sol, less than one km from the centre of town. To reach it, go south on Insurgentes/National Highway 200 to Pulpito and turn right. The beach is about two blocks straight ahead. Technically the Playa del Sol starts at the big dock, Muelle los Muertos, but I couldn't see much difference either side of the dock.

Something that has always intrigued me, and for which the locals have no reasonable explanation, is the openwork crown on the tower of the church by the zócalo, certainly a unique way of topping off an otherwise pedestrian structure.

It doesn't take very long for the quiet delights of Puerto Vallarta to pall on the average, or non-reading visitor, so nearly everyone takes a day trip out to Yelapa. This is a small village accessible only by boat. Yelapa has a beautiful white sand beach and resembles a South Seas' paradise of story and fame. There is also a rather primitive Indian suburb of the same name a short walk away. To get to Yelapa, go out the Malecón to 31 de Octubre and the dock where the larger sport-fishing boats land. There are regularly scheduled ferry boats aimed at the tourist trade. All are expensive, but some are more expensive than others, the price essentially determined by whether or not there is a bar aboard. Ask around and you can usually get a ride to Yelapa for a third the cost of the ferry price from one of the other boats making the run down with freight, mail, etc. But be sure your return trip is included, and that the boat is returning the same day, unless you intend to overnight.

Mismaloya Beach is 10 or 15 km south, where the road turns inland. Get there by way of the minibus that shuttles between the beach and town; you can catch it on Insurgentes. It is white with a multi-coloured stripe running fore and aft. Don't try camping on this beach without lots of DEET mosquito repellent unless you happen to be one of the lucky people mosquitoes dislike. Food and drink stands are plentiful.

Places to Stay

It is important to arrive early in Puerto Vallarta to be reasonably certain of getting a hotel room, with or without a reservation. Puerto Vallarta, even more than most Mexican towns, seems to fill suddenly during the late afternoon. If the low-budget hotels are full, and you dislike the idea of trying the more expensive resort hotels or sleeping on the beach out at Mismaloya, the surest bet is to catch a bus up to Tepic.

Madero, the street crossing Insurgentes to your left as you leave the Tres Estrellas and Pacifico bus stations, is the street of economical hotels in Puerto Vallarta.

On Madero, between Insurgentes and Constitución, is the *Casa de Huéspedes García Altos*, above a Mexican-style fast-food joint. The overall effect isn't helped a bit by the restaurant's ventilation duct, which runs up the front wall. But as you go up the stairs to the lobby you realize the off-white tile is spotlessly clean. Inexpensive.

Next door to the García Altos is the white-fronted *Casa de Hortencia*. This

Puerto Vallarta

Key:-
① Bus Terminals for Pacifico & Tres Estrellas de Oro
② Bus Terminal for Transportes Norte de Sonora

Area of budget hotels

one, too, is spic-and-span. Initially the Hortencia was a ground-floor-only operation, but business was good and recently the Hortencia added a couple more floors. I don't doubt the Hortencia will become a hotel and jack up its rates, but so far this hasn't happened. Inexpensive. Both the Garcia and the Hortencia are conveniently located within 50 metres of Insurgentes.

Hotel Lina is on Madero between Insurgentes and Aguacate. It doesn't seem quite as clean or as well run as some of the others on Madero, and the price isn't quite right, either, but it is pleasant. The Lina is built around a large and airy patio, and the rooms are ample. Expensive.

Farther up Madero is the *Hotel Analiz,* between Aguacate and Jacarandas. There is nothing pretentious about the Analiz; it's a typical, clean, small establishment surrounding a tiny, white-painted patio with a few plants in 20-litre cans. The hotel is competently managed by *simpático* people. It's also likely to be full. Recommended and moderate.

Casa de Huéspedes Bernal is next door to the Analiz, and is more a hotel than a run-of-the-mill casa de huéspedes. The two-storey white front overlooks the little-travelled street. Moderate.

Across the street from the Analiz and the Bernal is the much larger *Villa del Mar,* identified by a jumping fish in tile beside the front entrance. Over the years, I've stayed at both the Analiz and the Del Mar, and I'm well satisfied with both. The Del Mar has three floors and tall palms growing in the patio. Moderate.

Hotel Central, on Juárez just up the hill from Guerrero and opposite Shane's hamburger joint, is a typical small-town hotel for travelling telephone repairmen, mechanics, salesmen, scriveners, minor government officials and others who don't have access to fat expense accounts. If you would rather be close to the little zócalo than on Madero, this is the place for you. Inexpensive.

Most of the hotels listed herein are reached by going to the left out of the Tres Estrellas and Pacifico stations, and unfortunately they are usually the first to fill. An exception is the newish *Hotel Don Miguel,* which is to the right and several blocks along Independencia. The Don Miguel comes complete with swimming pool and sheltered loafing areas. I prefer the rooms facing the side street and about the second floor. Traffic doesn't seem to be too heavy. But I suggest you do as I do – keep a good supply of one-peso coins to pitch at the Doberman across the way, who is cursed with the twin sins of early rising and barking. Very expensive.

Places to Eat

As you cross the bridge on Insurgentes over the Río Cuale going toward the plaza, you can't miss the *Fuente del Puente,* also known as *Henry's Restaurant Bar and Cafeteria* – the name seems to change from time to time. The menu is no longer as extensive as it once was, but it is still a nice, shady place to have a snack or a meal and watch the people coming and going across the bridge. Moderate.

The city market is at Insurgentes on the north side of the Río Cuale, and as usual is the best place for economical eating. Here the restaurant counters are on the top floor, rear. At least once each time I'm in Puerto Vallarta, I eat at the *Cenaduría Elodia.* Technically, a *cenaduría* is a place that does suppers only, but the Elodia is open all day. If the Elodia doesn't appeal, there are several other good restaurant stands in the immediate vicinity, all inexpensive.

Benitos, on Zaragoza between Juárez and Morelos, opposite the plaza, is a pizza-and-spaghetti place that also serves a number of Mexican and seafood dishes. It is efficiently operated and very popular with local families. Mexican kids, like kids everywhere, go for pizza in a big way, so it is liable to be crowded Sunday afternoons with large family groups. Moderate.

If you're getting lonesome for a touch of home, perhaps *Shane's* hamburger joint is the place for you. Located on Calle Juárez up the hill a few metres from Guerrero, the sign says 'Shane's Hamburguesas', and in subscript, 'Roast Beef'. It's a sandwich joint that puts out some of the best burgers in Mexico. For some reason, every time I go to Shane's I find it crowded with stewardesses. Moderate.

Every town has to have a 'best restaurant'. It may not be the highest priced – in Puerto Vallarta it certainly isn't – but it is a place where the food, service and ambience combine for maximum customer enjoyment. In Puerto Vallarta the best restaurant is the two-storey *Casa Blanca*, on the Malecón just off Corona. The ground floor is the bar, the second floor the restaurant. In my opinion the perfect end for a delightful day is a plate of the Casa Blanca's fettuccine Alfredo sluiced down with a bottle of the red. Expensive, but worth it.

One block south (to the right as you leave) of the Tres Estrellas bus station, on the corner of Insurgentes and Cardénes, there is a fair-sized supermarket, the best of its kind in town. The cheapest way to eat well and heartily is to buy the necessaries here and meander down to the beach and eat by the pounding surf.

One reader, Craig R Gillispie, writes that 'I found the *Lonchería y Marisquetería Max* between Guerrero and Libertad on Morelos to be quite good and moderately priced. Breakfast at *El Tapatio* on the corner of Madero and Insurgentes is good but the dinners stink. Coffee refills free.'

Getting There

There's no central bus terminal in Puerto Vallarta, although one is sorely needed, but the various stations are fairly close together. Most foreign bus travellers arrive by Tres Estrellas, Pacifico, or Transportes Norte de Sonora (TNS); their stations are within 50 metres of each other.

The Pacifico and Tres Estrellas stations are on Insurgentes between Madero and

Cardénes. To get downtown from either, go out the front door and turn left. Cross the Río Cuale, turn left, and go along the right side of the market to Juárez, the third street. Turn right and you will be at the plaza in three blocks. Watch carefully lest you miss it – the plaza in Vallarta isn't very imposing. Walking time is about 15 minutes.

The TNS station is on Madero close to Insurgentes. To get to the plaza, turn left on leaving, then left on the first street, Insurgentes, and proceed as above.

There is frequent bus service to Guadalajara, Mexico City, Tepic and Manzanillo. Coming from Mazatlán and points north, service is less frequent, so I suggest you get the first available bus to Tepic and change there to the Vallarta bus. From Tepic to Vallarta is only 169 km, but it is 463 km to Mazatlán, an eight or nine-hour bus ride, and the break at Tepic provides a welcome opportunity for leg-stretching.

Puerto Vallarta has no railroad, and the ferry service to Cabo San Lucas and Cabo San José, at the tip of the Baja Peninsula, has been 'discontinued temporarily' due to a lack of paying customers. I hear that it is to be reinstated, but *quién sabe?*

Although Puerto Vallarta is pretty small as cities go, it has excellent air service and an international airport with service to Tucson, Phoenix, Los Angeles, San Francisco, Guadalajara, Mazatlán and Mexico City, among other places.

BARRA DE NAVIDAD, Jalisco

(elevation two metres, population 3500)
Barra de Navidad is easy to reach, either from along the coast or from Guadalajara, and I'm at a loss to explain why it is visited by so few foreigners – it is certainly popular with Mexican families who flock down from Guadalajara in droves, particularly on weekends.

The town is built on a small, sandy peninsula and is almost completely surrounded by the blue Pacific. The white sand beach is long and almost deserted.

Barra has no organized tourist activities

save fishing. Instead, it is the epitome of tropical towns, with palm trees, palapa shacks, an old movie set, open-air restaurants on the beach and a hotel that looks like a leftover from the movie *Rain*.

The movie set is the Bar Grif, which was built for a film that was to be called *Cabo Blanco*, starring Charles Bronson. For some reason it was never released in the US, as far as I know, but the well-made set still stands. It was intended to represent a South Seas saloon; the barroom is two floors high with a balcony running around the inside perimeter. Recently it has been recycled into a genuine saloon called the Bar Griff, with that extra 'f' for good measure. If you ever get a chance to see the movie on the late, late show, you'll recognize the set. It's just beyond the Hotel Tropical, on the left, and painted shocking pink.

Places to Stay

I've never seen Barra run out of hotel rooms, but I suppose it could happen, especially if some motion picture production unit is working in the neighbourhood. This happens all the time because of the beautiful tropical scenery.

On the street that parallels the beach is the *Hotel Barra de Navidad*, a fairly new beachfront hotel that is nowhere near as rapacious as the Tropical. Palm trees grow tall in the patio, and the waves just outside don't make the usual hissing noise – they fair boom on the steep beach, at times jarring the whole building. The bar and restaurant are inclined to close a little early for my taste, but are quite good value by local standards. Expensive and recommended.

Keep going about three blocks along the waterfront and you will arrive at the *Hotel Tropical*, a rather pretentious old beach hotel. This one catches the movie trade, and as a rule the better rooms are taken first, but they charge as much for the rooms equipped with cold water as they do for their very best. The Tropical originally offered excellent value for the

pesos, especially compared to the resort hotels around Manzanillo down the road. Not only have the rates skyrocketed over the years, but also the Tropical is not above charging singles the posted doubles rate now and again. Ridiculously expensive and not a lot for the money.

If you turn left on Sonora – the street that branches off the main stem just before you reach the Tropical from the bus station – and follow it to the bottom, you will shortly arrive at the *Hotel Delfin*, a typical tropical hotel of more or less contemporary design with four floors and arched balconies outside the rooms. It's expensive, but a far, far better deal than the Tropical.

A short distance farther along and across the street is the *Sands Hotel*, almost exactly the same price as the Delfin and very popular with the up-at-4-am sports fishermen. Try the Delfin first. Expensive.

Places to Eat

The new bus station doesn't have a restaurant, but the amiable woman next door sells sweets and refrescos.

The best place to eat in town has long been *Pancho's*, beyond the Tropical, so well appreciated that a good share of its trade comes from families who make the 285-plus-km drive down from Guadalajara just to put their feet beneath Pancho's table. Pancho's sign states, 'The best of the sea for you', and he isn't kidding. The restaurant doesn't get well underway until 8 pm. Moderate.

The restaurant in the Hotel Tropical is called *La Bugambilia*, and regardless of my remarks about the hotel, the restaurant is not bad and is the only place in town where you can get an American-style breakfast any hour they're open. It is only a little more expensive than Pancho's, and the food is almost as good. But don't order a drink at La Bugambilia. A copita of Viejo Virgil brandy cost me US$2.50, a stiff fee even during a two-for-the-price-of-one happy hour. Expensive.

Getting There

Barra de Navidad has direct bus service from Guadalajara, Manzanillo and Puerto Vallarta, making it easy to get to. The 280-plus-km trip down from Guadalajara takes six to eight hours over a twisty road that drops about 1500 metres in the process. It is only 73 km from Manzanillo along the coast, but to Puerto Vallarta is almost 200 km over a hill-then-valley-then-hill road that in at least one place rises to about 700 metres.

The bus station has moved. To get to downtown Barra, go out the front of the station and turn left, then right at the corner. One block away is the street that runs along the waterfront and past the Tropical, which will be to your left.

SAN PATRICIO, Jalisco

(elevation three metres, population 3500)
San Patricio is Barra de Navidad's lesser-known sister city. Located a few km north of Barra, it isn't even shown on most maps. Unlike Barra, San Patricio has a charming little plaza. There are quite a few hotels near the plaza, most moderate. You might want to keep them in mind in case Barra's hotels are full. Because Patricio isn't even on the majority of maps, it is unknown to most foreigners, so it is extremely unlikely to fill up. I can make no statement regarding the quality of the hotels; I've always stayed in Barra, although San Patricio looks to be cheaper.

Getting There

San Patricio is a stop on most north-south bus runs, and also for the buses on their way to Manzanillo from Guadalajara. Most foreigners arrive via the jitneys that provide a shuttle service from the plaza in San Patricio and back to the new bus station in Barra.

A few hardy souls have told me that they stroll along the beach between the two communities – it isn't very far, about six km.

MANZANILLO, Colima

(elevation three metres, population 40,000)
Manzanillo has one of the best harbours on Mexico's Pacific coast and there has always been a settlement there. It is believed that the local Indians had contact with Chinese traders around the 12th century. When Cortés visited the place, he realized immediately it was the ideal location for a shipyard, and to this day there are boatyards there.

The town does less business than Acapulco, which is odd because Manzanillo has a railroad connection with the interior, whereas Acapulco doesn't. Manzanillo today is the seaport for Guadalajara, and to a lesser degree, Morelia. Shipping is the principal business, with tourism and boat-building trailing by a considerable margin.

The town itself gives the impression of age, and there are a number of buildings dating from colonial days, but there has been a great deal of new construction. The ancient part of town is pretty much concentrated around the Jardín de Obregón (the plaza's official name). Manzanillo is a seaport pure and simple, and looks it.

Most of the tourist business isn't in Manzanillo at all, but at Playa Azul about 10 km south of town. Here you'll find most of the super-expensive hotels and restaurants.

The well-publicized Las Haidas is located near Playa Azul. Developed by the Bolivian tin magnate Antenor Patino, Las Haidas was intended as a haven for wealthy jet-setters, but it didn't take off. Eventually the Mexican government took over the operation, which didn't make business one whit better, and now it is mostly a monument to one individual's optimism.

Although the beach at Manzanillo is popular with the locals, foreigners staying in town mostly go out to the Playa La Audencia or Playa San Perdido, about one km from the plaza on the north. Of the two, I prefer Perdido because it has a gently

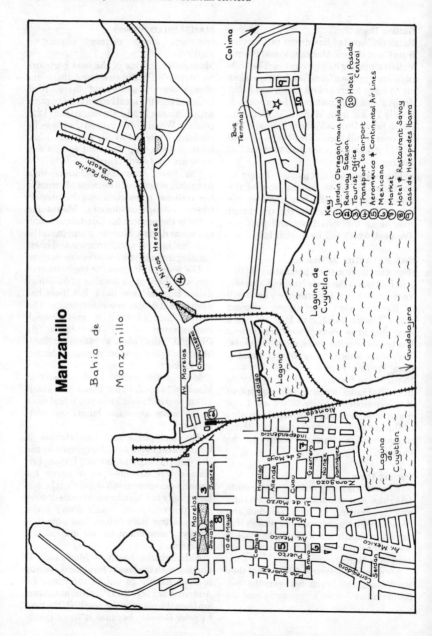

Manzanillo

Bahia de
Manzanillo

Key:
(1) Jardin Obregon (main plaza)
(2) Railway Station
(3) Tourist Office
(4) Transport to airport
(5) Aeromexico ✈ Continental Air Lines
(6) Mexicana
(7) Market
(8) Hotel ≠ Restaurant Savoy
(9) Casa de Huespedes Ibarra
(10) Hotel Posada Central

Colima

Bus Terminal

Laguna de Cuyutlan

→ Guadalajara

Laguna de Cuyutlan

sloping beach and is the closest to the plaza.

There is a sheltered lagoon on the inland side of Manzanillo that the residents use regularly, but I wouldn't recommend it. As with most coastal cities in Mexico, the town has no sewage treatment plant.

Places to Stay

Manzanillo is booming, and the rooms are usually full of longshoremen, fishermen, sailors, railroad workers, campesinos and all the rest of the people it takes to operate a busy port. Low-priced rooms are at a premium, especially near the plaza.

My personal favourite is the *Hotel Miramar,* upstairs on Juárez at 21 de Marzo. The sign on the side of the building is plainly visible from the plaza. The Miramar has been popular for years with seafaring folk who don't mind climbing the flight of steps to the lobby, and is very well managed by people who are helpful even when the hotel is full – which is most of the time. Moderate.

Hotel Savoy, on Davalos at Puerto, is overpriced by a factor of three. It should be inexpensive but is very expensive. I include it as a last resort, and by no means as a recommendation.

Hotel Emperador, on Davalos beyond the Savoy, is a pretty good go. It has fair-sized rooms, three floors with balconies, and a cream-and-maroon paint job on the front. It's quite good value. Moderate.

Hotel Colonial, on 10 de Mayo, is only a block off the plaza, and is without question the best hotel in town. It has the attributes we have come to expect in a Mexican hotel of its class: high ceilings, large rooms, small windows in proportion to the size of the rooms, and a lobby full of pseudo-colonial furniture. Although the Colonial looks quite elderly, it was built right after WW II. It is ridiculously expensive, but much better value than the Savoy.

There are a couple of hotels near the Central Camionera. If you go out the front of the Camionera and turn right, then right

again at the first street, you will come to the *Casa de Huéspedes Ibarra.* It has three floors and a cream paint job, and in my opinion is a cut above the Savoy downtown at about half the price. Moderate.

If you keep right on past the Ibarra and turn right at the next street, you will soon come to the *Hotel de Posada Central,* directly behind the bus station and easily visible from the bus stalls. Inexpensive.

Places to Eat

As with most seaport towns, Manzanillo is not noted for its excellence of cuisine, but there are a number of pretty fair, vaguely wholesome low-priced restaurants near the plaza.

At the corner of Davalos and Mexico is an easy-to-miss small restaurant without a name. It looks like a soda fountain but it is really a restaurant. It owes most of its considerable popularity to reasonable prices and good value for pesos. Moderate.

The restaurant *Savoy,* at the corner of the zócalo on Davalos and Puerto, has been feeding the local workers and myself for as long as I can remember. Being in Manzanillo, it is long on seafood but not to the extent of neglecting the remainder of the menu. The Savoy also puts out a fruit salad served on a platter heaped with everything in the way of available local fruit – delicious. The big Bogart ceiling fans are a Godsend a good 11 months of the year. Moderate.

The restaurant in the *Hotel Colonial* is easily the best in town, with white tablecloths, white-clad waiters, colonial-type furniture and chairs with thick cushions. Chilled mugs of beer come from a tiny barroom behind the restaurant. During the afternoon this bar becomes a sort of private club for the affluent and influential. The restaurant Colonial is for that inevitable time when you need a treat. It is not a tourist trap, as most of the customers are well-to-do locals and their families. It could use some ceiling fans, though. Expensive.

Getting There & Getting Around

Manzanillo has first-rate bus service, mostly from Guadalajara via Barra de Navidad, but there are also buses to Colima, Uruapan, Acapulco and Puerto Vallarta, among other places.

The Central Camionera in Manzanillo is easily the most grasping of the lot; this applies whether we are speaking of baggage-checking or the admission fee to enter the camionera. But on the plus side, I have never seen the station very crowded.

To get from the bus station to the plaza, turn left on leaving the station and continue on the same curving street to the second set of railroad tracks. Turn right and follow the tracks to the first cross street, Juárez. Turn left and the plaza is in the second block. Walking time: a busy 15 minutes.

Occasionally a rail fan or a die-hard arrives by the train that originates in Guadalajara and pauses in Colima for a while on the way down. This is supposed to be about an eight-hour trip, but it usually takes longer – sometimes lots longer.

Manzanillo has an international airport, with regular flights to Guadalajara, Mexico City and Los Angeles.

COLIMA, Colima

(elevation 503 metres, population 100,000)

Colima is a slow-moving, leisurely sort of town with several nice plazas. It's compact enough so that you can enjoy just about all its advantages by basing yourself downtown on the Plaza Libertad and spending a day or two simply strolling hither and yon.

The town is only a few km from Manzanillo, and because of its low altitude, shares much of the same climatic disadvantages. To put it another way, Colima is as hot, muggy, buggy and uncomfortable as the coast in the summer, but it has a winter climate that would be difficult to improve.

Colima is one of my favourite places to visit during early December – and not just because of the climate. It is one of those off-the-beaten-path towns that takes its religious observances very seriously, especially the Fiesta of the Virgin. On this occasion the townspeople dress themselves and their children in old-timey regional costumes and turn out in great numbers. In addition to more or less traditional Indian motifs, religious illustrations deck the women's white cloth shifts fore and aft.

The centre of these observances is, of course, the main plaza, the Plaza (or Jardín) Libertad. I never tire of lolling on one of the benches in the Plaza Libertad near the cathedral and watching the endless parade of passersby.

Another activity of which I never tire is prowling Colima's amazing collection of old cars and general machinery. Not really a museum, it is the personal collection of a man who liked everything in the way of vehicles. There are well under a hundred – ornate hearses (both horse-drawn and propelled by internal-confusing engines); Hudsons; Auburns; Packards; Buicks; Dodges – even a 1946 Diamond-T pickup, by all odds the handsomest pickup ever built in the US. The collection includes the first Fiat Topolino I've laid eyes on in 30 years, even in Italy. You'll also see an old Wayne parking lot sweeper, a one-lung Davenport hopper-cooled 3 HP stationary engine, and a venerable GE commercial broadcast transmitter. There's much, much more.

To reach the 'museum' from the Plaza Libertad, go out Hidalgo until it dead-ends at the Plaza (or Jardín) Nuñez. The collection is behind the auto parts store on the opposite side of the plaza. It's signed, but the paint has faded and it is easy to overlook. Enter through the parts store – the clerks will lead your way. I spend hours there every time I visit Colima. There will be either no charge or a small fee. As a gesture of appreciation, I make it a practice to give each employee of the parts

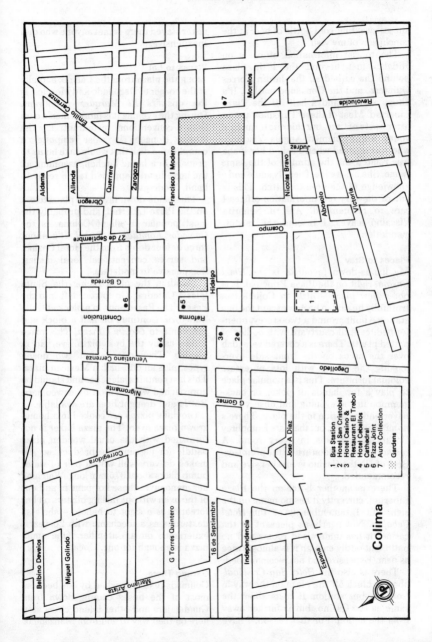

Colima

1 Bus Station
2 Hotel San Cristobel
3 Hotel Casino &
   Restaurant El Trebol
4 Hotel Ceballos
5 Cathedral
6 Pizza Joint
7 Auto Collection

:::: Gardens

shop a sweating-cold bottle of beer at the conclusion of my visit.

The tourist information office is on Hidalgo just beyond the little plaza behind the cathedral, the Jardín Torres Quintero, and the Conasupo market. It's about a block and a half off the Plaza Libertad. Most of these Turismos are an utter waste of time, but this one is run by a young woman named Angela Viscaino, who was amazed when I asked her if she was related the the admiral of the same name. She has a wide, friendly smile and a knowledge of the area to match. This is one of the very few information offices I care to recommend. And if Señorita Viscaino leaves, I rescind the recommendation.

Places to Stay

My hands-down favourite is the *Hotel Casino*, right on the Plaza Principal. It is not a new place – little in Colima can truthfully be said to be new except the bus station – built around a two-storey, open-topped, central courtyard with oodles of potted plants. There is a covered verandah over the arcos on the front side overlooking the plaza, with lots of ersatz colonial furniture. This is a popular place to play a few hands of poker or backgammon in the evening and observe the never-ending action in the plaza. There's no air conditioning, but there are Humphrey Bogart ceiling fans in every room. A restaurant and saloon are on the premises. Best of all, the Casino is inexpensive and recommended.

There is another hotel on the Plaza Libertad; currently it has no name on the sign, but I remember it as the *Hotel Ceballos*. Not nearly as pleasant as the casino, it has undersized rooms and no patio, but oddly enough it is almost twice as dear. Expensive and not recommended.

There is also the *Hotel San Cristóbal*, about a block off the plaza on the way in from the bus station. It costs about the same as the Casino, but is farther away from the action. For that reason, I have never stayed there or met anyone who did. Inexpensive.

Places to Eat

Along the plaza from the Casino, actually at the corner of Degollado and Morelos, is the upstairs *El Marquez* restaurant. During the evening it is more a men's club than a conventional restaurant. Try the lengua (tongue) in salsa chipotle, a complicated dish that would take hours to prepare in a home kitchen, assuming all the ingredients happened to fall ready to hand. Moderate.

The hands-down favourite place to eat on the Plaza Libertad, and probably the most popular in all of Colima, is the *Comedor Familiar el Trebol*. It's about three or four doors from the Hotel Casino, and serves conventional local dishes. Inexpensive to moderate.

Stand in the plaza facing the Santa Iglesia Catedral. Go to your left into the Paseo. The Paseo ends in a block at Calle Zaragoza. Continue on half a block and you come to *Giovini's Pizza*. This place makes easily the best pizza I've had in Mexico. They offer about two dozen types, plus an odd-ball: a Mexican pizza. This last contains jalapeños and should be approached with caution by newcomers. Bottle and draught beer are available.

Giovini's pizzas are cooked in a home-grown pizza oven. The pizza baker is not furnished with the usual wooden pizza paddle for juggling the product, so she makes do very well with a pair of water pump pliers about 375 mm long. Watching her manoeuvre those hot pans in and out of the oven without raising blisters on her forearms is a sight to behold – she's as dexterous as a mechanic with 20 years' experience on a Catapillar. One small pizza is enough for one. Cheap.

Getting There

Colima is readily reached by bus because most of the buses coming down from Guadalajara and other inland cities stop here on their way to and from Manzanillo.

There is a tiny central bus station built along the lines of an old-fashioned airplane hangar. To get uptown from the bus station, go out the restaurant end and turn left, then right at the next intersection. The Plaza Libertad is straight ahead. Walking time: under five minutes.

Although I can't imagine anyone taking the train, Colima is also accessible by rail, being on the Guadalajara-Manzanillo line.

There is no direct air service. If you feel you just have to fly, the easiest way is to fly to Manzanillo and take a bus the 150-odd km for the remainder of your journey.

LÁZARO CÁRDENES, Michoacan

This is a fairly large community on the coast between Manzanillo and Zihuatanejo. It's included in this book because it is the junction point for the coastal bus route's connection to the buses for Uruapan, Patzcuaro and Morelia. The Flecha Roja buses stop on a side street, so it is necessary to change to another bus line most of the time. The usual bus for the uphill shot is Galianos, and it stops about 150 metres from the Flecha Roja. Go left out of the Flecha Roja station, cross the heavily travelled street, and the other station is right at the corner. Walking time: about 5 minutes.

ZIHUATANEJO, Guerrero

(elevation three metres, population 25,000)

A mere 25 years ago, Zihuatanejo was a sleepy little fishing and banana-shipping port of about 1400 souls. Electric power came from a little Caterpillar light plant that (usually) ran from sundown until 11 pm or thereabouts.

Little by little, this idyllic tropical village was discovered by sun-worshippers and its population zoomed to over 20,000. Despite its growth, the town still manages to maintain much of its lazy charm.

Zihuatanejo has no intriguing colonial buildings because it was only established about a century ago. Much of it is of frame construction similar to that utilized by the French in their tropical enterprises, and the town as a result has a most un-Mexican aspect.

There are a number of beaches at Zihuatanejo, separated by rocky outcroppings. The beach in front of town is sheltered, but Madera, La Ropa and Las Gatas (The Sharks) beaches are more popular, even though open to Pacific combers. They are reached by taxi or by going down to the public dock on the waterfront and catching a small boat – you will probably be accosted by touts as soon as you set foot on the quay. Madera is below the Hotel Madera, and La Ropa is the beach by the Hotel Catalina. Many visitors simply take a boat from the waterfront out to Las Gatas and make a day of it – I recommend this. Food and drink are available from stands. It is possible to charter or rent boats for fishing and other aquatic activities, but so far there are no parachute rides or water skiing. I expect both these activities to arrive any day and turn Zihuatanejo into a full-fledged Mexican resort, right up in the same league as Puerto Vallarta and Acapulco.

Places to Stay

Although there aren't any organized entertainment activities, enough foreigners like the South Seas ambience, warm, sunny weather and sandy beaches so that every available room is taken during the winter. Recently the same thing has been happening during the summer vacation months. This is one place where it pays to make paid reservations or to arrive early in the day.

Even with all this tourist activity, there still remain a few reasonably priced hotels from the old days. They are near the centre of town, where they do the most good. Zihuatanejo is so small that the whole downtown area is less than 500 metres from salt water.

Hotel El Dorado is a small house on one of the shopping streets running down to the beach. As a rule, the more distant the beach, the less expensive the hotel. This is reflected in the price of the rooms. Moderate.

Hotel Guadalupe looks dingy from the outside, although it is quite clean inside. It is one of the last places in town to fill, probably because of the lack of its outward visual appeal to foreigners. Moderate.

Casa Aurora, practically next door to the Guadalupe, is neat, intelligently managed and often full. Moderate.

Go out the front door of the Estrella de Oro (not Tres Estrellas) bus station, and a few metres to the left is the *Casa de Huéspedes Lupita.* It's not much of a place, but for such low prices in Zihuatanejo you can't seriously expect the Dorchester. Inexpensive.

Posada Laura, a block from the market on the way downtown, is a two-storey white building. A verandah runs the length of its front and there's a functional balcony above it – a unique combination in Zihuatanejo. This is the very best shot in town for those fortunate enough to land a room. Moderate.

Places to Eat

There are lots of restaurants in Zihuatanejo. As usual, the cheapest eating is in the market, but there are a few other places I patronize each time I'm in town.

The first is *El Tapatio,* across the street from the Hotel El Dorado. Well-equipped with overhead fans, it isn't cheap, but it does a nice unhurried breakfast while the overhead fans keep the flies at bay. The waiters are helpful and attentive, and the food is typically Mexican, heavy on fish. Moderate.

My other selection is one I usually patronize just once each stay. *La Mesa del Capitan,* at Bravo and Guerrero, is a deluxe establishment catering to package tour customers fed up with hotel fare. It is the best eating place in the area if price is not a consideration. The wines are domestic and trustworthy; I've never had to send a

bottle back. In keeping with the pseudo-nautical theme of the place, the upstairs bar is a fairly honest facsimile of the aft cabin on a windjammer. There's a well-managed, well-stocked bar. Both saloon and restaurant are very expensive.

Getting There

Getting to and from Acapulco is a cinch, as is going up to Mexico City. Manzanillo, however, is more difficult, as very few buses run beyond Lázaro Cárdenes, which usually entails changing buses and bus stations.

There are two bus stations. The second-class Flecha Roja is on the other side of the market from town. Taxis are available, but the walk there is only 15 minutes. Go out the front door and straight ahead to the main-travelled street. Turn right, then left for a few metres. Pass the market, then turn right on the street by the Posada Laura. A couple of blocks more will bring you downtown.

The Estrella de Oro, or first-class bus station, is almost downtown. Go out the front door and turn left, then left at the next street, and you're there.

The more affluent tourists fly to Zihuatanejo from Mexico City and the United States west coast. Ask your travel agent.

PAPANOA, Guerrero

(elevation five metres, population 3000)
Papanoa, about a fifth as large as Zihuatanejo, is approximately 60 km along the coast on the way to Acapulco. It's very popular with surfers who prefer to camp on one of the beaches rather than stay at the costly Club de Papanoa. Even for non-surfers, some of the prettiest and most unpatronized beaches are near here. All supplies are available in Papanoa, which simplifies camping out.

ACAPULCO, Guerrero

(elevation three metres, population 600,000)
Almost as soon as the Spanish took Tenochtitlán, they discovered the superb

harbour at Acapulco. Immediately recognizing its worth, they established a shipbuilding business on the shore. The first two ships were constructed in 1532 – the *San Marcos* and the *San Miguel* – and were intended for use on an exploratory expedition by Hurado de Mendoza. In 1533, ships sailed from Acapulco to Peru, and in 1565 Fray Andres de Urdaneta opened commerce between the Philippines and Mexico via Acapulco.

Until the early 1800s, Acapulco was a lusty, brawling seaport through which most of the trade with the Orient was conducted. Apparently the profits went elsewhere, however, because Acapulco has very few of the fine old great houses that grace most older Mexican cities.

Came the revolution and Mexican independence, and the trade dried up. Acapulco slipped into a lethargy that lasted for over a hundred years. The pack routes running north to Mexico City were disused and overgrown, and by the early 1920s Acapulco was just another forgotten seaport, about as important as San Blas or Altata and certainly of far less account than Salina Cruz.

Acapulco would still be dormant today except for the road built in 1928 that allowed the first motorized vehicles to serve the town. Once the road to the interior was improved and reopened, it was again possible to haul freight, and ships started arriving. At first there were just one or two a month, but in a few years they came in fleets. Today Acapulco is Mexico's second port, its tonnage exceeded only by Veracruz on the Atlantic.

For some unfathomable reason there is still no railroad.

Most people think of Acapulco as strictly a resort city that has always been a tourist-oriented town, but it wasn't until just before WW II that the first of the fancy resort hotels was built, and business came only after the war.

After the tourist business started trickling in, clever advertising and promotion kept it growing. I don't know of a time since 1950 when there has not been at least one luxury hotel under construction. But even with all the tourist activity, Acapulco is first and last a seaport, and it is not unusual to see a couple of huge freighters tied up along the Costera Alemán, a few hundred metres from the zócalo, with half a dozen more awaiting berthing room.

Of recent years, Mexico has been assiduously promoting Acapulco and other Pacific coast towns like Manzanillo and Puerto Vallarta as the 'Mexican Riviera'. Another shot in the arm for the tourist business has been the successful television sit-com, 'Love Boat', probably the best free advertising any region ever received. The program is perfectly suited to the tastes of moderately well-off, older people who buy all-inclusive package tours that insulate them from contact with the local people.

The harbour at Acapulco is one of the finest and most interesting on earth. In my opinion, the best way to get an overall view of Acapulco is not to go up on a hill and look down, but to eyeball the city from the water. Several boats offer cruises around the bay, leaving from a pier immediately south-west of the zócalo. The best time is late afternoon, when the city is illuminated by the setting sun coming from behind you. There are also evening cruises intended for dancers and lovers of all ages. By night Acapulco is even more beautiful than the real Riviera. The blue-white and orange of the street lighting, the brightly illuminated hotels and the rank upon rank of workers' homes blanketing the hills all combine to create an unforgettable sight – one that by itself comes close to making the trip worthwhile.

Little Fort San Diego, on the hill just above the Costera Alemán, is a working military post and is often closed to the casual visitor. If you go up there and wander around, you might be fortunate enough, as I once was, to be invited inside, but don't count on it. The fort has a long and violent history. It was actually the second fort in Acapulco. The first was El Castillo de San Diego, which was flattened by an earthquake back in 1776.

This didn't discourage the Spaniards, however, and they promptly built the present one, El Fuerte de San Diego, with a star configuration unusual for the Spanish. During the revolutionary struggles, the fort was attacked by Morelos and a force he thought would be overwhelming. Overwhelming or not, the siege lasted four months before the Spanish were finally forced to run up the white flag, so the unusual shape can be counted a successful design.

The beaches at Acapulco start right at the zócalo and are much frequented by local families, although generally overlooked by tourists. For the price of a local bus ride, you can go down on the Costera and catch a bus out to the Caleta and Caletilla beaches, only a couple of hundred metres apart, or you can go the other direction to still more beaches along the south side of the bay.

Take caution – sunburn in Mexico does more harm than all the turista cases ever joked about.

Everybody goes out to see Acapulco's famous boy high divers. This show, primarily for the tourist trade, takes place every evening. Catch a Quebrada bus out to Quebrada and get off at El Mirador, or walk – it's only about two km. To reach Calle Quebrada, go through the zócala and past the cathedral on the street along the right side, Independencia. Quebrada is the second street. Turn left. Walking time from the plaza is an easy 20 minutes.

It is easy to forget that a great deal of fish are caught commercially at Acapulco. If you happen to be an early riser, you can saunter down on the Costera Alemán to watch the men launch their boats and later bring in their catch. The boats are beached well above high water; come launching time they are put on wooden rollers and wheeled down the beach. Landing is much the same thing, except more people are required.

Those odd boxes-on-wheels along the sidewalk are used to unload the catch and cart it up to the fish buyers, who congregate well before sunrise along the water side of the Costera. The bargaining involved in selling and buying the catch would do a Syrian arms peddler proud. This all takes place just below the Fuerte San Diego, a few hundred metres from the deep-water berths where the big ships unload.

Every movie filmed in Acapulco has at least one scene of either the Quebrada divers or the parachute riders. It wouldn't be too practical for you to try the high diving, but the parachute rides go on all the time. They aren't very dangerous, although every time I try one I get the living bejazus scared out of me. If this is your bag, or you just want to spectate, catch a 'Ciné Río-La Base' bus at the stop above Sanborn's. Just past the Estrella de Oro bus station, the bus turns down to the right and runs along the Costera past a lot of exceedingly expensive hotels. Get off at either the Playa Condesa or the Centro de Convenciones. Stand on the sand a few minutes and odds are that you will be hustled by a parachute-ride salesman. Try it – you might like it.

Sanborn's is the place to get English-language books, periodicals, ice cream sodas and other bits and pieces of Americana.

Places to Stay

Acapulco has probably the largest collection of low-priced hotels in Mexico, second only to Mexico City. They aren't out on the points among hotels that go for M$9600 a day or more, but most of them are positioned downtown near the zócalo. Each hotel is run by a *comedor familiar* – a family that does the cooking, serving and washing up.

There are also some economical hotels around the Flecha Roja bus station and the market. These aren't all that far from the centre of town but generally give less value than the places near the zócalo. There are exceptions.

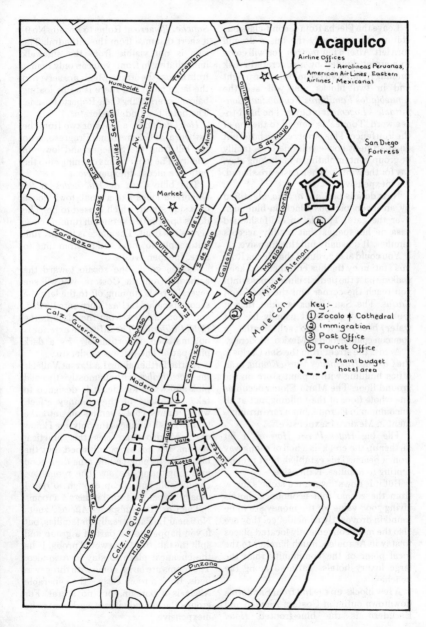

Leave the Flecha Roja second-class bus station the same way the buses do and turn left. After a few metres, you will come to a street divided by a concreted creek running right down the middle. Turn right and in two blocks you will see the *Amueblados Familiares Economicas Confortable – Logement a Loyer.* The hard-to-see word 'Tomles' is welded to the top of the iron fence. This is not really a hotel but an apartment house suitable for a family or group contemplating a fairly long stay, say for the winter. When costs are shared, it's inexpensive.

Next door is *La Casa del Río,* identified by an inconspicuous black-on-blue sign over the gate. This is an old-fashioned casa de huéspedes that readily accepts families. It's usually full. Inexpensive.

You could also go out of the Flecha Roja bus station by the bus entrance and keep walking past the pedestrian overpass until you reach the corner and the *Hotel San Carlos.* The San Carlos is older than it looks at first glance. It usually has hot water because it also sells baths, a common combination in Mexico. Moderate.

Across the street from the San Carlos is the *Casa de Huéspedes María Elonia,* in an office building with a paint store on the ground floor. The María Elonia occupies one whole floor of the building, not at all uncommon in Europe, but a rare arrangement in Mexico. Inexpensive.

The big *Hotel Playa Hornos,* a bit farther up the creek, is a hell of a long way from a beach. This establishment prefers renting to families. Expensive.

But it is downtown and a stone's throw from the zócalo that economical hotels giving good value for the money are to be found in droves. By coincidence, they are also the most conveniently located places to stay in Acapulco, much handier to the focal point of the community than the large luxury hotels scattered along the beaches.

A few blocks up the hill from Sanborn's downtown outlet at Costera Alemán and Escudero is the blue-fronted *Hotel*

Sanchez Romero at Roberto Posada No 9, a short distance from the cathedral. The sign is not visible from the sidewalk immediately in front; you can only read it from across the street. Meals are served in the large patio and there is a fine loafing balcony overlooking Calle Roberto Posada. The hotel is a find. Moderate.

Hotel del Patio, a block or two from the cathedral at Guerrero and Progreso, is up the hill from the Sanchez and lower in quality. The inner rooms opening onto the patio are nicest. Inexpensive.

The blue *Casa de Huéspedes* at 25 Quebrada looks like a small-town house on a side street, which it used to be. The doors open onto a verandah running clear across the front. The place is usually full, but people do come and go from time to time. Inexpensive.

As you go up the zócalo toward the cathedral from the Costera, you will see several streets running off to the left; the second is called La Paz. Turn onto La Paz, and about a block from the plaza is the *Hotel California.* The off-white exterior is not matched, unfortunately, by a dark pink patio. The price is moderate.

A little farther along La Paz, at Valle, is the *Hotel Isabel,* with its mostly stuccoed pink-and-white facade. It is designed to take advantage of the chimney effect, which draws cool evening air into the lobby. This building is the only one I know of in Mexico that uses this practical system. It's not air-conditioned, but the big, lazily turning ceiling fans do a good job of agitating the air. The rooms are comfortable and cheap enough so that I usually stay at the Isabel if there's a room.

The *Casa de Huéspedes Alicia,* Azueta No 9 near La Paz, is really for families, but if you happen to be part of a group and split the tab, the Alicia would probably be the cheapest place to stay in Acapulco. The rooms are large, some with three twin beds. Book a room early – the venerable Alicia is a bargain, but no secret. For groups the individual rate works out to be inexpensive.

Going up the hill and away from the plaza is almost like entering a separate small town, where money goes a long way. Stand on the corner of Hidalgo and Quebrada, for instance, and there are no less than six hotels in plain view, mostly moderate in price. The nearby *Hotel Mariscal* only rents to two or more people, but the *Hotel Pachis* just beyond is happy to room a single. Both houses are moderate.

Places to Eat

Acapulco is famous for its high-priced restaurants, such as the elegant *Normandie* and the high-camp *Carlos 'n' Charlie's,* but there are more good, reasonably priced restaurants in town by far than there are deluxe establishments worth their elevated prices.

The restaurant in the Estrella de Oro (not Tres Estrellas) bus station is better than most bus station restaurants and a safe bet for an early breakfast. Moderate.

For really down-to-earth eating, the market in Acapulco is a good choice. To get to the market, go out the back of the Flecha Roja bus station (where the buses enter,) and turn left. Cross the pedestrian footbridge by the OB clinic, and the market and its pleasures are all around you. This market is both wholesale and retail and gets a very early start. It is a good place for a cheap eye-opener before the rest of Acapulco wakes. Inexpensive.

Competing with the market in price is a ramshackle restaurant opposite the Canada shoe store and to the right of the bus exit from the Flecha Roja station. It runs 24 hours and does an enormous business, much of it to-go, but it has tables and chairs as well. The specialty of the house is a sort of open-face taco called a *sope,* as filling as the gordita it greatly resembles. Two or three of these and a Coca will hold most people the rest of the day. Inexpensive.

But take heed: this restaurant makes its own red sauce with *chilis arboles,* among the most potent on earth – almost on a par with the *habaneros* of Yucatán. If you really aren't up to the genuine article in Mexican labourer's provender, I suggest you order yours *sin salsa colorado.* It's no disgrace. Inexpensive.

On toward town, *Sanborn's,* a couple blocks short of the plaza on the Costera, has a typical Americanized Mexican menu – or Mexicanized American menu – for the benefit of those who value visible cleanliness and decor similar to the better type of stateside small-town restaurant. There are clean restrooms. Expensive.

The downtown *Denny's* – there are others in town – is located on the left of the zócalo at the corner of Juárez. It is the exception to my laudatory remarks about the universally fine state of their sanitary facilities. These are cleaner and better kept than the bus station facilities, but not much. Expensive.

The *Restaurante San Carlos,* on Juárez across the street from the back of Denny's and about 35 metres from the zócalo, is a tightly run establishment that puts the lie to the fable about Acapulco being strictly a deadfall for tourists. I've eaten there a number of times over the past few years, and I doubt I've seen more than a dozen travellers in the place, though it is fairly well patronized by foreigners staying for an extended period. The decorations consist mostly of red pillars and a large *parilla* at the front. The San Carlos serves both meat and seafood, and does them right well. Most things are cooked *al carbón,* and a mechanical breeze blows through the place, cooling customers and wafting good cooking smells out onto the street. Recommended and moderate.

For a top-notch seafood dinner without paying uptown prices, try the *Mariscos Milla.* Go through the zócalo and turn left at the cathedral. Continue to Azueta (formerly Arteaga) and turn left again. The white-fronted Milla is on the next corner. This is the place for the main meal of the day, from around noon to 4 pm. The Milla often closes very early for a Mexican restaurant. Good value, but expensive.

There are a number of low-priced restaurants on Azueta near the Milla, with little to choose from among them. Most feature seafood simply prepared; the day's offerings are usually chalked on blackboards on the sidewalk outside. Inexpensive to moderate.

There is a small bakery/grocery store on the corner of Hidalgo and Azueta. There are also several grocery stores nearby that can be combined for shopping purposes to knock the stuffing out of the high cost of living.

Also in the immediate vicinity are a casa de huéspedes or two which insist on renting on the American plan (with meals) when they can get away with it during the busy season, but they can be very inexpensive when the price of meals is not included.

Getting There & Getting Around

Most of the people who come to Acapulco by bus come by way of Mexico City, Cuernavaca and Taxco, and there is practically a shuttle service between the Central del Sur in Mexico City and Acapulco. Both first and second-class service are available, with all sorts of variations on the first class, such as 'Deluxe' and 'Pullman'. I usually take the

first seat available on a first-class bus and let it go at that.

I don't recommend the second-class service on that route. There is very little difference in cost between first and second class, and the second-class buses stop and pick up people along the highway constantly, detouring around the plazas of every collection of mud huts within 10 km of the highway.

To get downtown from the second-class Flecha Roja bus station, take a bus marked 'Zócalo' or 'Centro' near the bus exit from the station. If you prefer walking, leave the way the buses do and turn left. Go a few metres to a street divided by a creek and turn right. Follow this three blocks to the Costera Alemán, the main-travelled boulevard paralleling the beach. Make a right and walk for 30 minutes to the zócalo.

To get downtown from the Estrella de Oro first-class bus station, catch the bus that runs past the front door from right to left as you leave. The station is about four km from the zócalo, about an hour's walk. If you decide to hoof it, go out the front door of the station and turn left. Stay on this street until it crosses a street divided by a creek running in a concrete gutter. Turn left, and the Costera is about three blocks away. Turn right and keep going until you reach the zócalo.

To get back to the first-class bus station, catch a Cine-Rio bus at the next stop above Sanborn's. The buses make a left off the Costera by Sanborn's and often won't bother to pull over for a mere one or two passengers. The locals are well aware of this and catch the bus at the next stop.

The Estrella de Oro bus station in Acapulco is closed during the night insofar as ticket sales are concerned. If you want to take the 7 am bus for Mexico City, you won't be able to buy a ticket immediately before the bus leaves, so buy one a day or more in advance. If you don't have a ticket, you can still pay the driver in cash for the journey to the first open ticket office, probably Chilpancingo, where you will be required to buy a ticket for the balance of the trip.

Acapulco has a busy international airport and is served by a number of airlines, both foreign and domestic. It seems that a new carrier adds Acapulco to its list every few months, and promotional fares and excursions offering cut-rate tickets are constantly being advertised. Check with a travel agent, preferably one with some knowledge of Mexico, to get the lowest prices and latest schedules.

PUERTO ESCONDIDO, Oaxaca
(elevation four metres, population 6500)
The Spanish laid out their towns systematically, following approved-in-Spain plans, and using surveying instruments to make certain the streets intersected at correct 90-degree angles. Puerto Escondido, however, kept growing, and the lack of planning and a central plaza shows. The main street is called Perez Gasga, I'm told, although there are almost no street signs. It roughly parallels the beach at some distance inland so there is plenty of room for building along the west (ocean) side. It is a good place for high-speed sightseeing – about six minutes will suffice for viewing the whole town.

Escondido today is about what Puerto Vallarta was six months after Elizabeth Taylor and Richard Burton wrapped up the film *Night of the Iguana.* There's not much to do except loaf and enjoy the trade winds, sleep during the afternoons as any civilized person should, read, fish and surf. Surfing is Escondido's greatest single attraction, and most any dedicated surfer you meet has surfed at Escondido at one time or another.

Because Escondido attracts so many young and literate travellers from the US, and they have a lot of reading time available during their televisionless stay, there is an excellent book store on Gasga. It is called the Paperback Shack, and it's over at the Farmacia Cortés. There's also a branch at the local airport. The Paperback

Shacks are operated by an American, Dr George Bennett, who is a fountainhead of information about Escondido and environs, and Mexico generally.

Places to Stay
It is difficult to believe today that only 25 years ago Escondido didn't have a single hotel to its name, and anyone staying overnight had to make arrangements with a local family for lodgings or content themselves with sleeping on the beach with the mosquitoes for company.

A little way down the hill from the bus station is the *Casa de Huéspedes Las Dos Costas Precios Economicos,* formerly Habitaciones Amueblada. Just to make certain everybody gets the idea, there is also a sign saying 'Economical Rooms'. Maybe it was the name change, but business appears to be pretty good – they're adding another floor. Inexpensive.

Hotel Paraiso Escondido is the original grand hotel of the Puerto. It no longer stands out from the bus station because they've removed their name from their water tank on the roof, so you now have to pick it out from the street in front. This huge, meandering, tile-roofed funky establishment looks as if it were built by four masons who weren't on speaking terms. Moderate.

On down the hill, the three-storey *Hotel Roca Mar* has a genuine lobby at last. Guests should try for a top-floor front room to catch the ocean view and the trade winds. Moderate.

Continuing along Gasga, we come to *La Posada,* more a hostel than a hotel. The back of the hotel opens right out onto the beach. The Posada advertises 'Alojamiento Economicos y Restaurante'. There is *larga distancia* (long distance) phone service. Both the hotel and the restaurant are inexpensive.

Beyond the Farmacia Cortés is the *Hotel Las Almas* (sic) a brand-new, moderately priced house. Most of the time it has hot water.

A bit farther along, next door to the

Rincón del Pacifico Hotel, is a recreational vehicle and trailer park. In December of 1983 there were only two or three snowbirds in residence, but I expect them to flock down in droves as soon as word gets out.

Places to Eat

There are lots of restaurants in town, but here is my old favourite plus a couple of new listings:

The best place in town to eat used to be *La Palapa*, on the hill side of the street above the Roca Mar. The palapa roof that gives it its name makes for afternoon coolness, but the Palapa has fallen upon hard times. The roof is now patched with tar paper, and the hotel generally presents a ratty appearance. Food is still good, though. As with every other eating house in the area, the Palapa is long on fish, shrimp and langosta – this last is miscalled lobster in the western United States. Beef hereabouts is only for testing sharpness of tooth and strength of jaw, or for making hamburger. Expensive.

Probably a better bet in the evening is the *Restaurante Junto al Mar*. With approximately the same menu as the Palapa, it has more flair. The food is good, the ambience better. The Junto al Mar is popular with wayfarers. Expensive.

A sure sign of progress in a Mexican resort town is the flaunting of a pizza joint. This one is down the hill next door to the trailer park. Moderate.

Getting There & Getting Around

The best and least worrisome way to get to Puerto Escondido is to fly down from Oaxaca on an Oaxaqueña's DC-3 or Convair. If you're lucky, it will fly via Salina Cruz and then fly up to Escondido along the beach, which makes a grand sightseeing trip. There are several flights a day, usually three; the fare is about US$25. VW minibuses will take you into Escondido from the palapa terminal – the only one I know of in the Americas.

Escondido is currently having its airstrip overhauled, and will soon be able to receive jet planes that carry as many passengers a trip as the old Dakotas do in a week, which is why the town has so many hotels.

A second way to get to Puerto Escondido is by bus down the hill from Oaxaca. The buses leave from the second-class station in Oaxaca and take seven or eight hours.

You can also come along the coast from Acapulco via Flecha Roja, but in this neck of the woods Flecha Roja is a second-class bus operation all the way. Some buses continue on to Salina Cruz and Puerto Angel.

Running time from Acapulco is six or seven hours.

PUERTO ANGEL, Oaxaca

(elevation three metres, population 2500) Puerto Angel, a small town on the beach below Puerto Escondido, is very popular with Europeans. Lots of economically priced drugs are found there, bad news for Americans because the Mexican authorities dearly love to bust Americans as proof positive that they are cooperating with the US Drug Enforcement Agency.

Puerto Angel is the site of Mexico's next big computer-located tourist development, one that the government hopes will outdraw Cancún, but right now it has less to offer than Puerto Escondido. The town was originally a coffee port serving the *fincas* back in the hills behind town. Progress has pretty much passed it by. I mention Puerto Angel because sometimes it's easier to get to Escondido via Angel than directly from Oaxaca. There are several inexpensive hotels. Air service is available from Oaxaca. *Terry's Guide to Mexico* says, 'Winter is the only recommended season for a visit here' – a remark that pretty well applies to the whole coast south of Puerto Vallarta.

The best shot for the money in Puerto Angel is the *Hotel Sonaya*, overlooking Cemeterio beach. This is a small house with balconies and fairly spacious rooms. There's a pretty good restaurant on the premises. Best of all, it's moderate and recommended, according to Pat Noel of the *Mexico Traveler*.

Leslie Arough, of Old Bridge, New Jersey in the US, has high praises for a guest house called *La Posada Cañon Devata*, also on Playa Panteón. The Posada serves 'healthy vegetarian meals served in a communal atmosphere', which stretches a point by including seafood. The Posada is operated by a *gringa* from California and her Mexican husband. There are hammock facilities. Leslie says they fill up quickly, but they take reservations. Moderate.

Glossary

Albóndiga Meatball, usually cooked in soup or stock.

Arroz Rice, a staple of the Mexican diet.

Arroz con pollo Rice with chicken, one of the more popular dishes.

Barbacoa Barbecued meat, usually well spiced.

Bifstek Beefsteak, but don't expect it cut US style!

Billete Banknote (not ticket, as in Spain).

Bimbo White balloon-type bread, sliced. Found all over Mexico.

Birria de cabra or chivo Goat stew.

Bolillo An oblong raised bun made of white flour. If you feel it necessary to eat white bread in Mexico, this is the way to do it. Universally excellent.

Burrito Not all that 'Mexican.' A popular dish near the border and widespread in 'Mexican' restaurants in the US. Consists of a flour tortilla wrapped around a filling.

Caballeros Literally 'horsemen' but as meaningless as 'gentlemen' in the USA. Usually found on men's room doors.

Cabrón Literally 'little goat,' but that isn't what it means. The best definition I know is: a cuckold who does nothing about the situation. Either avoid the word altogether or say it with a friendly smile!

Cabrito al horno Baked kid, a delicacy popular in the north.

Caca Shit. Does not mean 'excrement,' which translates as 'excremento,' a word probably unknown to José Fulano.

Café Coffee.

Café con leche Coffee with milk. Made with strong coffee and hot milk, served in individual clay pitchers; it is a wonderful way to start the day.

Calle Street.

Callejón Usually an alley, but can also be a small, narrow or very short street.

(Al) carbón Literally, charcoal. Usually refers to food cooked over charcoal.

Carne asada Roasted or grilled meat, usually beef.

Cazuela Clay cooking-pot, usually sold in nested sets. One of the world's best cooking pots.

Cena Supper.

Cenaduría A restaurant that serves suppers, but in Mexico can be found applied to any restaurant.

Central Camionera Central Bus Station.

Central de Autobuses Central Bus Station.

Central de Camiones Central Bus Station.

Cerveza Beer or other malt beverage.

Chicharrón Crackling – the pork skin or other part that has had the lard rendered out. Often sold on street corners and occasionally served as a soup.

Chiláquile A sort of thick soup essentially made from corn tortillas and a stock base.

Chile rellenos Literally, stuffed chilis. Large, mild ancho chilis with the seeds removed are stuffed, dipped in batter and deep fried. Not at all 'hot.'

Chimichanga Similar to a deep-fried burrito. Delicious when made from the huge, thin Sonora tortilla. Mostly a regional dish in the states of Sonora and eastern Baja California.

Chingar The all-purpose, universal verb corresponding to the English 'to screw' – the threadless kind. Does not mean a Peruvian dance, a low dive or to become intoxicated (in Mexican Spanish.) For some reason omitted in most Spanish/English dictionaries. Or worse, mistranslated!

Churros Made from dough squeezed out of a pastry bag and deep-fat fried. The cooked churro is then coated with coarse sugar and served. Also applied to a 'donut' in some areas.

Cigarros Cigarettes.

Coca Coca-Cola.

Cocida de rez Beef stew, which no two cooks make the same way!

Comal A clay griddle.

Comida Lunch or dinner.

Comida corrida A multi-course meal usually much cheaper than the cost of its components would be if ordered separately. Usually available for lunch, but sometimes carries on into the dinner hours.

Completo Full. Usually found on signs near hotel desks in crowded cities.

Conquistador The early Spanish explorer-conqueror.

Damas Ladies. Usually found on restroom doors.

Desayuno Breakfast. In Mexico, the lightest meal of the day.

Diligencia Stagecoach or vehicle of like ilk. These were popular and widely used in Mexico before the Pilgrims wore out their welcome in the Old Country.

Descompuesto Broken, a far-from-uncommon state of affairs in Mexico.

Embarazada Literally, embarrassed. Usually means 'pregnant.'

Estación Ferrocarril Railroad station.

Excusado Toilet. In most of Mexico, 'bathroom.'

Ferrocarril Railroad.

Flan Dessert custard, one of the few Spanish dishes in Mexico.

Frijoles Beans, usually pintos. A staple, especially in the north.

Frontera Border between political entities.

Guayabera (also guayabarra) A man's shirt of thin fabric, more or less a 'dress' item, with pockets and with two appliquéd designs running up the front, over the shoulders, and down the back.

Guarache (also huarache) A sandal made of woven leather, with a sole of retired automobile tyre.

Hamburguesa A hamburger by another name. Not to be confused with a Big Mac. At best, more like a Wimpy.

Hay A verb meaning 'there is.' Mostly encountered as 'No hay,' which means 'there is none.'

Higado Liver.

Hombres Men.

Hot Kakes Pancakes.

Huarache See **guarache**.

Huevo Egg. Also testicle.

Jabón Soap. Easy to confuse with the next word.

Jamón Ham. Genuine ham is scarce in Mexico. What you usually receive instead is pressed ham.

Larga distancia Long-distance telephone.

Leche Milk.

Lechero Milk train or milker.

Lista de Correos General delivery or poste restante. Literally means 'mail list' because names of people with letters on hand are often posted on a list, supposedly updated daily.

Lonche A pochismo meaning 'lunch.'

Lonchería or lunchería Lunch room.

(de) Lujo Deluxe. As in the US, more often used than is warranted!

Lleno Full. This word is used in lots of places, but most tellingly in hotels. See **completo** above.

Mariscos Seafood, usually shellfish.

Machaca Shredded meat, either dried or pre-roasted.

Menudo A tripe soup or stew, something on the order of tripe a la mode de Caen with oregano and cumin. Popularly supposed to be a specific for crapulence.

Mexicana Literally 'Mexican.' Applied to food, it implies a method of seasoning heavy on tomatoes and spices, but not necessarily 'hot.'

Mole Usually a sauce made of chocolate and spices served over fowl.

Mordita Literally, the little bite. This is the trifle you pay a traffic cop in lieu of receiving a ticket.

Mosaico Pressed luncheon meat. Also mosaic.

Mujeres Women. Another sign often seen on restroom doors.

Palapa Thatched, usually thatched roof.

Pan Bread.

Pan Dulce Sweet bread, usually served in the form of assorted buns in a basket on the breakfast table. Eat as many as you will, and be charged for those consumed.

Papel higiénico Toilet paper. In Mexico it is in short supply.

Parada A bus stop, usually for city buses.

Paseo A walkway or pedestrian way. Usually grander than a path. Also the ancient custom of young men and women circling the plaza of an evening in opposite directions, then pairing off under the watchful eyes of chaperones.

Picadillo, picadilla Spiced minced meat. Also occasionally applied to hash.

Plazuela A small plaza.

Pochismo A word 'poached' from another language, usually English. 'Autobus' and 'trucka' come readily to mind.

Pollo Chicken.

Portales Arches supporting a roof extending over a sidewalk. Arcade.

Postre Dessert.

Pozole A soup or stew containing hominy and usually based on calves' or pigs' feet, and/or other outside parts such as tails or snouts.

Presidio Usually a fort or the garrison thereof.

PRI Stands for Party of the Revolutionary Institution, the dominant political party of the country. You will see a PRI sign on at least one wall in every village in Mexico, and in the larger cities PRI slogans can be seen strung side by side for many km. Pronounced 'pree.'

Propino, propina A tip or gratuity. Not quite the same as 'mordita,' and not to be confused with 'propio' which means proper, or one's own.

Puro cigar.

Quesadilla A folded-over, fried taco filled with cheese.

Queso fundido A Mexican fondue, nothing at all like the dish served around Zurich!

Rejas The handsome wrought-iron window guards that are the first thing the salvage artists take when stripping a ghost town.

Rico Generally means 'delicious,' but although most places advertise menudo rico or pozole rico, their claims are as much to be believed as political promises. Also means 'hearty' at times.

Salsa Sauce. Mole is a salsa. So is the stuff that appears in little dishes on tables. Approach warily. Can be hot, hot, hot!

Sanatorio Hospital, especially of the small, private variety.

Sanitario Literally, 'sanitary.' In Mexico, this word usually means toilet.

Simpático No equivalent English word. Translated variously as sympathetic, amiable, friendly, likeable and so on. Means all of the above, and more.

Sopa Soup.

Supermercado Supermarket. Can be a small mom-and-pop backstreet shop, or a veritable department store.

Taco A small corn tortilla folded or wrapped around a filling. Anything folded over. Not crisp.

Tacos al pastor Tacos made from strips of meat piled on a vertical spit and cooked in front of an up-and-down grate. As the spit revolves, the outermost meat is browned, then is trimmed off to make the filling for the tacos. Of the thousand and one tacos of Mexico, the taco al pastor is my hands-down favorite. Not generally street-corner food.

Taller Shop or workshop. A 'taller mecánico' is a mechanic's shop, usually for automobiles, and a 'taller de llantos' is a tyre repair shop, and so on.

Templo Church. Can be applied to a wayside chapel, or a very grand structure.

Típico Typical, characteristic of a region.

Tocino Bacon.

Tostón A 50-centavo coin, now obsolete. In Yucatán, Campeche and Chiapas it can refer to thinly sliced plantain, dipped in batter and deep fried.

Torta A sandwich, usually made on a bolillo that has been sliced lengthwise with some of the bread removed to make way for the filling.

Torta a la plancha A sandwich as above that is 'ironed' in a sort of smooth waffle iron. A kind of grilled sandwich.

Tortilla A flat, round, unleavened bread made from either wheat flour or – more likely – yellow field corn (maize). The basic item in the Mexican diet. In Mexico it is never an omelette, as it is in Spain.

Viajero A traveller, although some writers tend to use the word pejoratively. It can also mean 'passenger,' but this is relatively rare in Mexico.

Zaguán Usually vestibule or foyer, but occasionally porch.

Zócalo The town square.

Index

Lonely Planet travel guides

Africa on a Shoestring
Australia – a travel survival kit
Alaska – a travel survival kit
Bali & Lombok – a travel survival kit
Burma – a travel survival kit
Bushwalking in Papua New Guinea
Canada – a travel survival kit
China – a travel survival kit
Hong Kong, Macau & Canton
India – a travel survival kit
Japan – a travel survival kit
Kashmir, Ladakh & Zanskar
Kathmandu & the Kingdom of Nepal
Korea & Taiwan – a travel survival kit
Malaysia, Singapore & Brunei – a travel survival kit
Mexico – a travel survival kit
New Zealand – a travel survival kit
North-East Asia on a Shoestring
Pakistan – a travel survival kit kit
Papua New Guinea – a travel survival kit
The Philippines – a travel survival kit
South America on a Shoestring
South-East Asia on a Shoestring
Sri Lanka – a travel survival kit
Thailand – a travel survival kit
Tramping in New Zealand
Travellers Tales
Trekking in the Nepal Himalaya
USA West
West Asia on a Shoestring

Lonely Planet phrasebooks

Indonesia Phrasebook
China Phrasebook
Nepal Phrasebook
Thailand Phrasebook

South America
on a Shoestring

Lonely Planet travel guides are available around the world. If you can't find them, ask your bookshop to order them from one of the distributors listed below. For countries not listed or if you would like a free copy of our latest booklist write to Lonely Planet in Australia.

Australia
Lonely Planet Publications, PO Box 88, South Yarra, Victoria 3141.
Canada see USA
Denmark
Scanvik Books aps, Store Kongensgade 59 A, DK-1264 Copenhagen K.
Hong Kong
The Book Society, GPO Box 7804.
India & Nepal
UBS Distributors, 5 Ansari Rd, New Delhi.
Israel
Geographical Tours Ltd, 8 Tverya St, Tel Aviv 63144.
Japan
Intercontinental Marketing Corp, IPO Box 5056, Tokyo 100-31.
Malaysia
MPH Distributors, 13 Jalan 13/6, Petaling Jaya, Selangor.
Netherlands
Nilsson & Lamm bv, Postbus 195, Pampuslaan 212, 1380 AD Weesp.
New Zealand
Roulston Greene Publishing Associates Ltd, Box 33850, Takapuna, Auckland 9.
Pakistan
London Book House, 281/C Tariq Rd, PECHS Karachi 29, Pakistan
Papua New Guinea see Australia
Singapore
MPH Distributors, 3rd Storey, 601 Sims Drive #03-21, Singapore 1438
Spain
Altair, Riera Alta 8, Barcelona, 08001.
Sweden
Esselte Kartcentrum AB, Vasagatan 16, S-111 20 Stockholm.
Thailand
Chalermnit, 108 Sukhumvit 53, Bangkok, 10110.
UK
Roger Lascelles, 47 York Rd, Brentford, Middlesex, TW8 0QP.
USA
Lonely Planet Publications, PO Box 2001A, Berkeley, CA 94702.
West Germany
Buchvertrieb Gerda Schettler, Postfach 64, D3415 Hattorf a H.